Warriors for Social Justice and Equality

Maria Jiménez of Houston and Mexican American Activists

Linda J. Quintanilla

Number 12 in the Al Filo: Mexican American
Studies Series

University of North Texas Press
Denton, Texas

10 9 8 7 6 5 4 3 2 1

Permissions:
University of North Texas Press
1155 Union Circle #311336
Denton, TX 76203-5017

The paper used in this book meets the minimum requirements of the
American National Standard for Permanence of Paper for Printed Library
Materials, z39.48.1984. Binding materials have been chosen for durability.

Library of Congress Cataloging-in-Publication Data is available from the
Library of Congress.

ISBN 978-1-57441-912-2 (cloth)

ISBN 978-1-57441-923-8 (ebook)

Warriors for Social Justice and Equality is Number 12 in the Al Filo: Mexican
American Studies Series.

The electronic edition of this book was made possible by the support of the
Vick Family Foundation. Typeset by vPrompt eServices.

This book is dedicated to the memory of Maria de Los Ángeles Jiménez, her parents Raúl Jiménez Gómez and Elva Flores de Jiménez, and my father Sam Vargas Quintanilla, and all immigrant families who come to this country for a better life and, more importantly, where rights and dignity are respected.

Contents

Lists of Illustrations

Preface

In 2000 Dr. Tatcho Mindiola Jr., director of the Center of Mexican American Studies at the University of Houston, asked me to deliver a conference paper on Mexican American women of Houston. After delivering my presentation, a member of the audience suggested Maria Jiménez as a worthy research topic. That was my lucky day. I subsequently met with Maria many times. Each time she patiently endured my interviews and questions. I also participated in some of the events that she organized. She must have been surprised and amused that I wanted to write a book on her, but she cooperated because she strongly believed that history should be told "right."

My admiration of Maria led me to the complicated subject of immigration. I had never thought of myself as an immigrant, although I am a daughter of a Mexican immigrant. I was a proud Mexican American. However, as a student in Austin's public schools, I became aware of anti-Mexican prejudice and felt its sting from time to time. I wondered why these prejudices (which targeted Mexican Americans and Mexican immigrants alike) and the discrimination that racism promoted existed—everywhere, it seemed. But after I read the saying "Fish are the last [creatures] to recognize water," it became clearer to me why racist prejudices persist. If one is always surrounded by racist beliefs, they are a normal part of one's existence. Fish, having always been surrounded by water and flotsam or debris, take no notice of them. I concluded that water that is polluted is like an unjust society and that its debris represents specific racist prejudices and practices, which are so commonplace that they are not seen—that is, perceived. I later became intrigued when I read ideas from critical race theory. The theory said, first, that racism was normal (which is not to say everyone is racist), and second, that there were ways to tackle this problem in society.

Thus, with a theoretical framework (critical race theory), an impressive activist focus (Maria Jiménez), and the complex topic of racist discrimination, especially against Mexican immigrants, I started researching and writing this book. In it I tell the story of the struggles and achievements of Maria and earlier Mexican-origin activists for social justice and equality.

In my long and solitary journey to complete the book, I enjoyed the help of many kind and generous persons. First and foremost, my husband, Laurence B. McCullough, read every draft and encouraged me every step of the way. I also greatly appreciate others who read the manuscript: former graduate student colleagues at the University of Houston, Dr. Ann Brown and Dr. Valentina Hardin, both of Houston, and my sister, Anita Quintanilla, of Austin. When I had questions about Spanish quotes, my friend Marcela Espinos Martínez, of Mexico City, Mexico, gladly answered them. Also helpful were the dedicated archivists at the Austin History Center, specifically Kelly Harrell, Molly Hults, and Vanessa Hutchins. I also appreciate the technical expertise of Rene Renteria of Rene Renteria Photography in Austin. Critical to the book's final version were two peer readers, Dr. Cynthia Orozco and an anonymous reader. Their comments and suggestions helped me improve my book in countless ways. Last but not least, Director Ron Chrisman of the University of North Texas Press guided this nervous writer through every step involved in publishing this book. His steadfast encouragement and support were invaluable.

Abbreviations

ACLU	American Civil Liberties Union
AFL	American Federation of Labor
AFSC	American Friends Service Committee
AHS	Austin High School
AI	Amnesty International
ARCA	Association for Residency and Citizenship in America
ARMAS	Advocating Rights for Mexican American Students
BRC	Border Rights Coalition
CAC	Civic Action Committee
CAIFR	Coalition against Intolerance and for Respect
CIO	Congress of Industrial Organizations
CMAS	Center for Mexican American Studies
CRECEN	Centro de Recursos para Centroamericanos (Central American Resource Center)
CRT	critical race theory
DOD	Department of Defense
DOJ	Department of Justice
DOL	Department of Labor
DREAM Act	Development, Relief, and Education for Alien Minors
EEOC	Equal Employment Opportunity Commission
FAIR	Federation for American Immigration Reform
FBI	Federal Bureau of Investigation
FSMLA	La Federación de Sociedades Mexicanas y Latinas Americanas
GANO	Gulfton Area Neighborhood Organization
GAO	General Accounting Office
HISD	Houston Independent School District
HPD	Houston Police Department
ICE	Immigration and Customs Enforcement
IIRIRA	Illegal Immigration Reform and Immigrant Responsibility Act
ILEMP	Immigration Law Enforcement Monitoring Project
INA	Immigration and Nationality Act
INS	Immigration and Naturalization Service

xii   Abbreviations

IRCA	Immigration Reform and Control Act
JIFM	Jóvenes Inmigrantes por un Futuro Mejor (Young Immigrants for a Better Future)
KKK	Ku Klux Klan
KPD	Katy Police Department
LAC	Latin American Club
LIBRE	League for Immigration, Border Rights and Education
LIFE	Legal Immigration Family Equity
LULAC	League of United Latin American Citizens
MAEC	Mexican American Education Council
MALDEF	Mexican American Legal Defense and Education Fund
MAYO	Mexican American Youth Organization
MCDC	Minuteman Civil Defense Coalition
MOIRA	Mayor's Office of Immigrant and Refugee Affairs
NAFTA	North American Free Trade Agreement
NCDM	National Commission for Democracy in Mexico
NCLR	National Council de la Raza
NGO	nongovernmental organization
NLRA	National Labor Relations Act
NLRB	National Labor Relations Board
PADRES	Padres Asociados para Derechos Religiosos, Educativos, y Sociales (Priests Associated for Religious, Educational, and Social Rights)
PASO	Political Association of Spanish-Speaking Organizations
PRI	Partido Revolucionario Institucional (Party of the Institutionalized Revolution)
PRWORA	Personal Responsibility and Work Opportunity Reconciliation Act
RUP	La Raza Unida Party
SA	Student Association
SAWS	Special Agricultural Workers
SSI	Supplemental Security Income
UFW	United Farm Workers
UH	University of Houston
YWCA	Young Women's Christian Association

Chapter 1

Introduction

"Why are they like that?" I asked Cico. We skirted Blue Lake and worked
our way through the tall, golden grass to the creek.
"I don't know," Cico answered, "except that people, grown-ups and kids, seem
to want to hurt each other—and it's worse when they're in a group."
—Rudolfo Anaya, *Bless Me, Ultima*[1]

We were marginalized as a group from the mainstream activities at
the school . . . it not only produced suffering but an anger,
an anger that it was *wrong*!
—Maria Jiménez[2]

These quotes by Mexican Americans reflect the great harm that racial or
ethnic biases can do and indicate that when individuals are in groups,
they can inflict even more harm. Racial and ethnic biases unfairly deny dignity
and even rights to different individuals or groups and are therefore incon-
sistent with a just society. Far too many citizens in our nation have increasingly used demeaning racist rhetoric and supported racial discrimination that
unjustly targeted people of color. Of those so targeted, this book will focus
on the Mexican-origin community and Mexican immigrants. And while not

everyone is racist, everyone should want to oppose racist words and deeds. Critical race theory (CRT), discussed later in the chapter, addresses the harmful consequences of racism. To challenge racism CRT asserts, first, that it is necessary to acknowledge it in society and, second, that victims of racism must dedicate themselves to ending it.

This study's main assertion is that the activists described in this book have advanced social justice in the United States by fighting against racial discrimination and by promoting our nation's best virtues, especially equality and social justice. Not passive victims of social injustices, these Mexican-origin activists demonstrated impressive moral strength and determination in their fight against pervasive and long-lived racial prejudices. The second part of the book turns to Maria Jiménez, who is the epitome of a selfless, committed warrior for the rights and dignity of others.

Jiménez believed from a very early age that her role in society was to make it better. When only 21-years-old, Jiménez already knew what it meant to be an activist. In 1971 she said that being an activist "means to me that when I see a problem which I feel needs a solution, then I go out to solve it."[3] Her biography describes her lifelong battle against injustice, be it racist, sexist, or anti-immigrant. Of her several impressive achievements, the Immigrant Workers Freedom Ride in 2003, described in chapter 9, delighted her the most. The experience introduced its participants, undocumented immigrants, to historic places and to African Americans activists, or their descendants, from the Civil Rights Movement. The Freedom Ride, Jiménez asserted, not only provided an extraordinary history lesson but also inspired the immigrants in their long and difficult fight to gain legal status—a true victory for social justice.

The national debate on immigration has evoked strong emotions, polarized society, and frustrated efforts to achieve immigration reform. The anti-immigrant enmity reached an unprecedented level during the 2016 presidential campaign when the Republican candidate, Donald J. Trump, referred to Mexican immigrants as rapists.[4] Two years later, in 2018, President Trump commented on immigrants entering the country without documentation and said, "These aren't people. These are animals."[5] Why do emotions run so high on the topic of immigration? Critics of immigration predict the fall of American culture because of the influx of allegedly inferior groups. For example, Patrick J. Buchanan (b. 1938) asserted that the "invasion" since the 1960s of immigrants, particularly Hispanics, foreshadowed the decline of American society and constitutes "one of the greatest tragedies in human history."[6]

It is a serious injustice to brand an entire group with negative and false statements that try to demean them and rob them of their dignity. Why people do this to others is the query of Antonio, the boy in the excerpt from *Bless Me, Ultima* that opened this chapter. The harm of others' prejudices is expressed in the opening quote from Maria Jiménez and reveals what motivated her activism: anger.

The historical narrative that I provide describes the activism of individuals and groups, concentrating on one state, one city, and one activist: Texas, Houston, and Maria Jiménez, respectively. The choice of Texas is logical, given its large Hispanic, predominately Mexican, population. The same is true of Houston, where Jiménez resided. It has a highly diverse population and is Texas's largest city, the nation's fourth largest city, and projected to be the third largest by 2025. Its population reached 2,099,451 in 2010 and 2,304,580 in 2020, according to the US Census Bureau.[7] Although the book focuses on Mexican immigrants because of the nature of Jiménez's activism, it includes Mexican Americans because they share many of the historical experiences of and discrimination against Mexican immigrants. In addition, many Mexican-origin families are mixed status—that is, include citizens and noncitizens.

Fortunately, there are reasons for optimism regarding immigration. More and more citizens each year reject the claim that Hispanic immigrants, especially the undocumented, are dangerous criminals instead of prospective citizens who can enrich our culture.[8] A national survey in 2013 indicated that 63 percent of Americans "crossing party and religious lines favored a pathway to citizenship for immigrants living in the county illegally," and a poll in 2021 reported that the percentage had risen to 69.[9] A few years earlier, in 2018, Fox News, a pro-Trump news source, reported that its polling revealed that 58 percent of its respondents favored a pathway to citizenship for undocumented immigrants.[10]

A Society Strives for Equality and Social Justice

Racism in any form is anathema to a society that values equality and justice. Racism is defined by the CRT scholars Richard Delgado and Jean Stefancic as "any program or practice of discrimination, segregation, persecution, or mistreatment based on membership in a race or ethnic group," and, in the opinion of this writer, beliefs that support the problems described by Delgado and Stefancic.[11] A common target among racists is the immigrant community. Anti-Mexican immigrant bashing is not new in the sense that European Americans—that is, whites—view the Mexican-origin community as foreign and therefore a threat to the nation's identity and well-being. The "permanent foreigner" concept is one part of the Mexican American experience, as are its distinctive history, language, and culture. On the erroneous generalization that members of the Mexican-origin community are not native-born Americans, Jiménez commented, "We are constantly being questioned of the right to be here and about the right to belong. . . .We will always be foreigners."[12]

Despite being stigmatized as "alien" or the "other," the Mexican-origin community has contributed significantly to advancing social justice because of its strong belief in the equality of all persons. A prime example of minority-led progress in social justice was the African American Civil Rights Movement of the 1950s and 1960s led by the Reverend Dr. Martin Luther King Jr. and other committed individuals. Mexican Americans such as labor activists Cesar Chavez and Dolores Huerta rallied for equal rights during the 1960s and 1970s. Legal cases also advanced social justice. For instance, Mexican American lawyers argued the legal case *Hernández v. Texas* before the US Supreme Court in 1954, discussed in chapter 3.[13] *Hernández* addressed the exclusion of Mexican Americans on juries in Jackson County, Texas. The Mexican American lawyers successfully challenged this serious violation of Mexican Americans' constitutional rights.[14]

Jiménez fought for minority rights, immigrant rights, and women's rights, among others. However, what she eventually focused on were human rights. When human rights are respected, she believed, other rights are as well. This belief explains her excitement went she read the United Nation's

Universal Declaration of Human Rights of 1948. It asserts that all persons, regardless of nationality or national origin, have a moral claim to demand fair treatment.[15] The first sentence in article 1 of the declaration states that "all human beings are born equal in dignity and rights."[16] For Jiménez the article succinctly resolved, she said, "the issue of how do you deal with other people that are different . . . because it allows for diversity while defining our equality in the area of rights and dignity. . . . Our equality, the basis of our equality, is in rights and dignity."[17]

The narratives of Mexican-origin activists in this book reinforce the view that because of the efforts and courage of activists for social justice, the trend in our nation's history has been toward reducing inequality. The suffragettes of the early twentieth century, for example, led the fight for the right of women to vote. This right materialized in 1920 with the passage of the Nineteenth Amendment to the US Constitution. On the issue of inequality and intolerance for women and others, Jiménez was optimistic. She once commented, "I think that historically there's *conflict* between intolerance and tolerance, but there is *still* a questioning. There's a *soul-searching* in the American people on that. And it's not something you see in other societies."[18] As Jiménez suggested, there have always been Americans who believed that equality, including racial and ethnic equality, constituted a core national value and that deviation from it undermined our national character.

Interpreting Discrimination: CRT and Discrimination by Default

Strained majority/minority relations and citizen/noncitizen relations complicate efforts to reduce racism. Scholars offer various explanations for difficult interracial and interethnic relations, but this study primarily draws on concepts from law professors Richard Delgado and Jean Stefancic in *Critical Race Theory: An Introduction* and Lu-in Wang in *Discrimination by Default: How Racism Becomes Routine*.[19] They point out that pervasive racist beliefs and practices can become common—so common that they seem normal. People are therefore frequently unaware of their prejudicial beliefs and practices. A critical role for activists of color is to raise awareness of social inequities and to challenge them. Delgado, Stefancic, and Wang go beyond the narrow discussions that focus on the white/Black dichotomy or that suggest that only blatant racism should be addressed. On the complicated topic of racial relationships, Wang writes, "Our individual biases dovetail with a set of social practices, patterns, and norms that produce and reproduce unintentional discrimination and have become so familiar that they define our sense of what is 'normal,' and, in turn, what is 'real' and even 'natural.' "[20]

CRT, an outgrowth of critical legal theory, received national attention in September 2020 when President Donald Trump ordered the end of federal race-related training that used CRT, calling it "un-American propaganda."[21] However, a more accurate statement about CRT theorists, who are called "crits," is that they want to advance social justice by "studying and transforming the relationship among race, racism and power."[22] A subdivision of crits are "LatCrits," the abbreviation for "Latino crits." Two well-known LatCrits are law professors Kevin R. Johnson and Richard Delgado. They focus on Hispanic issues—for example, internal colonization, immigration, and bilingual education. LatCrits provide crucial insight since typical discussions on racial issues often concern relations between whites and Blacks and exclude many issues that affect Hispanics.[23]

CRT incorporates ideas from various sources that help activists of color combat forms of injustice. One major source is the Italian philosopher and political theorist Antonio Gramsci (1891–1937). Gramsci wrote about the concept of *hegemony* and oppressive structures of society. He used the term *hegemony*, which means domination or predominance, to express the fact that all individuals internalize the dominant beliefs of their society. In other words, members of a society often are conformist and passive, and "take part in a conception of the world mechanically imposed by the external environment."[24] One harmful hegemonic concept, discussed in chapter 2, is the "Mexican Problem," which perpetuated anti-Mexican antipathy and, to its adherents, justified racial discrimination.

Feminist crits also offered useful insight "on power and the construction of social roles" and how dominating systems, such as patriarchy, operate.[25] For the Latina who opposes the constraints of gender stereotypes and her "otherness" in white society, critical race feminism helps her to recognize and challenge oppressive powers. Besides mainstream society, Latinas also must deal with the patriarchy within their own culture. In this context the "Latina is defined by the *Latino* [male] in his dominant position in the family, church, and state."[26] A Latina who opposed constraints on her own needs and desires, Jiménez, for example, received harsh criticism and was told that she was a traitor to her people.[27] Jiménez's spirited response to her critics is described in chapter 4.

CRT posits that it is important that victims of discrimination tell their stories, including their responses to the injustices that they experienced.[28] I therefore offer their stories—in detail in the case of Maria Jiménez—and the historical context of their experiences. Life stories or personal narratives, indispensable to historical research, make books like this one possible.[29] On the value of the narratives of historical persons, historian David M. Kennedy asserts that history "is about people, not about abstract ideas or vast impersonal forces . . . about people who . . . shape the lives they lead and take responsibility for them . . . people who have agency."[30]

Among the central claims or tenets of CRT, the most important is that racism is normal, in the narrow sense that it is commonplace in society, but not in the sense that it is morally, socially, or politically acceptable. The term *commonplace* as used in this book indicates conformist attitudes and the subsequent actions of a dominant system of beliefs and values. Commonplace beliefs can be positive but often are harmful, as was the case when they supported Jim Crow laws and social attitudes in the South. CRT does not claim everyone is racist, but since many people have internalized commonplace racist ideas, prejudices and discrimination continue to exist. As crits explain it, "We each occupy a normative universe or 'nomos' (or perhaps many of them) from which we are not easily dislodged."[31]

Abusive beliefs and practices should never become normal, though this can happen. In the specific case of those victimized by border and immigration officials in South Texas along the US-Mexico border, this injustice has existed for so many generations that it seems routine, a part of "normal" daily life. On recalling in 1995 the harsh but common and routine treatment by Border Patrol, one resident of El Paso, Texas, explained why only a few victims of Border Patrol mistreatment ever complained. He remarked, "Maybe our parents have indoctrinated us and told us that this is the way it is here in the border, and that we just have to accept it."[32] Jiménez understood this comment, adding that, "We had the INS and Border Patrol in our midst for so many decades that a lot of abuse was no longer recognizable. . . . We thought it was *normal*. It had become normal [that] the *migras* stopped you."[33] For those so affected, Jiménez coined the term "abused-community syndrome," discussed in chapter 6.[34]

Since acts of discrimination may not be conscious or deliberate, crits believe that they must be made apparent to the offender. Once discrimination becomes apparent, the person can change his or her beliefs and behavior.[35] A vital role that activists of color have played, and continue to play, is to point out social inequities in our society. In the words of African American crit and pedagogy theorist Gloria Ladson-Billings, "A strategy of those who fight for racial social justice is to unmask and expose racism in all of its various permutations."[36]

In addition to the tenet that racism is commonplace, a second tenet of CRT concerns "white privilege" (i.e., the collective advantage of being white). Many whites are unaware of the concept or how white privilege conveys benefits to them. On whiteness, a component of white privilege, law professor Brant T. Lee asserts that it "has become the default race in our society. People are presumed to be white unless otherwise stated. Thus the 'standard' judge, teacher, student, or consumer—the standard person—is imagined to be white."[37] This assumption diminishes the role of people of color in society. Crits acknowledge, nevertheless, that whites sometimes reduce or eliminate racial discrimination. This happens, in the opinion of law professor and civil rights activist Derrick A. Bell Jr. (1930–2011), when there is "interest convergence."[38] Bell's thesis argues that "the majority group tolerates advances for racial justice only when it suits its interest to do so."[39] Examples of interest convergence are discussed in the chapters that follow.

A third tenet in CRT asserts that terms like *white*, *race*, and *ethnicity* are social constructs and their meanings can and do change over time.[40] For example, the US Census Bureau made changes in the category of *white* in 1930 when it removed Mexican Americans from it. The classification of *white* was so coveted by Mexican Americans because of the white privilege it entailed that they protested being put in the nonwhite category. Their protest is described in chapter 2. Law professor George A. Martínez interpreted the Mexican Americans' rejection of the nonwhite category thusly: being white "meant gaining access to a panoply of public and private privileges, while insuring that one would avoid being the object of others' domination."[41]

Maria Jiménez: Immigrant and Human Rights Activist

In the following chapters I will give voice to many Mexican-origin activists, telling of their victories against various injustices. Chapters 2 and 3 tell their story. The following chapters continue with their activism but will focus on the life of Maria Jiménez. The narrative about Jiménez and other activists will reveal the historical context in which they fought for rights denied them. Their life stories constitute important historical sources and provide readers with special insight into past events. As historian Alice Kessler-Harris believed, the biography of a public person "helps us to make sense of a piece of the historical process."[42] Similarly, historian Lois W. Banner, wrote, "Studying the life of an individual might be seen as a way of understanding broad social and cultural phenomena."[43]

The life story of Jiménez presented here adds to the limited literature on Mexican American women of Texas, especially of Houston. There are two important biographies of the famous singer Lydia Mendoza, a Mexican American woman of Houston.[44] There is also a biography for juvenile readers of Dr. Guadalupe Quintanilla, a well-known educator and admired community activist in Houston.[45] Clearly, more biographies are needed. A regrettable consequence of this neglect of minority women is that this group is unaware of the contributions of its members. Their life stories are important, LatCrit Richard Delgado explained, because they have a healing value, and represent "psychic self-preservation."[46] In other words, biographies can empower others. Scholar Teresa Cordova highlights another benefit: for a woman of

Mexican descent, the life stories "above all else, are defiance against definitions imposed on her—definitions that oppress her."[47]

This book addresses racial history, including discrimination, and the
controversial subject of immigration, including past policies and practices.
I describe how Mexican nationals and Mexican Americans in Houston fought
for their civil and human rights. Jiménez's remarkable life story stands out
in this history. Her accomplishments as an activist for social justice date
from the 1960s, when she became president of the Student Association at
the University of Houston, the first Hispanic and first woman to hold this
position. Later roles she would take on include immigrant and human rights
activist, writer, and university lecturer.

Although little has been written on Mexican American women of
Houston, there is more literature on the Mexican-origin community of
Houston. From the 1980s there are two admirable general histories and a
recent book that focused on a specific barrio. Thomas H. Kreneck wrote
Del Pueblo: A Pictorial History of Houston's Hispanic Community in 1989.
The book, a narrative of the history of the Mexican-origin community from
the 1800s to the 1980s, is graced with many photographs. The book's 2012
revision, *Del Pueblo: A History of Houston's Hispanic Community*, omitted
most photographs in the 1989 book and extended the history into the 1990s.[48]
Another noteworthy work, also published in 1989, was *Ethnicity in the
Sunbelt: A History of Mexicans in Houston* by Arnoldo de León, the well-
known historian of Mexicans in Texas.[49] In its 2001 revision, *Ethnicity in
the Sunbelt: Mexican Americans in Houston*, de León added a new chapter
to the earlier work that included a brief discussion on immigration. In the
2012 book, Kreneck addressed immigration and discussed problems associated with the new Hispanic residents, such as crime and low levels of education. In his 2001 book, de León asserted that the latest wave of immigration
from Mexico and Central America stimulated a cultural renewal, including
renewed interest in Mexican celebrations like quinceañeras and Día de los
Muertos.

Recent works that were used in this book addressed specific topics. First
is *The Spirit of Magnolia Park: Ethnic Pride in a Mexican Barrio, 1909–
2009*, published in 2013. It provided a more intimate history than those

of Kreneck and de León because it addressed only one Houston barrio.[50] The writers, Grisel Gómez-Cano and James Ross-Nazzal, described the challenges and achievements of the Mexican-origin leaders in the barrio of Magnolia Park and included information on Maria Jiménez. Another book, by historian Guadalupe San Miguel Jr., thoroughly researched the fight against educational inequities in Houston. I discuss his 2005 work, *Brown, Not White: School Integration and the Chicano Movement in Houston* in chapter 4.[51] An admirable biography by Thomas H. Kreneck, published in 2001, provided the life of an important League of United Latin American Citizens (LULAC) pioneer, Felix Tijerina.[52] Tijerina was a national president of LULAC (1956–1960) and well-known civic leader in Houston until his death in 1965.

The historical literature of Mexican-origin women in Texas is small but growing and provided information for this book, including a few sources on Maria Jiménez. For example, an important recent publication is *Las Tejanas: 300 Years of History*, coauthored by Teresa Palomo Acosta and Ruthe Winegarten.[53] It describes women from all backgrounds and is a major contribution to historical literature on Mexican-origin women in Texas. A very useful resource that includes information on Mexican-origin women is the *Handbook of Texas*—produced by the Texas State Historical Association, an independent, nonprofit association since 1897—available online.[54] Emma Pérez, a feminist theorist and historian, wrote *The Colonial Imaginary: Writing Chicanas into History*, which includes an insightful chapter on Mexican American women in Houston.[55] The book *Chicanas in Charge: Texas Women in the Public Arena*, by José Angel Gutiérrez, Michelle Melendez, and Sonia Adriana Noyola, discusses important public figures.[56] *Chicanas in Charge* offers biographies of twenty-five Tejanas, dating from the mid-1960s to the present. This book includes a short chapter on Jiménez and describes her early life and her later activism for immigrant rights. A recent publication, *Chicana Movidas: New Narrative of Activism and Feminism in the Movement Era*, includes a chapter on Jiménez coauthored by Samantha Rodríguez and Stalina Emmanuelle Villarreal, Jiménez's daughter. Their chapter focused on Jiménez's activism during the Chicano Movement era of the 1960s and 1970s.[57]

Literature about immigration abounds and reflects its multifaceted nature. Many excellent sources provided valuable information for this study. Historian David G. Gutiérrez, for example, wrote about California and Texas, focusing on ethnicity and the relationship between Mexican nationals and Mexican Americans up to 1980.[58] Historian Mae M. Ngai wrote a well-researched study that concentrated on the period from 1924 to 1965. Her work discusses Mexican, Filipino, Japanese, and Chinese immigrant communities in the United States.[59] Sociologist Timothy J. Dunn, who specializes on the militarization of the US-Mexico border, provided another dimension to the complex topic of immigration.[60]

In the never-ending national debates on racial justice and immigration reform, and the increasing level of nativism, a study that examines the Mexican-origin minority, especially the immigration issues this group faces, is timely. The racial discrimination against this minority, or any other, by individuals and official policies and practices erodes the moral fiber of the nation and its democratic ideals. To advance social justice, knowledge of the nation's racist past is indispensable. The life of Maria Jiménez is an untold part of this history. Her life mission was to promote social justice and to defend the dignity and rights of the Mexican-origin community, particularly its immigrants. Her efforts, and those of her predecessors, played a critical role in promoting our nation's cherished values of equality and social justice.

Chapter 2

Texas and Houston History through the Great Depression

The humanity and dignity of immigrants and of all people are lost in the midst of this confusion about "us" and "them."

—Maria Jiménez[1]

They would call you "Mexicano." That wasn't supposed to be nice.
I don't know. You really were, but I guess this is the way they wanted to hurt you.

—Mrs. Cruz Valdez[2]

Social justice, a major American ideal, exists when society regards all persons as human beings and equal to all other persons. There are no "us" and "them" divisions in a just society. However, race and other kinds of divisions and discrimination have existed throughout the nation's history. Persons of Mexican origin, for example, suffer from commonplace racist prejudices. These injurious beliefs are pervasive and tenacious and undermine the nation's sense of equality for all. However, despite a history of discrimination, the Mexican-origin community asserts its right to a life of equality and dignity. When it succeeds in fighting social injustices, it advances the nation's democracy.

The history of Texas and its Mexican-origin community, addressed in this and subsequent chapters, reveals why life is sometimes difficult, even dangerous, for Mexicans and Mexican Americans. This chapter will describe the period from Texas's early history to the 1930s, including bloody clashes between the Mexican-origin community and white Texans; the revival in the 1920s of the Ku Klux Klan (KKK), a white terrorist group; and the Great Depression of the 1930s, during which time Mexicans repatriated, usually involuntarily, to Mexico. Also in this period, Congress passed restrictive immigration laws that adversely affected Mexicans entering the United States. These immigration laws and others discussed in later chapters reflect the racism of society and will provide a historical context to the work of Maria Jiménez, an immigrant and human rights activist. In addition, the chapter will address the emergence of the "Mexican Problem," a nativist concept that vilified Mexicans and their culture. The chapter also will describe the ways that Mexican-origin activists challenged social injustice by, for example, joining or forming labor unions to fight for fair wages and work conditions.

Early Statehood

Persons of Mexican origin have long inhabited what is now the state of Texas. In the nineteenth century, inhabitants of this area experienced major transformations, both political and demographic, that greatly affected racial relations and at times incited racial conflicts. In 1800 the area known today as Texas was still part of the Spanish Empire. However, in 1821 Mexico won its independence from Spain, and Texas became part of Mexico. In 1836, after the Texas Revolution, also called the Texas Revolt,[3] Texas gained its independence from Mexico to become the Republic of Texas (1836–1845). In 1845 the republic became the twenty-eighth state of the United States. Relations between Mexico and the United States rapidly deteriorated, resulting in the Mexican-American War (1846–1848). After Mexico's defeat the war concluded with the Treaty of Guadalupe Hidalgo

(1848), which granted to Mexicans in Texas the right to become citizens of the United States.

In addition to the above political transformations that were very disruptive and violent to those involved, Texas underwent profound demographic changes.[4] Texas aggressively encouraged whites from the United States to settle in Texas, and they did so in large numbers. Prior to statehood, however, the pace of white settlement was slow. Attacks or threat of attacks from Indigenous tribes, especially the Comanche and Lipan Apache, discouraged emigration to Texas. Although attacks occurred, contemporary accounts indicate that fearful whites, as well as exaggerated news accounts, created the menacing construct of the "Indian problem."[5] Whites in Texas held the commonplace belief that Native Americans were dangerous, uncivilized, and were an obstacle to western expansion.[6] To end the "Indian problem," the Republic of Texas targeted Indigenous tribes for extermination. In 1832 Texans hired a group of frontiersmen, a precursor to the Texas Rangers, to kill Native Americans. The historian Gary Clayton Anderson described the violent assignment as "ethnic cleansing," an appropriate term given the zeal of the Rangers who performed this duty.[7] In addition, in 1854 the Texas legislature created two reservations for the Comanche. Other Native American tribes were relocated to present-day Oklahoma.

For Mexicans and Blacks, coexistence with white Texans became increasingly difficult. Interestingly, however, in the case of enslaved Black people in antebellum Texas, news reports in the 1850s indicated that they enjoyed freedoms not found elsewhere. They, for example, could hire themselves out as contract laborers and obtain guns and liquor. Nevertheless, they were not free, and Texas passed slave laws and established slave patrols to control them. Some Texans feared that enslaved Blacks might organize an insurrection. In 1860 the slave population totaled 169,000, or one-third of the state's population.[8] After the Civil War, formerly enslaved Blacks briefly enjoyed many legal rights during the Reconstruction, and forty-one Blacks served in the state legislature. However, after white Democrats gained control of the state government, African Americans' civil rights were suppressed or ended, and Jim Crow laws proliferated.[9]

Mexicans in Texas, or Tejanos, also had an uneasy relationship with whites. For example, white Texans vigorously objected to their socializing with enslaved Blacks. Fearing a slave insurrection, whites believed that interracial socializing gave enslaved Blacks a "false sense of freedom."[10] Whites punished Mexicans for their friendship with Blacks by expelling Mexicans from their homes and towns.[11] A wave of evictions in the 1850s occurred in different areas of Texas. Although Tejanos had the same constitutional rights that whites enjoyed—their rights, including naturalization, were guaranteed by the Treaty of Guadalupe Hidalgo of 1848—they suffered racial discrimination and even threats to their lives. White Texans violated the legal rights of Tejanos, secure in the prevalence of commonplace anti-Mexican prejudices. For example, in the 1830s one Texas resident remarked that he "looked on Mexicans as scarce more than apes."[12] Even in the case when whites murdered Mexicans for little or no reason, white society seemed unconcerned.[13] As a public official of Texas told the US Congress in 1878, "When it is known that a Mexican has been hung or killed . . . there is seldom any fuss made about it."[14]

Bloody clashes and other lawless acts between the races were far from rare. For example, Mexican cartmen, *arrieros*, who transported goods from the Gulf Coast to the interior of the state, enjoyed a lucrative business until whites violently seized their business. In this Cart War of 1857, whites killed at least seventy-five Mexicans and destroyed their carts.[15] In response to white vigilantism, Mexicans sometimes organized resistance, as in the Cortina War in 1859.[16] White vigilantes also lynched innocent Mexicans who were suspected of stealing horses or of other alleged crimes. In the opinion of historians William D. Carrigan and Clive Webb, mob violence in Texas against Mexicans was "state-sanctioned terrorism" since Texas Rangers contributed to these lynchings and did not discourage white vigilante groups from attacking Mexicans.[17] Fortunately, in 1919 Texas State Representative José Tomás Canales demanded that the state legislature investigate the Texas Rangers' actions during this deadly period and make recommendations for reform. These, however, according to historian Richard Henry Ribb, were merely "cosmetic."[18] For Mexicans and African Americans, the possibility of being lynched—unfortunately not a federal crime until 2022[19]—terrified these people of color in the 1800s and early 1900s. Among killings that were documented, records indicate that whites lynched three Mexicans in 1874 and fifteen in 1918.[20] Historians do not have accurate figures for the number of Mexicans lynched, especially since white Texans, indifferent to these deaths, did not leave reliable statistics. However, Carrigan and Webb estimate that the total in Texas from 1880 to 1930 was 282.[21] Lynching peaked in the early 1900s in south Texas during the Mexican Revolution era. A different kind of violence was the seizure of land from Tejanos, which occurred extensively. According to sociologist Timothy Dunn, the illegal methods whites used included "theft, intimidation, swindles, dubious challenges and the burden of related court costs, taxes, and other debts."[22]

The Mexican-origin community suffered great losses in land and lives, but it also claimed some victories and accomplishments. These improved their lives but also advanced social justice because they challenged racial discrimination. The landmark legal case *Re: Rodriguez* (1897) is one example. Whites in San Antonio, Texas, attempted to block Ricardo Rodríguez's application to become a naturalized citizen. Rodríguez eventually won his case, and during his legal struggle about two hundred Mexican Americans in San Antonio rallied to support his case. In addition activists tackled other problems by forming self-help organizations called *mutualistas*.[23] La Agrupación Protectora Mexicana (Mexican Protective Association) of San Antonio, for example, was formed in June 1911 following the lynching of 14-year-old Antonio Gomez. By August it was a statewide organization.[24]

The *mutualistas* and similar organizations provided the Mexican-origin community with welcome support and fellowship in a hostile society. These organizations reflected a community that was organized and prepared to address racial discrimination and violence. Their activism was timely because the Americanization movement emerged in the early twentieth century. Leaders in the movement offered classes that taught the traditional American culture— that is, white Anglo-Saxon Protestant—to the Mexican-origin community and other nonwhite, non-English speaking immigrant communities. The concepts of *white* and *citizen* grew in importance, and the nonwhite, noncitizen person was considered a threat to the American culture. Not surprisingly, in the early 1900s, according to historian Cynthia B. Orozco, whites created "a new paradigm—'the Mexican problem'—to racialize and subordinate La Raza."[25] The label "the Mexican problem," Orozco adds, became synonymous with "immigrant" and drew a sharp line between "us" and "them."

In addition to *mutualistas*, the Mexican American community organized labor unions in their struggle for social justice. Jiménez learned about labor unions as a child because her father was a union organizer, and she later followed in his footsteps. An example of an early union for Mexican-origin workers was the Federal Labor Union (FLU) No. 11953, organized in 1905 in south Texas. Its leadership emanated from Mexico, specifically from La Sociedad de Ferrocarril Mexicano, Mexico's first national railroad union. Railroad workers organized La Sociedad in 1887 in Nuevo Laredo, Mexico. The FLU was formed across the US-Mexico border in Laredo, Texas, and lasted until 1907. It was notable in its short existence, according to the historian Emilio Zamora, because of its "devoted adherence to the popular unifying value of mutualism and a socialist ideology with an international character."[26] Unfortunately, the most important organization of labor unions in the United States, the American Federation of Labor (AFL), opposed having Mexican workers in its unions and even advocated restricting Mexican immigration. The Industrial Workers of the World (IWW) took more interest in Mexican labor, but it lost much of its influence in the 1920s.[27]

The racial divisions did not prevent the Mexican-origin community from acculturating in varying degrees while at the same time embracing its Mexican heritage. Tejano activists in 1911, for example, organized El Primer Congreso Mexicanista (First Mexican Congress), which created the *Gran Liga* (Grand League). The league was short-lived, but, importantly, many of its leaders remained greatly motivated to promote social justice. Two important results of the 1911 initiative, according to Orozco, were the organizations the Order of the Sons of America (OSA) in 1921 and LULAC in 1929. From her research of the OSA, LULAC, and other organizations of the 1910s and 1920s, Orozco concluded that from these organizations emerged the Mexican American civil rights movement in Texas, and not much later, with the Chicanos/as of the 1960s and 1970s. The 1910s and 1920s, in other words, provided a critical foundation for later activists for social justice.

Federal immigration and naturalization laws of the time also shaped this period. These laws should be understood as egregious examples of social injustice whereby immigrants were treated unfairly and inhumanely. Unless of Anglo-Saxon and Protestant lineage, according to commonplace prejudices of nativists, immigrants were the inferior "other." Immigration laws and the recent heated national debates on immigration reflect the nation's inability to reach a consensus on immigrants and immigration policy and practices. Caught in this dilemma is the Mexican-origin community, especially mixed-status families, those whose members include US citizens and noncitizens.

From the beginning immigration laws have reflected the nation's desire to maintain a white society. As an immigrant and committed immigrant activist, Jiménez became keenly aware of this fact. The earliest federal law, passed in 1790, determined who could become a naturalized citizen. The Naturalization Act of 1790 granted naturalization to "free white persons," which, in practice, meant white male property owners.[28] In the following century, after the Civil War (1861–1865), Congress passed the Naturalization Act of 1870, which granted the right of naturalization to men of African descent. No other nonwhite group received this right. Finally, Congress passed an explicitly race-based immigration law that denied the right of naturalization to the Chinese with the Chinese Exclusion Act of 1882. It also denied Chinese people entry into the United States and was the first law barring an entire race.[29]

Mexican Labor: Early Twentieth Century and World War I

The labor demands of the growing US economy in the early twentieth century attracted immigrants from many countries. Mexicans emigrated to fill the jobs, and employers, in turn, welcomed a steady supply of cheap labor. Several transnational developments contributed to the demand for labor. Of these developments, Jiménez wrote, the "rapid pace of industrialization gave impetus to the development of agriculture in the Southwest and of transportation systems throughout the country, especially the railroads. This contributed to the initiation of streams of labor flows from Mexico."[30]

Mexicans emigrated to the United States for jobs, but they were also fleeing violence in their homeland during the Mexican Revolution era (1910–1920). Interestingly, the United States took the unprecedented step to grant refugee status to Mexicans.[31] The influx included not only ordinary Mexicans but also politically active Mexicans who opposed the Mexican president Porfirio Díaz. These Mexican exiles, who publicly espoused anarchism and called for the overthrow of Díaz, organized the Partido Liberal Mexicana (PLM) in Texas. The PLM greatly contributed to a volatile political climate in the United States, especially in South Texas. The tense situation sometimes resulted in bloody conflicts between Mexican nationals and Tejanos and white Texans. The latter, who feared an insurrection, included white vigilantes and the Texas Rangers. Unfortunately, whites killed Tejanos who were not involved in any political or seditious activities. Concerning bloody clashes in Texas history, Jiménez remarked, "Wanton acts of violence left a legacy of hatred between the two peoples. Mexicans engaged in armed uprisings against white society, and the Anglo-American political system legitimated police repression and gave law enforcement bodies like the Texas Rangers license to kill Mexicans."[32]

Other international events also strained relations between whites and Mexicans in the United States, increasing anti-Mexican prejudices. For example, political relations between the United States and Mexico deteriorated during World War I (1914–1918), especially after the publication of the Zimmermann telegraph from Germany to Mexico in 1917 and because of the rumor that there were German U-boat bases in Mexico.[33] Given the dangerous political climate of the war period, many whites distrusted Mexican nationals and Mexican Americans in the United States, not certain where they placed their loyalty. In fact, a significant percentage of Mexicans were immigrants, not US citizens, and retained a personal attachment to their homeland. According to this writer's father, Sam V. Quintanilla, his parents felt that attachment, although they decided not to return to Mexico. According to Quintanilla, "You know, that was the custom. Everybody was going back to Mexico."[34]

The tense war era put Mexican nationals in an awkward situation and illustrates another difficulty immigrant communities experience.

Mexicans held conflicting opinions on how World War I affected them. Some chose to stay and contribute to the war effort and others fled back to Mexico to avoid being drafted.[35] To assuage their fears, the federal government claimed that it would not draft them.[36] Tejano leaders such as the Houston teacher J. J. Mercado repeated these official assurances to nervous Mexican nationals.[37] Nevertheless, the government did, in fact, draft Mexican nationals. Mexican scholar Fernando Saúl Alanis Enciso estimated that about sixty thousand undocumented Mexican immigrants served on army bases in the United States and that almost fifteen thousand participated in the war abroad.[38]

Life for immigrants, especially the undocumented, became more complicated because of developments after World War I. This was a period when nation-states, according to political scientist Aristide Zolberg, established "hypernationalist" regimes that imposed greater restrictions on immigration. Specifically, historian Mae M. Ngai wrote, "Rigid border controls, passports, and state restrictions on entry and exit became the norms for governing emigration and immigration."[39] The new restrictions created tremendous hardships for Mexican immigrants and even problems for employers. For example, growers, who depended a great deal on cheap Mexican labor, needed to send recruiters into Mexico to solicit workers, a practice that violated Mexican law. Labor recruiters also routinely stationed themselves outside the offices of the US Immigration Service in El Paso, Texas, to hire Mexicans. The US government did not discourage these recruiters. According to historian George J. Sánchez, "Knowing that labor agencies immediately employed the immigrants, the Immigration Service established a policy of admitting all such aliens."[40]

Growers in Texas and other states competed for cheap Mexican workers. Labor recruiters for the Great Western Sugar Company in Colorado, for example, traveled to Texas in 1920 in search of workers. In Mexican neighborhoods the recruiters "worked from house to house . . . held public meetings, ran newspaper ads, and offered free transportation to the fields" in Colorado.[41] Aggressive out-of-state labor agents "recruited Mexican workers surreptitiously and spirited them out of the state on isolated country roads in overcrowded canvas-covered trucks."[42] Unfortunately, the recruited workers frequently endured harsh working conditions. According to historian Juan Gómez-Quiñones, Mexican workers "were often forced to ride standing [in trucks] for two or three days with few or no stops for food or the use of toilet facilities."[43]

It is difficult not to conclude from the contemporary sources that employers viewed migrant workers more like property than human beings. Texas, for example, attempted to prevent other states from reducing the state's supply of workers. Farmers in Nueces County expressed their claim on Mexican workers thusly: "We wish to prevent the transportation of Mexicans where they don't belong."[44] From 1923 to 1929, the Texas legislature passed the Emigrant Labor Agency Laws to discourage recruitment by out-of-state employers. The purpose of the laws was "to regulate the operations of the employment agencies that were directing the movement of Mexicans towards better job opportunities in the Midwest and the North." In other words, the laws' main purpose, according to historian Emilio Zamora, was to "immobilize Mexican labor" in order to have a secure supply of workers for Texas.[45] Historian David Montejano agreed with Zamora on the demeaning purpose of the Emigrant Labor Agency Laws and described the laws' control of the movement of Mexicans as "a set of racial labor laws."[46] These reinforced the commonplace belief among Texas farmers and out-of-state employers that Mexican migrant laborers could be treated inhumanely and should be denied better job opportunities elsewhere.

Ambivalent Immigration Policy and the "Illegal Alien" in the Early Twentieth Century

For decades the nation has needed comprehensive immigration reform to end the unjust and inhumane exploitation of undocumented immigration. Even though the nation's need for cheap labor persisted in the twentieth and twenty-first centuries, immigration policy and practices became increasing hostile to immigrant workers. This abuse reached an egregious level during the Trump administration (2017–2021) and violated the nation's belief in social justice. Reports of the abuse of immigrants included the unvoluntary removal of fallopian tubes from women in Immigration and Customs Enforcement

(ICE) detention and farmworkers forced to work without protective equipment for COVID-19.[47]

Immigration history clearly demonstrates the reasons that immigration activists like Maria Jiménez work tirelessly for reform. Although discussing the immigration situation in 1999, Jiménez's comments have relevance to the early 1900s. She wrote that for poor international migrants, mobility became more difficult because of "passports, exit and entry visas and militarized borders. . . . Erecting borders for international labor . . . creates the legal mechanisms for the increased exploitation of international migrants in dynamic and expanding economic sectors in receiving countries."[48] The unequal power relationship between the United States and Mexico adversely affected emigrating Mexicans with each new immigration law and increase in border control. For instance, the Immigration Act of 1917 introduced more obstacles for legal immigration, including literacy tests and a higher head tax.[49] Restrictive US immigration policy did not halt illegal immigration and, instead, increased the number of "illegal aliens." Indeed, Mexicans became "the largest single group of illegal aliens by the late 1920s."[50]

Mexicans continued to emigrate, though without authorization, to avoid the humiliating procedure that a legal entry involved. The procedures used at the El Paso, Texas, port of entry included many of those used at Ellis Island, although inspections at the Mexican border began earlier, in 1917, and ended later, in the late 1920s.[51] United States immigration authorities ordered Mexican immigrants who legally crossed the border to disrobe for medical examinations, to bathe, and to undergo treatment for lice. The embarrassing procedure was required every week for Mexicans who worked in El Paso.[52] José Burciaga recalled his experience, saying, "They shaved everyone. . . . They bathed everyone, and after the bath they doused you with cryolite [sodium aluminum fluoride], comprised of some sort of substance, it was strong."[53] Affirming this complaint, an inspector in El Paso in 1923 wrote that after passengers left the train from Mexico, they were inspected, vaccinated if necessary, and then most were "bathed and deloused and their clothing and baggage fumigated by that [Immigration] Service."[54] The gruesome process did not apply to wealthy Mexicans and Europeans, highlighting the class-based and racist discrimination most Mexicans had to endure. Immigration authorities exempted first-class passengers from "line inspections, the baths, and the literacy test" when they reached El Paso.[55]

Unfortunately, the immigration laws of the 1920s reflected the racist views of the time. Before 1921, unlike today, the number of immigrants who could legally enter the nation was not set. However, quotas were established with the National Origins Act of 1921, also known as the Emergency Quota Act of 1921, and later made permanent with the Immigration Act of May 26, 1924, also known as the Johnson-Reed Act. One of its provisions explicitly barred entry to any immigrant who was ineligible to become a naturalized citizen.[56] The 1924 law also reduced quotas for persons from central and eastern Europe countries who were more likely to be non-English speaking, Catholic or Jewish, and "racially inferior," according to the Dillingham Commission.[57] Larger quotas were granted for white, Anglo-Saxon, and Protestant regions of northern and western Europe. No limits applied to Mexicans because the commission claimed they were ideal laborers. They, like "homing pigeons," "work for a short time in the United States and then return to their families in Mexico."[58] Nevertheless, the presence of Mexicans in the nation troubled many whites. In 1928, the popular magazine the *Saturday Evening Post* expressed alarm concerning Mexican immigration. One of its issues claimed that "Mexican laborers often had nine children or even more" and, therefore, "any of these Mexicans who are coming in by the trainload might be expected to average 729 great grandchildren. . . . No temporary consideration of expediency should carry the smallest weight in preventing the proper economic protection of our own flesh and blood."[59] The writer described the immigrants as "Mexican Indians" and feared that they would taint the nation's bloodline.

A provision of the Immigration Act of 1924 established the Border Patrol. Since its creation the agency has violated the civil and human rights of countless Mexican immigrants and even US citizens of Mexican descent.[60] Initially organized to catch smugglers at the border, it became a division of the Immigration and Naturalization Service (INS) in 1933 and was given the authority to stop illegal entry into the country. According to historian Patrick Ettinger, Border Patrol agents' original targets were "European aliens."[61] Former INS Commissioner Leonel Castillo (1977–1979) disagreed, saying its objective was to "catch Chinese coming through Mexico. The Border Patrol was not set up to apprehend Mexicans, it was set up to apprehend Chinese. The Mexicans didn't want the Chinese either, so they were trying to deport them."[62]

In Texas, a state that welcomed neither Mexican nor Chinese immigrants, racist individuals and white supremacist groups spread terror among people of color. Many of the earliest Border Patrol officers in Texas were relatives of Texas Rangers, a racially intolerant force. Only one officer, Pedro (Pete) Torres was Mexican American.[63] Others were members of the terrorist organization the KKK, a white supremacist organization.[64] In addition to communities in South Texas, people of color far from the southern border also lived in fear. In 1922, for example, near Fort Worth in north Texas, "300 whites marched through the black and Mexican districts of a town . . . and drove out Mexicans and blacks by threatening to burn the homes of those who stayed."[65]

One objective of the Immigration Law of 1924 and the creation of the Border Patrol was to reduce the Mexican community by stopping illegal entries into the country. However, sometimes immigration laws produce unintended results; these will be discussed in later chapters. Regarding the 1924 law and its restrictive measures, its unintended result was an increase, not decrease, in the number of undocumented Mexicans in the country. They entered without documentation to avoid both the cost of visas and passports and any contact with immigration authorities. The number of persons from Latin America who emigrated to the United States during the 1920s rose significantly, especially from Mexico. Accurate totals for illegal crossing are not available, but legal Mexican immigration from 1911 to 1920 was estimated at 219,004, but for the decade 1921–1930, this figure more than doubled to 459,287.[66]

1920s and 1930s: A Time of Violence, Labor, and Community Activism

The early twentieth century witnessed important developments in the Mexican-origin community. The decades of the 1910s and 1920s, for example, gave rise to the Mexican American Civil Rights Movement, according to historian Cynthia E. Orozco. Its activists, she wrote, were "of a nascent Mexican American male middle class committed to combating racism as an obstacle to community empowerment."[67] Demographic changes facilitated their activism. As the percentage of native-born persons of Mexican ancestry increased and the percentage born in Mexico decreased, this minority community expected and demanded equality and social justice. Nevertheless, it faced significant obstacles in Jim Crow society, including racial discrimination and violence, or its threat. The Great Depression of the 1930s added severe economic challenges as well.

The possibility of violence against persons of Mexican descent and other people of color increased in 1920 following the revival of the KKK in Texas cities, most notably in Houston. According to historian Don Carleton, "booming Houston was the first Texas city to have a KKK chapter. In 1920, this 'secret society' formed the Sam Houston Klan Number One. George B. Kimbro, a former deputy sheriff of Harris County, led the chapter."[68] Houston's Mayor Oscar Holcombe (1888–1968) was greatly concerned by the group's violent tactics and its extensive influence on the local police that endangered public safety.[69] Alarmed by the Klan's actions, Mayor Holcombe eventually hired "West Texas lawmen to provide protection for individuals threatened by the KKK during the latter's ascendency in Houston during 1921 and 1922."[70]

The Klan members' interpretation of what they considered moral conduct, and their desire to enforce it, motivated them to target certain individuals, white or persons of color. For example, in May 1921 they castrated a Black Houston dentist because of his relations with a white woman.[71] The Klan also tarred and feathered a white Houston lawyer because he had Black clients.[72] The Klan's Houston headquarters was located across from the civil court at San Jacinto and Preston Streets. The Mexican American activist and lawyer John J. Herrera (1910–1986) recalled that "when they [the KKK] had their parades uptown during meetings, practically everybody from the courthouse, lawyers, judges, sheriffs, and everything, would cross the street and they come out with those white sheets and march up and down the street."[73]

The Great Depression struck in the spring of 1929. Federal and state aid became available, but its distribution to people of color was appallingly unfair. The Great Depression affected all Texans, especially the working class, including Mexican immigrants.[74] In this difficult period, Mexicans lost their jobs and were denied new ones. In addition, distribution of aid to those in need was not equitable and was influenced by racial prejudices. Texas offered little or no economic assistance to the persons of Mexican descent, even to those who were citizens. Mexican legal residents sometimes received aid, but if they were unable to prove their legal status, they were told to "take steps to obtain American citizenship."[75]

Personal and cultural beliefs besides racism also influenced public assistance. For example, the city government in Houston hesitated to provide aid because of the commonplace belief that aid to the needy, even for native-born whites, was a "dole."[76] This opinion applied especially to Blacks and Mexicans, who "were denied relief in Houston on the grounds that aid to minorities prevented the allotment of resources to deserving whites."[77] Many residents of the city took the assistance that was available, although not everyone. In the case of persons of Mexican descent, accepting aid was a difficult, even "traumatic," experience, and some refused it.[78] Proud Mexican-origin men, according to Mrs. Cruz Valdez, "found themselves stripped of their role as provider and protector."[79] Aid that was available varied from place to place. For example, the relief costs per capita for aid from January to September 1931 for Los Angeles, Chicago, and Minneapolis were $3.40, $2.41, and $1.69, respectively. In Texas the monthly welfare payments for families averaged only $7.08. Elsewhere, the amount per family ranged from $4.86 in Arkansas to $31.35 in California.[80]

The federal government took drastic measures during this economic crisis, including pressuring Mexican immigrants to repatriate—to voluntarily return to Mexico.[81] The pressure was so great that the "voluntary" aspect of the return was meaningless. According to Jiménez, "Viewed as a 'foreign' labor force, it [Mexican immigrant labor] is easily expendable in times of economic downturn. This is particularly true of the undocumented Mexican immigrant; anti-immigrant and anti-Mexican social attitudes trigger INS enforcement crackdowns when migratory flows coincide with economic downturns."[82] The exodus to Mexico was significant. One-third or more of the Mexican population in the United States repatriated during the Great

Depression. The Mexican scholar Fernando Saúl Alanis Enciso estimated 350,00 for the years 1930–1933, and historian Abraham Hoffman estimated the total at 400,000.[83] For Texas the total returning to Mexico between 1929 and 1939 was 250,000, which included a significant percentage of the Mexican community of Houston. Many returned to the United States and Houston in the late 1930s when the economy improved.

Fortunately, federally funded New Deal programs did provide work for citizens and, in some cases, for immigrants. Job programs included the Civilian Conservation Corp (CCC). Mexican Americans in Houston, including Herman R. Cortéz (1920–2011), were among the youths in the CCC. Cortéz spent four years in the CCC and sent part of his pay to his family.[84] Remarking on the New Deal programs, Houston activist Angelina Morales (1907–1994) said, "Everybody had hope and we really were not cheated. We were not [cheated] because President Roosevelt did a lot of things to upgrade the economy and the feeling of trust to know that we once again were a proud nation."[85]

As unemployment rose, Mexicans and Mexican Americans in Houston took jobs wherever possible, frequently confronting racial discrimination. Ernest Eguía (1919–2011), future LULAC activist, remembered that he "shined shoes at a barbershop and hawked newspapers at the corner of Washington and Houston Avenues."[86] Domingo Trevino (1921–2009), who later earned a Distinguished Flying Cross for his service in World War II, worked seven days a week in a motel and earned only seven dollars in a week.[87] Houston Mexicans who were unemployed or earned very little could not pay their rent and were evicted from their residences. This happened to the family of Jesús "Jesse" Reyes (1923–2017), later a World War II veteran who fought in the western front in Europe and who became a civil rights activist in Houston.[88] Another person trying to survive was Carmen Cortés (1913–2001). She learned shorthand and went to many job interviews in Houston, but businesses told her they had no jobs for Mexicans. She replied, "But I'm an American citizen . . . I'm a native," to which she was told, "I don't care; don't have a job for you."[89]

Members of the Mexican-origin community rallied to help one another— a welcomed development because they faced increasing intolerance. Jobs became scarce, especially for immigrants, as did available relief. Blatant racism influenced who received aid and how much, so the economic inequality of resources for all people of color was a grim reality. The trend of the federal and state governments to deny jobs to immigrants spread to Houston in 1931. That year the Houston City Council decided that "local relief supervisors could deny public employment to Mexican residents."[90] In the early 1930s, at least two thousand undocumented Mexican immigrants in Houston made the painful decision to return to Mexico.[91] In these cases local activists organized to help. Generous individuals and community groups in Houston provided the funding that immigrants needed for their return. For example, El Club Pro-Repatriación, founded by Bartoleme Casa in 1932, purchased a truck to transport Mexicans who decided to return to Mexico.[92] Mexico offered help, and even the US Immigration Service assisted by providing trucks to take families to the border.[93] Unfortunately, untold numbers of families were split by the repatriation process. In addition, the American-born children who went with their parents to Mexico found it difficult to adjust to a foreign, Spanish-speaking country.

Persons of Mexican descent necessarily relied on different organizations to survive, but they also contributed when possible. Two helpful sources were the Mexican Clinic in the Second Ward that provided free medical care and La Cruz Azul (the Blue Cross).[94] La Cruz Azul, originally located in the Mexican consulate, focused on health education. It depended on volunteers like Josefina Rosales Ypina, an immigrant from Aguascalientes, Mexico, who moved to Houston in 1918 and began volunteering a few years later.[95] Assistance also came from Our Lady of Guadalupe Church, a Roman Catholic church, and the Wesley House, founded by the Methodist Church in 1930. Parishioners helped, too, by pledging donations to their churches.[96]

Other sources of aid included a settlement house and groups composed of community activists, the *mutualistas*. First was the Rusk Settlement House, which provided food and other services in Houston. Like other settlement houses, its main goal was to promote mainstream culture in the immigrant communities across the nation. Félix Fraga, future popular activist, was only 3 or 4 years old when he first attended the settlement house. He recalled,

"They used to recruit us, but we went for that meal we got at noon! Back in the Depression, that was as important to us kids as whatever you learned in class."[97] A. B. Olmos of Houston also remembered the settlement house, recalling that it offered "milk and a sandwich of peanut butter for the children after school."[98] In 1932, when city budget cuts threatened to reduce the settlement house's staff, the appreciative Mexican residents committed to giving the settlement house one dollar a month for eight months.[99] Like settlement houses, *mutualistas*, or self-help groups, provided critical services during the Great Depression, but unlike settlement houses, the *mutualistas* promoted the Mexican culture. An important *mutualista*, founded in 1932 by Celesto Suárez, was the Sociedad Mutualista Obrera Mexicana (SMOM). It provided greatly needed funds for funerals. Its women's auxiliary was organized in 1936. Angie Morales, entrepreneur, activist, and strong advocate for women's issues, helped to create the auxiliary.[100] The organization remains active, serving, according to SMOM leader Mamie Garcia, hundreds of families weekly.[101]

During the Great Depression, an intense anti-Mexican nativism swept the United States. The media and other sources frequently expressed commonplace racist views, a problem that remains today. For example, in a 1930 report written for the House Committee on Immigration and Naturalization, Professor Roy I. Garis of Vanderbilt University in Tennessee wrote, "Their minds run to nothing higher than animal functions—eat, sleep, and sexual debauchery. . . . These people sleep by day and prowl by night like coyotes, stealing anything they can get their hands on, no matter how useless to them it may be."[102] Mexican children, unfortunately, were not spared racist opinions. A school official in Colorado expressed an opinion also found in Texas, that "respectable white people . . . did not want their children to sit alongside dirty, filthy, diseased, infected Mexicans."[103]

In the weak economy of the Great Depression, Mexican-origin workers became more radical, and some labor activists organized labor strikes. Strikes in the nation between 1930 and 1937 totaled about 4,700. Labor activism was especially difficult in the oppressive, racist Jim Crow conditions that existed in Texas. Nevertheless, the labor activism that did emerge reflected the ethnic pride and solidarity in the Mexican-origin community.[104] Many of the labor activists were women, native-born or immigrant, who bravely defied antilabor hostilities.[105] They faced anti-Mexican racism and sexism in their demands for better pay and working conditions, according to historian Irene Ledesma. She wrote, "Anglos believed that Mexicans, as dark-skinned people, expressed a threatening sexual licentiousness through prostitution," and, therefore, threatened the morality of the community.[106] Women-led strikes occurred as early as 1919 in El Paso. Although these striking workers fought hard against intense and violent anti-union opposition, their strikes were unsuccessful.[107] The same obstacles they faced persisted into the 1930s and beyond.[108]

Fortunately, during the Great Depression, federal help for workers became available. Specifically, the government granted urban industrial workers important legal rights with the passage of the National Labor Relations Act (NLRA) of 1935. The act, usually called the Wagner Act after its sponsor Senator Robert F. Wagner (b. in Germany 1877, d. 1953), created the National Labor Relations Board (NLRB) to enforce the act's terms. These provisions included guaranteeing workers bargaining rights with their employers and prohibiting the latter from interfering with union activities. Unfortunately, the NLRA did not apply to agricultural workers and domestic workers, who were overwhelmingly Mexican and who received extremely low wages.[109]

The workers had a few allies during the Great Depression. For example, the Congress of Industrial Organizations (CIO), formed in 1937, reached out to minorities in the late 1930s and provided them with valuable leadership experiences. As a result of this experience, especially in California and Texas, "the most active and militant Mexican American and Mexican immigrant political advocates often came from the ranks of CIO union," according to historian David G. Gutiérrez.[110] The CIO also helped workers in Houston and other Texas cities through affiliated unions such as the Texas State Industrial Union Council, also formed in 1937.[111] A well-known labor activist in the 1930s was Emma Tenayuca (1916–1999), a Mexican American and Communist from San Antonio, Texas.[112] Like Maria Jiménez years later, Tenayuca "took note of how the group victimized by capitalism was the same on both sides of the border: dark-skinned peasants and working-class people."[113] Tenayuca became an official for the CIO and, in 1938, organized the important Pecan Shellers' Strike in San Antonio in which several thousand Mexican American and Mexican immigrant women participated.[114] Her impressive labor activism ended, however, when she was forced to leave the city in 1940, a victim of Red-baiting as a Communist and labor leader. In the anti-Red political climate of the 1930s, she could not find work in her hometown and moved to Houston.

Besides the CIO, men and women of color turned to the Communist Party (CP) of the USA for support because of its favorable position on minorities. Minorities thought that the CP would help them in their struggle for equality and social justice because it demanded an end to racial discrimination. This position contrasted sharply with the Republican and Democratic political parties. The CP indirectly helped the nation's minority labor force. Although more concerned with the fascist threat in Europe, the CP attracted minority workers and labor activists because "as a whole, the party supported civil-rights activities, and the protection of the rights of the foreign-born. It protested police brutality and advocated the elimination of discrimination against Mexicans."[115]

In addition to the influence of the CIO and the CP, persons of Mexican descent became activists and leaders in their community through the organizations they formed. In the 1930s a major development that emerged in many cities, including Houston, was the establishment of civic organizations. One such organization was LULAC. Houston activists formed Council #60 of LULAC in 1934. Major organizers included Juvencio Rodríguez and lawyers John Henry Duhig and John J. Herrera. LULAC had originated in Corpus Christi, Texas, in 1929, and unlike older organizations that maintained strong ties with Mexico, it decided to focus on its members becoming successful citizens of the United States. This objective made sense given the anti-Mexican racism of the time, when lynching remained a threat.[116] Among the organization's early goals was to end the immigrant image typically attributed to persons of Mexican origin. In addition, because anti-Mexican prejudice was so great, the group chose the term *Latin American* instead of *Mexican* for the organization's name, resulting in the League of United Latin American Citizens (LULAC). The name also clearly indicated that membership was officially only open to US citizens.

LULAC led a protest after the US Census Bureau placed Mexicans in the nonwhite category in the 1930 census. Houstonian Juvencio Rodríguez claimed that objection was being placed in racial category of "yellow."[117] The nonwhite classification for the Mexican-origin community was also used in federal forms issued following passage of the Social Security Act of 1935. In the racist climate of the time, LULAC members and other individuals of Mexican descent, especially in Texas, valued their legal classification of "white."[118] The social construct of whiteness signified numerous advantages that whites had but people of color did not. The pressure from LULAC and its allies in Houston over the census changes probably was effective. The Census Bureau returned Mexicans to the white category and, after 1935, the Social Security Board reinstated the category of "white" for Mexicans. For Alonso S. Perales (1898–1960), the intellectual leader of LULAC from its inception in 1929, any classification of color reinforced prejudice in society and the law.[119] The disadvantage of nonwhiteness was a common experience for many people of color—for example, World War II veteran Antonio Campos (b. 1923), who lived in a town near Houston. Recalling an experience before the war, Campos said, "In the restaurants . . . if you wanted to get fed you had to go in the back. Mexican and dogs were in the back. You had to get a sandwich and go home."[120]

Fortunately, Houston members of LULAC and the Latin American Club (LAC) responded to racist discrimination, including against Mexican-origin city workers. In one case these workers' rights were violated because the city classified all its Mexican American workers as temporary, even those who worked full-time. The classification made them ineligible for benefits. Recalling his difficult work experiences during the 1930s, Juvencio Rodríguez said, "We couldn't get no jobs in the city, and those at the time putting Mexicans to work, would be classified as temporary employees."[121] In this case, however, Rodríguez and other workers received help from LAC. John Duhig, its cofounder and a lawyer, won "a court battle to have Mexicans accepted as permanent workers" and not temporary employees.[122]

LAC and LULAC sprang into action in another incident following a racist remark by S. A. Starkey, Houston's city commissioner.[123] Several Mexican city workers lost wages in 1938 when they took time off on

San Jacinto Day, April 21, a holiday granted to Houston city workers. The holiday commemorated the final battle of the Texas Revolution in 1836, east of present-day Houston. City Commissioner Starkey scoffed at the workers' request for the day off, saying, "What! Pay Mexicans for the day they were beaten." LAC and LULAC took umbrage at the derogatory remark since many Tejanos fought with whites in defeating Mexican forces at San Jacinto. The organizations sent the city council a list of Tejanos who fought and died at the battle. In LULAC's statement to the city council, the organization wrote, "These are the names of the Mexicans who were not beaten. They died, but in so doing they laid the foundation for the birth of the independence of Texas."[124]

Activists of Mexican descent responded energetically to the racism of this incident, although at other times they expressed a desire to be accepted by white society. As for the comments by the city commissioner, Juvencio Rodríguez said, "I'm telling you we just unloaded on him . . . the write up in the paper [Houston Press] there says Mr. Starkey done had enough of that. They gave more than Starkey could take."[125] A few years later, whites acted more positively, possibly due to the backlash that Starkey's comments received in 1938. In this incident in 1942, and at the suggestion of John J. Herrera, LULAC members placed a wreath at the San Jacinto Monument in the San Jacinto Battleground State Historical Park. LULAC members were not sure how the public would respond to this act. Evidently whites welcomed the LULAC members, who, according to Rudy Vara, "were so proud of ourselves that the gringos got so close to us and we were just accepted."[126]

In addition to insensitive racist remarks, another recurring problem that Houston's Mexican-origin minority experienced involved police brutality. Mexican immigrants in Texas felt particularly vulnerable. They also knew from experience to expect more help from the Mexican consulate than local Mexican American organizations. In one incident of police brutality, the consulate hired a Mexican American attorney from San Antonio in 1937 to represent the Mexican government in the trial of the death of Elpidio Cortéz, a Mexican immigrant. He died in April of that year while in police custody and two police officers were indicted. Although the police were acquitted, the trial was significant in Houston because, according to historian F. Arturo Rosales, it was "the first time a policeman accused of slaying a Mexican had been tried beyond the grand jury stage."[127]

Mexican American women's organizations, like their male counterparts, denounced social injustice. However, they also expressed, like Vara, the desire to be accepted by white society. According to Stella Quintenella, the secretary of El Club Feminino Chapultepec, her organization "wanted to show the Anglo-American community that we could be good Americans, not just Mexican girls."[128] El Club Feminino Chapultepec was active from 1931 to 1945 and had as its mission to project a cultured, positive image of Mexican American women.

Nevertheless, this middle-class social organization publicly criticized the racism in Houston. One incident that angered many club members was the Elpidio Cortéz case, mentioned above. It motivated the women to write a letter on June 11, 1937, to the office of the Young Women's Christian Association (YWCA) in Kansas City, Missouri. The club was affiliated with the YWCA and the letter outlined some of the social injustice that the Mexican-origin minority experienced in Houston. Recalling the letter, club member Carmen Cortes remembered that "we read it at the meeting before we sent it in," and that Olive Lewis, the YWCA sponsor of their organization, was "very proud" of the letter."[129] The women wrote, for example, that Mexican Americans were "falsely accused of many crimes in the city and because of some difficulty with the English language they [Mexicans] are taken advantage of frequently."[130]

Their letter listed many other grievances. Another problem the club mentioned was that "the Mexican people find it impossible to rent or buy in any decent section of the town and are forced to live in dirty crowded conditions in houses out of which Americans have moved."[131] A typical racist belief, then and now, is that any problem that people of color have is of their own making. An example of this belief included the idea that residents themselves caused the problems of substandard housing. In her 1944 report on the housing for the Mexican community in Houston, social worker

Bertha Wolf wrote that in Schrimpf Alley, a section of the Second Ward, "sanitary facilities are very bad. In fact, they have no toilet, no bathroom, no anything."[132] Conditions later improved in 1952, when the city built public housing, the Clayton Homes, in the Second Ward.[133]

Protesting racist conditions in Houston, as El Club Feminino Chapultepec did in its letter, was risky. Written the week after the trial on the killing of Cortéz, the letter created problems for the club and for Mrs. Lewis, who was fired by the YWCA. Stella Quintenella was especially affected.[134] The Federal Bureau of Investigation (FBI) kept her under surveillance until 1941 because they suspected that she was a Communist.[135] This allegation may have been the reason she was removed at the last minute in 1941 as a conference speaker when she planned to discuss racial discrimination against Mexicans in Houston. The conference was organized by La Federación de Sociedades Mexicanas y Latinas Americanas de Texas (FSMLA), a state-wide umbrella organization created in 1938 to address discrimination and to improve relations between Mexican immigrants and Mexican Americans. Mexican consul Luis L. Duplán, an active member of the FSMLA, personally asked her not to speak. Historian Emma Pérez believed that Duplán feared that Quintenella's address on racial discrimination in Houston would strain US-Mexico relations.[136]

Conclusion

By the early twentieth century, the Mexican-origin community was well established in Texas, having resided there long before European Americans emigrated from the United States. Many of these whites considered themselves superior to people of color. They held commonplace racial prejudices that considered Texans of Mexican descent a "problem" and undesirable, except as exploited workers. Mexican immigrants especially suffered in the early twentieth century from the increasingly restrictive immigration laws, fear of the Border Patrol and, during the Great Depression of 1930s, denial of work and much-needed aid.

Although the Mexican-origin minority faced racial injustices, it contributed positively to its community and its activists continued to promote social justice. In Houston the vibrant and diverse community included, for example, the *mutualistas* that provided funding for funerals, organizations that helped Mexican immigrants repatriate during the Great Depression, and barrio residents who pledged money to the Rusk Settlement House when the city threatened to reduce its budget. Other signs of growing activism were organizations, including LULAC, that responded aggressively to a racist comment by Houston's city commissioner and the woman's organization El Club Feminino Chapultepec that publicly criticized racial discrimination in Houston. Finally, activists for workers in Houston demanded that permanent city workers no longer be classified as temporary employees and, thus, be denied benefits.

The situation for Mexican immigrants varied but became progressively more difficult in the 1920s and 1930s. Then, as now, Mexican farmworkers were valued more as an economic resource and less as human beings who merited protection from exploitative employers. In Texas, the Emigrant Labor Agency Laws tried to prevent these workers from seeking better employment in other states. Furthermore, the NLRA of 1935, which defended the rights of workers, failed to extend protection to agricultural and domestic laborers who were overwhelming Mexican. Efforts by the NLRB to improve the wages and working conditions for people of color, in general, were disappointing. Anti-labor views and intractable commonplace racist prejudices in Texas prevented improvements for vulnerable workers. In addition, during the Great Depression Mexican immigrants were denied jobs and came under intense pressure to repatriate to Mexico.

The Mexican-origin community, especially its activists, continued to strive for social justice and equality. The growing community became more assertive as the percentage of immigrants declined and the percentage of native-born Tejanos increased. The community was more assimilated into the mainstream society than previous generations, although its words and actions sometime reflected insecurity in the Jim Crow society of Texas. Examples included the alarm raised in 1930 to the US Census Bureau's decision to removed Mexicans from the "white" category. Another example was the expressed goal of the woman's organization El Club Feminino Chapultepec for white society to believe that its members were "good Americans, not just Mexican girls."

Social injustices, in addition to increased activism among men and women of Mexican descent, will persist into the 1940s and 1950s. I turn to this history in the next chapter. There I also provide additional historical context of the later activism of Maria Jiménez and many other dedicated persons of Mexican descent who fought for social justice and equality.

Chapter 3

Texas and Houston History during the 1940s and 1950s

Who benefits by having the borders? The corporations . . . migration [should] be considered as an issue of labor mobility and an issue of labor rights and protection.

—Maria Jiménez[1]

Commonplace racist prejudices continued to support Jim Crow and policies in the 1940s and 1950s, like segregation, just as they had during the Great Depression with coerced repatriation to Mexico and other forms of social injustice. Aware of this history, Maria Jiménez once remarked that "the Mexican origin population long has been subjected to racism, prejudice and violence by the larger society."[2] Fortunately, the resilient minority challenged the commonplace belief in the inferiority of Mexicans. This chapter describes their struggles and successes in the 1940s and 1950s during the World War II period and the Bracero Program. In the postwar era, community activists of Mexican descent focused on reforms, particularly in the workplace and in education. The chapter also provides more historical context for the following chapter, which turns to the life story of Maria Jiménez, who moved to the United States as a young child in 1957.

Mexican American Organizations: American GI Forum and LULAC

When the United States entered World War II in 1941, the community of Mexican descent proudly served their country and many enlisted in the armed forces. After returning from the war, however, they encountered the same racism that they knew before the war. On this matter World War II veteran Ernest Eguía (1919–2011) remarked after fighting in Europe, "I thought that coming back to Texas, things would have changed."[3] His disappointment, and that of many other veterans, motivated members of LULAC to increase their activism and for other veterans to form the American GI Forum. Both organizations believed that the postwar racial discrimination was especially intolerable, given that Mexican Americans earned "proportionately more military honors than any other ethnic group."[4] In addition, a total of twelve Mexican Americans received the Congressional Medal of Honor, the nation's highest military honor.[5]

The American GI Forum formed in 1948 when veteran activists in Corpus Christi, Texas, organized it to serve the needs, and protect the rights, of returning World War II veterans. Many years later, in 2007, and true to its mission, the organization again sprang into action. That year professor of journalism Maggie Rivas-Rodriguez alerted the organization that a major Public Broadcasting Service (PBS) documentary series on World War II totally excluded the contributions of Hispanics soldiers to the war. Hispanic organizations, led by the forum, formed a nationwide campaign, Defend the Honor. Its goal was to have the contributions of Hispanic soldiers to the war effort included in the World War II documentary. Ken Burns, the well-known filmmaker and creator of the documentary, reluctantly added interviews of two Mexican American Marines, Bill Lansford and Peter Arias, to episodes one and six, respectively.[6] In addition, Burns added to the end of episode five the story of a Native American veteran, Chief Joseph Medicine Crow.

The American GI Forum tackled social injustices long before the Defend the Honor campaign. In its early years, the forum was under the leadership of Hector Pérez Garcia (1914–1996), a native of Tamaulipas, Mexico, who grew up in Texas and became a physician and surgeon. Garcia served in

Europe during World War II and was awarded the Bronze Star and later the Presidential Medal of Freedom.[7] Male veterans founded the forum, but women actively participated in it from the beginning. They were important members because the forum placed a high value on the family. The women eventually formed the American GI Forum Ladies Auxiliary in 1956 and organized fundraisers, promoted school desegregation, and encouraged voter registration. Their first conference, in 1956, addressed subjects such as education and rights for native-born Tejanas and Mexican immigrants. Beatriz Tagle Pérez (1923–1991), an important leader, was active in the forum and the auxiliary in the Corpus Christi organization for thirty years.[8] Elsewhere, in Austin, Texas, Margarita Muñoz Simon (ca. 1908–1998) organized the GI Forum and the auxiliary and edited the forum-sponsored newspaper *El Demócrata*.[9]

Organizations of the Mexican-descent community became increasingly alarmed by violations of its civil rights. Although the GI Forum focused on veteran concerns, it and LULAC addressed social injustice in general. In one instance of discrimination, Herminia Quiñones took her 6-year-old son for a haircut in 1945 to a barbershop on Canal Street in Houston. The white barber refused to cut her child's hair because the boy was Mexican. Herminia's husband was in the military at the time and in Europe. She recalled, "I felt so hurt. . . . I said, 'Well, his father is good enough to be in the service!'"[10] She informed LULAC of the incident. Although she did not know what the organization did, they apparently took some action, and the barbershop closed shortly after her complaint.

A few years later, the forum responded to another glaring example of white racism. The incident, which received national attention in 1949, concerned the wake for Felix Longoria (1920–1945), a World War II veteran. Longoria was killed in 1945 and was buried in the Philippines. The US Army later returned his remains to his hometown of Three Rivers, Texas. The owner of the town's only funeral home refused to allow the wake in its facility because Longoria was a Mexican American. The funeral parlor owner explained to Longoria's wife, Beatrice, that "the white people would object to that and I couldn't start that sort of thing."[11] Beatrice refused to allow this insult to the memory of her husband to go unchallenged. He had served his country with distinction, earning a Bronze Service Star and Purple Heart.[12]

In a short time, the Longoria incident became known nationally and internationally. It was eventually resolved through the tireless efforts of Dr. Hector Garcia of the American GI Forum with substantial assistance from the US senator from Texas, Lyndon B. Johnson (1908–1973). Patriotism was high in 1949, and many in the nation shared Beatrice's outrage. After she contacted Garcia, he sent out numerous telegrams to officials for help. Senator Johnson responded the next day, January 11, 1949, and wrote, "I deeply regret to learn that the prejudice of some individuals extends beyond this life. . . . This injustice and prejudice is deplorable. I am happy to have a part in seeing that this Texas hero is laid to rest with the honors and dignity his service deserves."[13] Senator Johnson arranged for Longoria to be buried with full military honors at the Arlington National Cemetery on February 16, 1949.[14] The forum, organized only a year earlier, had succeeded in addressing a grave injustice to a Mexican American veteran.

Racial Discrimination, Immigration, and the World War II Bracero Program

Historically, justice, social and racial, had been denied the Mexican-origin community, especially Mexican immigrants. It would become Jiménez's mission to reduce this injustice. As a student of history, she understood that her activism continued that of her predecessors. They encountered many obstacles in the Jim Crow era of the 1940s. Nevertheless, some positive developments emerged through the efforts of civil rights organizations, labor unions, and the federal government.

During World War II, as was the case in World War I, the United States government actively recruited Mexican immigrant labor. Also, as before, farmers and other employers exploited these workers. The federal government's recruitment of Mexican labor began in 1942 with the Bracero Program, officially called the Emergency Farm Labor Program. That year Mexico agreed to provide the United States with Mexican contract laborers. The first braceros, a term that signified "contract laborers," arrived in California in

September 1942. Unfortunately, the terms of the contract did not protect the braceros sufficiently from exploitation. For instance, their wages were low, and in many cases they had to pay for their own food and supplies, as well as other necessities.

Both whites and Mexican Americans reacted negatively to the presence of braceros in the United States. White nativists did not welcome braceros because they considered Mexicans inferior, and many white contractors (growers, factory owners, etc.) agreed. Employers therefore often disregarded the provisions in labor contracts that were designed to protect the braceros from racial harassment and to guarantee them reasonable wages and safe working conditions.[15] Mexican American civil rights organizations also opposed the Bracero Program and even supported restricted immigration. The organizations believed, rightly, that the guest worker program would exploit the braceros and that the employment of braceros would lower the wages for Mexican American workers. However, opposition to the bracero program varied. In Texas, for example, the relation between braceros and Tejanos was more adversarial than in other states because the job competition was greater and Mexican American activists in Texas strongly opposed the bracero program.[16]

Because of anti-Mexican immigrant prejudices, Mexican American organizations hesitated to attempt to protect braceros rights. The organizations feared that a rise in anti-Mexican racism, which typically accompanied an increase in Mexican immigration, would extend to native-born Mexican Americans. LULAC also claimed that braceros and "wetbacks," a term used even by Mexican Americans for undocumented Mexicans, undermined its organization's mission to promote the integration of Mexican Americans into mainstream society and to create a positive image of Mexican Americans in the eyes of white America.[17]

Regrettably, the concerns of LULAC and similar organizations about Mexican immigrants are understandable because society believed that immigrant minorities should discard their culture and assimilate to the dominant white culture. Nevertheless, a special kinship existed between many Mexican Americans and Mexican immigrants since, historically, both suffered racial discrimination. In fact, Mexican American organizations sometimes decided to help Mexican immigrant workers. For example, in 1943 LULAC and the Mexican consul, Lamberto Oregón, attempted to help Mexican workers at the Southern Alkali plant in Corpus Christi, Texas, in a labor problem discussed below. Southern Alkali and other refineries in the area opposed hiring Mexicans or Mexican Americans, even after the workers had received federally funded job training. Signs posted at these war-related industries in Texas said, "No Mexicans hired here." If they were hired, Mexican-origin workers were given only low-level positions, such as ditch digging or janitorial work.[18]

The Bracero Program, which ended in 1964, was originally designed to provide labor during the war period. It supplied agricultural workers to participating states except, in the early years, Texas.[19] In the case of Texas, Mexico officially blacklisted the state from 1943 to 1947 because of its well-known anti-Mexican racism and abuse of Mexican laborers.[20] As a consequence, Texas suffered a labor shortage and cotton wages in the state increased 236 percent. In contrast, cotton wages increased only 136 percent in California, a state that Mexico supplied with braceros.[21] Traditionally, growers in Texas preferred the well-established open-border arrangement for obtaining agricultural workers because growers believed that the "proposed guarantees of braceros' rights" were "onerous intrusions into the so-called free market."[22] In other words, growers wanted to continue to exploit, unhindered by federal regulations, the labor of noncontract Mexican nationals.

The racial discrimination against Mexicans that Mexico complained about during the Bracero Program even had serious international implications during World War II because fascists used it in their anti-Western propaganda. They publicized, for example, photos of Texas restaurant windows that said, "No Mexicans Allowed."[23] These signs also increased political tension between the United States and Mexico. Texas responded by organizing the Good Neighbor Commission (GNC). Historian Gutiérrez described the commission as "the first halting steps toward guaranteeing at least a modicum of rights to Texas's ethnic Mexican residents."[24] Established in 1943 to address racial discrimination against Mexicans and Mexican Americans, an important goal of the GNC was to improve relations with Mexico and other Latin American nations. The commission is an example of interest convergence whereby whites make changes that benefit people of color when it is to their (the whites') advantage to do so. The GNC, in the opinion of its critics, was more concerned with improving the image of the white-dominated government in Texas than with advancing racial and social justice for persons of Mexican descent. Supporting the criticism is the fact that, although it received complaints of discrimination, the commission did not order investigations. In the opinion of historian Matthew Gritter, the commission "served mainly as a token gesture."[25]

The bilateral bracero program required the cooperation of both nations. Neither was overly concerned with the well-being of the braceros; therefore, the exploitation of these guest workers in the United States continued. Regarding Mexico, the government favored the emigration of its workers because of the remittances that they sent home. The opportunity for workers to emigrate benefited Mexico also because it constituted an "escape valve" for poor Mexican peasants.[26] As for officials in the United States, they wanted cheap Mexican labor and even took steps to legalize "illegal" undocumented workers whom growers knew to be skilled and reliable.[27]

One form of formally legalizing Mexican workers, known as "drying out the wetback," revealed the nation's hypocrisy, then and now, about wanting to end Mexican immigration. The "drying out" procedure circumvented the legal requirement for undocumented immigrants to first cross the Rio Grande into Mexico before reentering legally as contract workers.[28] One ludicrous example of the drying out process, from California in 1953, described instructions immigration authorities gave to undocumented Mexicans on how to "dry out." Specifically, they were told to "run back to the official border crossing-point, put one-foot on Mexican soil, and then dart back so they could be legally processed."[29] In this manner and other versions of "drying out," employers acquired the workers they wanted. In 1947, in Texas alone, fifty-five thousand undocumented Mexican nationals had their legal status changed to braceros and given work permits.[30]

As for undocumented workers, their situation deteriorated in the 1950s because the nation responded to the rise of xenophobia of the Cold War with their mass deportation. The American GI Forum objected to the deportations and blamed the government for failing to address immigration problems. The forum also criticized the Immigration and Naturalization Service's "heavy-handed tactics" because "*mexicanos* were needlessly harassed by Immigration Service police."[31] The government's action, furthermore, alarmed the community of Mexican descent, which started "to realize how closely their own civil liberties were tied to the legal and political status of Mexican immigrants." [32] Aware of rising racial tensions in this period of "repression, fear, and witch-hunts," Mexican Americans also felt vulnerable.[33]

A flagrant example of social injustice was Operation Wetback, the massive deportation of Mexican undocumented immigrants. It began June 9, 1954, in California and Arizona, and ended mid-September of the same year. The militarized campaigns of Operation Wetback, which were organized by a former lieutenant-general of the United States Army, Joseph M. Swing (1894–1984), reportedly committed gross violations of human and civil rights in the deportation of 1,101,228 persons, Mexicans and Mexican Americans.[34] The Border Patrol boasted that during Operation Wetback, it made 41,951 apprehensions between July 15 and July 29, 1954.[35] Opposition to the deportations was greatest in the Rio Grande Valley in South Texas, where farmers objected not to any violations of the rights of the undocumented Mexican workers, but to the loss of cheap labor and the subsequent need to hire braceros. The farmers shamelessly asserted, according to a *New York Times* report, that "like the Southern slave owners of a century ago—it was a violation of their rights to take it [wetback labor] away, even if the 'wetbacks' are lawbreakers."[36] Local media in South Texas covered the activities of the unpopular Border Patrol, and newspapers referred to the Border Patrol agents who were in charge of deportations as an "army of occupation" and an "invading horde."[37]

The US immigration policy was problematic in domestic and international affairs. In Texas, the Border Patrol tried to appease angry farmers by permitting them to employ "dried-out illegals."[38] At the international level, the United States' claim of being a democracy was undermined by its immigration laws. These were clearly based on racist principles. In response to this fact, Congress removed racial and ethnic barriers to immigration and the naturalization process when it passed the Immigration and Nationality Act (INA) of 1952, also known as the McCarran-Walter Act.[39] Beyond this significant change, the McCarran-Walter Act retained the existing quotas that greatly favored English or northern European immigrants. Furthermore, the quota system effectively limited the number of Asians and Blacks from the Caribbean. Also greatly restricted were Jews and Italians from Europe, whom Senator Patrick Anthony McCarran (1876–1954) and others in the 1950s suspected of being Communists.[40]

The INA failed in large part to reform the racist nature of the nation's immigration policies. Instead, the 1952 act severely affected the Mexican immigrant community because it added more legal justification for denaturalization and deportation. It even made "aliens deportable for acts that were not grounds for deportation at the time they were committed."[41] The law also made all persons who had entered the United States illegally since the year 1924 subject to immediate deportation regardless of their good moral character, years of residence, or employment. Many Mexican American organizations criticized the new law. LULAC, for example, issued a resolution at its 1956 annual convention denouncing it as "oppressive and unjust and creating great hardships to thousands of families in the deportation of aliens who entered the country illegally but have established residences."[42] The lack of social justice revealed in the McCarran-Walter Act and the ruthless deportation campaign of Operation Wetback signaled to the Mexican-origin community an acute need for activism to create a better, more equitable society.

Decline of Jim Crow

The possibility for greater social justice and a decline in Jim Crow society increased after World War II. One factor, according to historian David Montejano, was "the defeat of the old city machines by Anglo business leaders in the fifties."[43] Postwar Texas also underwent an increase in urbanization. When Texas was overwhelming agricultural, its growers dominated Texas politics. According to Montejano, the "'heyday' of Texas growers" was the period between 1920 and 1940 when, he added, Jim Crow was its strongest.[44] They were also the major employers of undocumented Mexicans and the individuals who frequently exploited these laborers.[45] In the post–World War II era, however, the number of growers and their

influence in politics began to decline, in part, because of changes in traditional agribusiness. It became increasingly "'urbanized' as resident farm
ownership passed into corporate hands."[46]

Another significant factor contributed to a decline in Jim Crow. As
Montejano explained, this change emerged from within the Mexican descent
community itself and was the increase in its professional class. Growers
could not exploit this professional class, unlike Mexican migrant workers
whom they employed and who could not vote. In contrast, the rising middle-
class group had the power of leverage "(as workers, consumers, and voters)
to secure concessions and 'rights.'"[47] Merchants and politicians also began
to take a new interest in the Mexican American minority, especially its
middle class.

The Mexican American middle class included lawyers, and it was in law
that Mexican Americans achieved an important advance in social justice.
This progress resulted from the case *Hernández v. Texas* (1954), argued
by Mexican American lawyers before the US Supreme Court. The Pete
Hernández trial began in Edna, Texas, located in Jackson County, where
Hernández was convicted of murder. The lawyers included James de Anda,
Gus Garcia, John J. Herrera, and Carlos Cadena.[48] They argued against the
racist commonplace practice that excluded Mexican Americans from "any
jury commission, grand jury, or petit jury in Jackson County in the previous
quarter century."[49] Unfortunately, the charge of racial discrimination based
on race had proven ineffective in the past because Texas law defined Mexican
Americans as white.[50] Therefore, in the case of a Mexican-origin defendant,
an all-white jury was a jury of his peers and, in theory, not anti-Mexican.
However, Hernández's lawyers also asserted that the defendant's right
to equal protection of the law, guaranteed by the Fourteenth Amendment,
was violated.

By the time the case reached the Supreme Court, the commonplace
anti-Mexican prejudices of Jim Crow Texas made the lives of Pete Hernández
and his lawyers very difficult. Hernández's lawyers faced obstacles that white
lawyers of white defendants did not. First, as was true in the Hernández trial,
jurors were non-Hispanic whites; in other words, jurors were white and not
ethnically Mexican.[51] A second problem for the Hernández lawyers, as for

many other Mexican American lawyers, was that it was not safe to stay overnight in the towns where trials were conducted. These lawyers knew well, according to law professor Michael A. Olivas, that "rural towns were so inhospitable that the [Mexican American] lawyers trying a murder case could not safely find housing in the county seat."[52] Because of this danger, they needed to travel each day to a town for the trial but leave afterward. One of the lawyers for Hernández, James de Anda, recalled that "Mexican Americans could barely participate in the community, and restaurants displayed signs warning 'No Mexicans Served.'"[53]

Fortunately, the lawyers' second argument proved to be compelling. The historic *Hernández v. Texas* decision, 347 U.S. 475 (1954), was, according to LatCrit Richard Delgado, "the first Supreme Court case to extend the protection of the Fourteenth Amendment to Latinos/as, [and] it is among the great early triumphs in the Latino/a struggle for civil rights."[54] The court "held that Hernández merited Fourteenth Amendment protection because he belonged to a class, distinguishable on some basis 'other than race or color.'"[55] This legal case was historic for other reasons. Specifically, Gus Garcia, who presented the case, became the first Mexican American lawyer to argue a case before the Supreme Court. In addition, his oratory so impressed the court that "he became the first attorney in Supreme Court history to receive extra time at the lectern from the Chief Justice [Warren]."[56]

Equitable education was another major problem for the Mexican-origin community and a goal that energized many Mexican American activists. However, the political climate in the 1950s hindered their efforts. At the national and state levels, McCarthyism intensified the fear of threats to "traditional" American society. Therefore, "any action that lessened the power of the local elite—for example, calls for civil rights, expanded power of the federal government, and labor union growth—was identified by many as un-American."[57] Given this commonplace belief, the historic 1954 court decision of *Brown v. Board of Education*, making segregated public schooling unconstitutional, had little impact for many years in Texas because of a widespread resistance to this assault on Jim Crow. For example, the influential anti-Communist organization, the Minute Women of Houston, vigorously opposed school integration.[58]

The social injustice of racial discrimination against students of color enraged the Mexican American community and motivated its activists to demand equitable education. Even before the *Brown* ruling, LULAC and the American GI Forum had filed many suits against Texas school districts. The civil rights organizations charged school districts with violating the constitutional rights of Mexican-origin students under the Fourteenth Amendment. In *Hernández v. Driscoll CISD* (1957), a federal court ruled against the school district in Driscoll because it arbitrarily kept all Mexican American students in the first and second grades for a total of four years, without regard to a student's language skills. Although many of the students were from Spanish-speaking migrant families, their language ability in English varied, and at least one student, Linda Pérez, spoke only English.[59]

As a result of commonplace racist prejudices in the 1950s and 1960s, little progress occurred toward equitable schooling for minority students. Education historian Guadalupe San Miguel Jr. described this period as an "era of subterfuge" in which local school systems used tactics designed to maintain segregation. These included, for example, "freedom of choice plans, selected student transfer and transportation plans, and classification systems based on language or scholastic ability."[60] Two US representatives, Henry B. González (1966–1999) of San Antonio and Abraham Kazen (1967–1985) of Laredo, vigorously opposed the dozen bills that legislators introduced in 1956 and 1957 that would allow segregated schools to continue.[61] Among the state officials who opposed more equitable education for Texas students was the governor of Texas from 1949 to 1957, Allen Shivers (1907–1985). For example, he sided with whites in Mansfield, Texas, when they resisted the desegregation of their high school, and the governor even "sent the Texas Rangers to Mansfield in 1956 to prohibit Black students from attending public schools."[62]

Houston's Mexican-Origin Community in the 1940s to the 1950s

This section of the chapter will describe the history of the Mexican-origin population in Houston in the 1940s and 1950s and their struggle for a more just city. This history describes the city that Maria Jiménez and her family would make their home in 1957. There she encountered racial discrimination firsthand that would shape her views and fierce opposition to social injustice.

Houston's demography in the 1940s and 1950s primarily consisted of whites, Blacks, and persons of Mexican descent. Today it is an international metropolis with residents from all over the world. Harris County, where Houston is located, "added more residents than any other county in the nation" from 2022 to 2023.[63] By 2040 the percentage of Hispanics, whites, Blacks, and others will be, respectively, 44, 30, 17, and 10.[64] Mexicans constitutes the largest of Houston's Hispanic groups.

Mexican Americans and Mexican immigrants from other parts of Texas moved to Houston in search of employment. During and after World War II, jobs in Houston and surrounding areas were in the petrochemical and other industries that produced fuel and products such as synthetic rubber, steel, and lumber.[65] These industries boosted the local economy and Houston's population grew with the economy. In 1940 the total population in Houston was 384,514.[66] In the same year, the number of Hispanics, predominately Mexican, was about 20,000 and doubled to about 40,000 by 1950.[67]

Mexican braceros and Mexican Americans filled many of the new jobs, but not without encountering commonplace anti-Mexican prejudices and hostile working conditions. Records from the Santa Fe Railroad Company, an employer of several thousand braceros, indicated that braceros fled their railroad jobs to seek better opportunities in the cities. Wherever they worked, Mexicans often heard derogatory words like "greaser" and "spic."[68] In addition, companies offered only menial and low skilled jobs to Mexican nationals and Mexican Americans. The workers also received salaries lower than those paid to whites for the same position.[69] In his study of this period in Houston, historian Paul Alejandro Levengood concluded that "there is little evidence that Mexicans shared significantly in the city's wartime prosperity."[70]

Mexican nationals were especially vulnerable to workplace exploitation in Jim Crow Texas. They and other people of color, however, received some federal help from the Fair Employment Practices Committee (FEPC), created when President Franklin D. Roosevelt signed Executive Order 8802 on June 25, 1941.[71] Fortunately, the federal government reorganized the original and weak FEPC and granted it more authority when President Roosevelt signed Executive Order 9346 in May 1943. The FEPC was the only federal agency that conducted investigations and hearings on the discrimination of employees in the war industry because of race, creed, color, or national origin.[72] The agency established thirteen regions, and Carlos E. Castañeda headed Region X from 1943 to 1945. Castañeda was a naturalized citizen originally from Mexico, a distinguished professor of history at the University Texas at Austin, and one of the most important activists for social justice of his generation.[73]

Several Mexican-origin men benefited greatly from their experience with the FEPC under Castañeda's astute leadership.[74] Most importantly, these civil rights leaders—including LULAC members Alonso Perales, M. C. Gonzáles, and George I. Sánchez—learned how to work with the federal government. In the opinion of historian Gritter, "People of Mexican origin for the first time gained a foothold in a U.S. federal government organization."[75] In this period, Gritter also believed, a shift emerged "for some Mexican American civil rights leaders from trying to assimilate into American society to claiming rights and protections on the basis of their American citizenship."[76]

In 1943 the FEPC and Castañeda, operating within the rigid limitations of Jim Crow racism, "waged a two-and-half year challenge against thirteen refineries," according to historian Emilio Zamora.[77] As head of Region X, Castañeda unfortunately encountered many hostile men like C. N. Waterman, manager of American Smelting.[78] Waterman told Castañeda in 1943 that he considered Mexican workers lazy and believed that their complaints were lies.[79] One incident of discrimination against Mexican workers that Castañeda addressed concerned the limited number of these workers that the Southern Alkali plant employed. It was greatly limited by the company's hiring quota set in its 1937 contract. However, after an FEPC hearing in 1943, and through its efforts, the company removed the low quota for Mexican workers, allowing more Mexican workers to be hired.[80] In another incident of racial discrimination, LULAC leader John Herrera of Houston turned to the FEPC for help. In this case Brown Shipbuilding had unfairly laid off eleven Mexican women in 1944. The company denied that the women's termination was race related, even though no white women were dismissed, and when the company later hired more women, none of these new employees were Mexican.[81] After its investigation into the Brown Shipbuilding case, the FEPC ruled that the laid off Mexican employees should return to their jobs.[82]

Historian Emilio Zamora's thorough analysis of Mexican labor in *Claiming Rights and Righting Wrongs: Mexican Workers and Job Politics during World War II* confirmed that job discrimination against Mexican workers was the norm in oil refineries in the Houston areas.[83] Whites took most jobs, especially well-paying ones. Because of their commonplace prejudices, Zamora asserted, whites held "deeply engrained segregationist ideas" and strongly opposed fair employment practices, especially in the case of immigrant workers.[84] According to the findings of a 1943 survey by FEPC, 59 percent of the Mexican-descent employees were immigrants.[85] Fully aware of the racial prejudices that existed, the refinery companies claimed that labor unions would not tolerate measures to increase the pay and make other improvements for Mexican and Black workers. In fact, in 1943 white workers at Humble and Shell refineries effectively blocked union leadership or refinery management from improving the working conditions for minority workers. For Mexican government officials and Mexican American civil rights activists in Texas, the discrimination cases in Texas clearly demonstrated, Zamora wrote, the "deep-rooted racism and ineffective government intervention" on the behalf of exploited minority workers in Texas."[86]

Another problem that people of Mexican origin addressed was a rise in juvenile delinquency in Houston. Fortunately, activists of Mexican descent organized to help their troubled youth. For children and young adults, the tense wartime climate had produced new problems. Many men and women served in the armed forces, and unprecedented numbers of mothers entered the workforce. Some of the youths who became involved in criminal activities were called "zooters" because of the zoot suits they wore.[87] Zooter gangs in Houston included the Blackshirts in the Second Ward and the Long Hairs in Magnolia Park. Manuel Crespo (1903–1989), a detective for the Houston Police Department (HPD) from 1940 to 1946, remembered that people were afraid to walk around after dark because some zooters demanded protection money and beat persons who refused to pay it.[88]

Responses to the gang problem varied, but the Mexican American community organized to help, as did the HPD. The HPD, for example, created a six-man division, the Latin American Squad, in July 1944.[89] Mexican Americans objected to the squad in 1944 because they believed it stigmatized their youth. HPD did not establish similar squads for other groups in Houston.[90] Protests in 1944 against the squad were not immediately effective, however, and the squad continued to function until 1945.[91] What the youth really needed, especially during wartime, were social, educational, and recreational outlets. The Latin America Squad took credit for reducing gang-related crime but also acknowledged the role of Mexican American organizations in this reduction.[92] Another helpful resource was the Ripley House, which had been offering valuable services to the community since it opened in 1940.[93] Also important was the Juvenile Delinquency Committee of FSMLA that provided help for Tejanos and Mexican immigrants and organized sports activities for teenagers.[94]

After World War II, the Mexican American community continued to grow, and its activists for social justice continued to make incremental progress. For example, the Mexican Chamber of Commerce was established in 1940 with seventy-two members.[95] Other "firsts" occurred in the same decade. In 1941, for example, the pressure from the local International Longshoremen, LULAC, and other organizations helped Carmen Cortes to become the first Mexican American white-collar employee in the Harris County courthouse, located in downtown Houston. In 1944 Fernando Salas (1897–1982) became the first Mexican American to be in a grand jury in Harris County.[96] As for the size of the minority in 1950, when the total population in the metropolitan Houston area was 807,000, the Spanish surnamed population reached 40,000. In 1960 the city's total population was 1,243,000 and the Spanish surnamed population was 75,000.[97] The *Houston Chronicle* reported in 1958 that "eighty-four percent of Latin Americans in Harris County are native-born citizens of the United States; 8 percent are naturalized citizens, and only 8 percent are alien."[98] Unfortunately, the median income of Mexican Americans in Houston was low. In 1959 it was only $4,339, while the median income for Houstonians was $6,040.[99]

A significant source of pride in the Mexican American community in Texas was its returning World War II veterans. Most veterans were men, but women served too. For example, Felicitas Cerda Flores (1921–), of Houston, enlisted in the military division known today as the Women's Army Corps (WAC) in 1943 and, when 22 years old, rose to the rank of corporal.[100] The best-known veteran in the Houston area was Macario Garcia (1920–1972). Born in Mexico, Garcia grew up in Sugar Land, a short distance southeast of Houston. For his heroism in Germany during World War II, he received the Bronze Star, the Congressional Medal of Honor, and the Purple Heart. Unfortunately, like countless other veterans of color, and despite their distinguished military service, Garcia encountered racism in 1945 when he was denied service in a café in Richmond, a town west of Houston. Another veteran and Bronze Star recipient, Ernest Eugía (1919–2015), fought at Normandy in June 1944 but was harassed by the police the same week that he returned to Houston.[101]

In general, social injustice persisted in Jim Crow Houston as economic developments in the city evolved "from an essentially raw material and commercial base (e.g., oil and shipping) to one which is more technological (e.g., aerospace, petrochemical, and electronics industries)."[102] Economic progress did not mean social progress. Ambulances were segregated, with separate ambulances for whites, Blacks, and Mexicans.[103] Many employers hesitated to hire Mexicans or Mexican Americans. As one person at an employment agency expressed it in 1958, "In Houston, 95 per cent of what I consider good companies refused to hire Latin Americans."[104] Despite this bias, job opportunities for the Mexican-origin community increased. Specifically, the unemployment rate among males decreased in the decade 1950–1960 from 6.9 percent to 5.6 percent. The percentage of women working in the same period rose from 23 to 28 percent.[105]

Along with the demographic and economic changes, Mexican American men and women became more civic minded and fought for improvements, especially in education. School buildings that served a majority Mexican student population were dilapidated, and the teachers in these schools were the least experienced in the Houston Independent School District (HISD) system. Dropout rates were high and, according to a 1958 newspaper article, "no attempt is made to get Spanish-speaking teachers."[106] One problem that arose in the mid-1950s occurred after the school board closed Rusk Elementary School to make way for a highway. The Mexican American students thereafter needed to cross dangerous streets to attend another school. Community activists for education reform criticized this dangerous situation and pressured the school board to build a new school in a safer location.[107] It was completed in 1960.

Many women made significant contributions to their community in the 1950s, and Maria Jiménez followed in their footsteps in the following decades. The well-known businesswoman Maria Reyna (1911–1987), for example, helped found a Ladies LULAC Council in 1935 and was a leader in the Comité Patriótico Mexicano, serving as its president from 1980 to 1984. The Comité promoted positive relations between the United States and Mexico.[108] Sometimes women worked hand in hand with their husbands. For example, Angelina Morales (d. 1997) and her husband, Félix Hessbrook Morales (1907–1988), a Tejano of German Mexican descent, established a funeral home in Houston in 1931. In 1942 she became the first Mexican woman in Houston to earn a diploma in embalming from the Landig College of Mortuary Science.[109] Around 1940 the Moraleses cofounded the Sociedad "Unión Fraternal" that helped poor Mexican families with burial expenses and other forms of aid, sometimes in partnership with the Mexican consul. An impetus to the founding of the Sociedad, according to historian Arnoldo de León, was the refusal of Houston hospitals to admit Mexican nationals.[110] In 1950 Félix and Angelina Morales left their funeral business to their son and founded the Spanish-language radio station KLVL.[111] It was the first Mexican American owned station to serve Houston's Spanish-speaking audience. Another couple, Janie (1908–1997) and Félix Tijerina (1905–1965) were successful restaurateurs.

Although it was common for many Mexican Americans to strive to assimilate into the dominant white society, traditional Mexican culture continued to thrive. For example, the Morales' radio station KLVL, called La Madre de los Mexicanos (The Mother of the Mexicans), proudly broadcast in Spanish to a quarter million listeners in the Houston area.[112] In addition, the nationally known singer Lydia Mendoza (1916–2007) kept popular in Houston and elsewhere the traditional Mexican songs that she learned from her mother.[113] Born in Houston of Mexican immigrants, Lydia performed in 1977 at the inaugural celebration for President Jimmy Carter (1924–2024) and in 1999 for President Bill Clinton, when he awarded her the National Medal of the Arts.[114]

A major organization that promoted the civil rights of the Mexican-origin community was LULAC. During the 1950s two national presidents of LULAC resided in Houston. The national presidents were John J. Herrera and Félix Tijerina from 1952 to 1953 and 1956 to 1960, respectively. The organization's official policy on membership stated that only naturalized or native-born Mexican Americans could be members and only citizens were eligible to become officers.[115] In practice, however, LULAC's Council No. 60 in Houston and councils in other towns were not overly restrictive regarding membership. Noncitizens were voting members, although they could not hold any office.[116] LULAC members believed that it was important to allow Mexican immigrants to participate in the organization because, as LULAC member Angelina Morales asserted, "We felt a need for them to become American citizens."[117]

In addition to being a LULAC leader, Félix Tijerina wanted to improve the academic success of Mexican descent students by promoting English-language classes. Monolingual Spanish-speaking students were prohibited from, even punished for, speaking their language in Texas schools. For these children schools became hostile institutions. In 1958 LULAC reported that an "adult Latin American has an average of only 3.5 years of schooling," while the average for white and Black adults was 11.5 years and 7.5 years, respectively. The ideas that Tijerina promoted derived from a curriculum first developed by Isabel Verver in Ganado, Texas. Motivated by her traumatic experiences when a student and a desire to spare other children the same trauma, Verver opened her own school in 1957. She said that "I did not think it was right that I should cry and wanted to quit school because no one could understand me."[118]

Tijerina's idea of promoting English for Spanish-speaking schoolchildren attracted the attention of another important community and education activist, Dr. Guadalupe Quintanilla. She wrote her 1976 dissertation on

Tijerina's literacy project. Like Tijerina, she knew the emotional pain that students faced in Texas schools if they did not speak English. In fact, the school that she attended labeled her as mentally retarded.[119] Determined to succeed in school, Quintanilla eventually became a professor of Spanish at the University of Houston and that university's vice president of Academic Affairs for twenty-seven years.[120]

The curriculum that Tijerina advocated became formalized in the Little School of the 400, established in 1957. It taught children four hundred basic English words before they entered the first grade. By 1967 the school had taught over 150,000 Spanish-speaking students.[121] Other developments to aid students' language skills emerged in 1965, including Title I and Head Start.[122]

Conclusion

The 1940s and 1950s in Texas witnessed many changes, but social justice for minorities remained elusive in Jim Crow Texas because of deep-seated, commonplace racial prejudices. World War II provided opportunities for men and women of Mexican descent but did not protect servicemen and -women or their families from racial discrimination. Examples include the barber who refused to cut the hair of a soldier's child because he was Mexican. More egregious was the funeral director's refusal to allow a wake at his funeral home for the veteran Félix Longoria. In both instances, Mexican American organizations stepped in to help the mother of the child in the barber incident, and Beatrice, the wife of Felix Longoria. In doing so the groups advanced social justice in these two cases and, in general, democracy.

In the area of law and employment, some advances emerged. The federal agency FEPC addressed race-based discrimination in war industries. Under the skillful director of FEPC's Region X, Carlos E. Castañeda, and with the input and support of LULAC, the grievances of many oil refinery workers, both Mexican and Mexican American, were investigated and some improvements were made for them. In the area of law, a team of skilled Mexican

American lawyers presented the case *Hernández v. Texas* before the Supreme Court. In a historic ruling, the court extended the protection of the Fourteenth Amendment to Mexican Americans.

As for immigration issues, the federal government offered Mexican immigrants employment opportunities. However, Operation Wetback cruelly deported over one million Mexican immigrant workers and their families. The Bracero Program, designed to meet labor needs during World War II, required employers to offer jobs with reasonable wages and working conditions to Mexican immigrants, but these requirements were not enforced by the federal government. Another injustice, the ludicrous "drying out" process of legalizing undocumented workers reflected, like the Bracero Program, the commonplace low regard for the dignity and welfare of Mexicans. Finally, the INA removed race as a barrier to immigration but added onerous requirements for emigrating Mexicans.

As for the city of Houston, the future home of the activist Maria Jiménez, it experienced significant growth and attracted job seekers and those wanting a better life. During this period many instances of activism in the Mexican-origin community reflected a growing and robust minority. The FEPC, with the help of LULAC leaders of Houston, worked hard to reduce racial discrimination in Houston area refineries during World War II. Unfortunately, commonplace anti-Mexican prejudices frequently obstructed efforts by the FEPC in its mission. Nevertheless, Houston's Mexican-origin activists, many of them women, succeeded in improving the lives of their community. For example, they reduced the problem of juvenile delinquency among the zooters, helped the poor with their burial expenses, and demanded that the school board build a new school that, unlike the previous one, was in a safe location. Finally, the Little School of 400 prepared students of Mexican descent to succeed academically by offering them English classes.

In the decades to come, activists for social justice, including Maria Jiménez, continued the work of their predecessors to create a more just society, one with less racial discrimination where everyone had the same rights and was treated with dignity. Major concerns were education, police brutality, employment, and immigration. Jiménez became active in these areas and more. She became motivated by the anger she felt with the social injustice she experienced personally, but more from what others suffered. From her high school days, where she became radicalized, Jiménez became dedicated to protecting the rights of others. The following chapters will describe and contextualize her activism and reveal why she was admired by everyone who knew her.

Chapter 4

Activism from 1950 to the Mid-1970s
Maria Jiménez and Mexican American Activists of Houston

I learned from very early on that people who are poor suffer a
great deal of injustice.
—Maria Jiménez[1]

In 1957 Maria Jiménez and her family made their home in Houston, a city shaped by events discussed in the previous chapters. She would experience or observe many affronts to the rights and dignity of the Mexican-descent community that would instill in her a lifelong anger over injustices and make her a warrior for social justice. The quote above expresses a conviction that she formed as a young girl in Houston and foreshadows her mission as an adult to promote social justice. She and other Mexican-origin people in Houston became activists to oppose racist discrimination that violated the nation's belief in equality.

Consistent with the beliefs of CRT, a crucial role for minority activists like Jiménez is to reduce the commonplace—that is, widely accepted—racial prejudices against people of color. These prejudices guide the racist words and deeds of many individuals and constitute their nomos, their normative universe. The significance of racism being commonplace, or "normal," is that

61

a person makes no attempt to end it. Racist attitudes and actions, therefore, persist. Change is possible, however. Jiménez realized as an adult that individuals could reduce or eliminate injustice in their society only if they acted collectively. Expressing a belief that was central to her activism, Jiménez said that "the struggle for human rights is never, ever an individual attainment. It's always a collective one."[2]

Jiménez's many life experiences and accomplishments reflect her strong sense of justice and the belief that each person has a role in making justice possible. From her childhood her family instilled in her the idea that individuals can and should promote a society that treats every member equally and with dignity. As a child Jiménez struggled to understand the reasons for inequities in society. Later, as her perceptions and analytic abilities matured, she concluded that her own negative experiences were like others' and should not intimidate or demoralize her.

Like many immigrants Jiménez was knowledgeable about her native country, Mexico, and her adoptive country, the United States. Her ties to Mexico were renewed when she lived there during her marriage from 1974 to 1984. When she returned to Houston in 1985, the city had changed, in no small part because of a sharp increase in immigration. Shortly after her return to Houston, her activism for immigrant rights began. This path suited her, being an immigrant in an international city. As before, Mexican immigrants moved to Houston for a better life. In addition to these, countless immigrants from Central America came to Houston. By the late 1980s, the Houston area included one of the world's largest Salvadoran communities, with estimates ranging from 80,000 to 140,000.[3] Asians also came in increasing numbers, although in 1980 they totaled only 34,259 or 2.1 percent of Houston's population.[4]

Early Childhood and Education: The Making of a Radical

Jiménez's commitment to social justice impressed all who knew her. She attributed her drive to reduce injustice in society to her childhood experiences in Mexico and the United States. Jiménez was born in Castaños,

Coahuila, Mexico, on August 2, 1950, and her family moved from Mexico to Houston, Texas, in 1957. Even as a young child in Mexico, she was a keen observer of life. Jiménez recalled that she "learned at a very early age . . . this sense that there were injustices—[but] that you could participate in the political process to change them."[5] She was surrounded by intelligent, reform-minded adults, including her family. Her parents, Raúl Jiménez Gómez (1929–2020) and Elva Flores de Jiménez (1930–2002) had five children, Jiménez being the oldest. In Mexico Raúl was a skilled machinist and labor activist in steel plants and her maternal grandfather was a teacher and union organizer for teachers.[6] As a young child in Mexico, Jiménez observed class biases and how they affected her family. Her mother came from a middle-class family, but her father grew up poor. She recalled "sensing conversation sometimes which discriminated against the class origin of my father and his family, as opposed to my mother."[7]

Jiménez's childhood resembled that of other Mexicans. She lived, in her words, "in a very traditional Mexican family where my father was the breadwinner and absolute decider of family affairs." Given this context, one valuable lesson she learned from her mother "was how to deal with absolute power." Jiménez added, "She [her mother] would organize us children and say, '¡No le digan a tu papá!' (Don't tell your father!)" Her mother also conveyed to Jiménez a belief, perhaps atypical for the time, that the role of mother and housewife "wasn't as romantic" as society suggested. Her father was also atypical in an important respect. He believed that all his children, the boys and the girls, should go to college. Jiménez recalled the reaction of his friends: "¿Por qué educas a las mujeres, se van a casar?" (Why do you educate the women, they are going to marry.)[8] Her father, however, believed that his daughters should be educated so that they could leave an unhappy marriage, if necessary.

Jiménez's childhood memories of Mexico included those of her maternal grandparents. She remembered her grandmother, Manuela Guerra de Flores, as "a very strong woman." She was "one of the first women to drive in [her] town" and had a "practical, no-nonsense approach in running businesses from the home that kept her family afloat." Her grandmother's practical nature helped the family because her husband Ramón Torres Ortega

was an impractical idealist. He pioneered in adult education and established a school even though, Jiménez said, "there was no money. There
were no government resources. So he'd used his pay to sustain the school
and pay teachers."[9] Her grandparents influenced Jiménez in many ways.
For example, her grandfather gave her a violin and introduced her to poetry,
which she loved. Her grandparents also took Jiménez and her siblings on
trips to teach them Mexican history, geography, and culture. In addition, her
grandfather had a large library where she learned about the Mexican Revolution and the *soldaderas* (women soldiers) who made invaluable contributions during the revolutionary period.

On May 9, 1957, her family moved to the United States. Her paternal grandfather Jaime Jiménez Gómez (d. ca. 1960) had preceded them, seeking
better job opportunities. Jiménez's father emigrated for the same reason,
and later, in 1957, was joined by his wife and their three children: Maria,
the oldest; Raúl Enrique; and Elva. On their way to Houston, while in
San Antonio, Jiménez recalled seeing Black people sitting in the back of
the bus and thinking how that was not right.[10] Her family then settled in
Houston's largest barrio, Magnolia Park, usually called Magnolia, located
east of the downtown district. It is one of the two oldest Mexican neighborhoods in Houston. Adjacent to Magnolia is the Second Ward, called
El Segundo Barrio by its residents. By the 1960s Mexican communities
lived in other areas of Houston as well, and by 1980 their numbers in the
city exceeded 280,000 persons.[11]

Jiménez moved to a city with many examples of activists for social
justice that matched her own commitment to a just society. The city's Mexican
American leadership in the 1950s valued participation in mainstream society,
and one of its most important organizations was LULAC. However, the political climate changed in the 1960s, becoming more radical and less interested
in assimilation. Jiménez became part of that change.[12] As early as middle
school, she was interested in political science and maintained this interest
even though a counselor at Edison Middle School tried to discourage her.
Jiménez considered political science essential for "dealing with injustices
and inequities," such as the Jim Crow laws and practices that discriminated
against both Blacks and Mexican Americans.[13]

Activists of Mexican descent worked hard to improve their community's lives through political and other forms of activism. Concerning education, for example, the Civic Action Committee (CAC) joined forces with LULAC and the American GI Forum in 1960 to pressure HISD to provide a free lunch program. Their joint efforts, Houston historian Thomas H. Kreneck explained, followed a school board member's sarcastic remark that "Mexican American children did not need free lunches because they would rather eat 'pinto beans.'"[14] The conservative school board's opposition to the federal lunch program was not new; in fact, "from 1948 until 1967 the trustees refused to use federal moneys of the National School Lunch Act to provide free lunches to indigent schoolchildren."[15] Another concern of the Mexican descent community, politics, motivated many activists. For example, the CAC organized fundraisers in 1958 for Henry B. González's gubernatorial campaign.[16] González (1916–2000), the son of Mexican immigrants, lost the race but later was elected to Congress and served in the US House of Representative from 1961 to 1999, representing Texas's Twentieth Congressional District. CAC also launched a poll tax drive to increase the number of Mexican Americans registered voters.

The presidential campaign of John F. Kennedy, a Roman Catholic, also caught the attention of many Mexican Americans. In 1960 the CAC formed Viva Kennedy-Johnson Clubs to raise support for Senator Kennedy's bid for the presidency. A year later, in 1961, CAC's political influence rose when it became the Harris County chapter of the Political Association of Spanish-Speaking Organizations (PASO). In addition to CAC, LULAC members also organized Kennedy's political campaign and invited him to attend their banquet in Houston on November 21, 1963, which he did. Unfortunately, he was assassinated the next day in Dallas. The LULAC banquet room had a thousand seats, although four hundred were empty. John J. Herrera explained why so many people decided not to attend: they had wanted assurance that the presidential candidate would attend the banquet. Herrera, however, was instructed by the Secret Service to say only that Kennedy planned to attend. The Secret Service also had prohibited the LULAC leadership, for security reasons, from publicizing Kennedy's appearance on the radio.[17]

The anti-Mexican prejudices that Jiménez encountered after moving to Texas were still commonplace in Houston when Kennedy attended the banquet. Therefore, his interest in the Mexican American minority was significant. Another politician, Lyndon B. Johnson, also took an interest, as illustrated with the Longoria incident discussed in the previous chapter. The future US president became acutely aware of anti-Mexican racism when he was a teacher in a "Mexican school," in Cotulla, a Texas city near the Mexican border. Johnson observed that whites in Cotulla treated Mexicans, in his words, "just worse than you'd treat a dog."[18] Of his students he once commented, "My students were poor and often came to class without breakfast, hungry. And they knew even in their youth the pain of prejudice. They never seemed to know why people disliked them. But they knew it was so. I saw it in their eyes."[19]

As the quote from Johnson suggested, the schools in Texas perpetuated commonplace anti-Mexican prejudices. For example, Mexican American students typically dreaded classes when Texas history was taught. Luis Cano, who became a leading advocate for Mexican American studies in Houston public schools during the 1970s, had painful memories from his seventh-grade classes. He recalled, "When I studied Texas history in the seventh grade, I felt like crawling under the desk because I felt like my people were always made to look like bad guys."[20]

In the 1950s and 1960s, Houston schools were still racially segregated, and white Texans intended to keep it that way. In Texas Mexican-origin students did not attend schools with Blacks because they were classified as white. However, this arrangement did not mean that racial relations between the Mexicans and whites were positive. Jiménez recalled being in the home of Sharon Bradshaw, a white classmate, to complete a homework assignment. While she was there, the classmate's young brother went outside to play, after which the boy's grandmother said, "Don't play with those Mexican boys." Jiménez then asked her classmate, "Well, why am I in your house if that's the attitude your grandmother has?" Her friend replied, "Well, I told her you were French."[21]

Prejudice also existed between Mexican-immigrant students and Mexican American students. Jiménez recalled her experience at Franklin

Elementary School in the late 1950s and being prohibited from speaking Spanish, a school policy in this period. If caught speaking Spanish, a student might be expelled or, at the very least, required to stay after school. Jiménez's painful school memories included, she recalled, "being unable to ask fundamental questions like 'I need to go to the restroom' or [to say I] was thirsty." Even worse, she remembered, "being told by [Mexican American] classmates if I spoke Spanish, they would turn me in to the principal."[22]

A study conducted years later in 1978 by sociologist Dr. Tatcho Mindiola Jr. (1939–2024) examined anti-Mexican prejudice among junior high students in Houston. His findings revealed prejudices against Mexican immigrant students among students who were Chicanos—that is, students of Mexican descent who were born in the United States. Mindiola wrote that "Chicano students verbally and physically taunt the Mexican students."[23] Mexican students were called "*mojo*," short for "*mojado*," which is translated as "wetback" in English. The hostility toward Mexican immigrants appeared greatest among second- and third-generation Mexican Americans who typically did not speak Spanish and were not culturally connected to Mexico. Yet despite their high degree of assimilation, Mexican American students felt the sting of racial prejudices. As Mindiola explained, they encountered whites' anti-Mexican racism because whites did not distinguish between immigrants and Mexican Americans who were born in the United States.[24]

Jiménez started Milby High School in the fall of 1966. At Milby Jiménez became active in the debate club and acquired valuable public speaking skills. She described her debate coach, Mr. Thompson, as a "total contradiction" because his parents had been members of the KKK, but the coach believed in integration and was, she said, "very active in actually desegregating debate contests." Jiménez excelled in debate, even winning a women's state championship. Unfortunately, she and her female debate partner lost the opportunity to compete at the national level. The judges' decision favored the male duo whom she and her partner had debated. The university professor who voted for her and her partner told Jiménez the reason for the decision. He said that the other judges, two university students, voted against her and her partner because "they thought the boys would do better at nationals" than would a female team.[25]

In addition to blatant gender biases, Jiménez experienced other forms of prejudice. For example, she lost a debate because the judge did not like her accent.[26] Like other Mexican students, Jiménez encountered discrimination because she was an immigrant. She recalled being offered the opportunity to attend a mock state government session. However, the school withdrew this opportunity at the last minute because she was not a US citizen. Not long after this incident, in September 1968, Jiménez became a naturalized citizen.[27] Her earlier immigrant status, she believed, also prevented her from obtaining scholarships to attend the university despite having a 4.0 grade point average at Milby High School.[28] She, however, did receive a scholarship from Sembradores de Amistad for five hundred dollars.[29]

As a result of her high school experiences and the marginalization that she felt, Jiménez became, in her words, "a radical."[30] Many, if not most, white students did not consider the Mexican American students their equals. Jiménez was acutely aware of injustices toward minority, immigrant, and female students and became a strong advocate for all these groups. Reflecting on her high school days, Jiménez remarked, "It was very evident that we were, as a group, marginalized from the mainstream activities at the school. So, it in a sense, not only produced suffering, but an anger—an *anger* that it's *wrong*."[31] Another Mexican American student in Houston, George Xavier Cruz, agreed and remembered insults such as "the words 'Meskins,' 'beaner,' 'pepper-belly,' 'taco-bender,' and many others."[32]

Racial discrimination against minorities existed throughout Texas history, but their struggle against it and for equal rights began to intensify from the 1950s. Jiménez knew this discrimination well and participated in the struggle like other activists during the civil rights movements of the 1960s and 1970s. The fight for equal rights energized people of color, most notably by African Americans and Mexican Americans, but many other groups as well. In this volatile time, the Mexican American youth adopted the term *Chicano* or *Chicana* to express ethnic pride. Conservative and older Mexican Americans, however, rejected the term.[33] Félix Ramírez of Houston encountered this attitude in the late 1960s when he tried, with little success, to interest Mexican American organizations in his newspaper *Papel Chicano*. The word *Chicano* in the title, he believed, "hurt me."[34]

How one identifies oneself or what terms others use are sensitive matters and can affect one's relations with other people. Jiménez identified herself as a Mexican immigrant, as a gringa, and as a Chicana. She claimed an identity as a Mexican immigrant, she said, "because I was born in Mexico, [because of] my relationship to my parents and the country of Mexico." Her identity as a gringa, a term used to indicate a white woman from the United States, derived from her sharing the values this nation espouses—notably, tolerance. In her words, her identity as a gringa explained her "willingness to accept people for who they are as individuals. I see it more as something learned from the United States, a characteristic of the people of the United States." In contrast, she added, Mexico is "very intolerant to differences in class, ethnicity, and religion."[35]

Jiménez also self-identified as a Chicana "because since a child, I've had all the experiences of the Mexican growing up in the United States . . . a lot of conflict of the identity—who are we—is created by a dominant culture over another culture."[36] Unlike the terms *Mexican American*, *Hispanic*, or *Latino*, the terms *Chicano* and *Chicana* arose from Mexican-origin youths themselves during the Chicano Movement. Jiménez's preference for the term derived from her own activism in the Chicano Movement and the political party La Raza Unida. Another person in Houston who favored it was Daniel Bustamante. In 1979 he said, "Mexican-American is the polite term—it used to be Latin Americans. Some like it but it bothers me. I'm a Chicano." Others disagreed with Daniel and refused to use the term, like the woman who said, "Don't put me in with those radicals!"[37]

Farmworkers and Their Allies for Fair Wages

Politically active Mexican Americans of all ages, including Jiménez, were highly motivated in the 1960s and 1970s to end injustice in a wide range of areas. A major development that galvanized the Mexican-origin community in Texas was the 1966 Minimum Wage March. Its participants marched in support of Mexican and Mexican American migrant farmworkers who at this time constituted about 95 percent of the farm labor in Texas.[38] The immediate background to the march was the strike, or *huelga*, that farmworkers organized in 1965 against La Casita farms in Starr County in South Texas. The idea for the march to the state capital in Austin, according to Houstonian Alfonso Vasquez, came from an effort by Father Antonio González of Houston to calm the agitated and angry farmworkers. Vasquez reported that Father González instructed them to kneel and pray. He then said, "We're not going to have violence, we're not going to attack anyone. We are going to Austin and ask the governor and the legislature for a bill that will remedy the situation."[39] John Connally (1917–1993), the Texas governor from 1963 to 1969, refused to meet with the marchers at the state capitol building. He decided, instead, to meet with them in a small town near Austin.

The 1965 strike and 1966 Minimum Wage March became a major national news story. They represented "the first major civil rights event in Texas during the late 1960s," in the words of James C. Harrington, director of the Texas Civil Rights Project.[40] A 1960 news article reported that migrant laborers in Texas worked an average of 125 or 130 days a year and earned about $900.[41] The farmworkers were striking for a pay increase from $0.85 per hour, the highest pay rate and not offered to most workers, to $1.25 per hour.[42] Among the critics of the strike, besides the governor, was US Senator from Texas John Tower (1925–1991), a conservative Republican. Revealing a complete indifference to the workers' call for higher wages, Tower said, "The question of whether people can live on 85 cents an hour is not the point. The point is that 85 cents an hour is better than nothing."[43] Not only were wages low, but the working conditions were unsafe. Living quarters were "extremely substandard. There is no approved water supply. In fact, they sometimes must get their water from cow tanks or drainage ditches. Toilets are often near the eating facilities. Lack of privacy is almost on a level of animalism."[44]

Papel Chicano and other Chicano newspapers, as well as mainstream newspapers, covered the progress of the historic march of the striking farmworkers and the individuals and organizations that joined the strikers. The Houston paper *El Sol* expressed pride in the event and wrote that "the strikers have shown something which many Americans no longer show—guts and determination in trying to solve their problem."[45] Alfred J. Hernández (1917–2010) considered the strike and subsequent march very significant.

He described the march as "a turning point" and a break from the past when the Mexican American had been "passive" and "felt inadequate."[46] Hernández believed strongly in justice, as his activism demonstrated. He was born in Mexico in 1917 but had lived in Houston since 1921. In 1960 he was the first Mexican American to become a municipal court judge in that city and was a prominent leader in LULAC.[47]

The strikers and their allies in the Minimum Wage March endured many hardships in their 491-mile trek from South Texas to Austin. Like other activists in labor struggles in Texas, they encountered hostile local police and the Texas Rangers. Both were used by employers and influential individuals to intimidate, even physically assault, workers and union organizers.[48] The Texas Rangers, according to Bexar County Commissioner Albert Peña, were especially aggressive. Calling the Texas Rangers "*pistoleros*," or "gunmen," Peña complained that Mexicans were "under siege in Rio Grande City by the [Governor] Connally *pistoleros* and the [Texas Rangers Director] Garrison gunslingers who subjected them to harassment, fear, and intimidation, a little head cracking and jailing on nebulous charges."[49] Another critic was the US Senator from Texas Ralph Yarborough (1903–1996), a liberal Democrat, who called the Texas Rangers "Connally's strikebreakers" and union busters.[50]

The Texas Rangers' violations of the rights of people of color were well known, although white Texans had a high opinion of them. However, Texas state legislators, church organizations, university professors, the AFL-CIO, as well as Mexican American groups such as PASO, the American GI Forum, and LULAC, condemned the tactics of the Texas Rangers.[51] A 1967–1968 study by the United States Commission on Civil Rights criticized the Rangers as well. The study said that mistreatment "included physical and verbal abuse by the Texas Rangers and local officials, and the holding of union organizers for many hours before releasing them on bond."[52] The Texas Rangers' egregious intimidation of the marchers in 1966, not unique to this protest movement, resulted in a legal case against them that reached the US Supreme Court as *Allee v. Medrano* (1974). The court ruled in favor of the appellees, union organizers, and farmworkers, stating that the appellees "were subjected to persistent harassment and violence by appellants and other law enforcement officers."[53]

Many persons in Houston, including Jiménez, considered the march a historic and inspiring event. She recalled that she followed the progress of the march "on a daily basis in church and at home."[54] Jiménez believed that the protest march demonstrated the importance of collective action to advance social justice. In other words, for her the event demonstrated "that social movements lead to redress of injustices."[55] Although she did not participate directly in the march because she was in high school at the time, she and others in the Catholic Youth Organization of the Immaculate Heart of Mary Church collected items the striking farmworkers needed.[56]

Other Houston activists contributed to the historic event. For example, two Houston clergy who helped organize the march were Father Antonio González, mentioned earlier, of the Roman Catholic Immaculate Heart of Mary Church, and Reverend James Novarro of Kashmere Baptist Church.[57] Fathers González and Lawrence Peguero also organized a food drive and collected clothing for the strikers' families.[58] Judge Alfred J. Hernández, the LULAC president, participated in the march off and on, but as a private citizen and not representing his organization.[59] Lauro Cruz (1933–2017) was another marcher. He made history in Harris County, where Houston is located, in November 1966 by being the first Mexican American from that county elected to the Texas state legislature.[60]

The church's activism in this labor struggle was especially noteworthy. According to Robert R. Treviño, "The activities of Father González, Las Hermanas, and PADRES were clearly a break from any social action undertaken in the past by church personnel on behalf of Mexicans in Houston."[61] The groups referenced included Las Hermanas, founded by nuns in 1971, and PADRES (Padres Asociados para Derechos Religiosos, Educativos, y Sociales, or Priests Associated for Religious, Educational, and Social Rights), organized by priests in 1969. Judge Hernández agreed with Treviño's assessment and remarked that the new interest in social problems was "a completely new turn for the church."[62] During this period the church offered retreats (*cursillos*) that strongly encouraged activism for social justice. Participants who were inspired by the Cursillo Movement included César Chávez and, in Houston, Félix Ramírez, copublisher of *Papel Chicano*. About his retreat experience, Ramírez said that it "literally changed my life. . . . The Cursillo Movement caused a lot of awakening in our people."[63]

The historic march culminated in a massive rally on Labor Day, September 5, 1966, at the state capitol in Austin. News reporters believed that the crowd totaled ten thousand.[64] Alfonso Vásquez, editor of *Papel Chicano*, estimated that 90 percent at the rally were Mexican Americans. Also participating in the event, he believed, were many "[Mexican] nationals who were established residents in the United States. . . . So, you're talking about American citizens of Mexican descent. Even these farmworkers, many of whom were born on the farms in Texas."[65] These mixed-status marchers were joined by forty or more African Americans from Huntsville, a town north of Houston, who sang, "We Shall Overcome."[66] The rally was historic for its size and the number of officials of Texas present. They included US Senator Ralph Yarborough and US Representative Henry B. González; many state legislators, including almost all of those in the House of Representatives who represented Harris County; and the AFL-CIO president H. S. Brown. United States Senator Robert Kennedy (D-NY) wired a message of support for the marchers.[67]

Not surprisingly, the results of the march were limited, given the pervasive anti-Mexican prejudices, especially against immigrants. In the area of politics, Representative Cruz introduced a resolution in 1967 in the Texas House of Representatives, although it failed to pass. It demanded that the governor order the Texas Rangers out of Starr County.[68] The legislature also did not pass a minimum wage law. A more positive and enduring result of the march, Treviño believed, was that "Mexican Americans across the state showed an increased political awareness and a heightened ethnic consciousness that gave direction to their long-held resentment and energized the budding Chicano movement in Texas."[69]

Activist in Training: Jiménez at the University of Houston

Jiménez's participation in the Chicano Movement undoubtedly contributed to her later advocacy for human rights The activism of this period, according to Houston community leader Leonel Castillo, inspired "a degree of cohesion and unity of purpose among the main Mexican-American groups in the city."[70] In addition, according to historian Ignacio M. Garcia, at this time young Chicanos and Chicanas projected a "militant ethos" that evolved from "a political 'consciousness' of being *mexicano* in the United States."[71] The militant ethos included oppositional politics with new "platforms, manifestos, and tactics."[72] An example of the new aggressive tactics in Houston included the takeover of a vacant community center at the Juan Marcos Presbyterian Church in February 1970. The incident made a big impression on Jiménez. Years later, she recalled the incident and said, "My first picket line was in support of the people who had taken over the Presbyterian church."[73] She added, "I felt this is what I've been looking for, a real grassroots approach."[74]

The community-based Mexican American Youth Organization (MAYO) organized the three-week takeover, which had strong local support. MAYO leaders Gregorio Salazar, an avowed Marxist, and Yolanda Garza Birdwell, a Chicana married to a white political activist, led the takeover. At the time of the takeover at the church's community center, police and SWAT officers surrounded the building because they initially believed, incorrectly, that the activists were armed. Fortunately, according to MAYO activist Carlos Calbillo, the intervention of "cooler heads among the city's political leadership" prevented a violent confrontation between MAYO members and the police.[75] The barrio residents wanted the use of the building to provide services for the community, such as free breakfast for children and job training for adults.[76] Birdwell recalled the events leading up to the takeover, saying, "We went to three or four [church] meetings with different board meetings, etc., and nothing—so then we chose at that time to take it over."[77] During the takeover, the barrio residents supplied food for the breakfast program at the occupied church building.[78] A court order eventually facilitated a compromise between the Brazos Presbytery and MAYO that satisfied the latter's objectives. As Birdwell remarked, "Our fight was with the church, not the court."[79]

Jiménez's role as an activist for social justice intensified after high school. After graduating from Milby High School in 1969, she attended the University of Houston (UH). She became very active in student organizations because, as she expressed it, "I had to practically do something to end the injustices."[80] Jiménez first joined the Young Democrats for a semester, then joined the university's MAYO. When a position became available on the student traffic court, the campus MAYO encouraged her to apply to that position. After joining the traffic court in 1971, she was elected chief justice by its members, which included three other students and one professor. In one controversial move during her term, Jiménez led the decision to discard all parking tickets issued to students. Her sense of justice prompted this action. Parking spaces for students were often scarce and if students parked in faculty lots, they were fined. If faculty members parked in student lots, however, they were not forced to pay a fine.[81] Jiménez's traffic court attempted to change this inequitable policy. Concerning this episode, she commented, "When I was chief of the traffic court, we decided to throw out all the tickets that came to us from students until that (policy) changed . . . and I was *hated* by the faculty!"[82]

In another incident Jiménez angered some Chicanos and Chicanas when she wrote her essay "Women Still Powerless," an early example of her feminism. It was published in 1970 in Houston's Chicano newspaper *Papel Chicano.*[83] She recalled that it "made a lot of controversy. . . . The criticism was: you are adopting a gringo position and you're destroying the family."[84] Jiménez disagreed. She recalled, "I knew that women were active in Mexican history, so when I received this criticism, I just went back and put all those facts together I remembered seeing in my grandfather's books from Sor Juana [Inés] de la Cruz[85] to the movement for the right to vote, for the movement for public education for women in Mexico, to the feminist circles of the early nineteenth century, I mean, the early twentieth century, and different *strong* women."[86] In her essay Jiménez was saying that Mexican women had fulfilled and could continue to fulfill important political and social roles in addition to that of housewife and mother.

Jiménez held strong views about women, especially regarding power and leadership. A basic problem for women, she wrote, was that the Mexican male considered himself superior to females and that this attitude undermined women's ambitions and confidence. Jiménez had clear and specific ideas about women and leadership. She advised Chicanas who wanted to be activists and leaders to not get romantically involved with a Chicano and to remain a virgin, advice that she followed herself.[87] Her essay in *Papel Chicano* not only revealed her feminist beliefs but also included a critical assessment of her culture and the Chicano movement: "'*Justicia para el Chicano*' means just that, Justice for the *Chicano* and not the *Chicana*. In our urgency to '*levantar la raza*' (raise the people), we forget about one important segment of our people—the female. . . . The Chicana is oppressed in her educational advancement by the Mexican culture, the Anglo-oriented education system, and the Yankee business culture."[88] Jiménez also criticized the white education system for discouraging Mexican American students, male and female, from reaching their potential. White Texans held the commonplace opinion that Mexican-origin students were not intelligent or interested in education. For example, this writer's father, like other Mexicans in high school, was not expected to go to college. He and other Mexican students were assigned clerical or manual work in local businesses.[89] About thirty years later, Jiménez and other Chicanas had similar experiences. She recalled that school counselors would "channel [the Chicana] into 'practical' occupations such as secretarial jobs, beauticians, etc."[90]

Jiménez believed that many factors had a negative effect on women's self-image. In her controversial essay, Jiménez also attacked the "Yankee business culture" because she believed it encouraged women to marry in order to enjoy "wedded bliss." Once married, women's concerns would be no greater than "yellow floors" or "gray clothes." The Mexican culture, in addition, considered the roles of wife and mother to be the most important destiny for women. In the 1975 article "La Madre de Familia se Debe Cuidar" ("The Mother of the Family Should Take Care of Herself") in the Houston newspaper *El Mexica*, the writer gave women dietary advice so that they could better fulfill their role as mothers.[91] The end results of gender-based biases, Jiménez asserted in her essay, were fewer options and economic advantages for Chicanas. They also experienced early marriages and a series of pregnancies. Contributing to the latter was "our strong faith in the Catholic Church."[92] Although some of her readers believed that Jiménez was overly critical of the Mexican culture, she was expressing her pride in Mexican history and its strong women like Sor Juan Inés de la Cruz. As she phrased it, "So *my* history, the history of the people of Mexico, is a history of a struggle for the equality of women. So I don't know what *your* history is, but that's *my* history."[93]

In April of 1971, Jiménez ventured into politics. During her sophomore year at UH, she ran for vice president of the Student Association (SA) and Steven Umoff ran for president. Umoff believed that he could win with the support of the organizations that would back Jiménez. She did not immediately accept his offer to run. She commented at that time, "I had to ask the Latinos if they would be comfortable if I ran with this *white* guy. I had to ask the women if they would be comfortable if I ran with this *male*."[94] Umoff and Jiménez won their race and were sworn in on April 15, 1971. Halfway through their one-year term, Umoff reneged on his promise to step down from the presidency to allow Jiménez to become president, as he had agreed to do. Recalling this development, Jiménez related that "once we won, he didn't want to leave."[95] He later resigned, nevertheless, because of a funding scandal. The SA voted in November 1971 to replace him with Jiménez.

Jiménez was an admirable role model for Mexican American students, especially Chicanas. She was the first Hispanic elected to the SA at the University of Houston and the first woman ever to become its president. In November 1971 the newly inaugurated president told the *Daily Cougar*, the student newspaper at the university, that "my performance will be a reflection of the ability of women and chicanos."[96] Because of her strong belief in women's rights, Jiménez, for example, fought for a Women's Studies program at the university, supported the right to an abortion, and advocated free child care for students.[97] In 1972 the Houston-area chapter of the National Organization for Women (NOW) honored her with the Susan B. Anthony Award for advancing women's rights.[98] Two years later, in 1974, Jiménez graduated from UH with a degree in political science.

Jiménez promoted social equality and justice whenever possible in the turbulent 1960s and 1970s. In this era antiestablishment movements included the antiwar movement and the civil rights movements of African Americans, Chicanos, women, and gays. All these groups concerned Jiménez. Significantly, when president of the SA, Jiménez helped organize a conference for gays in 1971, which she believed was "the first gay conference in the nation."[99] She recalled that "nobody wanted to even lend them a place to have it. Nobody wanted to lend them any money at all," but the SA did because it supported, she said, "social justice issues."[100] She added, "We did it as a student government function. I remember we gave them a thousand dollars at the time to do this conference."[101]

Jiménez did not fear conflict in her goal to protect the rights and dignity of others. The conference for gays was one example. The event did not go unnoticed by a legislator in the state capital in Austin. State Representative Sid Bower called for an investigation of the funds used by the SA. He complained that the university funded "ultra-left-wing socialist organizations" and "a homosexual conference." Bower also asserted that the funding of political activities violated state law, but Jiménez rejected his characterization of Gay Liberation as "political."[102] Another contentious topic she addressed was the war in Vietnam. She did not hesitate to publicly criticize US involvement there and the atrocities against the Vietnamese women.[103] These were depicted in the film *Winter Soldier Investigation*, shown during a conference in October 1971 that Jiménez helped to organize at UH.[104]

Jiménez, who was an immigrant, unlike some of her friends, took a special interest in the immigrant community. Many in this group were farmworkers who frequently suffered from low wages and hazardous work conditions. Given this deplorable situation for Mexican American and Mexican immigrant farmworkers, the United Farm Workers (UFW) called for a nationwide boycott of nonunion lettuce in 1970. Jiménez helped organize the boycott in Houston. The experience provided her with important insight because, she recalled, the boycott "dealt with economic inequality . . . union organizing, and how the capitalist system worked."[105] Many years after the boycott, in 2014, Jiménez remarked, "This experience enriched my understanding of labor and social movements within a political and economic system that upheld the wealth and privilege of a minority of corporations and elites."[106]

Consistent with her concern for farmworkers, Jiménez served as president of UH's Students for Farm Workers (SFW), and off-campus she volunteered at the Texas Boycott Office of the UFW.[107] During the lettuce boycott, she worked with César Chávez and Dolores Huerta, cofounders of the UFW. At the University of Houston, MAYO, SFW, and several other student organizations pressured the school in 1971 and 1972 to use only union lettuce in its food service facilities but had limited success. Nevertheless, the boycott and many other experiences during Jiménez's years at UH advanced her skills that she would need later to promote social justice.

School Desegregation in Houston: Mexican American Activists Demand Reform

The CRT assertion that racism is commonplace was abundantly evident in the desegregation process of Houston's public schools. The intense battle between segregationists and integrationists illustrated the efforts of the former to maintain two kinds of schools, with superior education for white students and poorer quality education for students of color. After the *Brown v. Board of Education of Topeka* (1954) ruling, HISD continued to violate the rights of Black students, but racial biases also targeted Mexican-origin students.[108] These students knew the pain, like Jiménez, of being marginalized in a racist school environment. Among her earliest school memories, she recalled that "the threat to be expelled from school for speaking Spanish created insecurity."[109] Besides forbidding the use of Spanish, the school was hostile to the minority students' culture. Jiménez remembered that she "had to take a white bread and bologna sandwich . . . if we took a taco we were ridiculed."[110] As stressful as was her experience in elementary and junior high school, she believed that "the discrimination was even more glaring" in high school.[111]

The widespread opposition to integrating schools intensified Mexican Americans' activism in the early 1970s for desegregation. As historian Guadalupe San Miguel Jr. concluded from his research on Houston schools, this activism succeeded "in encouraging participation from all sectors of the Mexican American community—young and old, male and female, radical and moderate, and novice and experienced—and in keeping them united throughout the period."[112] The struggle against HISD was extremely difficult in part because HISD was the nation's largest segregated school system.[113] Its noncompliance with *Brown* illustrated the fact that laws or court decisions like *Brown* are not enough by themselves to advance civil rights if

commonplace racism resists change.[114] Laws and court decisions are undermined by "narrow interpretation, administrative obstruction, or delay," for
example.[115] HISD's opposition to integration frustrated many. For example,
a disgruntled HISD board member complained to the Texas State Advisory
Committee in 1967 that "a great amount of time, attention, and money has
been used in perpetuating segregation, which might have been used to better
educate the children of the Houston Independent School District."[116] Federal
District Judge Ben C. Connally (1909–1975) was also angry over HISD's
defiance and ordered it to create an integration plan for the fall of 1960.[117]
Despite this order, the subterfuge of the school system in the 1950s, described
by San Miguel in the previous chapter, continued in the 1960s.

The opposition to the integration of students of color, especially Black
students, varied from region to region in Texas. However, despite racial
intimidation, activists for equitable education vigorously pushed for desegregation. In December 1956 the NAACP in Houston filed a lawsuit on behalf
of two students, Delores Ross and Beneva Williams, after they were denied
admission at white schools in the fall of 1956.[118] Years later Beneva recalled
the jeers she heard as she left the school and that in the weeks that followed,
"The family phone rang with anonymous threats and racial epithets."[119] At the
college level, integration was also an issue. For example, the 1891 charter
of the elite Rice University in Houston granted admission only to "white"
students. In 1962 a large majority of the student population demanded an end
to the university's "color restriction on admissions."[120] The trustees, faculty,
and students believed that the policy was immoral, but also that the "discrimination made it difficult to attract faculty members and government research
funds."[121] The university's charter officially changed in 1966 and Black
students were admitted.[122] Integration became desirable to recruit faculty and
to continue receiving federal funding and not solely to advance racial justice.
The moral argument, nevertheless, was crucial.

Mexican American parents and students mobilized in the late 1960s
to protest HISD's continued failure to provide the education that minority
students needed. It was well-known that Mexican-origin students received
education that was inferior to that for white students.[123] Conditions that
existed in the 1950s continued into the 1960s and 1970s. An article by

Marie Dauplaise in 1958 reported that schools for Mexican students "are old and staffed by too many beginning teachers who are unable to speak Spanish."[124] Dauplaise added that the school system made no effort to hire Spanish-speaking teachers.[125]

In addition to dilapidated buildings and inexperienced teachers, the racial prejudices of the teachers directly affected students' self-image and academic success.[126] In 1970 students at Washington Junior High School in Houston, for instance, complained that teachers called them "brown monkeys" and made remarks like "half of you are on welfare."[127] For its part, HISD consistently denied charges of discrimination, inferior teachers, or the harassment of students. However, statistics on the education for Mexican Americans revealed serious decades-old problems. Data from the US Census Bureau indicated that the "7.4 median school years reported for Mexican-origin Houstonians twenty-five years and older in 1970" had improved by only one year over 1960.[128] Another example that illustrated HISD's poor record in serving the Mexican-origin community was a college-bound summer school program in 1969. In this case, most of the 120 male Mexican American students selected to attend the summer school could only read at a second- or third-grade level.[129]

In October 1969 Mexican American parents and students met with HISD officials to demand reform. The parents' own research indicated that only 11 percent of Mexican American students completed high school.[130] Nevertheless, according to San Miguel, "No specific measures were taken to address them [parents' grievances] by either the board of education or the superintendent."[131] During the 1968–69 school year, junior and senior high school students formed Advocating Rights for Mexican American Students (ARMAS). Students in ARMAS were inspired by the nationwide militant activism of the civil rights movements, but more specifically by the walk-out in 1968 at Edcouch Elsa High School in Edcouch, Texas. The high school students in this South Texas city organized a walk-out when the school board refused to hear their grievances and expelled the protesting students. The Houston Chicano newspaper *Compass* reported that "the fact that our youngsters are finally taking positive action (in the valley), should be a reminder—and hint for us to do our share." It added, a "revolution of walk-outs, sit-ins, or stay-outs is needed. . . . The Houston Schools are ripe for an internal revolution."[132]

Fortunately, the students and their parents of ARMAS had allies. A new organization, MALDEF, won a lawsuit in 1968 against the Edcouch Elsa High School for its unconstitutional actions that violated the students' right to protest. In addition, the United States Commission on Civil Rights conducted hearings in December 1968 that drew national attention to the discrimination against minorities in Texas.[133] ARMAS also organize walk-outs in Houston on September 16, 1969.[134] However, the walkout produced no concrete changes.

Students and their parents continued to fight for social justice and integration of Houston's public schools HISD. In 1970 activists protested HISD's latest desegregation plan because of its blatant unfairness to students of color.[135] The plan illustrated the "subterfuge" by HISD that San Miguel described when writing about the 1950s. The activists in 1970 pointed out that the desegregation plan paired schools that had majority Mexican American students (technically classified as "white") with schools with Black students.[136] In other words, the HISD plan moved Hispanic and Black students from one inferior school to another and left schools with white student populations almost untouched. Specifically, the pairing "affected 16,733 students, but included only 539 whites."[137] This kind of pairing was criticized by a judge (Judge Clark) in a similar legal case, referring to it as "mock justice."[138] HISD's desegregation plans exploited the category of "white" of the Mexican American students to maintain a segregated school system.[139]

To protest the HISD pairing plan, a coalition group of concerned parents, individuals, and organizations formed the Mexican American Education Council (MAEC). It called for a *huelga* (strike) against HISD, that lasted two and a half weeks. MAEC also organized *huelga* schools, officially called Huelga Enrichment Centers, for the years 1970–1971 and 1971–1972.[140] Of the 5,831 Mexican American students in the original pairing plan, over 3,500 boycotted HISD in the fall of 1970.[141] The *huelga* schools' principal organizers included Sister Gloria Gallardo, a Roman Catholic nun, and Tina Reyes, who years later was elected to the HISD school board.[142]

Mexican American youth were especially aggressive in their demands for equitable education. They demonstrated their enthusiasm in the so-called riot at an HISD board meeting on September 14, 1970. Leonel Castillo, the spokesperson for MAEC, could not convince the board to listen to the organization's concerns.[143] When the meeting was adjourned, the volatile members of MAYO, whose leaders included Gregorio Salazar and Yolanda Garza Birdwell, pushed forward to hand their list of complaints to the board. In the disorder that followed, the police arrested Salazar, Birdwell, and seven other MAYO members.[144]

Many factors contributed to the turbulent, emotional struggle for school reform in the early 1970s. Some Hispanic organizations did not actively support the MAEC-organized *huelga* schools. For instance, MAEC did not receive funds from older established organizations like LULAC, even though LULAC's state president, Tony Bonilla, personally expressed his support.[145] An angry writer of the barrio newspaper *Papel Chicano* in 1971 asked LULAC, "Do you really give a damn if the only Symble [*sic*] of resistance to the H.I.S.D. Pairing Plan, the Huelga School, continues to exist?"[146] Jiménez also was ambivalent about the schools because, although its leaders said they wanted equality for students, she believed that "the community was saying, 'I don't want to go with those black people.'"[147] It is not known if her assessment was accurate, but the *huelga* schools and other forms of activism ultimately succeeded in pressuring HISD to create a more equitable educational system. Improvements included more Mexican American teachers and programs benefiting Mexican American students.

HISD and other school systems, however, continued to circumvent *Brown v. Board of Education*. Achieving a more equitable desegregation plan in Houston hinged on the reclassification of Mexican American students as a distinct minority group instead of the race category of "white." In some cities in Texas, Mexican American students, in fact, were already classified as a separate ethnic group, but this was not true in Houston. Parents of the group Barrios Unidos were frustrated by HISD's pairing plans. The Barrios Unidos chair, Abel Alvarez, said Chicanos "were tired of being used."[148] The legal ethnic distinction Mexican American students needed in Texas was finally decided in *Cisneros v. Corpus Christi ISD* (1970) by the US District Court for the Southern District of Texas, and again in *Keyes v. School District No. 1* (1973), a district in Denver, Colorado. In the latter ruling, the US Supreme Court agreed with the lower court[149] and wrote that "the Mexican American educational experience was similar to the African American and that they should be accorded the same rights."[150] In 1974 HISD finally classified Mexican American students as nonwhite.

In the volatile period of the early 1970s, one of the most dedicated education activists was Luis Cano. Originally from Corpus Christi, Texas, Cano moved to Houston in 1970 and soon began his struggle with HISD to add Mexican American studies to its curriculum. Not long after Cano started teaching for HISD, he realized that HISD was failing to meet the educational needs of the Mexican American students. Despite their very high dropout rate, Cano noted that "there seemed to be so little interest or no interest at all in the educational problems of Chicano kids in Houston. I was appalled."[151]

Cano felt compelled to do something about this unjust situation. To alert the Mexican-origin community of his concern, he formed the theatrical group Teatro Chicano Sexto Sol in the spring of 1971. It was, in his words, "the first social issues theater in Houston." In addition, he offered a proposal for Mexican American studies. The HISD supervisor for social studies commented, "I'm concerned about this course . . . because I'm concerned it promotes communism. . . . Well, you talk about César Chávez in here. He's a socialist." In reply, Cano said he did not know or care if that was the case, adding, "The point is that he is prominent personally in Mexican American affairs and we have to teach about him." Fortunately, this supervisor left HISD and her successor allowed Cano to introduce Mexican American studies.[152]

HISD's response to the demands for educational reforms materialized in the 1974–1975 school year. That year it introduced magnet schools, which were district-wide schools that focused on specific subjects—for example, the arts, the sciences, and health. Another characteristic of the new schools was that its student population had to reflect the city's demographic makeup, which was 37.1 percent white, 42.6 percent Black, and 20.3 percent Hispanic.[153] The schools, according to sociologist Angela

Valenzuela, "were designed to attract students across neighborhood lines for the purpose of improving the quality of education and promoting integration, as well as to stem white flight."[154]

Some education activists questioned how much the magnet schools benefited minority students. The new schools, in the opinion of Valenzuela, were another example of what crits call interest convergence. Magnet schools, in fact, did reduce white flight because many white parents wanted their children enrolled in them. In the end, according to Valenzuela, whites "disproportionately benefited from them [magnet schools]."[155] Fortunately, the Association for the Advancement of Mexican Americans (AAMA) created another option when it established an alternate school for Mexican American students in 1973. The new school, the George I. Sánchez Junior and Senior High Schools in Houston's East End, was directed by Luis Cano.[156]

Public Education for Immigrant Children

An equitable school system is not one that provides education to some children but denies it to others. However, this social injustice existed in Texas because of anti-immigrant prejudices. Jiménez knew this firsthand. She said, "I was repressed because I was foreign-born . . . [it was] accepted if you're foreign born that you can be discriminated against . . . if you were a child, you couldn't go to public schools."[157] For immigrant children public schools were often hostile places. Nevertheless, immigrant parents fought hard to get their children into public schools. One obstacle was the price of education. Parents could not send their children to Houston's public schools because, since 1976, schools in Texas charged each undocumented child between $90 and $130 tuition per month.[158]

The exorbitant tuition charge for Houston's public schools became possible after the Texas legislature changed the Texas Education Code in 1975. The new code, Section 21.031, prohibited "spending state funds on students who were not U.S. citizens or legally admitted to the country." The amendment "also authorized school districts to exclude undocumented students, passed by voice vote, with no debate and no legislative history—no numbers, no studies of how many students would be affected or the amendment's financial impact."[159] In contrast to other states bordering Mexico, only Texas excluded "aliens from a tuition-free education."[160]

Fortunately, activist immigrant parents refused to accept this injustice and took legal action in 1977. The parents' long legal struggle against the discriminatory 1975 law began in Tyler, Texas, where the board of trustees decided to allow a tuition charge of $1000 a year to each undocumented immigrant student.[161] The parents' attorneys included Larry Daves and two lawyers from the MALDEF, Vilma Martínez (b. 1943) and Peter Roos. The US Department of Justice (DOJ) also sued the Texas Education Agency. The plaintiffs filed as John Doe to avoid the risk of deportation. The risk was real. In September 1977 the United States attorney had instructed INS in the Dallas area to conduct a raid against families who were plaintiffs in the suit. The raid did not occur because Leonel Castillo, the INS Commissioner (1977–1979), blocked it.[162]

The courageous parents and MALDEF succeeded in their efforts. In September 1978 US District Judge William Wayne Justice (1920–2009) ruled in *Plyler v. Doe* that the Texas statute and the Tyler schools' new tuition policy were unconstitutional. The ruling by Justice applied to the Tyler schools but its influence was statewide. Subsequent legal challenges by Houston and other school districts failed. In Houston Judge Woodrow B. Seals (1917–1990) ruled in July 1980 on *In re: Alien Children Litigation*. He upheld the lower court's decision that Section 21.031 was unconstitutional and "ordered the state to stop enforcing the law, and all local school districts to admit students without regard to their immigration status."[163]

Unfortunately, the legal battle continued because Judge Seals's ruling was appealed to the US Supreme Court as *James Plyler, Superintendent, Tyler Independent School District, et al. v. John Doe*. In a 5–4 decision in June 1982, the Supreme Court ruled that the Texas school districts had violated the Equal Protection Clause of the Fourteenth Amendment by denying free public education to undocumented schoolchildren, thus affirming the ruling of the Fifth Circuit Court of Appeals. The astute and sensible majority opinion of the court said, "It is difficult to precisely understand what the State hopes to achieve by promoting the creation and perpetuation of a subclass of illiterates within our boundaries, surely adding to the problems and costs of unemployment, welfare, and crime. It is clear that whatever savings might be achieved by denying these children an education, they are wholly unsubstantial in light of the costs involved to these children, the State, and the Nation."[164]

Conclusion

This chapter described the activism of Houston's Mexican-origin community in the 1950s and turbulent 1960s and 1970s and introduced the life story of Maria Jiménez. During these decades multiple civil rights movements emerged, and Jiménez contributed to many of them. She also experienced multiple forms of discrimination because of her gender, ethnicity, and immigrant status. However, rather than becoming disheartened, Jiménez eventually became a fierce defender of immigrant and human rights. Her life story and that of other activists of Mexican origin personified a principal belief of CRT: the narratives of people of color who have suffered discrimination must be told because their life stories undermine the commonplace view of people of color as the menacing "other." The counternarratives of the life stories also reveal the contribution of Mexican-origin activists in creating a more just society.[165]

In the period covered in the chapter, a major struggle concerned the need to end segregation in public schools and achieve a more equitable education. Mexican-origin students, especially those who were Spanish-dominant immigrants, had cultural and linguistic challenges. Jiménez personally knew the emotional pain from being in schools where Mexican-origin students felt marginalized. Fortunately, groups like the CAC, LULAC, and the American GI Forum demanded better education for their youth. The organizations succeeded, for example, in pressuring HISD in 1960 to provide free school lunches, despite the opposition of one school board member who said the students preferred pinto beans. Several other Mexican American organizations, including ARMAS, MAEC, and Barrios Unidos also demanded that HISD meet the needs of the Mexican-origin students, as well as comply with *Brown.* In protest to the school system, activists organized *huelga* schools and over 3,500 students boycotted the public schools in 1970. HISD's response was to form magnets schools. Another problem was the state's efforts to deny schooling for immigrant children. The efforts, however, did not intimidate activist immigrant parents who initiated a legal battle. With the help of the lawyers of MALDEF, their case reached the US Supreme Court, which ruled in their favor in *James Plyler, Superintendent, Tyler Independent School District et al. v. John Doe* (1982).

In this period Jiménez learned from her experiences and those of others. Her interests ranged widely from women to minority and to immigrant issues. She was greatly motivated by the anger she felt over racial discrimination in Jim Crow Houston. From an early age, her family had taught her that one should not tolerate injustices. Events in the 1960s and 1970s reinforced their teaching. From the Minimum Wage March of 1966, she witnessed the importance of collective action to advance justice. From the takeover in 1970 of the vacant community center of the Juan Marcos Presbyterian church, she saw the power of grassroots activism.

From the time that she was a young adult, it was natural for Jiménez to challenge inequities. Describing her evolution as an activist, Jiménez said, "I was repressed as an ethnic group, as a Mexican minority, so I'm in the Chicano Movement. I was repressed because I was foreign born, so I'm in the immigrant rights movement. I'm repressed because I'm a woman, so I'm in the women's rights movement. But ultimately what we are talking about in all those movements is the equality of rights and equality of dignity because we are human beings, period. It's a very radical concept."[166]

Chapter 5

Jiménez in the Era of Political Progress and Immigration Changes

Why do I do what I do? I do what I do because *tengo coraje* [I have rage] about social injustices and inequality. But I never feel disillusioned because the moment you do . . . they win.
—Maria Jiménez [1]

One of Jiménez's unwavering beliefs asserted that organizing the marginalized into collective action was the best way to fight against social injustices and inequality. She knew that commonplace racial prejudices and violations of rights persist if not challenged, and she insisted that individuals must organize to form a "collective to institutionalize the protection of [their] rights." [2] This belief dates to her childhood when surrounded by union activists, including her father. The civil rights movements of the 1960s and 1970s also provided more examples of collective activism for the rights and dignity of the Mexican-origin minority.

As this chapter will explain, the Mexican-origin community faced many challenges in the 1960s and 1970s. In this era activists for social justice and racial equality took to the streets and fought courageously for their civil rights. The civil rights movements, important in themselves, also influenced federal immigration policy. The federal government had removed racial and ethnic barriers in the INA of 1952, discussed in chapter 3, although quotas for immigrants from Western Europe—specifically immigrants from the United Kingdom, Ireland, and Germany—remained high.[3] However, a new immigration law in 1965, discussed below, would result in major demographic changes in the nation.

The chapter also addresses the challenges of the 1970s and 1980s for Mexican American activists for social justice, including Jiménez. During this period she ventured into electoral politics, married and divorced, resided in Mexico for a decade, and, most importantly, continued to mature intellectually as an activist for the marginalized. Her experiences would prepare her for her future role as an immigrant rights activist. As for other Mexican-origin activists of Houston, they would fight for more political power and tackle major problems, including one that remains a nationwide problem today: police violence against people of color, especially men.[4] An incident described in the chapter is the killing of Joe Campos Torres Jr. in 1977. It was an egregious example of police violence in Houston that united its Mexican-origin community against the racism in the city's police department.

Immigration and Nationality Act of 1965

Significant demographic changes affecting the Mexican-origin community followed the passage of the INA of 1965, also known as the Hart-Celler Act. It made possible a significant increase in the Mexican population in the United States. However, as the number of Mexican-origin citizens and undocumented Mexican immigrants steadily rose, so did anti-Mexican animus. In her life Jiménez had witnessed the periodic rise of commonplace anti-Mexican sentiment. Nevertheless, she was shocked in 1998 during the execution of Karla Faye Tucker when, she said, "there was just an intense anti-Mexican hostility." The hostile crowd verbally attacked Jiménez and other Hispanic death penalty protesters. The crowd shouted at the immigrant protesters, "They [Mexicans] should all be killed."[5] Sadly, President Donald Trump promoted this immigrant racism in his 2024 presidential campaign. At Green Bay, Wisconsin, he declared, "We are being invaded and we are being conquered . . . we will put these vicious and bloodthirsty criminals in jail."[6]

The important INA of 1965 went into effect in 1968 and ended visa quotas on individual countries, something the INA (McCarran-Walter) Act of 1952 failed to do. The 1965 immigration law instead created two quotas: 170,000 and 120,000 for the Eastern Hemisphere [Europe and Asia] and the Western Hemisphere, respectively).[7] These quotas did not include the number of family members of visa holders. Since the individuals with the visa were permitted to sponsor relatives abroad, the actual totals of visas issued each year far exceeded the 170,000 and 120,000 hemispheric limits. The migration pattern in which family members in the United States sponsored relatives abroad accelerated after the 1965 law and resulted in significant demographic changes. The growing Latino and Asian immigrant communities' impact on politics has increased since that time. Immigration has changed not only in its racial and ethnic nature since the Hart-Celler Act of 1965, but also in volume. For example, during the 1980s, "The nation absorbed 8.9 million legal immigrants, and by most estimates, at least 2 million illegal ones. In absolute numbers the 1980s saw more immigrants (legal and illegal) than any other decade in U.S. history."[8]

Although the elimination of race- and ethnic-based quotas was praised by many political leaders and Americans, historian Martha Menchaca asserted that the 1965 law was, in fact, an anti-Mexican immigration measure. For example, it reduced visas available for Mexicans without family in the United States. The law also imposed occupational restrictions on certain visas, allowing only designated professionals to immigrate. Mexicans who were unskilled or who were not professionals were not granted visas. Skilled or unskilled persons could be admitted, but only if the US Department of Labor (DOL) determined that they would fulfill current labor needs. According to Menchaca, the terms of the 1965 immigration law, passed less than a year after the Bracero Program (1942–1964) ended, were "the final stage in a series of congressional reforms passed to incrementally curtail Mexican immigration."[9] Immigration to the United States from Mexico, of course, continued, legally and illegally.

The curtailment of legal immigration without a reduction in the nation's demand for cheap labor assured the continued exploitation of voiceless and powerless Mexican immigrant workers. In some cases growers took measures to secure their supply of cheap labor in the post-Bracero era. Specifically, they "rushed to sponsor the legal immigration of former braceros and their family members under the relatively lax provisions in effect before the Hart-Celler Act [INA of 1965] took effect" in 1968.[10] In the case of some American trans-national corporations, they established factories, or *maquiladoras*, within Mexico itself where they could pay workers less than in the United States. This option materialized in the mid-1960s when the Gustavo Díaz Ordaz government created the Border Industrialization Program. The Program allowed *maquiladoras* to be established in northern Mexico. Years later, in 2000, Jiménez criticized the transnational corporations' control over global development and the mobility of workers symbolized by the *maquiladoras*. As Jiménez explained, the corporations' goal was to "restrict the mobility of workers to areas where labor-intensive industries, or the *maquiladoras*, are being placed, so they can have an available labor supply and take advantage of low wages."[11]

Regrettably, although immigrant workers knew to expect exploitation, they needed jobs. It is difficult to determine the number of jobseekers who came to Houston. One study of the population in Harris County, where Houston is located, estimated the population growth from 1970 to 1980. The number of Hispanics, of which most were Mexican and which undoubtedly included many undocumented immigrants, increased from 180,738 to 369,075. This total represented an increase in the percentage of the county's population from 10.4 percent to 15.5 percent. In the same decade of 1970 to 1980, the number of Blacks increased from 350,668 to 473,698, but their percentage of the population dropped from 20.1 percent to 19.7 percent. Whites increased from 1,377,118 to 1,701,719, and their percentage decreased from 79.1 percent to 70.6 percent. In the case of white Houstonians, the lower figure for 1980 may have been "due to a greater identification and increase in the 'Other' category," which was 9.7 percent, an increase from 0.8 percent in 1970.[12]

In addition to Mexicans, Houston witnessed a sharp rise in the number of non-Mexican Hispanic immigrants during the 1980s, many fleeing warfare in their homelands, especially in Central America. The immigrants significantly altered Houston's demographic makeup and created new challenges. Agencies emerged to help the newcomers avoid being victimized by unscrupulous persons. The organization Centro Para Inmigrantes (Center for Immigrants) was helpful because it offered legal services for undocumented immigrants.[13] The agency stayed busy since it was estimated that 140,000 Central Americans moved to the Houston area between 1980 and 1984. Estimates of the number of undocumented Mexicans in 1980 varied widely. Centro Para Inmigrantes estimated that total at about 150,000 and the immigration scholar Frank D. Bean estimated a range from 80,954 to 130,688.[14]

Labor Issues and Immigrant Workers

A background in the complex topic of immigration, some offered above, is important because Jiménez's life work focused on protecting immigrant rights. She demonstrated her interest in immigrant issues as early as 1965 with the labor strike by migrant workers that precipitated the Minimum Wage March of 1966. The exploitation of immigrant labor, on farms and in cities, continued, as did the demand for cheap labor. By the 1970s Houston and surrounding areas needed large numbers of workers. The region had "matured as an industrial center," according to sociologist Nester P. Rodríguez, because "several multinational corporations established or expanded their energy-related operations" there.[15] The world oil shortage of the mid-1970s also motivated the change and greatly benefited Houston's economy.

Immigrant workers were a well-established part of the local economy and an integral part of the new "requirements of the global economic system."[16] The workers represented, in the words of Jiménez, "a human manifestation of the global integration" who were "needed as part of the exploitation in profit-making companies and sectors."[17] However, the growth of the Mexican immigrant community alarmed whites with commonplace anti-Mexican prejudices. It was difficult to assess the actual number of undocumented Mexicans, but one method of approximating the total used the number of apprehensions and deportations that INS made. Nationwide in 1968 the INS deported 151,000 Mexicans, but in 1976, "when the

20,000 per country quota was imposed, the INS expelled 781,000 Mexicans from the United States."[18]

An increase in immigration often had political consequences. For example, the influx of immigrants created problems for President Jimmy Carter (1977–1981) and worried many nativist individuals and groups. One virulent nativist, the Grand Wizard David Duke of the KKK, planned patrols for a weekend in late October 1977 along the Mexico-Texas border because of "an invasion that threatens our American life."[19] Duke compared the "invasion" to that by Mexican troops in 1836 when they attacked the Alamo in San Antonio. The KKK said that it would report immigrants who it saw crossing the border to the Border Patrol. The latter, however, said it would ignore these calls.[20] At least two Mexican American groups in Texas, the Brown Berets and the Barrio Club of Crystal City, announced that they, in turn, would protect Mexican nationals at the border from the Klan. However, the weekend passed without any contact at the Texas-Mexico border between the KKK and the Brown Berets. For its part, Mexico worried more about clashes at the border between the KKK in Arizona and Mexican nationals. The Mexican government sent a patrol to the Sonoran border, but no clashes occurred. In fact, an Arizona sheriff reported that the KKK did not show up.[21]

President Carter attempted to address the immigration issue in August 1977 by sending an immigration reform plan to Congress. Mexican Americans vigorously opposed the plan. For example, Mamie Garcia (b. ca. 1942), director of LULAC's District 8 in Houston, complained that "[Carter] is not sensitive to Mexican-American peoples' needs nor understands our culture or our heritage."[22] The Carter Plan, as it was known, called for employer sanctions for hiring undocumented workers, greater border control, and an identification card for workers. The latter measure was required for immigrants and for all US residents.

The president's plan may have had unintended results. Political scientist Christine Marie Sierra asserted that the Carter plan "triggered a rebirth of Chicano activism, which had been in relative decline since the early 1970s."[23] Leonel Castillo (1939–2013), who had been appointed commissioner of the INS by Carter, defended the Carter Plan and was heavily criticized by the Chicano leadership for doing so.[24] In reaction to the Carter Plan, organizations large and small organized the First National Chicano/Latino Conference on Immigration and Public Policy in the fall of 1977. José Angel Gutiérrez (b. 1944), a well-known political activist in Texas, and the political party La Raza Unida organized the conference. Mexican American organizations like LULAC and the American GI Forum even participated.

The conference, according to historian David G. Gutiérrez, marked "a dramatic departure from the traditional Mexican American position on the immigration issue" and indicated how "the immigration controversy had become a major civil rights issue in the 1970s."[25] Over two thousand people met in October 1977 in San Antonio, Texas, and issued a call for action that criticized almost all the Carter administration's proposals. For example, they believed that the proposed economic sanctions on employers of immigrants would increase unemployment among immigrants and Mexican Americans alike. The conference declared that "the truth of the matter [was] that Latinos are to be made the scapegoat for this administration's ineptness at solving economic problems of inflation, unemployment, wage depression and rising consumer frustration."[26] Ultimately, the Carter Plan did not become law. Chicano opposition to the plan contributed to its failure, though to what extent is not known.

The Chicano Movement

The backlash against the Carter Plan emerged in the context of increasing political activism of the Mexican American minority, particularly its youth. Young Chicanos and Chicanas, including Jiménez, publicly demonstrated their new pride and identity, Chicanismo. Their tactics, which alarmed their parents, "were the tactics of the time. They were mostly direct confrontation," according to Jiménez.[27] She also recalled "There was resistance and I think we all faced it."[28] Young Chicanos believed that the activism of their parents' generation was too accommodationist. The younger generation also rejected the older generation's insistence on being categorized as "white" and pointed out that this classification did little to prevent the racism and discrimination that targeted Mexican Americans. Instead, young Chicanas and Chicanos took pride in their Indigenous and nonwhite lineage. As playwright

Luis Valdez expressed it, "We are, to begin with, Mestizos—a powerful blend of Indigenous America with European-Arabian Spain, usually recognizable for the natural bronze tone it lends to human skin."[29]

For Jiménez the Chicano Movement and its activists represented many important ideas. In an interview years later, in 1998, she concluded that the movement's activists "were part of a global struggle for national liberation."[30] In an interview in 2012, she described the Chicano movement as a "cultural renaissance" whose activists "tried to basically recover that which had been denied like our cultural pride and our language and [was] a look back through our history."[31] Similarly, in 1971 she remarked, "We have been denied our history. And it is to everyone's advantage to learn it—consider the education majors who might find themselves in a classroom of Chicano children."[32]

Mexican Americans in the 1960s and 1970s, especially their youth, strongly objected to society's tradition of ignoring, undermining, or distorting contributions made by the Mexican-origin community. Extolling the history and culture of mainstream white America but not that of people of color was racist. The social constructs of race and commonplace racist stereotypes permeate our society and are harmful. At the level of the individual, if the resulting constructs are demeaning and internalized, then that individual's self-image suffers. On the societal level, if society believes that a false construct is true, then social injustice results. For example, the construct of a Black or Hispanic man as being criminally inclined can justify police brutality, as in the police killing of Joe Campos Torres, described later in the chapter.

Activists in the Chicano movement expressed pride in their culture and history in various ways. A specific manifestation of this new cultural pride took place on April 21, 1970, at the San Jacinto Battleground Monument near Houston where MAYO organized a demonstration. April 21 commemorated Texas's victory over Mexico in 1836, but many Chicanos believed it was also an occasion for whites to denigrate Mexicans and to accuse Tejanos of being treasonous.[33] With their appearance at the San Jacinto Battleground Monument, the MAYO students challenged, in the words of historian Thomas H. Kreneck, "Anglo-Texan's ethnocentric view of history which had shaped Anglo attitudes toward people of Mexican descent."[34] The students' conduct on April 21 contrasted greatly with that of LULAC members in 1943, who laid a wreath at the San Jacinto monument and were pleased by the approval they received from whites. MAYO also organized a very well attended antiwar march in the Houston barrio of Magnolia Park in July of 1970. The march expressed Chicano outrage at the high mortality rate of Mexican American soldiers fighting in Vietnam, a percentage that far exceeded those of other groups. Chicanos in the Southwest represented about 11 percent of its population in 1960 but "represented close to 20 percent of the region's soldiers killed in battle during the following decade."[35]

Chicano activism occurred on university campuses as well as in the community. Jiménez became active in both areas. For example, as spokesperson for the University Information Program, established in 1971, she promoted university education at UH among barrio students. Her encouragement was needed. In 1971 UH's student enrollment was 25,000, and of this total only "four hundred and fifty were Mexican American and 1,000 were Negroes."[36] Also in 1971, Jiménez, while a member of the Black-Brown Education Committee at UH, helped to obtain scholarships and funds for Chicano and Black students to pay for their SAT tests.[37] Off campus, as noted in chapter 4, Jiménez volunteered at the Texas Boycott Office of the UFW from 1970 to 1971 to organize the lettuce boycott.

Jiménez and members of MAYO at UH contributed significantly to one of the most important developments at their university, the establishment of the Mexican American Studies Program in 1972, which later became the Center for Mexican American Studies (CMAS) in 1995. To make the program a reality, a few students, including Jiménez, wrote a proposal and took it to Austin where the state legislature was in session in the spring of 1971. Reflecting later on her experience with the Texas legislature, Jiménez said, "We were very young, and we didn't know you couldn't do those things in the state legislature, [and] because we didn't know we couldn't do it—we did it!" The students also were unaware of the complex political scene in the state legislature. On this matter, Jiménez later recalled, "We didn't know there was like an internal fight there . . . some of the state legislators thought this was a way of pushing their issues."[38]

From its inception the Mexican American Studies Program lacked adequate support from the administration and faculty at UH. Jiménez criticized the university because of its weak support of the program. For example, she pointed out that the salaries it offered its professors were not competitive. She told the *Daily Cougar* in 1972 that "UH is not offering as much as the others . . . Chicanos with Ph.D.s know there are better salaries elsewhere." Another problem was an "extreme lack of Qualified Chicano faculty members." Jiménez also observed that UH's faculty "see Mexican-American Studies Programs as a fad, not as a legitimate field of study. They give the program to the students to keep them quiet. They think it will go away after a while."[39] In other words, the university agreed to create the program, not because it believed in its value, but to silence a vocal student faction. Funding for the program became another, and chronic, problem. Dr. Tatcho Mindiola Jr., who became the program's director in 1980, knew this problem well.[40] In 1983 the frustrated director told his dean, "I had spent three years trying to get funds from the university . . . but every request had been denied."[41] Fortunately, under his skillful directorship, and after many difficult years, CMAS became a valuable part of UH and invaluable to students of Mexican descent.

The National Chicana Conference

Young Chicanas like Jiménez gained valuable political experience in the Chicano and feminist movements of the 1960s, but they had their own needs and aspirations. The women in the Chicana Movement, which emerged from the Chicano Movement, faced specific challenges, such as the sexism of Chicanos, and developed their own feminist discourse.[42] One of the most important events during the Chicana Movement occurred in Houston, May 28–30, 1971, and Jiménez helped organize it. The event, officially called *La Conferencia de Mujeres por La Raza*, is usually referred to as the National Chicana Conference. Approximately six hundred women from more than twenty states participated. The Magnolia YWCA in Houston sponsored the event. The conference was famous, or infamous, because it was historic—the first national Chicana conference—and for the contentious split that arose among the participants. Differences of opinion at the Houston conference became so intense that about half of the participants walked out on the second day, including Jiménez.

The political differences that surfaced reflected tensions of the time. Many of the participants who walked out of the conference were from California or Texas. They asserted that the barrio women of Houston were not sufficiently represented in the conference and resented the participation of white women, the so-called "*gabachas*."[43] Some objected to the conference being associated with a white organization, in this case the YWCA. Jiménez offered another perspective. She said, "The clash was between the Latinas who wanted to be part strictly of the feminist movement and those of us who wanted to be part of the Chicano movement and fight for women's rights, but within the context of also fighting for the rights of all members of the community." Jiménez added that white feminists were "always much more radical than we could be"; for example, they performed self-examinations and "would do their own checkup of their vagina . . . which was for us too radical."[44]

Jiménez was a leader of the conference's second group that preferred to align with the Chicano Movement. Following the split up of participants at the conference, the second group relocated to a local park but had no clear agenda for the remainder of the conference. Jiménez reflected many years later about this experience. Commenting on the volatile political climate then, Jiménez said, "It was common for us to question organizations that were institutionally white . . . [but] after years of being in politics, I don't think I would have handled that that way again." The split-up provided a valuable experience that taught her, she admitted years later, "when you take a political action, you should not just create controversy. You'll be controversial anyway, but you should have other objectives."[45]

Jiménez: Political Candidate

Consistent with her belief that social change is not an individual but a collective achievement, Jiménez ventured in a new direction in the fall of 1974. While still a student at UH, Jiménez ran for public office as the La Raza Unida

Party (RUP) candidate for the Texas House of Representatives, District 87.[46]
Dr. Tatcho Mindiola Jr., the chair of the RUP for Harris County, urged her
to run. He had a high regard for Jiménez and once told *Houston Chronicle*
reporter Jo Ann Zuniga that "she [Jiménez] has always been dedicated to the
dispossessed . . . she does what she does, not for recognition, but because
she sincerely believes."[47] His assessment of Jiménez was true at the time
and remained one of her most admirable qualities. As for entering electoral
politics, Jiménez resisted the offer to run for office because she preferred to be
part of a team and not in the limelight. Nevertheless, Dr. Mindiola persuaded
her to run against the incumbent, Ben Reyes. Concerning her political race,
she said, "even my acceptance of running was because it was a *party* decision, not because *I* had wanted to run. And so I saw it as an obligation and a
duty to the party."[48]

The leadership ability that Jiménez revealed while still a student at
UH became well known locally. According to Dr. Mindiola, the Democratic
Party hoped that she would become a candidate for their party and attract
Mexican American voters. Dr. Mindiola knew that the "Democrats paid a
lot of attention to her . . . they just kind of assumed that after college she
would step into a very liberal Democratic slot and continue her work."[49]
This did not happen. Her values drew her to the RUP instead. According
to Daniel Bustamante (b. 1948), former Harris County chair of RUP, the
party "felt so sure about our candidate . . . and her ability to defend herself
and to speak up for the principles of the party."[50] Bustamante correctly
believed that Jiménez and the idealism of RUP were a good fit. Specifically, the party called for a "humanistic alternative" government that would
"abolish racist practices within the existing social, educational, economic,
and political system so that physical and cultural genocidal practices will
be discontinued."[51]

RUP presented an unexpected challenge to the Democratic Party because
it scored several political victories after it formed in 1970. However, the
party lost many races in 1974, including that between Jiménez and Reyes.[52]
Nevertheless, Bustamante believed that her campaign was the best organized of all RUP campaigns in Texas. He also thought that the votes that she
received were "pretty outstanding for this city," and noted that the voter

analysis indicated that "we pretty well beat Ben Reyes with the Mexican vote."[53] Dr. Mindiola agreed, commenting that Reyes received votes from Blacks and whites but did not carry the Latino vote.

The number of votes that Jiménez received was especially impressive because she did not begin actively campaigning until she finished the spring semester of 1974 at UH. She then went from house to house in the barrio and in African American neighborhoods. Jiménez and the RUP "made appeals to African Americans in an effort to achieve state and national viability."[54] She and the party believed they could win the Black vote because Blacks and Hispanics suffered from racial discrimination and shared many political views. As a result of this outreach, and connections that Jiménez had made, a group of African American leaders, including community activist Omowali Luthuli (b. 1948), joined Jiménez in her door-to-door campaign.[55]

Jiménez's campaigning impressed many. She was especially success-ful in getting out the vote in Magnolia Park, where she lived. The selection of Houston as the site for the RUP state convention may have been due to the energy Jiménez spent on her campaign. Bustamante believed this was so "because of her dynamic ability to influence people . . . people knew her, and they respected her . . . she was a woman, she was young, and everything was just right for us here."[56] At the convention itself, Jiménez continued to impress others. Dr. Mindiola recalled that at the convention, Jiménez was "selected permanent chairman and she did an excellent job of running it."[57]

The political race challenged Jiménez's skills and endurance. Fortu-nately, she had a lot of both. Nevertheless, she readily agreed with the description in a news article that the campaign was a "nasty political battle."[58] She told the *Houston Post* that Reyes used the staff of an antipov-erty program to promote his candidacy and that his supporters destroyed her campaign literature and signs.[59] She also said that someone shot into her political headquarters and that Leonel Castillo rode through her district broadcasting that she was a Communist.[60] Bustamante also recalled that, on election day, Castillo attacked the RUP, "referring to us as communists and instigating troubles."[61] Irregularities at the polls also occurred. For exam-ple, voters were told that "if they voted for Maria Jiménez, they could not vote for Barbara Jordan. In other words, you couldn't split the ticket."

Also, voters who could not speak English but wanted to vote for Jiménez allowed precinct judges to vote for them, but they actually voted for Ben Reyes and Dolph Briscoe (1923–2010), the Democratic candidate for governor.[62] Luthuli, the African American who campaigned for Jiménez, pretended that he could not read when he went to vote. The precinct judge told him to vote for Ben Reyes.[63]

The contentious race between Jiménez and Reyes revealed to her the dark side of electoral politics. She and other RUP members were naïve, she concluded, about "the very vicious nature of electoral politics . . . [but] because . . . we were young, we felt that if we ran fairly, we would be treated fairly, and we would have fair results." Jiménez believed that Castillo and Ben Reyes further tried to influence voters "with all sorts of rumors about my being a woman. [And] I was planning to marry . . . and leave the country."[64] They were thus implying that a vote for Jiménez would be a wasted vote. It was true that she was engaged and that her fiancé wanted to live in Mexico, but Jiménez would have remained in Houston had she won the election. It did not happen, however. She lost her race like many other RUP candidates in 1974. Years later, commenting on the results of the campaign and electoral politics, which she disliked, Jiménez asserted, "I believe that it doesn't matter who is in office. If we don't have active groups of citizens, then we don't have what we want."[65]

Jiménez's strong character became apparent during her campaign, and the experience proved instructive. Her insight impressed others. Dr. Mindiola believed that she was "a sharper person [than Reyes], a much more politically conscious person. . . . Ben does not take a public stand on issues where Jiménez has and will." For example, she addressed a topic that was as controversial then as it is today—the undocumented immigrant. Dr. Mindiola noted that she publicly discussed the "undocumented issue. She took a stand on that and she ran into all kinds of opposition . . . about their taking our jobs. . . . She took a stand in that. She held to it."[66] Regarding the political decline of RUP following her and other campaigns, Jiménez astutely concluded, "It failed because we were dealing with the effects rather than the causes . . . the most important . . . [was] economic inequality." She added, "We were reacting to our reality and organizing around it. We didn't have a theory."[67]

Although RUP's successes were short-lived as a political party, it presented an unprecedented challenge to white-dominated Texas politics. This was especially true in the southern Texas counties of Zavala, La Salle, and Dimmit, and most notably in the city of Crystal City in Zavala County. Even the menacing presence of the Texas Rangers in Crystal City did not prevent RUP's electoral success in that city.[68] Writing in 1975, Richard Santillan lamented that "the partido [RUP] has not fulfilled its potential. It is still in its preliminary stage of development. . . . There is no doubt that the Partido has developed a political arm in the Chicano struggle . . . a new political consciousness among the people in the barrios."[69] It was the people of the barrios, according to Bustamante, that RUP wanted to serve and from where it received its inspiration. He commented, "I think the creative, intellectual impulses came from the people that we were organizing . . . we were effectively reaching the unorganized people of Texas that were interested in bettering themselves through political activities or economic activities."[70]

Jiménez, only 24 years of age, had matured politically and had learned a great deal. The 1960s and 1970s provided valuable experiences for her and other Mexican American activists. In 1974 she moved to Mexico to begin the next stage of her life. Her years there greatly influenced her future activism when she returned to the United States in 1985.

Marriage and Mexico: Making of a Human Rights Activist

After busy and fulfilling years while a university student and following a grueling political campaign, Jiménez began another enriching period of her life when she moved to Mexico. There her political views became more sophisticated and international, and her skills as a community activist and organizer improved. She moved to Mexico as a young bride. However, when her future husband first proposed marriage years earlier, Jiménez had said no. She had many personal goals and believed that "being a political woman was the most important thing."[71] Later, after some reflection, she realized that she could be political on either side of the US-Mexico border, that people on both sides of the border faced similar problems. In other words, Jiménez concluded that "the same struggle here in the United States was the one in Mexico . . . we were fighting an economic system that created inequities which were social, economic, and political inequities. So whether I was here or in Mexico was immaterial."[72] With this conclusion in mind, she told her future husband, "Yes, now I will marry you."[73]

On April 23, 1974, Jiménez married Francisco Javier Villarreal González, a Mexican citizen. They moved to Mexico, where her husband preferred to live. Commenting on her husband, who was a Marxist, Jiménez said, "The reason I married the man I married was because he *was* a Marxist. And he was the only Mexican man I knew who believed in women's liberation. I didn't change my name." She added that "we were both atheists," and they were married in a civil ceremony, not in the Roman Catholic Church.[74] Three years after they married, the couple had twins, a boy named Carlos Federico Villarreal, who was named after Karl Marx, and a daughter named Stalina Emmanuelle Villarreal, who was named after the famous Russian revolutionary Stalin.[75] Reflecting many years later, she thought that the names given to her children perhaps should have been less political.

Jiménez believed her years in Mexico were instructive and enlightening. She liked the fact that Francisco "had an advanced ideology" and "offered me the ability to grow politically. And I did!"[76] She read Karl Marx (1818–1883), Frederick Engel (1820–1895), Mao Zedong (1893–1976), and Vladimir Lenin (1870–1924) in "a search to understand a framework, an ideology." Later, she admitted that she was not sure that she understood this literature. She remarked, "I've always said I'd never call myself Marxist-Leninist. Other people have called me a Communist, but I never did."[77] The couple joined "leftist circles in Mexico," she recalled, adding that its members "were more leftist intellectual circles . . . as opposed to practicing, political circles."[78] However, Jiménez, as her later activism revealed, did not adhere tenaciously to any ideology. As a fellow activist, Pancho Arguelles, observed, "She does have this Marxist analysis without being dogmatic."[79]

The young couple first moved to Sinaloa, Mexico. By 1975 Jiménez's husband was employed as a rural development worker for the government. Jiménez worked in a variety of positions. At this time she became politically active when she, her husband, and his boss participated in a student movement at the University of Sinaloa. One of the students' objectives was lower bus fares. However, their employer, the Mexican government, opposed the students' protest and told Jiménez, her husband, and his boss, she recalled, "We'll either fire you or you go to Yucatán."[80]

Her political activism, however, continued in Yucatán. After two years in Sinaloa, the couple relocated to Mérida, Yucatán, where she worked in various jobs and became a volunteer union organizer and where, in 1978, their twins Carlos and Stalina were born. Many years later, she told Jo Ann Zuniga, a reporter for the *Houston Chronicle*, that she "wandered from field to field, lecturing farmworkers on everything from history to health and safety."[81] For Jiménez the experiences proved valuable. For example, she said that she "worked directly with marginalized people in the agricultural sector" and learned "how to plan and develop sustainable economic community projects."[82] She believed that activists should organize, and not control, the community that fights discrimination or other problems. In other words, she said, "You actually had to create entities where the common folk would participate and be equal with the intellectuals and others."[83] Reflecting on her experiences and her friends who organized labor unions in Mexico, Jiménez said that "people who are organizing in a system that is autocratic are really admirable. And so it helped me to strengthen this concept of how the only protection individuals had was through organizing the many."[84]

Jiménez always believed that real change came from the collective efforts of many persons. She was fearless in her job, even though organizing *campesinos*—that is, farmworkers—and other workers in Mexico came with risks. Jiménez was following in the footsteps of her father, Raúl G. Jiménez, who had been a union organizer in Mexican steel plants.[85] She did the same in the Yucatán. However, it was not long before she learned firsthand, she recalled, the "tremendous repression of the Mexican government and political leaders." Specifically, the Mexican riot police crushed the steel workers' strike she helped organized. The police arrested fifteen people, and Jiménez was forced to go underground briefly. She and other union organizers remained in the union hall until negotiations with the government succeeded in allowing her and others in the hall, she said, "to walk freely." Commenting on this episode, she said, "It was the only time I was really in a situation of danger . . . it ended in . . . a fourteen-day lockout. And we would have riot police come, consistently and constantly. There was an attempt to bring in scabs [strike breakers hired by the company] who were carrying iron bars." She added, the government "closed all media—all our ability to communicate through the media."[86]

Jiménez's firm commitment to social justice for workers may have cost her her marriage, which ended in divorce in October 1985. Reflecting later on the incident when the government crushed the steel workers' strike, she said, "I think that [the incident] did in the marriage because I put myself in danger, put the children in danger, put him in danger, put the household in danger."[87] Upon the breakup of their marriage, Jiménez recalled that the "question for us was not who kept the children, but how to split up the books," which totaled about four thousand. Francisco kept "a lot of original literature" and she took "the political, economic stuff, and of course . . . the children's books."[88]

Despite the effect on her marriage of her participation in union activism, Jiménez believed that her years in Mexico were very beneficial and informative. It was the time, she said, of "the growth of primarily popular movements in Mexico and . . . the demise of the sectarian political groups that were very popular in Latin America in the 60s, 70s, 80s. And [I] saw how the Mexican left matured and integrated into popular movements that have democratized in Mexico." Jiménez added, "I've always felt that those ten years in Mexico were very important to my development politically because it gave me the opportunity to study." She sharpened her analytical abilities and learned, she said, "how to deal with repression, how to deal with building popular movements."[89] Jiménez concluded that she "learned a great deal about how to develop strategies, how to understand the differences between tactical means and strategic means."[90] Her new knowledge served her well when she returned to the United States. On this point, she said, "That was why, when I returned and worked for the [American] Friends [Service Committee] at the local and national level, why I had a leadership position, amongst the *many* leaders, because that period in Mexico helped me to refine my political skills at organizing."[91]

Police Violence in Houston

While Jiménez organized *campesinos* and steel workers in Mexico, activists in her hometown also fought for social justice. People of color, especially their youth, were prominent in the civil rights movements that swept the nation in the 1960s and 1970s. In Houston African Americans and Mexican Americans tackled the major problem of segregation. Both communities also focused on the serious problem of violent racist attacks by the HPD. When Jiménez returned to Houston years later, she would also need to address police abuses against the Mexican-origin community.

Regarding segregation, a major advance in social justice in Houston began with the peaceful desegregation of its lunch counters. The Progressive Youth Association (PYA), headed by Texas Southern University (TSU) law student Eldrewey Stearnes (1931–2020), provided critical leadership in the movement for desegregation. On March 4, 1960, the PYA organized its first sit-in, "the first sit-in west of the Mississippi,"[92] at a lunch counter in a Weingarten store near TSU, a historically Black state university located near the University of Houston.[93] Eventually, Stearnes and other TSU students succeeded in desegregating many businesses by using, or threatening to use, demonstrations, boycotts, and damaging news coverage. White business owners and Black leaders also worked together to advance integration in Houston.[94] Interest convergence played a role, as well, because of the city's desire for national prominence. Specifically, in the early 1960s, Houston wanted the National Aeronautics and Space Administration (NASA) to choose it as the location for the planned manned spacecraft program. Houston also wanted to acquire a Major League Baseball (MLB) team.[95] It succeeded in both goals.[96]

During the Civil Rights Movement, the Black and Mexican-origin communities frequently engaged in separate struggles, but they shared one major concern: police harassment and killings. According to a *Time* article in 1977 that examined Philadelphia and Houston, both cities shared "a common problem. Their police forces had reputations for brutality against minority citizens."[97] The following year, a study by the US Commission on Civil Rights reported that HPD "officers were involved in the deaths of 155 citizens, mostly Hispanic or Black, during the 12-year period ending in 1978."[98] In 1979 another news article reported that the HPD routinely followed a "search and kill policy," a policy with deadly consequences for many people of color, when the police pursued a criminal suspect who had entered a building.[99]

In two notable assaults, the first against African Americans and the second against a Mexican American, the HPD's problem with racism stood out. In 1967 TSU students organized protests against police brutality in late March, April, and May. In this tense climate, shots from men's dormitories in mid-May were aimed at passing police cars.[100] The HPD reacted quickly when Police Chief Herman Short ordered an assault on two TSU dormitories. Before it was over, "police fired thousands of rounds of ammunition into the buildings, arrested 489 male students, and destroyed thousands of dollars of property looking for weapons." One police officer was killed by a police bullet that ricocheted and struck him. Five TSU students, the TSU Five, were indicted for inciting a riot and murder, but charges were dropped because of insufficient evidence.[101]

The police department later faced an even greater problem, the killing of a young Chicano, Joe Campos Torres, on the night of May 5–6, 1977. The incident alarmed Chicanos from all walks of life throughout the city. The killing reflected the racial bigotry, particularly anti-Mexican bigotry, of some HPD officers. The troubles for Torres began when he became rowdy after a few drinks at a bar. Police officers arrived and, in the course of the evening, beat him twice at the Hole, a location along Buffalo Bayou, a water-way that runs through downtown.[102] Heated words that night from the officers included, "Let's see if the wetback can swim,"[103] and "Hey, Mexican, you going to whip our ass now? You're really stupid, but since you think you're so tough, come on, let's go." To the latter remark, Torres replied, "You're nothing more than a bunch of pigs."[104] At that point events turned fatal for Torres.[105] Two officers were charged with beating Torres and pushing him into the bayou.[106] His body was discovered floating in the bayou two days later, on Mother's Day, May 8. Police involvement in his death came to light two days after the incident only when one of the officers, a rookie who witnessed the killing, reported it to police officials.[107]

The crime was covered extensively in Chicano newspapers in Houston, as well as by major newspapers.[108] There were two trials. The venue of the first trial, a criminal trial at the state level, was moved from Houston to Huntsville, seventy miles north of Houston and the location of the Texas Department of Corrections headquarters and a large prison complex. The jury was all-white in the state trial, which ended in October 1977.[109] The two former officers accused of killing Torres were found guilty only of negligent homicide, a Class A misdemeanor, not the felony charge of first-degree homicide.[110] The convicted former officers received a probated one-year sentence and a fine of two thousand dollars. After the sentencing LULAC members wore dollar bills. According to Mamie Garcia, district director of LULAC, the dollar symbolized what the low fine represented, that "all we were worth [was] one dollar."[111] As for Margaret Torres, the mother of Torres, she said, "I heard all they get is one year in jail and I'm disgusted. The Mexican American community will continue to fight for justice."[112] An angry Chicano community pressed for a federal trial for the violation of the victim's civil rights. The federal trial took place in February 1978, this time in Houston. An all-white jury found the defendants, three former officers this time, guilty of violating the civil rights of Torres. None of the officers served more than nine months.[113] In both trials the juries were not convinced that Torres was deliberately pushed into the bayou to "cause serious bodily harm."[114]

The Torres incident exposed different, sometime contentious, forms of Chicano activism. Within the community the response to the officers' sentences varied. LULAC brought in lawyers and held meetings with the new police chief, Harry Caldwell. Because of her persistent efforts to seek justice for Torres, Garcia reported that some in the Chicano community called her "Joan of Arc."[115] Another group, Barrios Unidos, included Margaret Torres, the victim's mother. This group pursued confrontational tactics, including marches and rallies. The Chicano community remained embittered over the light sentences given to the former police officers. Its anger turned violent one year after Torres's death, when a major riot in Houston occurred on Cinco de Mayo (the fifth of May) 1978 between Chicanos and the police, resulting in injuries and extensive property damage.[116]

The Mexican American community continued its struggle for social justice and demanded improvements in the HPD. In the late 1970s, the community's pressure on the HPD to reform was intense, and the department made some changes in 1977.[117] For example, the police department made its new Internal Affairs Division a permanent department and established a strict policy on the use of deadly force. Caldwell also created a new position of liaison between the HPD and the Hispanic community. He offered the position to Mamie Garcia on the same day that he first met with LULAC about the Torres killing.[118] In addition, HPD started to offer Spanish lessons and classes on the Mexican American culture to its police officers. Dr. Guadalupe "Lupita" Quintanilla, a professor at UH, was the instructor. The excellent course that she organized, Cross Cultural Communication Program, won national recognition from the Department of Defense (DOD) and the DOJ.[119]

The Torres case represented a troubling aspect of society in Houston: anti-Mexican prejudice. The racist comments and attitudes of the police officers in the Torres killing were not sui generis but arose from long-held anti-Mexican racism. The Torres case continues to resurface whenever suspected police misconduct against Hispanics in Houston occurs.[120] Interestingly, many years later, in 2021, the HPD issued a formal apology to the family of Torres.[121]

Jiménez did not live in Houston when Torres was killed, but she would address police brutality after she returned to Houston in 1985. Her activism then, as earlier in Mexico, was guided by a firm belief in social justice. As she once told an interviewer, "It is our obligation and our responsibility to create societies that, in all its laws, in all its policies, in all its practices, recognizes this principle: that all of us human beings are equal in dignity and rights. And if they don't exist, they must be created."[122]

Mexican Americans of Houston in the 1970s and 1980s

The Mexican American community in Houston was pleased with signs of a more equitable society, such as the integration of schools, but more needed to be achieved.[123] Some activists, including Jiménez, turned to politics in order improve the lives of their community. Regrettably, the Mexican-origin minority was greatly underrepresented in politics. In 1975 Vilma S. Martínez (b. 1943), president and general counsel of MALDEF, spoke on the topic of underrepresentation in politics before the US Commission on Civil Rights. She reported that of the 4,770 elected Texas officials, only 298 were Chicanos. She concluded that this small number was "no mere coincidence. It is the result of manifold discriminatory practices which have the design or effect of excluding Mexican Americans from participation in their own government and maintaining the status quo."[124]

Fortunately, in Houston there were some political victories in the 1970s for men and women. In 1971 Leonel Castillo was elected as Houston's city controller and David López became the first Mexican American elected to the HISD School Board. In 1972 and 1974, Ben T. Reyes (b. 1947) was elected to the state legislature from District 87. In 1979 he was elected to the Houston City Council, becoming the first Mexican American on the council. Raúl Martínez, a veteran police officer, was appointed in 1973, then later elected and reelected, to the position of Harris County constable of Precinct 6. Women also gained prominence—for example, Rosemary Saucillo, who in 1974 became the first Mexican American woman to become a judge in the Municipal Court in Houston. In 1976 she also worked jointly with Police Chief Harry Caldwell to establish Spanish classes for police officers who were assigned to the Mexican American community.[125]

As Houston and the nation emerged from the volatile era of civil rights movements, the political climate became more moderate. As Jiménez herself observed after returning to Texas in 1985, her former activist colleagues had turned to "community development, affirmative action, and similar programs."[126] They were more likely to be on organizations' boards than to be found protesting in the streets. Jiménez's earliest reaction was, "What in the world are all these boards?"[127] Did the change reflect real progress in social justice? Perhaps, but Jiménez's future position with the American Friends Service Committee (AFSC) indicated that more work was needed to reduce racial injustice. Commonplace racist beliefs in Houston and the nation continued to justify violent assaults on people of color.

By the 1980s an important result of the civil rights movements of the 1970s was the "politics of inclusion."[128] As historian David Montejano wrote, "Inclusion refers, in the most specific sense, to the extension and exercise of first-class citizenship."[129] Minorities strove to promote their inclusion in society, but demographic changes, including a rise in the number of immigrants, complicated this process. When Jiménez returned to Houston, the city's Hispanic community was larger and more diverse. In Harris County, where Houston is located, the total population in 1980 was 2,409,547 and the Hispanic population was 369,075 or 15.5 percent.[130] Estimates for the new immigrants are difficult to reach, but for Salvadoran immigrants, the range was from 75,000 to 150,000.[131] The growing Hispanic population meant that the police department needed more Spanish-speaking officers to help victims of crimes and to interrogate suspected criminals. HPD, therefore, created the Chicano Squad in 1979.[132] The urgent need for the new unit followed a bloody weekend in Hispanic neighborhoods that included seventeen homicides. Improvements in the relationship between the HPD and Houston's minority communities began in 1982 when Mayor Kathy Whitmire (1982–1991) appointed Lee P. Brown (1937–) as the new police chief. Brown, the first African American police chief of Houston (1982–1990), introduced important reforms, such as neighborhood-oriented policing.[133]

Although Blacks welcomed the new chief, Hispanics expressed concerns that were unique to their minority group, including immigrant-related issues. Community activist Félix Fraga (1929–2024) organized a meeting in 1984 between the HPD and the Mexican American community because "the police were stopping cars with Hispanic-looking drivers in an effort to nab illegal aliens."[134] Another problem was the small number of minority police officers. In 1987 Hispanics were estimated at only 10 percent of the department. Black officers constituted about 13 percent of HPD.[135] The percentages in 2024 of Hispanics and Blacks were 42 percent and 18 percent, respectively. In addition, whites and Asians were 37 percent and 3 percent, respectively.[136]

Politically, Mexican Americans made progress, but only slowly. According to sociologist Joe R. Feagin, "Disenfranchisement in effect characterized the minority communities of Houston until the 1970s."[137] Although Houston was founded in 1836, it was not until 1979 that the first Hispanic, Ben Reyes, was elected to the city council. His election became possible after minority groups fought to change the city's election system. This legal battle began in 1975 when they "filed a suit seeking a court order requiring single member districts. They complained that the current system diluted the minority vote and was discriminatory."[138] The DOJ concluded that the "city's annexation of outlying white areas in 1977 and 1978 diluted the city's minority voting strength, a violation of the Voting Rights Act,"[139] and it ordered reforms in the election system. Fortunately, the persistent pressure by minority activists resulted in a more equitable election system.

Conclusion

This chapter addressed important developments in the 1970s and 1980s that affected the Mexican-origin community and continued with the life of Maria Jiménez. During the 1970s and 1980s, Chicano activists in Houston challenged many forms of social injustice and Jiménez became immersed in this struggle. In addition, from her experiences in Mexico, her perspective on social justice began to broaden to include human rights.

A significant development in this period was a new immigration law, the INA of 1965, that eventually contributed to the "browning" of the United States. Immigration opportunities both increased and decreased with the passage of the law. For example, the small number of visas granted to Mexican immigrants resulted in a rise in illegal immigration. On the positive side, visas became more available for relatives of US citizens and legal residents. With the passage of time, the number of Mexicans and other Latin Americans, especially Central Americans, who emigrated to the United States rose steadily. As these numbers increased, so did the commonplace anti-Mexican prejudices, a problem Jiménez would fiercely challenge in a few years.

During the 1960s and into the 1980s, activism among the Mexican-origin minority increased significantly, especially among its youth. Participants in the Chicano and Chicana Movements expressed pride in their Mexican heritage and demanded, for example, classes in schools and universities that taught their history and culture. Jiménez led in this effort at UH, which established the Mexican American Studies Program in 1972. In addition, Chicanas created their own movement to fight sexism in society and within the Mexican culture. Another development among a wide range of Mexican American organizations, illustrated by their strong opposition to the Carter Plan, was an alarm over the exploitation of immigrants. Although the organizations in the past had opposed labor programs like the Bracero Program, they now viewed the exploitation of Mexican immigrant workers as a civil rights issue.

Mexican Americans also became more active in politics in their pursuit of greater social justice. For example, Jiménez became a candidate of the RUP, disappointing the Democratic Party that had wanted this dynamic young woman as one of its candidates. Although the RUP's successes were short-lived, the political party motivated other Mexican Americans to run for political offices. Reflecting in 1998 on the short history of the RUP successes in electoral politics, Jiménez astutely concluded that its problem was that "We didn't have a theory" and were "dealing with effects rather than causes." With this assessment in mind, she recalled, "I started to look for a theory and I became a socialist."[140]

In addition to the political gains in the 1960s,1970s, and 1980s, Mexican-origin activists contributed to social justice in other areas—for example, in the fight against segregation and police brutality. As for Jiménez, she continued her role as an activist after returning to the United States in 1985. She returned with a strong belief that it is the victims of discrimination themselves who must organize for their rights and dignity. In other words, she explained, "For me the important thing is that communities are organizing—and I have a great deal of faith . . . in their humanity, their ability to spot contradictions, injustice, and inequality and to try to redress them to establish better societies."[141]

Ku Klux Klan Initiation, Houston, Texas, December 8, 1921. Courtesy of Hulton Archive via Getty Images.

"Group Portrait of the Texas Rangers," 1932. AR-X-016-D091, Frank Caldwell Texana Collection. Courtesy of Austin History Center, Austin Public Library, Austin, Texas.

"Four Men Standing," 1948. *Left to right*: Dr. Carlos Castañeda, unknown, Father Duffy, unknown. Neal Douglass Photograph Archive, nd-48-425-02. Courtesy of Austin History Center, Austin Public Library, Austin, Texas.

Braceros being fumigated with DDT, Hidalgo Processing Center, Texas, 1956. Leonard Nadel Photographs and Scrapbooks, Archives Center, National Museum of American History, Smithsonian Institution.

Political poster of Maria Jiménez, Raza Unida Party candidate, Houston, Texas, 1974. Maria Jiménez Collection.

Bayou, location of the police killing of Joe Campos Torres, Houston, Texas, 1977. Orie Collins, *Houston Chronicle*.

Maria Jiménez with Mark Zwick and Susan David protesting the detention of 111 undocumented workers at Cleveland Park in Houston, Texas, by the INS, November 1993. Carlos Antonio Rios, *Houston Chronicle*.

Maria Jiménez in Washington, DC, with Redford, Texas, residents in 1997 to meet with government officials to protest the killing of Esequiel Hernández. *Left to right*: Enrique Madrid, Ruby Madrid, Belén Hernández, Maria Jiménez, Jesús Valenzuela, Dianna Valenzuela, and Reverend Melvin La Follette. Maria Jiménez Collection.

Maria Jiménez testimony in US Congress, no date. Maria Jiménez Collection.

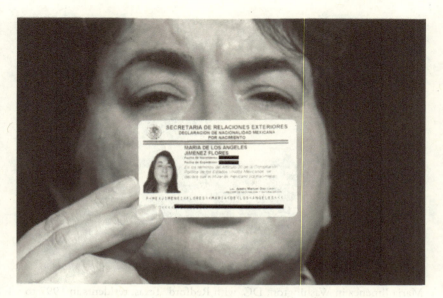

Maria Jiménez with her nationality card of Mexico, 1998. Carlos Antonio Rios, *Houston Chronicle*.

Maria Jiménez in her office at Central Aztlan, 5115 Harrisburg, Houston, Texas, 2004. Maria Jiménez Collection.

Maria Jiménez with two other persons at the Capitol, Washington, DC, late 1990s. Maria Jiménez Collection.

Maria Jiménez with Bill Chandler at the Immigrant Workers Freedom Ride Rally, Jackson, Mississippi, 2003, across the street from where Medgar Evers was assassinated in 1963. Maria Jiménez Collection.

Maria Jiménez teaching "Latino Activism and Organizing," University of Houston, Houston, Texas, 2005. Carlos Javier Sanchez, *Houston Chronicle*.

Medical Examiner Dr. Corinne Stern, Webb County, Texas, in 2007 with remains of an unidentified immigrant. Mayra Beltran, *Houston Chronicle*.

Activists of the United We Dream organization in the conference room of Speaker of the House Nancy Pelosi, 2021. Photo by Vivianne Peckham.

Chapter 6

Jiménez Monitoring the Border, the "Abused-Community Syndrome," and the Era of Globalization

In the context of immigration law enforcement, the international Mexican labor force is placed in a position of illegality, vulnerability, exploitation, and socio-political marginalization. . . . The only change currently is that this fervor takes place in the context of the inequalities produced by a global economic system.

—Maria Jiménez[1]

This chapter turns to the late 1980s when Maria Jiménez tackled problems not only at the state level but also at national and international levels. In her new position as director of the Immigration Law Enforcement Monitoring Project (ILEMP) of the AFSC, she will aggressively pursue her mission to fight injustices that targeted undocumented immigrants. In addition, the problems that she and other advocates for immigrants will address included the harsh consequences of globalization and federal immigration laws, especially the Immigration Reform and Control Act (IRCA) of 1986.

Commonplace prejudices against "illegal aliens" contributed to the discriminatory nature of the nation's immigration policy, practices, and attacks on Mexican immigrants. For example, an alarmed Jiménez complained about "gangs of white supremacists [who] have since 1988 regularly beaten, attacked, robbed, and with paint-bullets, shot Mexican immigrants" in San Diego County, California.[2] In addition, border authorities' violations of civil and human rights seemed to be justified, if not directly encouraged, by the negative stereotypes of undocumented immigrants.[3] IRCA increased the number of border patrols, increasing the number of violations of civil and human rights. Fortunately, an important, and positive, provision of IRCA granted legal residency status to three million undocumented immigrants and offered them a path to citizenship.[4]

Houston, Globalization, and Immigration

A background in some economic and social changes that affected Houston will reveal how these changes affected the Mexican-origin community and immigrant community. Of the "push-and-pull" factors in migration—that is, factors that push someone out of their country and factors that attract someone to another country—Houston was a strong pull because of its growing job market. The estimate of undocumented Mexicans in Houston in the early 1980s exceeded eighty thousand.[5] Central Americans also came in large numbers. Their migration reflected the globalization of the economy but was attributable more to the unrest in their homelands. Many fled the civil war in El Salvador, a repressive government that received US military aid, including training for its armed forces.[6] An estimated one hundred thousand Central Americans settled in Houston after 1981.[7] By 1985 the total number of undocumented Hispanic persons in the Houston area reached almost two hundred thousand.[8] Fellow countrymen who had settled earlier in Houston made it easier for the new arrivals. Guatemalan migrants who traveled to Houston, for example, knew "exactly which neighborhood in Houston they must go in order to settle among hometown people."[9]

By the 1980s Houston was a major world center of petroleum technology with a strong economy that attracted large numbers of immigrant workers. According to the sociologist Nester P. Rodríguez, "Undocumented workers from rural and urban Mexico became a preferred labor force, especially among construction employers who paid low wages and offered poor working conditions."[10] Unfortunately, these and other migrant workers had little or no job security, a fact that benefited their employers and increased their profits. During the 1970s and early 1980s, for example, construction and office-cleaning industries enjoyed large profits in part because of "low-wage, nonunionized Latino immigrant work forces (much to the dismay of unionized U.S. workers)." Men usually worked in construction and service industries, while women typically worked in "restaurants, cafeterias, middle- and upper-income homes, and office-cleaning crews."[11]

Aware of the exploitation of foreign labor, Jiménez lamented the fact that these workers were "part of our global system" that insured "inequalities at an international level."[12] Found in major cities like Houston, this global system resulted in labor exploitation and human rights abuses. Sociologist Beth Anne Shelton concurred with Jiménez and wrote that large cities "in the advanced capitalist economies" have a "migrant-labor system." The system favored employers who could easily exploit foreign workers. Undocumented workers were the most exploited, but authorized workers were too. According to Shelton, foreign migrant workers in the migrant-labor system were largely defenseless because they were "substantially restricted from joining working-class movements and can be sent home in times of economic downturns."[13]

The Houston economy, which had suffered from a drop in oil prices in the mid-1980s, improved in the late 1980s. Unfortunately, the situation did not improve for Hispanics, especially undocumented workers. Rodríguez believed that many factors contributed to this problem. For example, when industrial plants reopened, they did not operate at their previous capacity. The businesses reduced staffing, wages, and vacation time. In addition, labor unions were too weak to demand better salaries. Therefore, "menial jobs that use to start at $8 per hour now paid less than $5 an hour."[14] Despite the low wages, Rodríguez's research in 1986 of a group of Central Americans revealed that their employment rate was 81.3 percent.[15] Fortunately, some help was available for the Central Americans. Church and community organizations in Houston, for example, the Ripley House, provided the underemployed or unemployed with as much food and other assistance as possible.[16]

Mexico

A discussion of immigration in the United States should include information about its neighbor to the south, Mexico, the source of most immigrants. A background in Mexico also offers insight to Jiménez's activism. She was born in Mexico and later resided there from 1974 to 1985, and her experience there became very useful when she became director of ILEMP. On a more general level, some knowledge of Mexican history, especially economic, is important because it explains the push-and-pull factors in Mexican immigration to the United States.

Fortunately for Mexico, its economy grew substantially from 1965 to 1982. In this period the push factor subsequently declined. The country followed the import substitution industrialization development model with the objective to "create and sustain internal markets to serve as springboards for economic growth."[17] Mexico's economic growth appeared especially notable during the years 1976–1982, called *el boom petrolero*, or the oil boom era. The political leadership also changed. Previously, the nation's presidents originated from Mexico's provinces, but after 1970 the leaders had their roots in the capital, Mexico City. This new breed of leaders and government officials included technocrats, and many had advanced degrees from foreign universities. Other changes had long-term significance as well. Beginning in the early 1980s, the Mexican population became increasingly dissatisfied with their government corruption, and civic action groups began to multiply.[18]

Besides the economy, other critical events influenced the direction of the government. The administration of Gustavo Díaz Ordaz (1964–1970) is remembered for the bloody crackdown on October 2, 1968, of student protesters in Tlatelolco Plaza in Mexico City. That year student protests broke out in many countries, including the United States. However, since the Mexican government was hosting the 1968 Summer Olympics, which started on October 12, it suppressed any civil disturbance that might disrupt this world event. The number of the students killed at Tlatelolco Plaza remains unknown, but estimates range from forty-four, the Mexican government's estimation, to three hundred. In the opinion of the Mexican intellectual

Carlos Fuentes (1928–2012), the government's action in the Tlatelolco massacre demonstrated that "it had no response to the demands of the young men and women that were educated in the ideals of democracy and freedom and participation."[19]

The long-term consequences for the ruling party of the massacre of student protesters were significant. According to the Mexican historian Roderic Ai Camp, after the Mexican government's egregious action in the plaza, "Mexicans began to question the efficacy and morality of an authoritarian state that required violence against middle class students to maintain its position of authority and legitimacy to govern."[20] The government had suppressed the student movement for the time. However, following the 1968 massacre, the Mexican president faced unprecedented criticism. In addition, the traditional loyalty to the federal government and the ideals set forth during the Mexican Revolution (1910–1920) appeared shaken. The government needed to address the concerns of its citizens, especially its youth, because student protests continued. Fortunately, according to Mexican historian Enrique Krauze, "The supposedly revolutionary country accustomed to obedience and silence" was transformed, became more democratic, and offered more freedom.[21]

President Luis Echeverría Álvarez (1970–1976) succeeded Díaz Ordaz and took a more populist approach to dealing with pressing needs of the country and to appeal to young Mexicans. The government funded, for example, improvements in health services and public works such as road construction and rural electrification. Many changes reflected Echeverría's belief that "a culturally and politically expanded state could solve of some of Mexico's most significant social inequalities."[22] His administration wanted to attract the young Mexicans who were critical of the government. The reforms it introduced included "slightly opening the political system, lowering the voting age, proposing reforms in the electoral system, and revising the representation system in Congress."[23]

José López Portillo (1976–1982) succeeded Echeverría. López Portillo benefited politically during his early administration from the high oil prices that boosted the Mexican economy. Oil prices rose when the Arab Oil Embargo of 1973 stopped oil shipments to the United States in October and greatly reduced oil production in November and December. Oil producers in the Organization of Arab Petroleum Exporting Countries (OAPEC), led by Saudi Arabia, were retaliating against US support of Israel in its conflict with Egypt and Syria.[24] Mexico also benefited from the 1976 discovery of new oil deposits. On the other hand, Mexico faced difficulties, such as the drought in 1977, which contributed to a rise in migration to the United States. A greater problem was that during the oil boom period of 1976–1982, Mexico took out large loans with very high interest rates from foreign banks. Unfortunately, an oil glut occurred in the early 1980s, oil prices dropped, and the Mexican economy rapidly deteriorated. The middle class suffered greatly because of the acute inflation, but the poor suffered more. Many moved into the cities or emigrated to other countries, especially the United States, in search of employment. Because of the economic problems in the 1980s, this decade became known as *la década perdida*, or the lost decade.

Miguel de la Madrid (1982–1988), who succeeded López Portillo, was the first Mexican president to have studied in the United States. In 1965 he earned a master's degree in public administration from Harvard University. Regarding Mexican politics, the Party of the Institutionalized Revolution (Partido Revolucionario Institucional, PRI) and de la Madrid faced strong opposition from other political parties. The opposition won many local elections, which forced PRI to make some changes. Reversing previous government policies, de la Madrid's administration, for example, reduced the government's control of the economy by selling enterprises, previously state-owned, to the private sector. In addition, the president ended the import substitution strategy in favor of a neoliberal approach, including lower tariffs, more trade, and more foreign capital investment. The austerity measures that the government took to pay its debts and improve the economy became extremely unpopular. Nevertheless, de la Madrid received credit for "setting Mexico on a path toward a free-market economy, which culminated in the country's entering into the North Atlantic Free Trade Agreement with the United States and Canada in 1994."[25]

One serious blemish during his administration was his mishandling of the devastating earthquake, centered in the nation's capital, in September 1985. De la Madrid's inaction after the earthquake weakened the reputation of his political party, the PRI, and strengthened opposition parties, including the National Action Party (Partido Acción National, PAN). Damages from the earthquake extended over a hundred miles, and the quake was felt as far away as Houston, located 745 miles to the north.[26] The president hesitated to order the established disaster plan because, William H. Beezley asserted, he "feared the catastrophe might result in a military takeover of his government."[27] Mexican citizens, instead, organized their own rescue efforts, assisted by the Roman Catholic Church.[28] Sympathetic organizations and individuals outside of Mexico also aided Mexican victims of the earthquake. Jiménez had returned to Houston before the earthquake. However, she and many other concerned Mexicans collected and sent needed supplies to earthquake victims in Mexico.[29]

Jiménez's connection with Mexico was strengthened during her residence there, and the knowledge that she gained served her well in her future positions. Events in Mexico, some of which Jiménez observed, altered the nation's political landscape. In her opinion, as noted earlier, "The Mexican Left matured and integrated into the popular movements that have democratized in Mexico."[30] In regard to unauthorized immigration, the impact of the economy was key, however. In the opinion of the researchers of Mexican immigration Marcela Cerrutti and Douglas Massey, "The probability of illegal migration appears to be connected more strongly to changes in the Mexican political economy than to shifts in U.S. policy."[31]

Immigration, Houston, and United States Immigration Policy

A major development affecting the lives of undocumented immigrants in the United States was the passage of the IRCA. President Ronald Reagan signed the law on November 6, 1986. A major objective of the law concerned halting the immigration of undocumented immigrants into the United States. Since the impact of IRCA required Jiménez to draw extensively on all her leadership skills, it will be discussed in this section.

To end or reduce unauthorized immigration, Congress greatly increased funds for the INS to patrol the US-Mexico border. Another provision of the law imposed sanctions on employers if they knowingly hired undocumented workers. From the perspective of immigrants, the sanctions reduced their job opportunities and persuaded some of them to return to Mexico. In 1988 the *Houston Chronicle* reported that the Mexican consul general in Houston, Hermilo López Bassols, said that "more people had gone back across the border since publicity about employer sanctions increased last year."[32] However, as predicted by researchers at the time of the act, and confirmed by the majority of post-IRCA studies, the law had negligible success in reducing migration or reducing the number of undocumented persons in the United States.[33] As Jiménez observed, greater border control "simply transformed a heretofore circular movement into much more of a unilateral flow . . . [and] increased the number of undocumented Mexicans living in the United States."[34] In other words, unable to recross the southern border, Mexican immigrants chose to settle in the country.

On the positive side from the immigrants' perspective, the IRCA granted amnesty to immigrants who had illegally entered the United States by January 1, 1982. These applicants were required to support themselves, not use public assistance, and provide documentation of their continuous residence since January 1, 1982, although brief absences were allowed. The deadline for applicants was May 4, 1988. In Houston the total number of applicants for general amnesty totaled 110,924, with an additional 25,774 applicants in a program specifically for agricultural workers. By April of 1989, 80 percent, or about 89,000, of general amnesty applicants had been recommended for approval.[35] Not all immigrants benefited from IRCA, however. Many could not produce a work record because their employers were unwilling to provide one. In addition, Central American and other immigrants who came to the United States after 1982 did not qualify. For the successful amnesty applicants, the five-year residency requirement for citizenship ended in 1994 or 1995, at which time large numbers applied for citizenship. In Houston alone the INS office received over 2,000 applications per month by mid-1994. In August 1994 the total reached a record 2,700 applications.[36]

A major part of the IRCA was the sanctions it imposed on employers who knowingly hired undocumented workers. Undocumented individuals who became unemployed because of the IRCA faced personal economic hardship.

However, Dr. Dorothy Caram (b. 1933), a community activist in Houston, identified another problem. She pointed out that Hispanic businesses also would suffer since they relied on immigrant labor and customers. In addition, Dr. Caram remarked, "These people [immigrants] will be hungry. We'll have to feed them. What will happen to them?"[37] William P. Hobby Jr. (b. 1932), the Texas lieutenant governor from 1973 to 1991, also criticized employer sanctions, but for another reason, saying the sanctions "would make felons of most employers in South Texas."[38] His remark revealed how much employers depended on undocumented Mexican workers.

The negative impact of sanctions became obvious. By 1987, according to Joe R. Feagin, "fearful employers [in Houston] had begun to fire workers they knew or suspected to be undocumented . . . and have slammed the door on others looking for jobs."[39] Employers were "refusing to interview anyone who looks foreign, especially Hispanics."[40] The AFSC criticized employer sanctions., believing that since work was a critically important right, it should not be denied to anyone. The organization decided, according to Jiménez, "to sue the government based on [its] religious beliefs . . . [that] work is fundamental for people to survive on and no one could outlaw it."[41] Also affirming this right, she added, was the United Nations in its Universal Declaration of Human Rights. The United States is a signatory of the declaration.[42]

Jiménez criticized the sanctions in her 1992 article "Labor Mobility and the North American Free Trade Agreement." In it she wrote, "Its [IRCA's] employment sanctions provisions effectively denied to the two-thirds of Mexican immigrants in the United States who are undocumented the internationally recognized human right: the right to work."[43] Pro-immigrant groups in Houston organized to help Mexicans and other immigrants in this difficult situation. The groups formed the Community Task Force on Immigration Affairs in 1988 to address human and civil rights issues, Jiménez said, for "the many people that did not qualify for legalization."[44] The task force set up a hotline to provide accurate information on the law's provisions to employers and immigrants. The task force members included the Justice and Peace Action Forum, Catholic Charities, and the Council of Houston Hispanic Organizations.[45]

The IRCA affected immigrant groups in various ways. Salvadorans in Houston worried the most about the possibility of deportation because, they believed, returning to their war-torn homeland was "often a death sentence."[46] Juan, an undocumented Salvadoran in Houston said, "If I went back now, I wouldn't live a year." In desperation, some Salvadorans moved to Canada. The sudden rise in the number of Salvadorans in their country alarmed Canadians, and its government passed a law in February 1987 to discourage this movement. The law required immigrants to fill out an application and denied their entry into Canada until their applications had been processed. The new requirement angered some Canadians—for example, Nancy Pocock of the Quaker Committee for Refugees, who said she was "ashamed" of her government's action.[47]

Agricultural employers endeavored to make profits despite the IRCA, but workers had few options. One effect of the IRCA was lower wages. Jiménez noted in her 1999 article "Mobility, Human Rights, and Economic Development" that research on immigrant labor indicated that, "before IRCA immigrants without documents earned the same wages as those with them and that specific rates of pay was determined by a person's education, duration of US experience, and English-language ability."[48] After the IRCA, according to findings by immigration scholars Katharine M. Donato, Jorge Durand, and Douglas S. Massey, "undocumented migrants appear to suffer deterioration in their labor market position."[49] For example, Jiménez reported that wages were 28 percent below that of documented workers and "working conditions likewise worsened, with higher proportions of migrants earning wages below the legal minimum and working under irregular circumstances."[50]

Even before the IRCA, migrant workers had little or no power to negotiate for better pay or working conditions. As for the growers, the federal government tried to help them by offering more work visas. Some growers employed immigrant workers known as Legally Authorized Workers (LAWS). Farmers with perishable products frequently hired Special Agricultural Workers (SAWS), an option that a provision of the IRCA allowed. SAWS were immigrants who could prove that they had worked at least ninety days each year in agricultural jobs during the years 1984–1986.[51] SAWS allegedly had special skills, but growers applied the term to "any bracero they wished to retain."[52] In response to pressure from growers' demand for even more SAWS, Congress established agricultural "replenishment programs" in 1989. Opponents of these programs, including farm-worker advocates, insisted that the claim of labor shortage was only a ploy to supply growers with a surplus of cheap, exploitable immigrant labor. Guadalupe Luna, attorney for MALDEF, asserted that the agricultural program meant "supplying those growers with cheap labor and continuing to cultivate poor working conditions." Luna added, "There's plenty of unemployed workers already available."[53]

Others agreed with Luna, including US Senator Alan Simpson (R-WY) and US Representative Howard Berman (D-CA), about the injustice of exploiting workers for greater profits. These legislators objected to pressure from the "perishable agriculture industry, who have always sought to maintain an oversupply of labor."[54] Critics of replenishment programs predicted easy legalization for many of these agricultural workers. The agricultural worker program of IRCA was administered so inefficiently, according to a study in California, that it attracted "many Mexicans who would not otherwise have left for the United States."[55] In addition, it was plagued with fraud. An INS official estimated that at least one-third of the 1.2 million applications nationwide were fraudulent.[56]

The massive problem for the INS in dealing with undocumented workers motivated the Border Patrol in June 1988 to open a new office in Houston. The fourteen officials' assignment required them to locate, investigate, and deport unauthorized workers. The officials were very efficient. Of all INS districts in the nation investigating fraud, reportedly none "matched Houston's success in ferreting out fraud and obtaining sworn confessions from false applicants."[57] In April 1989 the Houston INS office reported that about 75 percent of SAWS applications were recommended for denial; specifically, only 6,300 out of 25,774 applicants were successful.[58]

The employer sanctions had serious consequences for Texas growers because it nullified the well-known Texas Proviso that they liked because of its advantages. The proviso had "specifically excluded employment [of undocumented workers] as constituting harboring under the law." In all other situations, it had been "illegal to 'harbor' anyone who entered the United States without documents."[59] With the IRCA, however, all employers were required to verify that their employees had a legal right to work in the United States or risk fines or worse. As of late April 1989, the INS in Houston had served sixty fine notices to these employers, totaling $232,550.[60] Anthony L. Hutchinson, owner of a Houston landscaping company, and his foreman became the first men in Harris County to face criminal prosecution. Following a ten-month investigation, the authorities arrested him on May 27, 1989.[61] Hutchison was found guilty in December 1989 and sentenced in March 1990 "for conspiracy with intent to commit bribery, two accounts of presenting counterfeit government documents and one count of harboring illegal aliens."[62]

Jiménez, Director of ILEMP

Jiménez returned to Houston in 1985, more mature and ready for the next stage in her life. Her years in Mexico included the birth of her twins, Stalina and Carlos, learning political theory from Mexican intellectual leftist circles, and work experience in union organizing. Houston and the people she knew were different too. What she found especially interesting included how her former associates had changed and how "social movements had been institutionalized." On this matter she remarked, "And so when I returned to the United States, I find that all ex-colleagues of La Raza Unida Party are either integrated into institutional work or they're into cultural work, but nobody's actually doing political work anymore."[63]

Initially, Jiménez continued her union work after she returned to Houston. The Service Employee International Union hired her to help unionize janitors, mostly Central Americans. She later commented, "I didn't know Central Americans, but I got to know them after I came back."[64] By December 1985 the unionizing efforts successfully organized janitors who worked in a building downtown. Two months later, in February 1986, the INS targeted the new union, Jiménez recalled, by raiding the "only building where the union had won—clearly a union busting tactic. And so that told me how important it was, how important the immigrant labor was for the economy. . . . In Mexico the reaction was to beat you up and put you in jail. Here it was to deport you." The INS action that February increased her commitment to seek justice for immigrants and eventually, she said, "led me into the national circles of immigration." Jiménez's next job, from 1986 to 1987, was as a labor organizer for the Texas State Employees Union. However, she was not satisfied with this position because among her co-workers and the clients, "there were very few Chicanos . . . and there were very few immigrants."[65]

In 1987 Jiménez began a career that would become her mission in life, to promote and protect human rights. That year, she became the director in Houston of the ILEMP, a new division of the AFSC. She remained with the Quaker organization until 2003. The ILEMP's general purpose was to protect the civil and human rights of immigrants. Specifically, according to Jiménez, the ILEMP had decided to document "law enforcement abuse on the southern border, generating written evidence of the daily occurrence of border violence perpetuated by these [US] government forces."[66] To her surprise, Jiménez noted, no one was documenting abuses at the border at this time. She commented, "Nobody was doing anything about it. It was very interesting to me because I thought, well, why didn't MALDEF or LULAC or National Council of La Raza start this [ILEMP] project?"[67] Perhaps, as asserted in CRT, abuses against Mexicans and Mexican Americans by border authorities had been so commonplace that they did not attract the attention of these major national Hispanic organizations.

Jiménez's position at the AFSC brought together an organization concerned with human rights violations with an exceptional woman who had the skills it needed. Nevertheless, her earliest contact with the AFSC, the job interview, was arduous. As she recalled, "You're interviewed by one or two people per hour every hour for about, all day, from eight to four. And so, you had, eventually in the end of the day . . . about thirteen interviews. And they get together and decide who to select." She added, "But one of the interesting things was [that] they asked on the application about everything that I hid in the other applications in a normal job situation. I mean, who would want to hire a union activist who had to go underground or who was an atheist or who studied Marx or who had belonged to a third party, La Raza Unida—[who] was considered a radical. If I applied to Exxon, I'd have to not declare all those activities."[68]

Hired in April of 1987, the AFSC asked Jiménez to create a work plan by May for its National Community Relations meeting. About fifteen other persons who were involved in social justice attended the meeting. The prospect of developing a plan did not worry Jiménez. She remarked, "Well, because I had been part of these circles in Mexico in which one *did* plan social movements in terms of defining goals and objectives—and then developing strategies in writing—it was the most normal thing." Jiménez impressed the AFSC with her plan. As she recalled, "So they were shocked! And I was told they never had anybody present such a detailed program, with each component and—but that had been something I learned in Mexico."[69]

Jiménez's exceptional organizational skills became apparent immediately. Her new position required documenting human rights abuses of immigrants, but she strongly believed that documentation was not enough. The innovative plan that she presented to the AFSC required the participation of the local communities whose rights were violated by border officials. Specifically, she asserted, "We couldn't just describe human rights violations and the enforcement of immigration laws. We had to create conditions for change . . . to organize the communities themselves . . . and so part of the program implementation which I designed, which had been something I had done in Mexico—which was the first thing I did—was to design a training course, which was offered to many organizations in each community."[70]

The project Jiménez proposed was greatly needed. Since IRCA increased funding for border agents by 50 percent, the potential for the abuse of immigrants at the border increased. In 1988 Jiménez wrote the article "Police Policies and Practices: The Case of the Border Patrol," criticizing the federal government's harsh border control tactics and insisting that the Border Patrol and other immigration authorities must be held accountable for violating human rights.[71] Accountability, in fact, became her most important goal in her fight for social justice and protecting the rights and dignity of immigrants, documented or undocumented.

The risk to border crossers increased each year. In addition to more agents involved in the control of the border, IRCA's funding equipped these agents with more arms, including semiautomatic M-14 rifles. Unfortunately, when officers used excessive force, immigrants died. Jiménez reported that "two undocumented immigrants were shot in the back while handcuffed by the Border Crime Prevention Unit" in the San Diego area in December 1988. The unit was a joint task force composed of the Border Patrol and San Diego police. She added that even in large cities like New York and Houston, INS agents made arrests "with guns drawn in non–life-threatening situations."[72] It was even common practice for border enforcement authorities to patrol Mexican American neighborhoods in South Texas. Border Patrol harassment and flagrant violation of the civil rights of south Texas residents eventually culminated in the legal case *Murillo et al. v. Musegades, INS, et al.*, discussed in the next chapter, which was heard by the US Supreme Court.[73]

The same year that IRCA became law, 1986, Congress passed the Anti-Drug Abuse Act. This act increased the agency's responsibilities because it "officially broadened the Border Patrol's duties to include narcotics as well as immigration enforcement, and soon one-third of all Border Patrol agents were cross-deputized to enforce U.S. drug laws."[74] The 1986 act also had a retroactive aspect; that is, it said that "a person who—before the passage of the act—had been fined in the United States or in his or her country for the possession of, for instance, a small quantity of marijuana now faced deportation or was barred permanently from entering the United States."[75]

The change in the Border Patrol's role and the new "war on drugs" was an ominous development. The Anti-Drug Abuse Act converted border surveillance, Jiménez wrote, into an "intense multi-agency anti-smuggling operations coordinated by the Drug Enforcement Administration, the FBI, the Customs Service, the Coast Guard, and the INS (Border Patrol)." These operations, she explained, included "extensive use of a wide range of technologies, including data links, computer systems, seismic, magnetic and infrared sensors, low-light television systems, airplanes, and helicopters."[76]

The border regions had become, according to Jiménez, a "deconstitutional zone" where border authorities were not held accountable for their misconduct.[77] In 1992 Jiménez wrote "War in the Borderlands," in which she predicted that the increase of border control agents and the militarization of the border would lead to more violations of the civil and human rights of immigrants and residents along the border. Commonplace racist beliefs about Mexican immigrants equated to a high tolerance for the violation of their rights. In its zeal to apprehend undocumented immigrants and drug traffickers, the Border Patrol also victimized US citizens and legal residents in Texas. Authorities viewed this abuse, Jiménez wrote, as "collateral damage" that was considered "regrettable but necessary if the nation is to protect its territory and its sovereign power to define who 'belongs.'"[78]

Jiménez considered justifications like "collateral damage" intolerable. South Texas residents, she believed, were denied social justice, and those living in the border Texas town of El Paso suffered more "collateral damage" than other towns. According to sociologist Timothy J. Dunn, a Hispanic, any Hispanic in El Paso, Texas, had to endure a kind of repression by Border Patrol agents that represented a form of "ethnic policing."[79] In response to actions by the Border Patrol, the Border Rights Coalition (BRC) was organized in 1989 to document and report cases of abuse committed by the Border Patrol to the local media.[80] Jiménez had urged BRC members to form their organization, and she even provided them with funds from ILEMP for their new organization.

Abused-Community Syndrome and Abuse by Border Agents

Jiménez's alarm over the situation at the US-Mexico border increased with each passing day. The militarized southern border constituted a grave danger for job-seeking migrants. Fortunately, as director of the ILEMP, she could try to mitigate the situation with the support of the AFSC, parent organization of ILEMP. Jiménez knew personally that Mexicans who crossed the border expected, at the very least, a stressful experience, even when entering legally, as she did. Jiménez recalled, "As a Mexican immigrant, my earliest childhood memory is my parents instructing us not to speak as we reached a checkpoint because the border agent might yell at us."[81] Jiménez pointed out that there was a popular salsa song in which a man proposes marriage to his sweetheart. He says to her, "Let's live together until the INS separates us." Jiménez often mentioned this song to border agents, telling them, "That's how predominant you are in our lives. It's no longer until God do us part, it's until the INS do us part."[82]

Sociologist Timothy J. Dunn greatly admired Jiménez's work. He believed that, under her direction, the ILEMP became "the first group to promote efforts to systematically monitor human rights concerns in the border region as they related to border enforcement."[83] Jiménez concurred. She asserted that the ILEMP was "probably the first human rights organization to elaborate reports not only on a case-by-case basis, *pero* [but] on a statistical analysis of human rights violations that were happening on the border." In other words, the ILEMP documented civil and human rights violations by border officials and presented its findings to the US Congress and the media. Jiménez added, "And from our work then, we got other organizations of an international level interested. Human Rights Watch, for instance, the Americas Watch component, has done several reports. And many of our cases go now directly to them."[84]

Civil and human rights violations, including harassment and profiling of the Mexican-origin community in the border area, increased in the 1980s and 1990s. For this problem Jiménez coined the phrase "the abused-community syndrome," because although profiling was constant, "nobody ever raised the issue that it was profiling. Profiling, basically, is the violation of the Fourth and Fifth Amendments."[85] Explaining the problem Jiménez said, "It's gone on for so many generations that we no longer see the abuse. It's become a way of life. Part of our work is increasing public awareness that we are an abused community."[86]

Jiménez understood that because the abuse was commonplace, even the people being victimized saw it as part of their normal life. The study by Dunn echoed Jiménez's observations. From his interviews of residents of El Paso and their experiences in the 1970s with the Border Patrol, Dunn wrote that "what stands out is the acceptance, passivity, and fatalism reinforced by fear of retaliation (especially of deportation) among the 'subject population'—particularly parents instructing their upset, complaining children not to publicly complain and to just accept mistreatment."[87]

Practices by border agencies, Jiménez predicted, would "result in denial of due process to undocumented immigrants and, in extreme cases, in their death."[88] Dehumanizing measures against individuals by the Border Patrol, well-documented by the ILEMP, ranged from threats to actual blows with a cattle prod or worse. Striking undocumented immigrants on the head with a flashlight was a common practice by border agents. Victims of this practice were called "tonks" because of the sound made when the flashlight hits a head.[89] Of course, some Border Patrol agents were sympathetic to the job-seeking immigrants, but many were not. In an ILEMP report in 1992, former Border Patrol agent John Quirindongo compared the dehumanizing attitude of the Border Patrol toward immigrants to the attitude of US troops toward the Vietnamese during the Vietnam War. In 1991 Quirindongo said, "It is easier to shoot them if they are gooks . . . you do this for psychological protection."[90] In other words, Jiménez wrote in "War in the Borderlands," it was helpful in the minds of the Border Patrol—as well as the American public—to view immigrants as "the enemy" and the Border Patrol as "the embattled troops" with the right to assault undocumented immigrants, or even US citizens, at the border.[91]

Many of the desperate immigrants, despite the dangers of unauthorized entry, traveled to Houston to join their predecessors. It was a city that knew "chain migration" and had organizations that aided the immigrant community. One was Centro Aztlan, established in 1975, in Houston's East End. Ray Rodríguez, a paralegal at Centro Aztlan, noticed an interesting trend in the late 1980s. Before that time, young single males constituted most immigrants to the United States. However, as of the late 1980s, Rodríguez said, "it has become a 50-50 split"; that is, men and women began to migrate in about equal numbers. Jiménez explained this phenomenon, saying that "the war [in El Salvador] has been such that the men have been killed, or are in the armed services or guerilla movement. The women are left as heads of households. The women have to migrate to support whoever is left."[92]

Amnesty and Anti-Immigrant Animus

The topic of amnesty, a heated topic for both pro-immigration and anti-immigration groups, was and remains a major obstacle to immigration reform, a lifelong goal of Jiménez's activism. As described above, the IRCA granted amnesty to immigrants who had entered the country without documentation by January 1, 1982. The considerable number of undocumented immigrants rushing to apply for amnesty before May 4, 1988, the deadline set by the IRCA, alarmed many in the United States. Organizations that objected to any form of amnesty included the Federation for American Immigration Reform (FAIR). Patrick Burns, assistant director of FAIR, complained, "Amnesty has exacerbated the flow of nonworking dependents. . . . Now that we've given them legal residence, families want to come here legally. The hubby has gotten amnesty, and he sends for the wife and kids."[93] A skinhead group in California was more direct, saying, "We don't want any more greaseballs coming up here illegally . . . the white man is going to act to stop you in your tracks."[94]

Many more persons opposed the newest wave of immigrants who were from Central America, creating the potential for racial conflict. To study the impact of the new immigrants on white, Black, and Hispanic Houstonians, the Ford Foundation awarded a $150,000 grant for a two-year study (1988–1989) to UH. Sociology professor Nester P. Rodríguez directed the field study. He concluded that the rise in racial prejudices was due to a "great lack of familiarity."[95] The fear of the unknown, the study revealed, even emerged among white leaders of Houston churches that had a majority Hispanic congregation. The whites deliberately drove away Hispanics by ending bilingual Bible classes and masses in Spanish. In the case of apartments, managers segregated their Hispanic tenants in the rear-most units to not drive away prospective white tenants.[96]

White Houstonians were not alone in their opposition to immigration from Mexico and other Latin American countries. Blacks and Mexican-origin Houstonians also worried. Blacks, for example, believed that the immigrants who received amnesty created an economic burden on the nation. Blacks told researchers that they also worried about losing jobs to "ignorant" squatters who were "getting on welfare," although one Black Houstonian remarked, "We are all God's children."[97]

The persistent belief in Houston and elsewhere that immigrants were a drain on social services, a major source of anti-immigrant animus, belie the findings of research on the topic. In the first place, individuals in the process of becoming a citizen were barred from receiving social services, with some exceptions, from their state.[98] In fact, the nation benefited greatly from a "immigration surplus"—that is, "a simple and frequently cited metric of natives' total gain from immigration." For example, the immigration surplus in 1996 totaled $14 billion, according to a study published in 1997 by the National Research Council.[99] Jiménez also wrote about the immigration surplus in her 1995 editorial to the *Houston Chronicle*. She reported that documented and undocumented immigrants paid more in taxes than they received in public services. Specifically, she pointed out that "in 1992, for example, immigrants who arrived after 1970 paid $70.3 billion in taxes to all levels of government, but used only $42.9 billion in services, producing a surplus of $27.4 billion."[100]

Although Blacks feared, incorrectly, a drain on the economy because of immigrants, Hispanics had additional concerns. For example, the Ford Foundation study found that some Hispanics believed that immigrants would reinforce the racial stereotype that Hispanics were "mainly poor, illiterate, and impotent."[101] Another concern asserted that immigrants, legal or not, undermined the progress Hispanics had made in areas such as education and employment. A study by the National Association of Latino Elected and Appointed Officials (NALEO), like the Ford Foundation study, challenged many unfounded beliefs about new immigrants, including their contributions to their adopted country. NALEO's five-year national study, published in September 1989, found that 81 percent of Hispanics who became citizens had registered to vote. In comparison, the percentage for all Hispanics Americans was lower, only 57 percent. In addition, about 27 percent of naturalized Hispanics reported that they participated in political fund raisers and gave money to candidates.[102]

INS, Immigrants, and Immigrant Advocacy in Houston

Jiménez, as the director of the ILEMP in Houston, became intensely involved with the IRCA for many years. Therefore, more background on this important law is useful. One provision of the IRCA created the possibility of amnesty for millions of undocumented immigrants. As the deadline, May 4, 1988, to apply for amnesty approached, conditions for this group worsened because immigration officials also prepared to increase deportation. To facilitate this process, the Border Patrol, a division of the INS, worked closely with HPD. In addition, the Border Patrol established a new office in the George H. W. Bush Intercontinental Airport in north Houston. The IRCA's sanctions on employers of undocumented workers also made life more difficult for immigrant workers. The employer sanctions became fully effective on June 1, 1988. Given the dire situation they faced, immigrants applied for political asylum in increasing numbers. In response to the increase in applications, the INS needed to establish a special unit by late 1988 in Houston.[103]

The large presence and increased role of the INS and the Border Patrol in Houston worried Jiménez. She had observed that "during the year of legalization, the INS attempted to change its image into a new INS—one of professionalism and service. But it never ceased to be the old INS." Its agents' primary objective, according to Houston's INS District Deputy Director Mike McMahon, was to raid "outdoor targets such as construction sites and illegal labor pools that gather on street corners awaiting piecemeal work." Commenting in the *Houston Chronicle* on the raids, Jiménez predicted that the large number of Border Patrol agents in Houston would increase the desperation of the undocumented community. In other words, the agents would create, she said, "a reign of terror." Jan Pena, head of the immigration ministry of the Roman Catholic Diocese of Galveston-Houston shared Jiménez's concern about the raids and described the situation as "very scary."[104]

The INS raids at workplaces and elsewhere, in fact, did heighten tension in immigrant communities. Jiménez and other immigrant advocates reported that the INS raids targeted Houston neighborhoods with large Central American populations, a charge that the INS denied. One INS raid, conducted in early April 1989, covered a twelve-block area, including apartments, job sites, and street locations where immigrant laborers sought day work. Employers at targeted businesses could demand a search warrant. They did not, Jiménez explained, because they "don't know (they can ask for a

warrant) so they don't ask." Instead, employers and their employees cooperated with the INS. However, as Jiménez interpreted the situation, "How
voluntary is it when you're surrounded by armed officers?"[105] INS questioned
a total of about five hundred persons in the April raid, sixty-two of whom
were jailed. Sixty of these agreed to "voluntary" deportation, which was paid
for by the federal government. Local groups that protested the raid included
the human rights organization La Resistencia, led in Houston by the community activist Travis Morales. James Collins of the Houston Chapter of the
National Black United Front also criticized the INS raids. He called for "fair
treatment of all people, rich, poor, black, Nicaraguan, or European." Ron
Parra, INS district director and a Hispanic, understood his critics, but said
that "every single one of us can sympathize with their economic plight, but
they are here in violation of immigration law."[106]

Fortunately, there were groups and organizations in Houston willing to
help the frightened and intimidated immigrants—for example, Casa Juan
Diego. The refugee shelter opened in 1981 in west Houston. It was one of
many Catholic Workers Houses of Hospitality in the nation and the only one
that aided Spanish-speaking immigrants, legal or undocumented. Its director
Mark Zwick said that Casa "accepted people whether they were Catholic,
Protestant, or had no faith at all."[107] Evidently some Houstonians did not
approve of Casa Juan Diego's mission to help immigrants since arson was
suspected in the two fires at the shelter during the 1980s.[108] The fires did not
discourage Mark or his wife, Louise, however. By 2001 Casa Juan Diego
had grown to include fifteen houses that provided shelter, food, and health
care.[109] Mark Zwick told the *Houston Chronicle* in 1994 that his activism was
consistent with Catholic teaching and that "people who reject immigrants are
committing sins and are going to hell."[110]

The Zwicks and many other community groups also provided English
classes for any immigrant who wanted to learn it. English classes were
extremely important because the second phase of the amnesty process
required individuals to pass an English proficiency examination. Besides
Casa San Diego, KXLN-Channel 45, Fiesta Marts Inc., the *Houston Chronicle*, and the Houston Community College worked with Opportunity USA to
offer free English lessons to recently legalized immigrants.[111]

Conclusion

This chapter discussed a period when Mexican American activism had become more inclusive and included, among its concerns, the exploitation of immigrants. Jiménez's position as the ILEMP director was timely because she focused on the civil and human rights of immigrants and, more generally, social justice. She had the skills and knowledge from her experiences in Mexico to address the problem of immigrant exploitation in a global economy.

As the 1980s came to end, the nation's economy continued to be well integrated in the global economy and had been for a long time. Competing successfully in the global economy depended on cheap labor, which usually meant foreign workers. These workers, Jiménez often said, personified the human manifestation of globalization. However, many in the United States feared these "aliens," especially Mexican and Central American immigrants, and even equated them with criminals. The American public, therefore, demanded restricted immigration and more secure borders. Anti-immigrant prejudices became intense. Racist and xenophobic comments like "greaseballs," "ignorant" squatters, "tonks," and "gooks" alarmed Jiménez. In 1986, in response to the public's demands for more border control, Congress passed the IRCA and the Anti-Drug Abuse Act in 1986.

Fortunately, positive developments, including some initiated by Jiménez, emerged for undocumented immigrants. First, the IRCA granted amnesty to qualifying immigrants who had lived in the nation for many years. Ultimately, almost 2.7 million persons received permanent residence.[112] Another development was the creation of the ILEMP by the AFSC. The ILEMP's original mission, to monitor and report abuses committed by border authorities, however, seemed too limited to Jiménez. Therefore, as the ILEMP director, she created a plan that offered training that empowered the immigrant community itself. For example, groups in the community, such as the Border Rights Coalition (BRC), were trained to collect data on violations of their rights committed by immigration authorities. Jiménez helped to create the BRC and provided it with the funds it needed.

This chapter also examined some push-and-pull factors that influenced immigration. The history of Mexico provided examples of the push factors, especially when economic conditions in Mexico deteriorated. The pull to the United States, with its demand for cheap, undocumented labor, was constant, except during periods of economic recession. However, for job-seeking migrants, the difficulty and danger of unauthorized crossing of the border became more acute after the 1986 laws were passed. Because of the danger to border crossers, Jiménez called the area near the US-Mexico border the "deconstitutional zone." The INS and the Border Patrol intensified their pursuit of immigrants, sometimes even violating the civil rights of US citizens in South Texas. This abuse was not new, only more intense. Because it was not new, many Mexican-origin residents in South Texas seemed to have acquiesced to it, a situation that Jiménez called the "abused-community syndrome."

Social justice for immigrants, especially those who were undocumented, was often elusive. Jiménez did not object to immigrants being part of globalization if it was fair to these workers. For her, globalization was positive "if it can lead to economies that will develop decent standards of living for people and decreases the inequalities in both wealth distribution and social and political expression." In her work Jiménez committed, she said, to "organizing those impacted by globalization policies to have a voice in the way that integration is happening," as a way of "reaching more equitable social systems."[113] In other words, it became her mission in life to strive to create conditions that reduced inequities and to advocate for the rights and dignity of all persons. The next chapter continues with the activism of the Mexican-origin community, as well as that of Jiménez. The challenges ahead required her to use all her exceptional analytical and organizational skills. Although she focused on immigrant rights as the ILEMP director, she also dedicated herself to helping her community in Houston.

Chapter 7

Jiménez Challenging Nativism and Border Militarization

In the historical continuum, this (marginalization) is nothing new for the
Mexican-origin population in the United States. Racism, exclusion, and
segregation are all too familiar.
—Maria Jiménez[1]

Many developments in the 1990s affected Houston's Hispanic community negatively, especially immigrant groups. These developments
kept Maria Jiménez increasingly active, fighting for social justice and dealing
with challenges to immigrants, especially the undocumented. She personified
an important concept in CRT, that minority activists are essential, both in
promoting social justice denied to minority groups and to reducing prejudices
that they encounter. Jiménez, as director of the ILEMP of the AFSC, devoted
much of her energy to challenging federal immigration policies and practices and the alarming militarization of the US-Mexico border. Other activists
were also busy, focusing on the fight for better education for Mexican-origin
students. Through their struggles, the nation's best virtues, like equality and
social justice, were promoted.

Houston Hispanics and Education

In few areas was racial discrimination in Houston, especially for immigrants, more glaring than in public education. Jiménez knew this well from personal experience. For example, although her grade point average was 4.0 in high school, only one organization, Sembradores de Amistad, offered her a scholarship. She believed that she did not receive more funds because, at the time, she was not a citizen. However, the discrimination she experienced when young left her with the desire to help others. Therefore, an important consequence of her hurtful experiences in Houston's schools was a stronger commitment to fighting for social justice, especially for the marginalized. Reflecting on her experiences at Milby High School, she said that there, "I realized the injustices that occur. I felt that the blacks and browns weren't ever in the mainstream. I think Milby made me radical."[2]

Commonplace racial prejudices played a part in the woefully inadequate education that HISD provided its Hispanic students for decade after decade.[3] However, activist students and their parents were not passive in the fight for equitable education. For example, in the late 1980s, parents organized to protest the problems at Austin High School (AHS). Their complaints included the school's "record of poor academic achievement, its culturally insensitive administration, and its tolerance of high dropout rates."[4] HISD's chronic indifference, or at least failure to improve the students' education, reflected what crit scholar Lu-in Wang, author of *Discrimination by Default*, interpreted as educators' low expectations for minority students, an attitude that impaired students' self-confidence and learning.[5]

The worsening situation at AHS prompted student activists to organize a walkout on October 20, 1989. Students objected the most to class scheduling. For example, students were assigned to classes they had already passed. Some classes were assigned in girl's bathrooms or even broom closets. One student recalled, "I remember I was in a classroom without a teacher for the whole first six weeks . . . I ended up getting a grade for just showing up. This was the first time I really saw how the school didn't care for me or any of us."[6] Sociologist Angela Valenzuela, who wrote about the walkout, drew the same conclusion as the student assigned to a classroom without a teacher. A major problem at the HISD was its lack of "caring" for the Mexican-origin students. From this lack of caring, Valenzuela wrote, other problems followed, including an inadequate counseling staff, bad food, restroom plumbing that did not work, and computer rooms without computers. She also discovered that the high school "spends 599 fewer dollars per student than the district average."[7] The HISD made some changes following the walkout, including firing the school's unpopular principal, hiring Spanish-speaking counselors, purchasing more textbooks, and making improvements in the cafeteria, which had several fire code violations.[8] Valenzuela reported that HISD also agreed to two important demands, a bilingual advisor and a ninth-grade relief school.[9] She believed that the protest by the students and the community achieved "a thorough disruption of the harmful isolation that had characterized Seguín [Valenzuela's pseudonym for the school in her book] up to that point."[10] However, the few changes that the HISD made failed to correct major problems, such as high dropout rates and low academic achievements.

Another major challenge for the HISD was meeting the pedagogical needs of immigrant students, especially if English was their second language. The HISD failed these students as well. Although schools, including the HISD, typically viewed immigrant students as disadvantaged because they were deficient in English, Valenzuela's research indicated otherwise. Hispanic immigrant students, her study concluded, "do better in school than third or fourth-generation Hispanics whose parents have lived in the United States all their lives."[11] Jiménez's academic accomplishments in school supported Valenzuela's research findings. Furthermore, like Valenzuela, Jiménez viewed immigrant students positively. She believed that Mexican immigrants or first-generation Mexican Americans, unlike second- or third-generation Mexican Americans, were more likely to challenge injustices because they "are faced with the concrete obstacles that have to be overcome."[12]

Sometimes schools took a special interest in immigrant students. For example, educator Ana Acevedo obtained federal funding in the late 1980s for the Migrant Education Program at HISD. In an unprecedented community outreach, the HISD "hired recruiters to go into the community, door-to-door, distributing information about their migrant education program." Statistics from the Department of Education (DOE) revealed the dire need for this program. The DOE estimated that 75 percent of the ten thousand migrant students in Houston dropped out.[13]

Mexican-origin students dropped out in alarming numbers. To address this problem, AHS established a dropout prevention program called Communities in Schools. Nevertheless, the dropout rate remained high. Robert Rivera, the Communities in Schools project manager, said in 1995, "It's a pretty scary situation . . . I think we are losing whole generations of kids. It's happening. . . . The long-term evaluation is that things aren't better, they are worse."[14] The problem with the HISD, according to Valenzuela, was that it ignored the most important needs of its minority students: to be respected and to have their culture respected. Instead, the HISD offered minority students, Valenzuela asserted, "subtractive schooling"—that is, schooling where there are "subtractively assimilationist policies and practices that are designed to divest Mexican students of their culture and language. A key consequence of these subtractive elements of schooling is the erosion of students' social capital, evident in the presence and absence of academically oriented networks among immigrant and U.S.-born youth, respectively."[15] The HISD's willful indifference to the students' culture reflected the school system's racism.

FAIR: Nativist Group Targets Houston

In January 1990 Jiménez responded to a virulent racist attack on immigrants in Houston. That month immigrant bashing reached a new level because of anti-immigrant radio messages produced by FAIR. The organization chose Houston as a test market to determine the effectiveness of their ads, which blamed economic and social problems such as unemployment, even traffic congestion, on immigrants.[16] The ads exploited negative perceptions about immigrants to create more anxiety among Houstonians, many already nervous about the "other" in their midst.[17] Six Houston radio stations broadcasted the FAIR ads. The ads were scheduled to run from January 17 through January 31. The Houston press reported that former INS Commissioner Alan Nelson said that the FAIR ads represented an "American point of view" of immigration and that Ronald Parra, the INS district director in Houston, did not consider the organization's ads inflammatory.[18]

Hispanics, including Jiménez, became outraged and extremely critical of the FAIR ads. Jiménez lamented, "I think FAIR does an injustice to the American people by using inflammatory advertisement to basically encourage prejudice and hatred . . . (FAIR) knows that this is the easiest way to inflame hatred and opposition to immigrants." Margaret González, vice president of the southwest region of LULAC, described the "political propaganda" ads as "racist in tone and certainly not conducive to good human relations in this country." Houston activist Leonel Castillo complained that the radio ads were "clearly filled with distortions and misrepresentations and innuendo" that would exacerbate "racial and ethnic tensions in the city, particularly toward Hispanics."[19] In addition to Hispanic organizations, groups objecting to the ads included the Catholic bishops of the diocese of Galveston-Houston, the Asian American Bar Association, the Social Action Committee for Temple Beth Israel, and the ILEMP of the AFSC.[20]

Jiménez, the ILEMP director in Houston, organized a candlelight vigil on January 17, 1990, at the Houston hotel where FAIR representatives were staying. Participants in the silent vigil included UH professor Dr. Fernando Galán. He said, "We cannot be neutral. If we do not protest, take a position, we are giving tacit approval to this ad campaign." The attorney Gordon Quan of the Asian American Bar Association added, "We are here to protest any ad campaign that would suggest any one group is culpable. This is not the kind of Houston we want. . . . Of all the things that bother me the most was that they picked Houston, like we would accept this kind of racism." Jiménez agreed. She remarked, "We feel it is very serious that Houston should be used as a lab. They will come and test us and go. They will leave us with problems of racial tensions that we will have to deal with."[21]

The protests by Jiménez and many others ultimately succeeded in ending a grossly racist campaign that targeted the city's vulnerable immigrant community and that tried to damage Houston's prized reputation for diversity and internationalism. FAIR may have decided that anti-immigrant prejudices were commonplace enough in Houston that the city would be receptive to their ads. Speculating on FAIR's choice of Houston for the ads, González of LULAC said, "I think they picked Houston because of the recent events in the city; the [police] killing of Ida Lee Delaney and Byron Gillum."[22]

Kathy Reiser, cochair of the Social Action Committee for Beth Temple Israel, agreed, adding that "they [the ads] are unfair, they're distortions, they're oversimplifications. . . . To link immigrants with drugs, crime and traffic is really absurd." FAIR Executive Director Daniel Stein indicated that he would meet with Hispanic leaders to discuss the ads. In response to the offer, Jiménez said, "We invite them to talk but not until they remove the ads. We cannot have a balanced discussion while they are still trying to influence people out there to share their opinion."[23] FAIR stopped the radio ads but a meeting with FAIR and Jiménez did not occur. Although FAIR originally wanted the aids to run through January 31, the aids were pulled from all six radio stations on Friday, January 19, only two days after first being aired.[24] Fortunately, activists for social justice, including Jiménez, succeeded in the abrupt ending to the virulently racist ads.

Job Discrimination and IRCA

In her effort to reduce racism and injustice in Houston, Jiménez tackled another problem, job discrimination against immigrants. This social injustice stemmed from a provision of IRCA that imposed harsh sanctions on employers who knowingly hired undocumented immigrants. However, as Jiménez pointed out, the "people who are primarily affected are the legal permanent residents and the newly legalized."[25] In fact, immigrants who had authorization to work filed 76 percent of the complaints in Houston.

Jiménez attempted to correct this injustice. She represented the Community Task Force on Immigration Affairs, discussed in chapter 6, at a press conference in March 1990. Jiménez called on the Houston City Council to pass a resolution that urged Congress to repeal employer sanctions. The news conference coincided with a publication of the General Accounting Office (GAO) that "found that as much as 10 percent of 4.6 million employers in its survey may be biased against hiring workers according to national origin because of the law."[26] The report confirmed what was happening in Houston. To inform Houstonians of the findings, the Community Task Force offered seminars at the First Unitarian Church and other locations. It also, Jiménez recalled, sent "a large mail-out to different civil rights associations and social justice organizations" with information on the GAO report.[27]

The Community Task Force also released the results of a national survey by nongovernmental organizations (NGOs) on job discrimination in Houston and elsewhere. The NGOs reported that 241 complaints of discrimination in Houston were recorded from June 1988 to June 1989. Residents legally in the country filed most of the complaints. The major complaint was "wage theft," when unscrupulous employers failed to pay workers for their labor. Undocumented workers were the most vulnerable. Jiménez angrily commented, "The worst thing . . . is the theft of wages, people who are contracted and then not paid."[28] These corrupt employers justified their wage theft in these incidences by saying that the workers lacked the appropriate documentation.

Anti-Mexican immigrant racism, in addition to greed, explained the countless cases of wage theft and other forms of exploitation. Sometimes, however, immigrant workers took legal action by suing their employers. For example, men recruited by La Pisca in Houston for jobs in Florida were plaintiffs in a federal lawsuit in 1992. One plaintiff said of his employers, "They didn't bring us water; they didn't bring us anything to eat. Sometimes I ate and sometimes I didn't. It was exploitation." Even the trip from Houston to Florida was degrading. Thirteen men were crammed in a van "for a 30-hour drive. They stopped only to refuel, and the only food available was at filling stations." Unfortunately, according to Ray Rodríguez of Centro Aztlan in Houston, this exploitation was "nothing new."[29] Workers often could not escape from their situation because contractors confiscated their identification documents. In the Florida case, contractors also threatened workers with a gun.[30] The pervasive, commonplace racism that justified inhumane treatment in the minds of employers, as in the La Pisca case, was promoted by FAIR and other anti-immigrant organizations. The company later lost a lawsuit for similar cases and the plaintiffs were awarded $300,000.[31]

The Immigration Act of 1990 and Jiménez's Congressional Testimony

President George H. W. Bush (1924–2018) signed the Immigration Act of 1990 into law on November 29, 1990.[32] Before it became law, pro-immigrant activists, including Jiménez, went to Congress to speak with the legislators.

The activists strongly urged the lawmakers to enact measures that would mitigate civil and human rights violations of immigrants crossing the border without authorization. Despite their efforts, in its final form, the 1990 law authorized "INS personnel to carry firearms, execute warrants, and make arrests for any federal felony which the officer has reasonable grounds to believe has been or will be committed. INS officers will be authorized to use force, including deadly force, after regulations have been promulgated and officers have been properly trained and certified in arrest procedures."[33] Ultimately, the law depended largely on the actions of individual border agents. In other words, unauthorized immigrants were likely to be arrested solely on the subjective judgment of a border agent. The new law also eliminated all judicial recommendations against deportation, thus leaving immigrants without legal recourse when their deportation was unwarranted.

The new law greatly increased the danger to border crossers, granted too much authority to border authorities, and denied immigrants any judicial recourse. In this period of heightened xenophobia and nativism, Jiménez, as director of ILEMP, did not hesitate to respond to this new danger and assault on due process and social justice. In April 1990 she traveled to Washington, DC, to report on border authorities' abuses of immigrants. Jiménez spoke on April 18, 1990, before the Subcommittee on Human Rights and International Organizations of the US House Committee on Foreign Affairs. She told the subcommittee, "Not only immigrants and refugees suffer abuses by immigration officials. Residents of the southern border, including U.S. citizens, whose language, culture, and skin color make them appear 'foreign,' are considered suspect. Incidents of exclusion, illegal arrest and illegal deportation of citizens and immigrants legally in the country are frequently reported."[34]

Jiménez presented to Congress the findings from the ILEMP's one-year study from May 1988 to May 1989. She wrote the introduction to the report, entitled *Human Rights at the Mexico-US Border*.[35] The five areas studied included San Diego, Tucson, Florida, and, in Texas, the Rio Grande Valley and El Paso. Community-based groups collected the data for this important report after they attended the course "How to Document Abuse in the Immigrant Context," cosponsored by the ILEMP. The groups sent their data to Jiménez at her ILEMP office in Houston. "Abuse of authority" in the study was defined as "any action by an immigrant official that, without regard to motive, intent or malice, tends to threaten personal safety, trespass upon human dignity, and/or violate an inherent legal right."[36] Data collection faced the usual obstacles regarding immigrants, legal or undocumented. Obstacles included their fear to report abuses, not knowing that they could report abuses, or believing that their complaints would be ignored.

One of Jiménez's greatest concerns, and a motivation for the study, included the lack of accountability of the border officials' abuse of and violence against undocumented immigrants. The officials too often acted with impunity. It is difficult to explain this social injustice persisting for decades, but Wang believed that norm theory explains the tolerance of abuses by border authorities (i.e., blaming the victim). She wrote, "We also tend to blame victims of discrimination for the negative treatment they receive . . . our subsequent assessments of discriminatory outcome may reinforce the perception that discriminatory outcomes are appropriate and justified."[37] Jiménez's also offered an interpretation of the abuses. She viewed the problem as systemic, not an aberration, in law enforcement and the judiciary. Jiménez expressed this view in her introduction to *Human Rights at the Mexico-US Border*. She wrote, "When it comes to border regions, constitutional safeguards normally employed to constrain police power in the United States are minimally defined. Existing jurisdictional interpretations define INS functions as civil and administrative, rather than criminal law enforcement. As a result, few constitutional safeguards protect the individuals who come under its purview. Violations of rights and abuses of authority are daily occurrences."[38] The ILEMP and Jiménez hoped that the results of their study would convince lawmakers to write policies with new standards for immigration agents. Specifically, Jiménez wanted standards that would end agents' violation with impunity of the civil and human rights of immigrants.

In the process of creating standards to recommend to the INS and Congress, Jiménez's efforts were impressive. She organized four study groups that included, she said, "professors who deal with criminal justice in the area of monitoring law enforcement, people from civilian review boards, grassroots people." Mark Geller from the Police Executive Research Forum, a research and policy organization, also offered information, specifically on the use of force. Jiménez's project was intense. She recalled, "I think I must have sent at least fifteen pounds of paper!" Paraphrasing the study group's message to the INS, Jiménez reported that it said, "This is what we think is the model policy on high-speed chases. This is the model policy . . . that should be appropriate for an adequate complaint process that is functional."[39]

A key ILEMP recommendation to Congress, which eventually became Section 503 of the Immigration Act of 1990, was "to enact national standards and guidelines, defining the proper exercise of INS police power."[40] The recommendation had four parts, including "safeguards for individual rights." Another part, which Congressman Howard Berman (D-CA, 1983–2013) introduced in 1989, called for "a national code of conduct and ethics for (INS) officers." Berman objected to the vast power that INS officers possessed. According to Jiménez, his response to the Border Patrol's demand for more power was, "If you want more authority . . . you have to basically review and redo your use of force policies, deadly force policies, your standards of enforcement. You have to have certification for training in those, and then you have to develop a system to quickly deal with the evaluation of those standards."[41]

Berman's support of ILEMP's demand for the accountability of immigration agents was decisive. Because he pushed for the recommendation, Jiménez explained, it "became known in our circles as the Berman amendment, but it's Section 503 of the '90 law."[42] It required that border agents receive instructions on the authority granted them in the 1990 law, as well as instructions on established standards of conduct. The objective of Section 503 was to reduce the incidences of unwarranted violence by border authorities against unauthorized border crossers.[43]

Jiménez knew that without accountability for misconduct, the human and civil rights of immigrants and US citizens in the border area would continue to be violated. Therefore, she was delighted that Section 503 called for an "expedited, internal review process for violations of such standards."[44] The ILEMP study that impressed Berman had documented a total of 380 incidences of human and civil rights violations, which involved at a minimum 814 victims. More than half of the cases involving victims occurred in Texas.[45]

Of the documented clashes between border agents and immigrants, Jiménez wrote, "Six resulted in death (San Diego; Rio Grande Valley) and 8 (in four areas) in serious injuries. In most of these cases, victims were killed or injured by gunshot wounds to the back as persons obviously attempted to return across the border into Mexico."[46] Victims in the El Paso area had submitted complaints to the American Civil Liberties Union (ACLU), Texas Rural Legal Aid, and the Mexican consulate.[47] Some victims filed class action suits. In addition, "The shooting victims (all Mexican nationals) received support from the Mexican government, which sent the U.S. State Department an official note of protest."[48]

In addition to Jiménez, persons testifying at the Congressional hearing in 1990 included a colleague, Roberto Martínez (1937–2009), director of the US-Mexico Border Program of the AFSC, Representative Jim Bates of California, Steven García of the Border Patrol, and James R. Dorcy, a former special agent of the DOJ. In a congressional hearing titled *Allegations of Violence along the United States-Mexico Border*, the ILEMP denounced border enforcement. However, Jiménez also expressed sympathy for border agents. Her testimony before Congress included the following:

> The flip side of the accountability coin, we believe, is the need to free immigration officials from a "mission impossible." National policy makers have decided to treat the complex socio-economic problems of international migration and illicit drug traffic as domestic police problems. The result is that enforcement authorities on the U.S./Mexico border have had placed on their shoulders responsibility for dealing with our nation's policy to curtail domestic drug consumption, the human exodus from wars in Central America, and the movement of people resulting from the growing debt crisis and capital flight in Mexico and the rest of Latin America. Casting such massive social and political phenomenon into problems of border control is a recipe for disaster and is grossly unfair to immigration officials, particularly the Border Patrol agents.[49]

Nevertheless, Jiménez argued that despite its "mission impossible," the Border Patrol should not ignore or tolerate civil and human rights.

Many organizations knew of, and documented, the violation of civil and human rights by border officials. For example, Amnesty International's

1998 report revealed that victims were subject to "cruel, inhuman or degrading treatment" and that there was "a perception that I.N.S. officers act with
impunity."[50] Human and civil rights violations of US citizens living along the
border also occurred frequently, a fact that led Roberto Martínez to conclude
that "people have come to accept that abuse. . . . It's sad." Martínez reported
that border violence in the San Diego area since 1974 totaled thirty-three
known deaths. The true total was unknown. Enforcement officials, including
the Border Patrol, wounded another forty-eight individuals.[51]

    Martínez and other researchers never obtained accurate statistics on
death and injuries at the border. This was true, Martínez explained, since
"many injuries go unreported because the Border Patrol sends victim back
across the border without filing a report."[52] Besides undocumented immigrants, immigration authorities also violated the civil rights of US citizens.
Agents searched their residences without search warrants and sometimes
confiscated their US birth certificates. Some persons were arrested when
entering the United States, even though they were US citizens and entered
the country legally. In explaining the situation that the Border Patrol sometimes encountered, García said that "hostile crowds of people hurl rocks,
bottles, and insults at Border Patrol agents who venture close to the border."
Regarding allegations of abuses by agents, García countered that any large
organization has a few "officers who exceed the scope of their authority.
These situations are dealt with harshly as soon as they are discovered."
Dorcy, formerly of the DOJ, added that "serious misconduct has never been
tolerated."[53]

    Although Jiménez acknowledged the predicament that border control
entailed, she did not believe that cases of abuse represented aberrations.
Instead, they were "systemic" and were even "reinforced by the agency."
To support her claim, she referred to a meeting with a high-ranking INS official in Washington who "repeatedly referred to undocumented immigrants
as 'wets,'" short for the derogatory term "wetbacks" for undocumented
Mexican immigrants.[54] Undocumented immigrants reported that immigration officials called them *"mugrosos"* (dirt balls), *"marranos"* (swine), and
"putas" (whores). Immigrants also reported that Latino agents were the
most abusive verbally. A problem with demeaning terms, civil rights experts

believed, was that "brutal language itself foments an atmosphere conducive to brutal acts."[55] Statistics indicated that border authorities unfairly targeted Latino immigrants. Jiménez noted that although the Border Patrol in 1987 interrogated 18.5 million individuals, only 1 million were arrested. She therefore concluded that "over 17 million were legally entitled to be in the country."[56] A few years later, in 1994, Jiménez reported that "while Mexican nationals account for only about 55% of the undocumented people in the United States, 90% of the people arrested on United States borders are Mexican nationals."[57]

Jiménez knew that violations of civil and human rights of Mexicans by border authorities and white vigilante groups also happened to other Latino immigrants. In a meeting with Jiménez in 1990, Daryl Borquist, an official of the US Justice Department, denied that violence at the border was racially motivated. However, Jiménez later reportedly "scoffed at Borquist's assessment. She said that violence on the border was selective primarily against Mexicans and secondarily against Central Americans."[58] Besides the Border Patrol, white vigilante groups were a threat to border crossers.[59] Vigilantes attacked two border crossers who reported the assault to Martínez. He later told the congressional panel that the victims had "their heads split wide open with flashlights."[60] Salvadorans experienced their own kind of harassment. Specifically, although they could seek political asylum according to US immigration law, immigration authorities often coerced them into "voluntary" deportation. The practice of dissuading Salvadorans from seeking asylum culminated in the *Orantes* injunction from *Orantes-Hernández v. González* (2009), which "prohibits DHS [Department of Homeland Security] from coercing or otherwise improperly encouraging Salvadorans detained by immigration authorities to waive their rights."[61]

Problems within INS itself greatly contributed to the nation's difficulties in controlling illegal immigration. Evidence of mismanagement dated from the 1970s and continued into the 1990s. This problem was well documented in a study published by the GAO. The GAO reported in 1990 that the INS had not improved in its "overlap" in investigations. An example of overlap occurred in Houston in January 1990. In this case INS agents went to Houston to set up a sting against a counterfeit green-card operation in some motel rooms. They asked the motel desk clerk who the persons in the rooms were. The confused clerk answered, "Well, you guys are." It became obvious that the group being targeted in the sting were themselves undercover INS agents. Other findings of the GAO revealed that "the agency's books are in 'chaotic' and 'deplorable' conditions and that its decentralized management promotes 'fragmentation' that borders on anarchy."[62]

Militarization of the Border: Violation of Human Rights

Jiménez and other immigrant rights activists became very troubled by the new border enforcement measures in the Immigration Act of 1990. Section 503, the Berman Amendment, was designed to provide accountability of the abusive actions of the Border Patrol against the undocumented immigrants they arrested. However, immigrant and human rights groups knew border authorities would not always comply with regulations. A part of Jiménez's work as the director of the ILEMP in Houston, which she did effectively, included recording and reporting these abuses.

The violation of immigrants' human rights concerned many organizations—for example, the AFSC and Human Rights Watch. They both documented abuses of immigrants by INS agents. Aryeh Neier, executive director of Human Rights Watch, criticized the INS because, he believed, "agents behave as if they are accountable to no one." Although agents were officially prohibited to violate civil and human rights, the Border Patrol exercised broad authority, including entering homes without warrants within twenty-five miles of the border. Wherever the agents went, Neier reported, "Beatings, rough physical treatment, intimidation tactics and verbal abuse are routine."[63] For instance, in Jiménez's 1992 article, "War in the Borderlands," she reported that violent action against immigrants included striking or threatening to strike them with a flashlight or cattle prod and "unjustified shootings resulting in death."[64]

The ILEMP and Jiménez never ceased monitoring the activities of border authorities in communities at the United States–Mexico border. Monitoring became necessary because, as Jiménez astutely observed, "fanned by drug and xenophobic hysteria, the borderlands have become, in effect, a 'deconstitutionalized' zone."[65] In its zeal to crack down on drug traffickers and ordinary undocumented job-seeking immigrants, the INS frequently also harassed US citizens in the border regions. In El Paso the Border Patrol routinely stopped residents who, consequently, "had to be prepared to prove their rights to be in the country at all times or face the prospect of arrest, detention, and possibly even deportation by Border Patrol agents."[66]

An out-of-control Border Patrol was evident at Bowie High School in El Paso, Texas.[67] The violations of civil rights at Bowie High School eventually resulted in *Murillo et al. v. Musegades et al.* of 1992.[68] According to sociologist Timothy J. Dunn, the legal case became "the most successful, formal, and large-scale challenge to Border Patrol enforcement excesses in local history, and arguably along the entire border."[69] Violations at the high school illustrated the fact that discrimination was commonplace and that harassment was a daily occurrence for border residents. In the 1980s, however, local activists organized to end this abuse. In 1986 the El Paso community formed the League for Immigration, Border Rights and Education (LIBRE). The organizers, according to Dunn, included "a small group of mainly leftist Anglo and Chicano activists and intellectuals (many college students or recent graduates) from both El Paso [Texas] and Juárez [Mexico]."[70] One of the activists' effective tactics involved persuading the local media to report incidences of abuse by the Border Patrol. Previously, the Border Patrol had controlled the information given to the media, but the new media coverage put it on the defensive.

Jiménez provided valuable advice to LIBRE. With her encouragement LIBRE members and other local groups formed the BRC in 1989. More importantly, as noted in chapter 6, she sent the new organization greatly needed funds. The funds enabled the BRC to hire a person to collect statements from the residents who had been harassed, even beaten, by border authorities. The statements provided valuable information for the plaintiffs in the *Murillo* case. Jiménez's imprint and the focus of ILEMP's mission in the border areas were unmistakable in the legal struggle in El Paso. There, Dunn wrote, the BRC "raised the issues of human rights in border enforcement and the near total unaccountability of federal enforcement agencies to local communities."[71]

Testimony in the *Murillo* case revealed questionable conduct and abuse committed by the Border Patrol against El Paso residents. For example, agents frequently entered Bowie High School looking for undocumented immigrants and often raced through school grounds in their green-and-white utility vehicles. Testimony also revealed that Border Patrol agents observed female students during their physical education classes through their binoculars.[72] In a specific example of misconduct, a Border Patrol confronted Suzie Díaz, a 16-year-old US citizen. The agent questioned her about her citizenship status and then, she recounted, "shoved me, pushed me, and I fell to the ground. He put his foot on my chest and started kicking me."[73] In his ruling on *Murillo v. Musegades*, Judge Lucius D. Bunton III (1924–2001) of the Western District of Texas wrote:

> A review of the actions of the INS and its Agents [Border Patrol] in this case demonstrates Defendants violated Plaintiffs' Fourth Amendment rights. . . .The INS in this case discriminated against Plaintiffs in violation of their Fifth Amendment rights to equal protection. The INS has repeatedly and illegally stopped, questioned, detained, frisked, arrested, and searched Plaintiffs and numerous other students from the Bowie High School District . . . the illegal and abusive conduct of the El Paso Border Patrol was directed against Plaintiffs, staff, and residents in the Bowie High School District *solely* because of their mere immutable appearance as Hispanics.[74]

The Border Patrol agreed to comply with the out-of-court settlement to cease their practices that violated the Fourth and Fifth Amendments rights of Mexican Americans and legal Mexican immigrant residents in El Paso. Significantly, Judge Bunton ruled that the court should supervise the Border Patrol's compliance with the settlement for five years.[75]

The Border: A Deconstitutionalized Zone

As director of ILEMP, Jiménez focused on immigrant-related issues at the US-Mexico border and on what alarmed her most, the militarization of the border region. Dunn defined "militarization" broadly as "the use of military rhetoric and ideology, as well as military tactics, strategy, technology, equipment and forces."[76] On the twenty-fifth of February 1992, ILEMP published its third study, a sixty-four-page report entitled *Sealing Our Borders: The Human Toll*. It documented over 1,200 cases of abuse by the INS, including the Border Patrol, in the period from 1989 to 1991. The ILEMP had trained its staff and volunteers, training that Jiménez created when hired to head the ILEMP, in border communities to document immigration law enforcement transgressions. The ILEMP staff and volunteers used a software program called WINSTON in the collection and analysis of the information they collected.[77] Jiménez told the *Houston Chronicle* that the report was timely "in light of the preoccupation in particular areas of the country with increasing the presence of immigration agents, Border Patrol or military troops on the border."[78]

The 1992 report was one of several produced during the 1990s that criticized the INS's violations of civil and human rights. The other reports included five between 1992 and 1997 by the Human Rights Watch, a 1997 report by four state advisory committees to the United States Commission on Civil Rights, and a 1998 report by Amnesty International (AI), mentioned earlier.[79] The Mexican newspaper *Notimex* wrote about the AI report and included comments by Jiménez. She said, "We have to acknowledge the weight that Amnesty [International] has and for that there is hope that this report has an impact not only among immigration agencies but also before Congress."[80] In other words, she hoped the AI report would help to end the civil and human rights violations by border authorities.

ILEMP's *Sealing Our Border* addressed major problems at the border. It documented 1,274 cases accusing the Border Patrol of "sexual, verbal, and physical abuse, false arrest, and illegal deportation."[81] The report's recommendations included the following: (1) that there be on-site congressional hearings in major cities along the border, (2) that the complaint process, which was handled by the DOJ, be made more accessible to complainants, (3) that civilian oversight of federal immigration officers be established, (4) that the DOJ investigate and prosecute incidences of abuse, and (5) that, in the course of its activities, the Border Patrol not violate the human rights of immigrants, refugees, and residents of the US-Mexico border.[82] Significantly, a bill for a citizen advisory panel, ILEMP's third recommendation, was introduced to Congress by Senator Dennis De Concini (D-AZ) in 1992. The US Commission on Immigration Reform supported the idea of the panel. Unfortunately, Congress did not pass the bill.

Jiménez criticized the increased militarization of the border on many occasions. She stated in a 1987 article that the grave situation dated at least to 1981. In "Border Militarization: The History, the Effect, the Response," she wrote that "the historical separation of police and military authority was revised by adding amendments to the Posse Comitatus Act (1878), relaxing proscriptions against using military equipment and personnel for civilian law enforcement."[83] The Posse Comitatus Act limited the federal government's use of the military for state law enforcement. The concept of maintaining a separation between police and the military emerged as early as the colonial period. Colonists objected bitterly to Great Britain maintaining troops in the colonies, even during peacetime, a practice Parliament authorized with the Quartering Act of 1765. The act "cast the British forces in the role of overseers and, even, oppressors." A century later, the Posse Comitatus Act reflected another unpopular situation, the US Army's ten-year military occupation of the former Confederate states following the Civil War. Enacted shortly after the Civil War, the Posse Comitatus Act "largely prohibits the use of the active duty armed forces in executing the domestic laws of the United States."[84] Unfortunately, President Ronald Reagan (1981–1989) later broke with this important and long-standing separation of the police and the military during his War on Drugs.

Jiménez knew that the militarization of the border would result in human and civil rights abuses. The Texas border with Mexico was populated by Mexican Americans and legal residents of Mexican descent. The possibility of these groups being mistaken for undocumented persons because of racial profiling, therefore, was very real. When Congress passed the Anti-Drug Act in 1986, the Justice Department, and INS, Jiménez recalled, "held the view that the military could also be used to combat the flow of undocumented immigrants," and the "Border Patrol received M-14 rifles, created counterinsurgency units and received training in riot control."[85] In addition, the military doctrine of low-intensity conflict (LIC) emerged during the 1980s.

Dunn defined LIC as "the establishment and maintenance of social control over targeted civilian populations through the implementation of a broad range of sophisticated measures via the coordinated and integrated efforts of police, paramilitary, and military forces."[86] Jiménez also understood the economic implications of the militarization of the border. It was clear to her, she wrote, that "the use of military force is a tacit indication of the high priority placed by elites in their quest for dominance and wealth," including large profits and low wages.[87] In the elites' pursuit of power and wealth, the most vulnerable workers—the undocumented immigrants—paid a high price, even their lives at the border.

Operations Hold-the-Line and Rio Grande

The militarization of the border included a series of operations by the Border Patrol designed to block unauthorized entry into the country. The operations made entry more difficult or impossible along much of the border. Unfortunately, the border operations also contributed to thousands of preventable deaths of emigrants when they passed through sweltering deserts in their attempt to enter the United States. Referencing two studies on the known deaths between 1994 and 2009, Jiménez reported that, at a minimum, one migrant died every day.[88] She also noted in 1999 that the Border Patrol's increased vigilance at the border had not ended emigrants' unauthorized entry into the country in search of jobs.[89] In other words, she and researchers concluded that the operations' objective to reduce the immigrant presence in the country failed. Furthermore, studies proved the opposite development occurred because "the probability of return migration [to Mexico] has fallen, yielding an increase in the number of long-term undocumented residents."[90]

Operation Hold-the-Line, originally called Operation Blockade, started September 19, 1993, in El Paso and became the model followed elsewhere on the southwest border. It presented a change in border control because its goal was to prevent entry of undocumented immigrants instead of apprehending them after entering the country. Dunn called the change the "deterrence-displacement strategy." It involved stationing Border Patrol agents for their

entire shift at fixed locations, called "X's," at the border between El Paso
and the Mexican city of Ciudad Juárez.[91] The highly visible placement of
the Border Patrol succeeded in discouraging illegal entry into the United
States. At the international level, however, the operation strained the relationship between the United States and Mexico at a sensitive time. The US
Congress had scheduled a vote on the North American Free Trade Agreement (NAFTA) in November, only two months after Operation Hold-the-
Line started.

The second part of Operation Hold-the-Line was the "displacement" of
the apprehended immigrants. Specifically, the Border Patrol took the immigrants to the port of entry of Palmas, Chihuahua-Columbus, New Mexico,
where the immigrants continued on foot to El Paso, sixty miles away.
The location in New Mexico required them to "walk home through the desert,
[which] sparked protest from Catholic Church officials."[92] As for the unauthorized immigrants who decided to avoid border crossing in the El Paso area
altogether, they entered the country through the deadly deserts of Arizona,
where many of them died.

Although entering the United States became even more deadly with
this and later operations, undocumented immigrants continued to cross the
border in pursuit of work. The second deterrence operation, Operation Rio
Grande, started August 25, 1997, in the Brownsville, Texas, area called the
McAllen Border Patrol sector. It continued the strategy introduced with
Operation Hold-the-Line that placed border agents at fixed intervals, "X's,"
along the border. Operation Rio Grande reduced the number of illegal entries.
However, the number of persons entering with fraudulent documents rose.
According to an official in Brownsville, "There's a lot of fraud out there, and
a lot is attributed to Operation Rio Grande. When they can't come across the
river, they're going to try to come through another way."[93]

Houston's Demographic Changes and
Police Harassment

Houston's demography became more diverse in the 1980s with the arrival
of Central Americans who fled their war-torn homelands. Unfortunately, the
xenophobia that emerged in the 1990s complicated racial-ethnic relations

in Houston, and the possibility of racist conflicts involving the immigrant community increased. Jiménez believed that the xenophobia resulted, in part, from concern over the newcomers' impact on politics. She told Jo Ann Zuniga of the *Houston Chronicle*, "It's not the weakness of immigrants that is causing the hostility, but their perceived strength and growing potential political power. When politicians get United States citizens worked up about immigrants taking away their jobs, the politicians are worried about their own jobs being taken away."[94]

Nativism and xenophobia typically increase whenever the economy is weak and immigration is or is perceived to be on the rise. The economy in Houston, in fact, weakened in the 1980s following a major downturn in the petroleum energy sector. For Houston's Hispanics, that decade became especially difficult and "households at the bottom of Houston's economic ladder nearly doubled," according to the US Census Bureau. Demographer Steve Murdock added, "It is likely that continuing immigration played a very large role in the dramatic income changes recorded among Hispanics."[95] The explanation for the change was that most Hispanic immigrants took low-paying jobs, and their salaries depressed the average salaries of all Hispanics. However, despite this explanation, Edward Castillo, director of the counseling center Centro Aztlan, viewed the new immigrants positively. In 1990 he said, "They don't know they are supposed to be humble. They see the struggle as more of the haves vs. the have-nots, and while they see a gap between what they have and what '*los Americanos*' have, they figure they can pretty much close it with enough hard work."[96]

The new immigrant groups joined the older Hispanic community in Houston who had made only incremental political progress over the years. In 1990 Hispanics, who were only 8 percent of the voters, totaled 288,494, or about 20 percent, of Houston's population. However, only 154,400 were citizens.[97] In other words, Hispanics were not a significant force in politics.[98] A study of the Houston barrio of Magnolia Park in 1990 revealed that political candidates for city and county offices usually did not campaign there. In addition, "Some local candidates had little or no knowledge of Magnolia [Park], Houston's largest barrio."[99] Leonel Castillo, a well-known community activist, believed that "Hispanics still feel they are on the bottom of the totem pole. But the transition has already begun."[100]

Besides a lack of political influence, another situation greatly concerned Jiménez in the 1990s. It was the joint operations by two or more law enforcement groups, typically the INS and local police departments, who targeted immigrant communities. The trend of joint operations significantly increased the possibility of violations of human and civil rights. This, in fact, occurred in 1994 in Katy, a city in the greater metropolitan Houston area. On May 18, 1994, the Katy Police Department (KPD) and INS officials conducted a joint sweep in which they arrested eighty persons at an "informal labor pool." Many more persons suspected of being undocumented were questioned.[101] Police action reportedly included entering homes without warrants, a violation of the Fourth Amendment. Civil rights groups, including LULAC, the ACLU, the AFSC, and the Lawyers' Committee for Civil Rights, strongly criticized the joint raids. A week after the raids, LULAC held a press conference. Johnny Mata, LULAC's district director, claimed that the KPD had created "an atmosphere of fear, intimidation, and distress within the Hispanic community of Katy . . . [and] . . . went far beyond the intended scope of assisting INS in its enforcement of immigration laws."[102]

The civil rights organizations denounced the harsh actions of the INS and KPD, who, in turn, insisted that they acted on complaints about the local immigrant population. However, the heavy-handed tactics of the INS and KPD that included "blanket neighborhood searches" were unconstitutional, according to immigration attorney Joe Vail. He added, "They (law officers) have to have reasonable suspicion of alienage. Brown skin is not enough."[103] Debbie Perkins of the ACLU agreed, adding that the US Constitution "provides protection to all, not only to citizens, to due process," a fact lost on officials in Katy where persons "were stopped and questioned because they looked Hispanic."[104] Authorities in Katy pulled over drivers as they were exiting a highway or were driving down a road and conducted sweeps near two landscaping companies and corners where day laborers stood to get work. One man was arrested while shopping at a grocery store, and a woman was questioned as she was picking up her child at a school bus stop.[105] The INS arrested any individual who could not produce proper documentation.

Jiménez publicly criticized the joint operations in Katy, as well as similar raids in nearby Conroe and Spring Branch and in Georgetown, near Austin,

Texas.[106] In the Katy operation, eleven immigrants who were legally in the country were caught in the sweep. Most of the remaining persons were arrested and deported the next day.[107] Jiménez sympathized with persons harassed by the police and INS. A Mexican immigrant herself, it angered her that "it's accepted that if you're foreign born that you *can* be discriminated against."[108] Joint operations continued in the area. In July 1994, two months after the Katy raid, Jiménez reported that the INS and the local police conducted a joint operation at a Houston apartment complex. There, she added, "HPD closed the entrance while INS went from apartment to apartment."[109]

Following the Katy incident, twelve Hispanics sued the KPD. In 1997 US District Court Judge Melinda Harmon approved a settlement ending two lawsuits against the KPD. The plaintiffs, who received guidance from Jiménez, strongly objected to the discriminatory action by the local police but they did not seek damages. Instead, they asked that the KPD establish a policy against targeting persons based on their appearance. Raúl Gutiérrez, speaking for the plaintiffs, said that they wanted "civilized treatment" from the police and "wanted all Katy residents to be treated fairly and in accord-ance with the law."[110] The KPD also agreed not to question persons about their immigration status.

What concerned Jiménez the most was the unfortunate repercussions in Katy from the combined forces of the police and the INS. On this point, she said, "When local police work with the INS, like they did in this case, it undermines the trust for police in the immigrant community . . . community-based law enforcement requires the trust of the community to work."[111] Immigrants then and now are less likely to report crimes against them to the police and, there-fore, are more vulnerable. The public is also potentially at risk whenever criminals can evade arrest. In other words, society benefits, and is more just, when it seeks to protect every person, without exception.

Conclusion

In the late 1980s and the 1990s, the period discussed in this chapter, the racist discrimination against and marginalization of Mexican Americans and legal residents of Mexican origin, as well as the victimization of the undocumented

Mexicans by immigration authorities, became serious problems. However, Jiménez and other Mexican Americans responded to the problems time and again. Their victories, large and small, represented the fight against common-place racism, a fight to make society truer to its values of social justice and equality. The issues tackled included, for example, HISD's failure to provide pedagogically appropriate education to its minority students, or, in Houston and South Texas, the violation of the civil rights of citizens and immigrants alike by the police and/or border patrol.

Jiménez, as director of ILEMP, focused on immigrants' rights issues at the border, but she and other activists also dealt with local problems, such as job discrimination, wage theft, and joint police and INS harassment of the immigrant community. For example, Jiménez and many other individuals and organizations reacted vigorously to the racially inflammatory radio ads by FAIR. Their criticism of FAIR's anti-immigrant campaign was strong enough that FAIR stopped its ad campaign after only two days. Job discrimination, another problem, became significant because of the sanctions imposed on employers by IRCA. A subsequent rise in unemployment affected Hispanic citizens, legal residents, and undocumented immigrants alike. The Commu-nity Task Force initiated measures to minimize the harm that job sanctions created. Sometimes workers took direct action against discrimination, exploitation, and wage theft, such as the successful lawsuit against the La Pisca company.

Jiménez objected to the social injustice that targeted the immigrant community in Katy, creating an "atmosphere of fear." Specifically, the police and the INS created fear by their coordinated sweeps and other activities to arrest undocumented persons. Authorities violated the rights of the targeted community, for example, by entering homes without warrants and using racial profiling to arrest individuals. Jiménez offered advice to Hispanics in Katy who successfully sued the Katy Police Department. In their settlement the plaintiffs did not ask for money damages but only to receive "civilized treatment . . . in accordance to the law."

As director of the ILEMP, Jiménez was most concerned with the civil and human rights of immigrants at the southern border of Texas. The new federal "deterrence-displacement" strategy forced unauthorized migrants entering the country to pass through deadly Arizona deserts, routes that the federal government knew would result in fatalities.[112] Fortunately, immigrant rights activists enjoyed some victories, such as Section 503 of the Immigration Act of 1990. It provided for the accountability of border agents in their mistreatment of the undocumented. Jiménez was a major advocate of this provision and contributed to the inclusion of Section 503 in the 1990 law. Still the danger to residents because of the militarization along the Mexico-US border remained and will, in fact, result in the death of a young US citizen, discussed in the following chapter.

Chapter 8

Jiménez, Anti-Mexican Immigration Laws, and Hispanic Activism

> The demilitarization and the strong accountability methods for the border
> policing will come only when people view people that cross the border,
> and the residents of the border, as human beings.
> —Maria Jiménez[1]

Jiménez and the pro-immigrant community faced new and ominous challenges in the mid- to late 1990s when the commonplace prejudices against immigrants, especially Mexicans, reached new levels. First, a harsh anti-immigrant law passed in California, followed by similar laws in other states. Tougher border control created hardships and led to a significant increase in the deaths of individuals entering the country without authorization. In addition, the militarization of the border led to civil and human rights violations, including the unjustified killing of a young US citizen. Domestic and foreign developments also created difficulties for the Mexican-origin community. For example, new laws passed by Congress in 1996 resulted in tremendous hardships for undocumented and legal residents. Finally, developments in Mexico resulted in an increased emigration of Mexicans to many cities in the United States, including Houston.

Although the 1990s were difficult years, Jiménez remained as dedicated as ever to protecting the human and civil rights of the immigrant population as the director of ILEMP in Houston. Her desire to advance social justice even extended to the Zapatista rebels who fought for Indigenous rights in Chiapas, Mexico. Jiménez exemplified important concepts in CRT: it is imperative for activists of color to engage in critical storytelling, to be the voices for the voiceless, and to attack "embedded preconceptions that marginalize others or conceal their humanity."[2]

Anti-Immigrant Legislation, Proposition 187, and Jiménez's Reaction to Nativism

As the ILEMP director for the AFSC, Jiménez focused on problems at the border between Texas and Mexico, but she also fought racial injustice in Houston. For example, in 1993 she led a coalition that organized a pro-immigration march and rally in response to a rise of nativism. She explained her belief thusly: "We are promoting understanding and tolerance. . . . The whole mood of the country is so strongly against immigrants as to deny their humanity. The government is set to deny citizenship to children born here from the undocumented. That has not been denied since slavery days."[3]

Unfortunately, politicians, motivated by their political ambitions, exac-erbated the enmity toward immigrants. California Governor Pete Wilson, for one, aggressively called for an end to services that were legally granted to undocumented immigrants, including education and healthcare for their chil-dren. In 1994, Wilson urged Californians to vote for Proposition 187, called "Save Our State" by its advocates. Voters passed Prop 187 on November 8, 1994, at the same time that they reelected Wilson. Proposition 187 became an international controversy when hundreds of protesters in Mexico shouted, "Racism, racism!" in front of the US embassy in Mexico City. Over a hundred Mexican riot police were summoned to protect the embassy compound.[4]

Prop 187 was significant for the precedent it set for other states, although it alarmed many organizations. For example, the ACLU and MALDEF imme-diately challenged Prop187. The day after it was passed, a US district court issued a temporary restraining order that barred it from being implemented.

The court barred the new law almost in its entirety because the "state law intruded on the federal law to regulate immigration."[5] In other words, a state could not legally pass and regulate immigration laws because these were the responsibility solely of the federal government. The California law, and similar measures in Arizona a few years later, clearly reflected the intense anti-immigrant sentiment of the time. Governor Jan Brewer of Arizona (2009–2015) exploited this enmity for political reasons.

The hostile political climate created havoc in immigrant communities.[6] Undocumented workers were vulnerable and their deportation rates broke records. The American public felt reassured by media coverage that showed undocumented workers in chains being arrested by immigration authorities at worksites. The raids comforted the viewers because they believed that the federal government was cracking down on "illegals." Jiménez and other pro-immigrant activists, who also knew the value of public events, organized protests and rallies for October 17, 1994, against Prop 187. The largest protest occurred in Los Angeles, with about sixty-five thousand persons participating. The number of marchers in Houston was lower, estimated at "several hundreds."[7] Despite these efforts, California voters approved Prop 187 a month later.

Jiménez, referencing the protest march in Houston, said, "People are tired of this anti-immigrant sentiment. This is a first step to show that we're not going to take it anymore." Proposition 187, she added, imposed morally questionable measures against Hispanics. For example, she said, it "would require teachers to turn over children they suspected of being illegal immigrants to authorities. It obligates doctors to turn in patients they suspect."[8] The Houston groups that participated in the protest included the Centro de Recursos para Centroamericanos (or CRECEN), the Hispanic Education Forum, LULAC, the Gulfton Area Neighborhood Organization (GANO), the Magnolia Multipurpose Center, and Hispanic Vietnam veterans.

Jiménez believed that the voters' approval of Proposition 187 "was sort of the bell that woke up the sleeping giant" and "sparked a lot of concern all over the country."[9] Had it not been barred by the court, Proposition 187 would have eliminated public benefits for undocumented immigrants—for example, public education for undocumented immigrant children and prenatal care for undocumented women. However, Governor Wilson held the commonplace belief that Mexican women were "hyper-fertile baby machines" and issued an executive order in November 1994 to deny them prenatal service. The public outcry against his action included an "organized response of immigrant rights groups, civil rights lawyers, and concerned health practitioners."[10] The executive order was to go into effect December 1, 1994, but the San Francisco Superior Court Judge Stuart R. Pollak "issued the first temporary restraining order against the measure."[11] Subsequent restraining orders also blocked the executive order until Wilson's successor, Governor Gray Davis, signed a bill that allowed prenatal service for pregnant immigrant women to continue.[12]

Jiménez considered Proposition 187 a serious blow that was "devastating for the civil and human rights of immigrant communities, in particular Latino immigrant communities." It also, she believed, would "create a great deal of polarization between ethnic groups and increase hate between peoples."[13] Ultimately, Wilson suffered politically for his support of the proposition because Hispanics strongly objected to his views, which they considered racist. Republican politicians took careful note of this reaction and wanted to avoid alienating Hispanic voters, as Wilson had.[14] Critical legal scholar and LatCrit Kevin R. Johnson concluded that the backlash against "Wilson's support for Proposition 187 in 1994 taught Republican politicians the potential downside of taking strong anti-immigrant positions that angered Latinas/os."[15]

The public's views on immigrants and immigration, in general, were uninformed and misguided. Regarding the rise of nativism in the 1990s, Jiménez wrote in 1995 that the "anti-immigration hysteria that exists in America today is really an anti-Mexican hysteria. . . . It's about the Spanish-speaking, southern border-crossers." Fortunately, most people believed, correctly, that the typical border-crosser came to work and not to commit crimes. They emigrated for a better life, but, at the same time, they contributed significantly to the nation's economy. For example, Jiménez reported that "the total immigrant income in 1989 was $285 billion, most of which is spent on U.S. goods and services."[16]

Another major misconception was that immigrants who migrated to the United States were a drain on the economy. On the contrary, many legal immigrants who qualified for public benefits did not use them. A study that used data from the 1996 census indicated, like the 1989 American Public Welfare Association study before it, that legalized households underutilized public services and other benefits for which they qualified.[17] Ken McDonnell, analyst for the Employee Benefit Research Institute, based in Washington, DC, claimed that these persons "don't apply for it because of cultural or linguistic reasons, or because they fear using public health services will harm their chances at obtaining citizenship."[18]

Although most immigrants, legal and undocumented, struggled to survive, they often encountered the false belief that they came to exploit this country's social services and to do so without working. A study in 1996 by the DOL confirmed, according to Labor Secretary Robert Reich (1993–1997), that this group "faced extraordinary obstacles to achieving the American Dream."[19] The 1996 DOL report also found that the males in the study were "working or actively looking for work" at a higher rate "than other minorities or Anglos."[20] Women were also eager to work and wanted US citizens to believe this fact. As one Honduran woman in Houston explained, "If the people here who are not in favor (of immigrants) would see the way we have to live, they wouldn't be so against us coming. They would see the *pobrecitos* (poor little ones). We come out of such need. We're willing to do any work."[21]

Immigrants who settled in Texas expected to work hard to survive. It was not like California, where more social services might be available.[22] In addition, a news article in the *Houston Chronicle* claimed that a movement in 1995 in Texas like the one behind Proposition 187 was less likely because the "level of hostility is lower" against immigrants. It added that "if there is anything approaching universal sentiment about the undocumented in Texas, it appears to be the perception that those who come here do so to work." The situation in Texas also differed from that in California because Texas had a "skimpier social service net" for the undocumented, as well as for Texas citizens.[23] For example, a 1996 study found that the Houston area had the highest percentage in the nation of residents without "guaranteed access to health care."[24] A later study by Washington-based Center for Immigrant Studies reported in 2000 that 59 percent of Houston's immigrant families had no health insurance, the highest percentage in the nation. The same study revealed that "Houston also had the highest overall uninsured population."[25]

Push-Pull Factors: Mexico and the United States

Jiménez, as a Mexican immigrant and immigrant rights activist, understood the push-pull factors that contributed to the emigration to the United States. Push-pull factors were a reality in Texas because the conditions there affected those in Mexico and vice versa. The Texas-Mexico connection has been a constant part of the state's history. In the 1990s Jiménez focused on many problems, including political asylum, Mexico's weak economy, NAFTA, and the Zapatista rebellion in Chiapas. For example, in the case of asylum, Mexican applications for political asylum in the United States rose sharply when the political and economic situation in Mexico deteriorated, a push factor. Many of these asylum applicants had criticized the Mexican government and feared persecution.[26]

Obtaining asylum status was a difficult process. Jiménez noted that the number of asylum grantees from Mexico had been zero in the years 1990–1993. Fortunately, a few immigrant judges believed that Mexican applicants who reported "abuse, torture, and fear for their lives" might qualify for and could apply for asylum. The possibility of asylum increased because "individual Federal immigration agents and judges [ruled] on a case-by-case basis." The judges' decision to grant political asylum to Mexican political dissidents was unusual and significant because it acknowledged that there were human rights abuses in Mexico. As for Jiménez, she told the *New York Times* that the judges' decisions "corroborate what Amnesty International and Americas Watch have reported, that there are no prosecutions of persons—the police, or army or anyone—who commit these (human rights) violations" in Mexico.[27] Unfortunately, in the fiscal year of 1994, ending in September 30, the United States granted asylum to only five Mexicans, far short of the number of applications for asylum for that year, which exceeded nine thousand.[28] In the fiscal year of 1995, fifty-five Mexicans were granted political asylum from over nine thousand applicants.[29]

Political persecution was one of reasons that Mexicans emigrated to the United States. However, Jiménez believed that a major reason in the 1990s for legal and unauthorized entry into the United States was NAFTA of 1994. It was a push factor because it failed to include a provision to protect Mexican workers in Mexico. This failure led to job losses in Mexico and the emigration of large numbers of workers to the United States in search of employment. Besides losing their livelihood in their own country, Mexicans crossing the border without visas would encounter border authorities. Jiménez criticized the policies and practices that viewed unauthorized immigration as a law enforcement problem, instead of a labor issue. The indifference to the plight of workers was intolerable and needed to be changed, according to Jiménez, "from the corporate standpoint . . . (to) our standpoint, from the human rights standpoint, from the standpoint of social justice."[30]

Jiménez believed that the flawed NAFTA negotiations did not address the universal right for labor to migrate legally from where jobs were lost to where they were available. The AFSC, Jiménez wrote in 1994, "went on record in hearings in San Diego and in hearings in Houston (conducted by the US Trade Representative), as asking that the issues of migration and labor mobility be included in NAFTA negotiations. These issues should now be considered regulatory issues and they should be recognized as an important part of economic development."[31] Recommendations that would benefit workers did not materialize because concessions to labor would reduce profits to businesses in the United States and, Jiménez asserted, because of "old prejudices toward the Mexican immigrant population."[32]

Jiménez and the AFSC had very few allies in their opposition to NAFTA. Labor unions feared the loss of jobs to Mexican immigrants and the National Council de la Raza (NCLR) opposed the possibility of another Bracero Program. Fortunately, Jiménez wrote, the Southwest Voter Registration Institute acted and "started a nationwide series of conferences on the implications of NAFTA for the Latino communities in the United States."[33] In addition, MALDEF took the major step of convincing the NCLR to cosponsor a Latino Summit on NAFTA. Although it did not directly address the right of workers' mobility, it was, Jiménez believed, "the first time that Latino organizations took a position on creating a tri-national commission to look at migration issues."[34]

In 1995 the weak Mexican economy, an important push factor, alarmed the administration of President Bill Clinton (1993–2001). A spike in immigration of about 3 million immigrants, in fact, did occur between 1995 and 2000 because of the "peso crisis," which dated from December 1994.[35] To address the peso and immigration problems, President Clinton proposed a $40 billion loan package for Mexico. Jiménez questioned the effect of the loan on reducing Mexican immigration because, she said, "the whole issue of immigration was independent" of the United States' efforts to stabilize the peso. The controversial loan had supporters and critics in Houston. For example, the city benefited from the aid to Mexico because, as the Houston's Hispanic Chamber of Commerce explained, the city had "about 560 companies with business ties with Mexico that provide more than 650,000 direct and indirect jobs to Houston-area residents."[36] On the other hand, a critic in Houston, Tony Cantú of the Committee of Solidarity with the People of Mexico, believed that the loan would "only empower certain elite groups in Mexico and the people will be left paying for it." In fact 3,000 businesses failed and 2 million workers lost their jobs.[37]

Jiménez and Danger at the Border

In her commitment to social justice, Jiménez tackled a variety of problems. Among her greatest concerns was the violence, especially by border authorities, committed against immigrants. In the case of undocumented immigrants, their deaths also resulted from drowning when crossing dangerous waterways or dehydration when passing through scorching hot deserts. Frequently the identity of the victims remained unknown. Jiménez, therefore, became active in the Desert Angels and other groups that formed to identify dead border crossers using their remains and DNA testing.[38] Another activity that Jiménez pursued, beginning in the mid-1990s, was to urge politicians and academics to address the problem of deaths at the border.[39] The indifference or disinterest of the deaths frustrated Jiménez. In 2004 she told the *Houston Chronicle*, "Back then, no one even knew how many people were killed on the border. No one cared."[40]

As director of the ILEMP, Jiménez contributed to several studies on immigration—for example, "The Human Costs of Border Enforcement at the Texas-Mexico Border."[41] The ILEMP sponsored the study, and the Center for Immigration Research at UH conducted it. It examined the years between 1985 and 1994. The study reported that at least 1,400 persons, and perhaps twice that number, died trying to cross the border and that most deaths resulted from drowning. Jiménez announced the publication of the study in a press release on March 14, 1996. In it she wrote, "The immigration bills now before Congress would worsen the problem of violence and abuse on our southern border. . . . We believe that the proposed border enforcement legislation is fundamentally misguided because it does not respond to the two major forces driving people to risk attempting illegal entry into this country: the terror of war and the crushing burden of poverty and economic dislocation."[42]

Years later, in 2009, Jiménez wrote *Humanitarian Crisis: Migrant Deaths at the US-Mexico Border*. It covered the years 1994 to 2009 and detailed the tragic fate of undocumented immigrants who encountered many hardships and even death.[43] Although accurate numbers were not known, she wrote that the total of known deaths was 5,607.[44] Sadly, the border crossers knew the risks they took. In *Humanitarian Crisis* Jiménez wrote, "Every time they attempt to cross the border and risk suffering and death, migrants knowingly risk their lives for the higher commitment to a dignified life for self, family, community, and humanity."[45]

Later studies confirmed Jiménez's greatest fears because they also reported high mortality rates among the undocumented persons crossing the border. She told the Spanish-language newspaper *Diario de Juárez* that "1996 has been a violent year. . . . The high temperatures produced by the drought worsened the passage for hundreds of men and women who come to this country to work and many times what they find is death."[46] In some cases those entering Kenedy County in South Texas were Chinese, which explained why the Border Patrol named the route "Ho Chi Minh Trail."[47] UH conducted another study, this time for the years 1993–1997. It estimated that the deaths exceeded 1,600 in the "United States-Mexico border region in circumstances that indicate they may have occurred during an attempt to enter the United States without inspection."[48] The UH study also reported that, in Texas, more than five hundred people drowned during the same years in the Rio Grande River (Rio Bravo).[49]

Jiménez hoped that the second study would help to reduce deaths by placing "in the center of the national debate another human face to immigration that some seem to want to deny."[50] The border authorities kept incomplete records; therefore, accurate statistics on the number of deaths could not be determined. The significantly understated total of deaths that the Border Patrol reported, estimated at 564, was the subject of a major CNN report.[51] As for the researchers at UH, they estimated that as many as 330 undocumented immigrants died each year in their efforts to cross into South Texas.[52] The 1993–1997 study revealed that, in the case of drowning deaths, most victims' names were unknown and family members never learned the fate of the deceased. In 1998 Mexico and the United States announced a joint effort to address the high death rate.[53] Jiménez was pleased by the binational agreement but added that "they did not address the fundamental causes of migration such as the economic problems that the people who abandon their country face."[54]

The heartache for the families in Mexico of the deceased was immeasurable, although the counties near the border were also greatly affected year after year by the high number of deaths. For the families, the fate of their loved ones remained unknown, in part, because of improper burial and record-keeping procedures in South Texas. Economic factors explained these problems, as well. For the counties in South Texas, among the nation's poorest, the cost for the burials of the immigrants was significant, especially for Webb and Brooks Counties. For example, in 2007, Webb County needed to designate $95,000 for indigent burials, the majority of which were undocumented immigrants.[55] As for Brooks County, in 2013 eighty-seven known deaths occurred, and it reportedly cost the county about $2,250 "to handle each migrant death."[56] Brooks and the other counties usually did not attempt to identify the deceased because of the cost of the procedure. Documentary filmmaker John Carlos Frey reported another problem—specifically that the counties repeatedly violated the laws for burial and record-keeping procedures in the case of immigrants. Frey wrote, for example, that in one location, "Remains were placed in red biohazard bags; four in what appeared to be grocery trash bags. Five were covered only in plastic wrap and packing tape. One set of remains was buried in a milk crate."[57]

A tragic border incident occurred in 1997 that revealed the dangers of a militarized border and low-intensity covert military operations. For Jiménez the incident, the killing of a young US citizen, highlighted the danger inherent in the use of military forces to patrol the border. Commenting on this killing, Jiménez said, "This was a predictable death. Having the military engage in civilian law means it will happen again."[58] The tragedy was not about an immigrant illegally entering the United States but, instead, a US citizen. In the incident a US Marine shot and killed Esequiel Hernández Jr.[59] The high school sophomore, who turned 18 years old six days before his death, was shot on May 20, 1997, as he herded his family's goats near Redford, Texas, at the US-Mexico border.

The four-man Marine unit involved in the incident was on a "covert drug surveillance mission to assist the Marfa sector of the U.S. Border Patrol."[60] Surveillance missions were conducted in the evenings and the unit wore camouflage uniforms when they passed near Hernández after 6:00 p.m. Hernández carried a seventy-year-old single shot .22-caliber rifle to protect his goats from wild boars and other predators. Believing that the motion he detected was an animal, he shot in its direction. One of the Marines shot back with his M-16 rifle, killing the youth. None of the residents of Redford, including Hernández, were aware that the Marines of the Joint Task Force-6 were conducting covert operations in the area. The Marines, who were stationed at the US Army Fort Bliss in El Paso, Texas, provided military support to the Border Patrol. After Hernández was shot, medical personnel did not reach him for twenty minutes. By then, he had bled to death from the single shot by Marine Corporal Clemente Banuelos.

The case went before two grand juries, but Banuelos was no-billed each time. Congressional investigations, however, later determined that there were a number of inconsistencies in the reports by the Marines and that "forensic evidence contradicted their accounts." The report following the investigation of the incident described "a series of failures," including, for example, that the Marines were not given "any training on civilian law enforcement or a briefing on local conditions," such as the practice of local residents being armed when in the desert.[61] The decision to acquit the Marine was based on the fact that soldiers on this kind of assignment acted "within the rules of engagement [ROE] which allows soldiers to fire if fired upon, even in domestic enforcement situations." The navy and DOJ later agreed to a $1.9 million wrongful death settlement with the victim's family to avoid a civil lawsuit.[62]

Jiménez knew the inherent risk whenever the Posse Comitatus Act (discussed in chapter 7) was violated—for example, whenever the Border Patrol, a police force, and the military engaged in joint operations. The BRC, a group in South Texas that Jiménez gave advice and funds, "played an active role in organizing educational and protest activities for some months after [the killing of Hernández]."[63] Jiménez, who had been following the situation at the border, also took action. When she arrived in Redford, she recalled, "We proposed a legal strategy because by this time we had developed a network of attorneys working on these issues."[64] Within a week of the shooting incident in May, Jiménez offered to provide the Redford residents with any support and advice that they wanted. Reflecting on the town hall meeting she attended there, Jiménez told the *Houston Chronicle*, "It was terribly hard for them. The grandfather, the mother, the sisters were all there. All I could tell them was 'Let the pain you have be turned into a light for other people and democracy.'"[65]

Fortunately, the AFSC provided the funds for Jiménez to help the Redford citizens. She was able to arrange meetings in July, two months after the young man was killed, between the citizens' group from Redford and officials in Washington, DC. These meetings confirmed to her the military aspect of the killing. When she inquired who they would meet with, she recalled that they told her that they "had to meet with Assistant Secretary of Defense in charge of Special Operations and Low Intensity Conflicts."[66] Besides officials at the Pentagon, Jiménez and the Redford group met with INS Commissioner Doris Meissner.[67]

The Redford group that Jiménez organized reported about the Border Patrol's mistreatment of persons in their area and complained that border agents were not held accountable for their abusive conduct. From her meeting with Meissner, Jiménez concluded that the commissioner showed real concern and "sensitivity" to the Redford killing. Jiménez hoped that congressional hearings on the incident would lead to "a way of giving oversight of agencies. They have to give an account to Congress of what they're doing."[68] The Redford group also expressed their strong opposition to the militarization of the border. Fortunately, after intense public and political pressure, the DOD temporarily suspended the military antidrug patrols on the border. The DOD made this decision the same month that the Redford civic group went to DC.[69] The DOD, Jiménez reported, "announced that they would suspend those operations and could only be re-instituted if they got permission directly from the Secretary of Defense. Up until then, it was the Border Patrol Sector Chief who said, '. . .we want a covert operation here.'"[70] Jiménez welcomed the DOD decision, which was, she said, a first step "towards a possible demilitarization of the border," but insisted that what was needed was a complete separation of the military from civilian law enforcement.[71] This separation lasted until 2005, when troops were ordered back to the Texas border.[72]

As undocumented immigrants continued to enter the United States illegally, the killing of immigrants at the border continued by border authorities and, sometime, by vigilante ranchers. For example, in September 1998 the Border Patrol shot at undocumented immigrants, killing two in San Diego, California, and one in Arizona. In January 1999 an officer of the federal Drug Enforcement Agency program in Texas shot an unarmed 19-year-old Mexican in the back while he was crossing the Rio Grande River. The Mexican government sent a formal protest over the incident, which left the youth paralyzed, to the US government. Lisa Navarrete of the National Council of La Raza also complained, asserting that "improper training is precisely why we have this kind of problem."[73] In late 2000 the officer who shot the young man pleaded guilty.[74] He was convicted of aggravated assault.

In addition to the danger of troops at the border, Jiménez knew that another danger was also the anti-Mexican racism of some border residents. Vigilante ranchers, for example, shot at and killed immigrants who crossed their land. Two facts were common to this type of violence: many of the ranchers were new to South Texas, and the victims were shot in the back. For example, an Arkansas retiree was charged with murder after killing a 25-year-old immigrant. In this case the immigrant was near but not on the

rancher's property. The newer owners of land in South Texas had less tolerance to immigrants passing through than did the older residents. According
to a local ranch hand, "The new landowners are doctors or lawyers from
Houston. . . . They're not use to being approached by immigrants, and some
of them are prejudiced."[75]

Some ranchers in South Texas also objected to the presence of border
agents, whose tactics included driving their vehicles over fleeing immigrants.
Jiménez, who received many reports of these incidents, commented, "We're
hearing many more complaints in recent years about their tactics . . . (border
residents) are beginning to object to the numbers of Border Patrol agents
coming onto their property." Kenedy Ranch, for example, banned these
agents from its property, a vast and sometimes inhospitable stretch of land
where immigrants have died of heat stroke. In 1995 and 2000, the Kenedy
Ranch demanded that the Border Patrol stay off its land, the second time after
the agents twice ran over undocumented immigrants in March.[76]

Immigration Laws of 1996

Jiménez's mission to help immigrants became more difficult with the
passage of laws in 1996 that made the path to citizenship more difficult,
resulting in an increase in the number of illegal immigrants.[77] Instead of the
laws' punitive measures, Jiménez thought that a better way to reduce the
number of undocumented immigrants should include, for example, offering more citizenship classes.[78] Unfortunately, the hostile political climate
continued to target Hispanic immigrants, especially the undocumented,
because of the commonplace racist belief that they increased the nation's
economic problems and the level of crime, for example. One of the laws
that targeted immigrants, even those in the country legally, and even US
citizens, was the Personal Responsibility and Work Opportunity Reconcilia-
tion Act (PRWORA), also called the Welfare Reform Act. It was signed into
law by President Bill Clinton on August 22, 1996, and went into effect in
July 1997.[79] The harsh terms of the new law motivated many immigrants to
become naturalized citizens. The number that did so in the fiscal year ending
September 1996 was unprecedented, totaling 1.1 million. In Houston, in one
day alone, six thousand took the oath to become citizens."[80]

The Welfare Reform Law barred legal immigrants from receiving aid—specifically food stamps and Supplemental Security Income (SSI). The law granted states flexibility in determining eligibility requirements of legal immigrants for major federal and state programs. Commenting in 1997 on PRWORA, Jiménez said, "Maybe welfare does need to change, but it sparks outrage when people understand that legal immigrants are the ones going to be hurt." Joe Higgs of The Metropolitan Organization, a coalition of ministries in Houston, added, "This is merely a punitive measure taken against the people who are most powerless in society."[81] The bill projected to save $55 billion in six years, most of which "would come from stopping benefits to most legal immigrants until they become citizens or have worked here for 10 years." In 1996 the Center for Public Policy Priorities "estimated that 186,000 immigrants in Texas would be cut from the Food Stamp Programs, 22,000 from Aid to Families with Dependent Children, and 53,000 from the Supplemental Security Income."[82] Fortunately, later amendments to the law restored food stamps and SSI.[83] The undocumented immigrant community received needed services. For example, the Harris County Hospital District, which included the city of Houston, continued its practice of "providing free and discounted preventive care to undocumented immigrants who are ineligible for many services because of federal law."[84]

The heated anti-immigrant climate mobilized pro-immigrant groups and activists, including Jiménez, but they soon became dismayed by another immigration law. The Illegal Immigration Reform and Immigrant Responsibility Act (IIRIRA) was signed into law September 30, 1996, and became effective on April 1, 1997. It significantly increased the INS's budget and manpower, making it the nation's largest federal law enforcement agency. One egregious provision of the IIRIRA made deportation, now termed "removal," of immigrants easier and converted minor legal offenses into felonies; in other words, the law greatly expanded the definition of aggravated felonies. Committing a felony was justification for removal. Protests and marches against the new law took place across the nation. Jiménez organized the protest march in Houston. She informed the newspaper *La Jornada* of Mexico in early April of 1997 that protest activities were scheduled for a whole week.[85]

The Welfare Act and the IIRIRA imposed painful terms on the immigrant community, whether legal or undocumented. From a human rights perspective, IIRIRA was very troubling because "punishment for a removal is more serious, judicial oversight is often eliminated, and mitigating circumstances are rarely considered."[86] INS also deported immigrants more quickly, sometimes in less than twelve hours. Often arrests followed job raids, which meant that a man or woman who went to work in the morning did not return home to his or her family that evening. In Houston a Guatemalan immigrant said, "The people feel vulnerable. They're scared to leave the house for all the roundups. I don't even send my children on the bus."[87]

There was widespread fear in the immigrant community in the late 1990s. Jiménez told the *New York Times* in December 1998, "It is as if, suddenly, war had been declared on immigrants. Stopping immigrants from entering the country has become more important than the war against drugs."[88] With its inflated budget, which was $3.1 billion in 1997, INS increased raids and other activities that frightened and intimidated the immigrant community. Between October 1996 and May 1997, INS deported almost two thousand immigrants from Houston alone, twice the number deported during the same period of the previous year. For the entire fiscal year that ran from October 1996 to the end of September 1997, the INS's deportation goal was about ninety-three thousand immigrants nationwide, about 35 percent more than the preceding year, including three thousand from Houston.[89]

The emotional and economic stress on the families of deported unauthorized immigrants, usually the provider, was incalculable. Legal residents also became deportation targets, the *Houston Chronicle* reported, "because changes in the law," for example, "considered driving while intoxicated convictions as felonies."[90] The IIRIRA law, in other words, added "retroactive punishment and the INS deported persons who committed crimes that were in the past non-felonious but were redefined as felonious by the IIRIRA."[91] Fortunately, the retroactive punishment provision was eventually overturned by the US Supreme Court in 2001 when the provision was ruled unconstitutional.[92]

The IIRIRA also greatly increased INS's manpower, equipment, and technology at the US-Mexico border. With these changes the possibility of the violation of human rights along the border rose. An alarmed Jiménez told the Mexican newspaper *Cronica,* "I believe that we must insist in the respect of human rights, the end of discrimination and the selectivity of the immigration laws against the Mexican population."[93] However, she also acknowledged the tension the Border Patrol felt because of a heightened pressure to crack down on the border. The stress from long nightly patrolling of the Texas-Mexico border contributed, she believed, to the mistreatment of immigrants caught by immigration officials.[94]

Jiménez's profound objection to the militarization of the border became a major focus of her activism. She told *Diario de Juárez* that the main tactic "of the military who responded to a call was to shoot to kill," whereas police were trained to pursue other options.[95] She also said that "the growing presence at the border is not only a threat to public safety, it also undermines the constitutional rights of native-born and immigrant alike."[96] In one incident a Green Beret shot a Mexican national near Brownsville, Texas, a border town, on January 24, 1997. The presence of "Green Berets was an open secret at the southern tip of Texas," which put "civilians at risk of being confronted by the military."[97]

Jiménez and other pro-immigrant activists organized in 1996, even before the killings in Redford and Brownsville, to protest commonplace anti-Mexican prejudices. An apprehensive Jiménez told the *Houston Chronicle* that "the situation was worsening and we had to defend our rights."[98] The unjust conditions at the border and elsewhere in the United States, like Proposition 187, created a political awakening that materialized in the historic Latino and Immigrants' Rights March in Washington, DC, on October 12, 1996. Another contributing factor to the march was the brutal beating on April 1, 1996, of undocumented immigrants by deputies in Riverside County in California. A video of the beating was shown on news programs nationwide.[99] The Coordinating Committee '96, also known as *Coordinadora* '96, organized the protest march in Washington, DC. Created in 1994, it was a national coalition of community organizations in about twenty-five states. Jiménez chaired the Coordinating Committee '96 in Houston. On May 23, 1995, at Houston's city hall, she announced the committee's plans for marches in Spring Branch on May 27, 1995, and the nationwide march in Washington, DC, the following year.

The successful event in October 1996 was an unprecedented "nationwide effort to organize Latinos to come to Washington, D.C. and march for immigrant and civil rights."[100] Among those caught up in the enthusiasm of the moment was Representative Nydia M. Velasquez, a New York Democrat. She said, "Newt Gingrich was the wake-up call. If we can't get engaged politically, we will be subjected to the abuses of the Washington establishment."[101] The estimates of the total number of marchers by "mainstream papers" ranged from twenty-five thousand to thirty-five thousand. Demands of the marchers included universal human and constitutional rights, "equal opportunities and Affirmative Action . . . citizens' police-review boards; labor law reform . . . and an extension of the date of eligibility for amnesty for all those who entered the U.S. prior to January 1, 1992."[102]

Referring to the historic march and the enthusiasm of its participants, Jiménez declared, "We are no longer an invisible population."[103] She lamented that the major Hispanic organizations initially did not endorse the march, including MALDEF, LULAC, or NCLR. However, once aware of a rise in pro-immigrant activism, "and because of pressure from below, now they see that they need to participate," Jiménez said.[104] For example, Raúl Izaguirre, the executive director of the NCLR, spoke at one of the rallies, as did Jiménez.[105] Many Hispanic Houstonians also participated in the march. In Houston Mary Champion Closner made plans to participate in the march, even though her parents said only troublemakers went to rallies. Mary disagreed, saying that "this is the strongest feeling a Latina or Latino can feel"— that is, to demonstrate on behalf of immigrant rights.[106]

Public events like marches and rallies had an important role in activism because, Jiménez believed, they are "part of a process of increasing awareness to regain our dignity . . . creating political power." Blanca Blanco of Houston added that the march gave voice to the voiceless undocumented immigrant. Jiménez's and Blanco's activism challenged discrimination and thus advanced social justice. Recalling earlier times, an animated Blanco said, "Back then you didn't see unity among Hispanics. . . . Now you see a unity. We have to remember we came from the same wombs. Our grandfathers, our

great-grandfathers were all immigrants. We are the fruit of that."[107] Jiménez
agreed, adding that the Latino and Immigrants' Rights March asserted "the
idea that Latinos were here to stay."[108] She added, "We needed to create a
political movement to defend the interests of Latino immigrants . . . to defend
our civil and human rights in this country. . . . This represents an emergence
of a new Latino movement."[109]

Jiménez: A Dual Citizen

In 1998 Jiménez made a major decision, starting a process that she helped
to make possible. In March of that year, the government of Mexico passed
a nationality law, *la ley de doble nacionalidad*, that allowed Mexicans who
had become citizens in another country to recover many of the rights they
had as Mexican citizens. Since she identified with the culture in Mexico
as well as the United States, Jiménez joined other like-minded immigrants
to make the law a reality. She said, "I join with other Mexican immigrants
throughout the United States sending delegations to Mexico to change the
constitution to allow for dual citizenship, dual nationality. I went myself to
Mexico City to lobby in the Mexican congress . . . and so when the law went
into effect . . . I was the first one at the Mexican consulate signing and I was
invited to the national palace in Mexico City with one hundred others to
receive, to recuperate my Mexican nationality. The 110 of us . . . received it
from the president of Mexico.[110] President Ernesto Zedillo presided over the
ceremony and Jiménez was given the honor to speak at the event. Jiménez
didn't want to participate in an event with the president because she was,
she said, "very involved with progressive politics."[111] She expressed similar
views in an email to this writer when she wrote, "I believe that as a human
rights activist I should not be part of any government because it compro-
mises my ability to hold any government accountable for polices, laws or
actions that violate human rights."[112] She was well-known in Mexico as a
defender of the rights of Mexican immigrants in the United States, although
she was also known as a critic of Mexico. For example, she said, "I've
been an official observer in Mexican elections before and also protested the
Mexicans' actions in Chiapas."[113]

For Jiménez and many other Mexican Americans in the United States, the 1998 dual nationalist law was an emotional and legal victory. Although dual nationality as granted in the 1998 law did not include all the rights of Mexican citizenship, more rights were added later, such as the right to vote. Nevertheless, Jiménez believed that the new law was "a step forward. . . . For me, it's legal recognition for most Mexicans' reality. Our existence is in both countries."[114] She was very proud of being bicultural. Jiménez also hoped that she and others could have a voice in Mexican politics, which the right to vote provided. As for one of the initial legal rights given in 1998, property rights benefited Jiménez personally. This allowed her to claim half of the Mexican property that she and her ex-husband had owned.[115] Important as were the specific rights that the Mexican law granted, Professor Jorge Durand offered an interesting interpretation of *la ley de doble nacionalidad* in 1998. In his opinion the law was in response to IRCA because it had motivated large number of Mexican nationals in the United States to rush to become US citizens.[116]

Developments that startled nativists in the United States followed the passage in 2006 of a subsequent Mexican law that granted the right to vote in Mexican presidential elections to individuals like Jiménez.[117] For example, in 2006 Mexican politicians running for office "organized community events in California in attempts to garner votes," and "some Mexican nationals living in the United States initiated electoral campaigns to seek office in Mexico."[118] The alarmed nativists included US Representative Tom Tancredo (R-CO, 1999–2009), chair of the Congressional Immigration Reform Caucus, who called dual citizenship an "oxymoron."[119] In addition, FAIR, which advocated restricted immigration, questioned the loyalty of dual citizens. According to Houstonian K. C. McAlpin of FAIR, dual nationality or dual citizenship "raises unnecessary and dangerous questions that should not exist in the minds of many Americans (about) the allegiance of citizens of Mexican origin. Citizenship in any country should mean commitment to that [country]."[120] Jiménez rejected the criticism, noting that thirty-one nations in the world granted dual citizenship. Regarding Mexican-origin individuals, she added that many US Mexicans, herself included, were highly critical of the Mexican society and government. She also pointed out that Mexican

Americans who served in the military had earned Congressional Medals of Honor in disproportionately high numbers relative to their percentage of the population.[121]

Jiménez's advocacy of social justice and human rights was not exclusive to one city, state, or even country. In 1994 she became interested a movement in Chiapas, Mexico. It organized an uprising to defend the Mayan Indians' rights, which included the right to speak their own languages, to control the natural resources in their territory, and to have their own political and economic organizations. The Chiapas rebels, known as the Zapatistas, took their name from the followers of Emiliano Zapata (1879–1919), a revolutionary in the Mexican Revolution (1910–1920). The army of the neo-Zapatista army, still active, is the Ejercito Zapatista de Liberación Nacional (EZLN), the Zapatista Army of National Liberation. The significance of the EZLN extended well beyond Mexico because it represented a new form of conflict, the social "netwar," which used the internet to promote their cause. John Arquilla and David Ronfeldt, scholars at the RAND Corporation, coined the term "netwar," which "refers to an emerging mode of conflict (and crime) at societal levels, short of traditional military warfare, in which the protagonists use network forms of organization and related doctrines, strategies, and technologies attuned to the information age."[122] The Chiapas Indigenous insurgents' successes in their fight were possible in part because they attracted massive support from many local and international NGOs who "wanted to foster a form of democracy in which civil-society actors would be strong enough to counterbalance state and market actors and could play central roles in making public-policy decisions that affect civil society."[123]

Jiménez's involvement in the Zapatista movement is of interest because it reflected her broad commitment to aiding the marginalized. She shared many of the ideas and values of the Zapatistas—for example, respect for human rights, nonviolence, and the belief that achieving goals was a collective and nonhierarchical process. Jiménez called the Zapatistas the "authentic voices of the oppressed" and added that "their revolution has sparked hope worldwide."[124] She respected them, she said, "because they begin with a very traditional Left ideological concept, and as they go into indigenous communities and begin to organize, and then their ideas are confronted by the indigenous way of thought and life, their whole ideas are restructured." She continued, "One of the things that the Zapatistas offer is an ideology of understanding marginalized communities in our current period."[125]

The activists of Chiapas, Jiménez asserted, shared her belief on how to bring about change.[126] The Zapatistas believed, she said, "If social change comes about, it has to be the people changing," but, she added, "They [the Zapatistas] have to change also. I mean, there is an interaction."[127] In fact, the Zapatistas did change their tactics over time, according to Jiménez, because "there is no longer one formula for resistance."[128] Reflecting on another historical situation, she asserted, "You can't be stuck in a dogmatic ideological position. I mean, I think we saw the tremendous harm done by the Left or the Communists that directed the revolution in Cambodia, the . . . Khmer Rouge. I mean, they had the ideology that everyone had to be a peasant . . . It was absurd."[129]

Jiménez and the Zapatistas knew of the harmful effects of globalization. Like them, Jiménez believed that globalization "is being directed by economic elites . . . not being directed by the majorities." Therefore, she added, to decrease inequities and exploitation, it was necessary "to organize those who are globalized from below."[130] Significantly, the Zapatista rebellion started the day that NAFTA took effect, on January 1, 1994. The rebels insisted that the treaty was a "death sentence" for Mexican Indians "who stand to be forced from traditional lands by agribusiness and development projects."[131] Mexican peasant growers could not compete with modern commercialized farmers in Mexico and the United States.[132]

Zapatistas and other persons knowledgeable about Mexican politics questioned the benefit of NAFTA. For example, according to Roberto Martínez, director of the US-Mexico Border Program of the AFSC, NAFTA would not help average Mexicans because "there is no trickle-down theory in Mexico. The rich are going to get richer and the poor are going to get poorer."[133] Organizations in the United States sent aid to Chiapas, including the AFSC and Mexico Relief, a group based in Houston.[134] Nevertheless, the economic hardships due to NAFTA contributed to the great spike in emigration to the United States between 1995 and 2000. The result was to strengthen the push in the "push-pull dynamics that encouraged unauthorized migration" to the United States and contributed to falling wages in Mexico since NAFTA was enacted.[135]

Always eager to promote social justice, Jiménez traveled to Chiapas in August 1996 to attend an *encuentro* (meeting). The Zapatista meeting was the International *Encuentro* for Humanity and Against Neoliberalism. Human rights activists from fifty countries participated to learn about the Indigenous Mayan Zapatistas and their struggles. Jiménez attended as a representative of a Mexican NGO, established in the United States, called the National Commission for Democracy in Mexico (NCDM). In addition to her support for Zapatistas, Jiménez felt a kinship with them, a feeling that she believed was mutual. In fact, after the *encuentro* the Zapatistas met with a large group of Chicanos, whom the Zapatistas considered a "priority relationship." Jiménez also believed that there was a "special bond" between the rebels and Chicanos. The Zapatistas believed that both they and Chicanos and Chicanas had endured, according to reporters Roberto Rodríguez and Patrisia Gonzales, "exclusion and discrimination in their own homelands."[136]

Jiménez's involvement with the Zapatistas motivated the feminist in her to respond to the problem of rape in Chiapas. An impassioned activist for women's and human rights, she was alarmed when she learned of the sexual assaults of women in Chiapas. One incident was the rape on October 26, 1995, of Cecilia Rodríguez, a native of El Paso, Texas, and an official NCDM spokesperson for the EZLN. Rodríguez's sexual assault "by military or paramilitary elements" was at least the fiftieth assault in Chiapas since 1994. Regrettably, Jiménez said, Mexican President Ernest Zedillo did not have the "power to take on the Chiapas landowners or [their] White Guards, so there is little hope for redress."[137]

Jiménez, nevertheless, needed to act. She told the *Houston Chronicle*, "We felt we really need to raise awareness of this issue in Houston." Jiménez became a leader in the Coalition to Raise Awareness of Rape as a War Crime and, in 1996, organized a presentation in Houston about the problem. The speaker she invited to Houston was Dr. Shana Swiss, executive director of Women's Rights International. A physician and expert on rape as a war crime,

Swiss was pleased to tell her audience that the United Nation Commission on Human Rights acknowledged the disreputable use of rape in war zones and other hotspots and that in 1993 the United Nations added rape to its list of war crimes.[138]

Houston: Changing with Immigration

Jiménez followed with concern the increasingly tense situation in the late 1990s for people of color, especially the immigrant community. However, indications that Houston was becoming more diverse and tolerant emerged. Jiménez welcomed this trend, if true. In 1997 the National Immigration Forum published a report on Houston. In it Executive Director Frank Sherry praised Houston's civic leadership because it "minimizes racial and ethnic intolerance and works together to solve problems."[139] The year before Rice University sociology professor Stephen L. Klineberg offered his assessment in his publication *Houston Ethnic Communities*. An expert on the city's demographics, Klineberg believed that the city was undergoing a "rapid transformation . . . (into) a multiethnic metropolis." Less optimistic than Sherry, however, Klineberg added that "Houston is now having to compete in the much more complex and problematic environment of a worldwide, knowledge-based, high-technology community." Klineberg concluded that the city was "increasingly unable to produce enough well-paid jobs for the workers who are already here."[140]

As for the immigrant population, it had always contributed to the economic growth in Houston, although public opinions toward them continued to be unfavorable. Commenting on the Klineberg survey, Jiménez said that she tended "to think (that the more positive attitudes are) on the surface because even within the last few months I've personally seen strong reactions against immigrants."[141] Jiménez was referring to an anti-Mexican racist mob at a demonstration against capital punishment on February 3, 1998, the execution day of the convicted murderer Karla Faye Tucker. Jiménez said that a mob at the demonstration verbally assaulted her and other Hispanics. Most of the Hispanics were immigrants. The mob that turned on Jiménez and the other capital punishment protesters, Jiménez recalled, said, " 'This is our state, you go back to where you came from.' Some other person said, 'Yeah, Mexicans just come in to trash our country,' and another one said, 'they should all be killed.'" Although not naïve about racial attitudes, Jiménez confessed that she was alarmed by the remarks. She said, "In a short while there was just an intense anti-Mexican hostility. I was very shocked to see how instantly we became the focus of hate." From this experience Jiménez concluded that the hecklers' belief that immigrants were inferior and a drain on social programs was "very much alive."[142]

The sharp rise in the number of immigrants in Houston strained racial relations. The large numbers of recent immigrants in Houston from Mexico and Central American created unprecedented situations. In December 1997 the US Census Bureau released population figures for the years from 1990 to 1996. In Harris County, of which Houston is the largest city, the "white population rose from 1.5 million in 1990 to 1.6 million in 1996 while the Hispanic population jumped from 644,916 to 819,216 in the same period." Many Houstonians believed that the total was much higher because undocumented immigrants avoided being counted. Demographer Steve Murdock was not so sure. He believed that the undercount was "not an immigration issue. It's always difficult to count any population that is highly mobile, poor, and living in a diversity of households."[143] Census statistics were considered inaccurate for another reason. The Hispanic immigrant community, fearing that information gathered by the Census Bureau would be shared with the INS, frequently did not provide the necessary information. Whatever the reason, the undercount in the 1990 census cost Texas about $1 billion in federal aid. Hispanics in Texas were undercounted 5.4 percent, and the undercount in Houston was the largest of any major city in the nation.[144]

Conclusion

The developments of the mid- to late 1990s revealed a disturbing degree of inhumanity and social injustice. Commonplace racist prejudices reflected poorly on our democratic society, but the Mexican-origin community's activists, including Jiménez, fought to advance values like equality. In the 1990s, in brief, harsh laws at the federal and state levels violated the civil and human rights of the Mexican-origin community, especially undocumented immigrants. In addition, the militarization of the border predictably resulted in violations of human rights, even death. Pro-immigrant groups and individuals protested these developments, and Jiménez led many of the efforts to protect the vulnerable. Her concern for social justice even extended to Mexico, especially for the rights of indigenous people in Chiapas.

Welfare reform laws targeted undocumented immigrants, although the new laws in 1996 also created hardship for legal residents and poor citizens. Against this wave of laws, Jiménez took actions such as speaking out, organizing marches, and many other forms of protest. In 1994 one proposed state law, the draconian Proposition 187, was specifically designed to drive legal and undocumented immigrants from California. Immigrants and pro-immigrant activists responded by organizing the nationwide Latino Immigrants' Rights March. Jiménez organized the march from Houston and participated in it at the national level. In 1996 the federal welfare laws PRWORA and IIRIRIA greatly limited, or even ended, social benefits to the immigrant community. The commonplace racist belief that immigrants were a drain on the nation's economy motivated the passage of the 1996 laws. This anti-immigrant myth persisted, even though many studies, including one by the DOL, proved otherwise.

Other disturbing developments emerged in the 1990s, including the militarization at the US-Mexico border—a violation of the Posse Comitatus Act—and a rise in deaths of border-crossers. Tragically, one result of the militarization of the border was the killing of Esequiel Hernández Jr., a US citizen. Jiménez's timely action after his death included organizing a delegation from the young man's town to Washington, DC, to speak to government authorities. Soon after these meetings, the federal government ordered the withdrawal of troops at the border. Jiménez and the Redford group believed their pressure contributed to the withdrawal.

Another tragedy at the border was the high number of immigrant deaths, frequently from drowning in the Rio Grande River or succumbing to dehydration in deserts. The preventable deaths were the reason that Jiménez strongly advocated for the right of workers to cross borders legally. While undeniably a tragedy for the deceased and their families, the deaths had other consequences—for example, the cost for burials for local, financially strapped county and city governments. South Texas towns became overwhelmed financially by these burial expenses. In many cases the dead were even put in garbage bags. Fortunately, organizations formed to identify the deceased through DNA testing, and Jiménez contributed to their efforts.

In the 1990s Jiménez's attention turned to Mexico for two reasons: first, her desire to regain her Mexican citizenship, and, second, her desire to support the struggle for Indigenous rights in Chiapas. As for citizenship, Jiménez was part of a group of Mexican American citizens who lobbied, successfully, the Mexican government to allow them to regain their Mexican citizenship. Initially, the applicants gained nationality status, but later laws added more of the rights that Mexican citizens possessed, including the right to vote for the Mexican president. Jiménez welcomed having a political voice in Mexico. As to the Chiapas revolution, it was, she believed, an important fight against social injustice. She had always had an interest in the marginalized because she personally knew what their experience was like. Jiménez's participation in the movement in Chiapas included attending international conferences there and being a representative of the NCDM.

Many troubling developments emerged in the 1990s, but there were also positive developments. Jiménez contributed to these, such as the withdrawal of troops at the border after the killing of Esequiel Hernández. In the 2000s there would be more fights for social justice because of commonplace racism and anti-immigrant prejudices. However, there would also be victories, including the emergence of young immigrant activists, the Dreamers. From these and other examples of activism, the idea became increasingly clear, Jiménez declared, that "Latinos are here to stay."

Chapter 9

Jiménez and the New Era of Immigrant Activism

Any place you begin to facilitate a process for an organized, collective
voice that challenges power opens up the possibility for change . . . the
soul of organizing for social change is the people.
—Maria Jiménez[1]

The rise of nativism in the country distressed Maria Jiménez. She knew
that a just society could not coexist with pervasive forms of hatred
like nativism. It exacerbated commonplace prejudices in Texas, including
anti-Mexican and anti-immigrant animus. In 2014 Jiménez commented,
"We have grown up in a society of inequalities and the reinforcement of
privilege. We all have to work to deconstruct these aspects of our world
view and examine actions that exclude and marginalize."[2] Her comment
on deconstruction recalls the concept of hegemony associated with the
Italian political theorist Antonio Gramsci. The difficulty with hegemony,
he believed, is that it is an invisible form of domination and "involves no
coercion but the consent on the part of the dominated."[3]

The goal of activists like Jiménez is to help create an equitable society
where no one is denied social justice. She believed that commonplace racism
constituted a pernicious form of hegemony. Jiménez also understood what
Critical Race theorist Lu-in Wang meant when she wrote in her book *Discrimination by Default* that "social group stereotypes are 'normal.'" In the case
of Mexicans immigrants and Mexican Americans, common stereotypes were
"alien," "foreigner," and the "other." Demeaning stereotypes are harmful and
insidious because, Wang explained, they "come easily and often unbidden
to mind and are difficult to shake—but they tend to be neither accurate as
descriptive matter nor egalitarian in their prescriptions."[4]

This chapter continues the life story of Jiménez and her struggles against
virulent nativism and unjust immigration policies. She addressed dangers,
which sometimes resulted in death, to undocumented immigrants by the
Minutemen, a nativist group, and agents of the INS. Jiménez also initiated
a successful nationwide process for immigrants who had been unfairly
disqualified from becoming naturalized citizens. With Jiménez's guidance,
these individuals formed the Association for Residency and Citizenship in
America (ARCA). This chapter includes other positive developments, including Jiménez's teaching position at UH, where she taught Latino activism
and organizing. Another very positive development was the emergence of
the Dreamers, youth who, when minors, had been brought illegally to the
United States. For older activists like Jiménez, these young adults and the
movement they created represented a new phase in the fight for immigrant
rights and the legalization of immigrants. These were persons who, in many
cases and for many years, had contributed positively to the nation but, nevertheless, were denied the right to become citizens.

Immigrant Issues: Nativism, Hate, and Crime

During the racially tense period of the late 1900s and the early twenty-first
century, commonplace anti-Mexican prejudices contributed to police violence
in some cities against the Mexican-origin community. This was true in Texas.
One case that concerned Jiménez reflected both class and race discrimination. Specifically, she strongly objected to the murder conviction of Ricardo

Aldape Guerra, a Mexican citizen who was convicted of killing a Houston police officer in 1982.[5] Jiménez believed that "Ricardo went to death row because he was not a rich man. Ricardo went to death row because he was a Mexican."[6]

Fortunately, Ricardo's situation changed in 1997 when a judge dismissed his case. The judge ruled that the police had intimidated witnesses into accusing Aldape Guerra of the crime. In addition, the gun used in the crime did not have his fingerprints.[7] On hearing the news of the dismissal of his case, Jiménez remarked, "Wow! That's good news. There was so much proof that he was innocent. He became the symbol of the injustices against the undocumented immigrant."[8] The Mexican Consul General in Houston expedited his return to Mexico, where Mexicans gave him a hero's welcome. Sadly, he died there in a car accident a few months after his release. A tearful Jiménez commented, "I don't have any words . . . so many years and so many people fought for his life. . . . It's really a shame that he could only enjoy his life and liberty for such a short period of time."[9]

In the area of law enforcement, Mexican nationals were particularly vulnerable to injustices and sometimes to police violence. In 2000 Consul General Rodulfo Figueroa expressed intense displeasure in a letter to Harris County District Attorney John B. Holmes Jr. The Mexican official believed that the district attorney's office failed to adequately handle cases in which Mexican nationals were killed by police. Houston police killed four Mexicans from September 1997 to mid-2000, but no officers were ever criminally charged with the murders. Following the police killing of Mexican national Jaime Santiago on March 5, 2000, Figueroa wrote another letter to Holmes. In the letter he said, "This episode is the latest in a series of acts by your office demonstrating disregard for the rights of Mexican nationals who are the victims of police violence in the Houston area."[10]

The best-known killing by the Houston police was that of the Mexican immigrant Pedro Oregón Navarro. After his death an official from the Mexican government met with the victim's family and HPD. On July 12, 1998, the Houston police shot Oregón Navarro twelve times, nine of which were in the back, and all were from a position above his body. The shooting occurred after police invaded his apartment without a warrant in search of drugs. The police found no drugs. One officer was wounded during the invasion, but he was shot by another police officer, not the victim.[11] The raid was the result of misinformation from a confidential informant. Later examination of court records revealed that from 1994 to 1998, the drug "task force had conducted 432 similar drug investigations without warrants."[12] The six officers involved in the incident had their employment terminated. Jiménez was pleased with the firings but added, "Justice is not just in the firings. Criminal indictments are still needed."[13] Only one officer was found guilty of a crime. The grand jury charged him with trespassing, a misdemeanor.[14]

A crime of a much different nature in Houston involved a serial murderer from Mexico, Angel Maturino Reséndez, wanted for murders in Texas, Illinois, and Kentucky. He was called the "railroad killer" or the "railcar killer" because he traveled around on trains. In 2000 the 42-year-old immigrant, who said he was half man and half angel and could not be killed, was sentenced to death for the murder of a local woman, a physician, in December 1998. Maturino Reséndez apologized to the victim's family on the day that he was executed in 2006.[15]

Of course, the Mexican-origin community, including Jiménez, was shocked by the crimes that Maturino Reséndez committed. Unfortunately, in this case as in other serious crimes involving a Mexican immigrant, the public demonized the entire Mexican immigrant community. The public attributed to the murderers a litany of negative qualities, and political figures readily seized the opportunity to accuse immigrants of any alleged rise in crimes. For example, in July 1999 then Republican presidential candidate Pat Buchanan added to the nativist hysteria by claiming that the serial killer was "the poster boy for what is happening in illegal immigration."[16] In Houston Jiménez reported that "our (AFSC) office has been getting some terrible calls from people, sounding mostly elderly, about Mexicans looking alike, saying they were 'small, dirty, and ugly.'"[17] She added, "So with thousands of calls coming from all over the country, law enforcement and others need to be cautious while engaging in a search. They need to make sure they're individualizing their search instead of generalizing a whole population. We as Hispanics are stereotyped."[18]

Besides the police, immigration authorities also made life very difficult for Hispanic immigrants and Hispanic citizens. Harassment by the Border Patrol occurred so frequently that it seemed normal—that is, commonplace—although not just or fair. For example, the Border Patrol angered Mexican Americans in Cameron County and elsewhere in South Texas when the agents unfairly pulled them over for questioning. In this tense climate, the police stopped Judge Gilberto Hinojosa, the judge in Cameron County, in 2000 because they suspected that he was an undocumented immigrant. Police also stopped Judge Filmen B. Vela. Remarking on his experience, Hinojosa said, "It feels like occupied territory. It does not feel like we're in the United States of America." According to another Mexican American, Fernando Garcia of El Paso, "Here on the border, it's almost normal to be detained." However, during the manhunt for Maturino Reséndez, the so-called railroad killer, Garcia added, "The climate is that the sheriff's deputies and Border Patrol are stopping almost everyone if they look like a Mexican. People are getting arrested for just walking on the tracks. It's getting out of hand."[19]

The apprehension that Jiménez felt over anti-immigrant biases, and the violence it encouraged, alarmed the federal government as well as Hispanic organizations. In 1993 the federal government started tracking hate crimes. That year there were 472 reported hate crimes that victimized Hispanics, but in 1997 the total exceeded 600.[20] In addition to the government's research, the NCLR decided to study the problem. In 1998 it documented abuses against Hispanics, including illegal "street sweeps" like the ones conducted in Katy, Texas, in 1994.[21] The NCLR also worked with ILEMP, headed by Jiménez in Houston, to collect statistics. The NCLR released its first study on hate crimes in July 1999. In a meeting in Houston, NCLR President Raúl Yzaguirre said, "It seems as if open season has been declared on our community. These crimes are not only perpetuated by hate groups but also include acts of systemic discrimination and violence by ordinary citizens." The disturbing trend suggested, he continued, that "hate is being mainstreamed." Unfortunately, too many assaults were ignored by the DOJ, Yzaguirre concluded, causing him to rename the DOJ the "Department of Injustice."[22]

In this troubling period, Jiménez was active in many nonprofit organizations that offered help to immigrants, including the undocumented. A few organizations had been in existence for years. For example, Casa Juan Diego was established in 1981. CRECEN, an immigrant rights group for Central Americans and other Latin Americans, was organized in 1985. Its energetic director is Teodoro Aguiluz. In 2005 he hired Jiménez to be CRECEN's special project coordinator. Another organization, the Central American Refugee Center / Gulfton Area Neighborhood Center (CARECEN/GANO) was founded in 1983. It offered many services, including assistance in the citizenship and permanent residency application process.

Jiménez provided invaluable assistance to organizations for immigrants in Houston. One needed service was specific to immigrant workers. The total number of immigrant workers in Houston approximated 150,000, including about 10,000 who were undocumented. These workers congregated daily in the city at over thirty informal sites where local companies and contractors hired them. To improve this unorganized and haphazard situation, in 2001 the city created a day-labor site and authorized CARECEN/GANO to operate it. The center provided "a safe, orderly 'hiring hall' for large numbers of low-income and immigrant workers" where they set their own rules.[23] In the same year, the city government added another service, and it would directly involve Jiménez. In 2001 Mayor Lee P. Brown (1998–2004) formed the Mayor's Office of Immigrant and Refugee Affairs (MOIRA). Mayor Brown said that the purpose of the new office was "to provide these citizens with the city services they need. On the municipal level, we understand that these communities have different needs than the rest of the community."[24]

MOIRA's original staff was only one person, Benito Juárez, an immigrant from Guatemala and well-known labor activist. He was the former coordinator of the Houston Immigration and Refugee Coalition. Juárez and Jiménez led the coalition and had urged the Houston City Council to declare Houston a sanctuary city, which it declined to do. Although definitions of a sanctuary city vary, "It is a broad term applied to jurisdictions that have policies in place designed to limit cooperation with or involvement in federal immigration enforcement actions."[25] Despite the city council's position on

Houston as a sanctuary city, Jiménez welcomed the creation of MOIRA. She believed that it would protect workers from exploitation, and she gladly served as the chair of the Mayor's Advisory Committee for MOIRA. It had many supporters, including Councilman Gordon Quan and Caroline Alvarado, senior executive assistant to the mayor.[26] In addition, the Harris County AFL-CIO Council "worked with prominent immigrant advocates to support [its] establishment."[27]

Immigrant workers encountered many problems, including job discrimination. It persisted because workers hesitated to complain, fearing losing their job. Other problems for the workers included the lack of legal aid, or the indifference of persons, groups, or organizations that could help. However, a legal case of job discrimination that ended well for its plaintiffs involved the Quietflex Manufacturing Company in Houston. The brave actions of the employees, many of whom were undocumented, initiated the process when they attracted the attention of the Harris County AFL-CIO and other organizations. These groups stepped up to fight the blatant discrimination of the Hispanic immigrants at Quietflex. The conditions were so unjust that 83 walked off their job in January 2000, complaining about poor wages and working conditions. Quietflex employed 250 workers, of which approximately 91 percent were immigrants, either Hispanic or Vietnamese. The company used the "divide and rule" strategy to control its immigrant employees.[28] The Vietnamese worked in a department where the pay and working conditions were better, and the company would not allow the Hispanic workers to transfer to that department. In addition, they, and not the Vietnamese workers, were required to clean the lunchroom. Quietflex fired the protesting Hispanic employees, who subsequently walked off the job, but the NLRB forced the company to rehire them. In addition, the Equal Employment Opportunity Commission (EEOC) required the company to turn over its employment documents in order to investigate the work conditions at Quietflex.[29] Finally, MALDEF successfully sued the company, which was ordered to award the Hispanic plaintiffs, 78 current and former employees, $2.8 million.[30] Happily, in the case of Quietflex, the Hispanic immigrant workers fought for, and received, social justice.

Jiménez and ARCA: Fighting an Unjust Law

One of Jiménez's most important achievements was the creation of the ARCA. It launched a nationwide "late amnesty" campaign for IRCA applicants who were unjustly disqualified from this 1986 immigration law. A major provision of IRCA, discussed in chapter 7, granted amnesty to qualified undocumented immigrants. One requirement of the law was continuous residence in the United States from 1982 to 1986. These years included a period before IRCA was signed into law on November 6, 1986, and during which many amnesty applicants had returned briefly to their country of origin. This absence, the INS believed, disqualified them for amnesty.

A legal struggle for late amnesty followed, ending in 2000, organized by many energetic, very focused, and well-organized undocumented immigrants. For those active in the campaign, the act of coming "out of the shadows" was extremely risky because they faced the possibility of deportation. They felt, Jiménez recalled, "a lot of fear."[31] Many of the original amnesty applicants who had been denied amnesty filed a class action suit against the INS in 1986, as did other groups on their behalf, including Catholic Social Services in 1986 and LULAC in 1987.[32] The long legal battle encountered many setbacks, and a court ruling in 1998 even temporarily derailed it. In addition, the INS repeatedly appealed court rulings over the years, stalling the application process each time.[33]

The late amnesty applicants were in "legal limbo" for years. They, Jiménez recalled, "thought they were here to stay. They bought homes. Some of them are business owners."[34] But, she added, "as a result of that ruling [in 1998 against a class action suit, discussed further below], people have lost work permits, jobs, homes, cars, and access to healthcare."[35] One Houston amnesty applicant complained bitterly, saying, "We had faith the lawsuit wasn't going to fail. I'm buying a house. My children were born here. They don't even speak Spanish."[36] Work permits were canceled, and immigrants became deportable. In other words, the amnesty applicants "went from legal workers to illegal workers overnight."[37] This unfortunate development meant, Jiménez noted, that "thousands of families will be broken up when one or more of its members are required to leave the country."[38] Nationwide, 350,000 persons were potentially affected, including 20,000 in Houston.[39]

The struggle for late amnesty, guided by Jiménez, took three long and difficult years. The organization ARCA, formed in April 1998, led the effort. It spread to other cities, including New York, Chicago, Miami, and San Francisco. ARCA represented a grassroots movement in which hundreds of thousands of immigrants eventually obtained their green cards and later became citizens. ARCA's eventual success, according to immigrant rights activist Pancho Arguelles, was "the only real victory the immigrant rights movement has had in the last ten years or many more . . . the only real victory we have had was the late amnesty cases."[40]

Jiménez's guidance was crucial for ARCA members' campaign to succeed in obtaining late amnesty. According to Anna Nuñez, a political activist in Houston, Jiménez "headed up ARCA . . . and thanks to her, national laws got changed. She mobilized communities nationwide and hundreds of thousands of people were legalized who had gotten left out of the late 80s amnesty."[41] Jiménez's concern about the amnesty problem began in the Spring of 1998 "after noticing a violation of the 1986 law on one man's deportation order."[42] She immediately called a meeting and told the three hundred in attendance, "The only thing you can do is to organize and try to get your own law through Congress. We will help you organize."[43]

Within a month ARCA had had several meetings and had created a web page. Jiménez provided ARCA with a national strategy for their late amnesty campaign and obtained funds for the new group from the AFSC. Although the Quaker organization willingly helped ARCA, other national organizations hesitated, such as the National Immigration Forum and the National Council of La Raza. They made statements, according to Arguelles, like, "No, that's not possible. . . . Winning is not possible. This is not winnable." They also referred to the "current political climate," which was the reason that Arguelles called these pessimists "meteorologists."[44]

This dire situation of being denied a pathway to citizenship was the background to the creation of ARCA and Jiménez's invaluable advice to the organization's fight for justice. As Jiménez explained,

Their struggle took three years. And they needed a law from Congress to legalize their situation which had been pending for over twelve

years when they started their struggle. And so, they [Congress] passed
it [the LIFE Act]. . . . And they [the activists] were the ones that gave
it life or kept it going . . . I, think it was May [1998)], took a hundred
immigrants, mostly of Latin America, to lobby in DC. So we trained
them how to lobby. . . . They began to organize other late amnesty
applicants in Chicago. And I went with them at the beginning to the
organizations which they did in Chicago, in Miami, in LA, and San
Francisco, New York and Houston. And we set up chapters. It started
working all over the country.[45]

As was her custom, Jiménez worked with a group in their initial stages but
urged them to continue on their own. She was impressed with their effort,
saying, "They were particularly motivated . . . the leadership was very
smart. The only thing I did was . . . direct them . . . [as] an organizer does."[46]
One exceptional member in Houston who emerged as a leader in ARCA
greatly appreciated Jiménez's organizational strategy. This person, Adriana
Fernández, remembered that Jiménez "told us we were the ones with the
problem and we would have to take care of it ourselves."[47]

Jiménez helped ARCA, but at the same time, she learned a lot from
them. The national campaign involved a wide range of activities, including
conference calls and the extensive use of the internet. Recalling this experience, Jiménez laughed, "Well, they taught me how to use the internet. I didn't
know how to use the internet. Some of them are very savvy." Many ARCA
members were not Latinos. The ARCA group in San Jose, California, for
example, included Sikhs. Jiménez was not certain that they always understood her because she did not speak Punjabi. Nevertheless, they lobbied in
Washington, DC, with other immigrants. A well-pleased and proud Jiménez
remembered saying at the time, "Even if they just walked the halls of Congress
with their turbans and so forth . . . people would ask, 'What's happening?'
'What are they doing here?'" She also commented that, "in terms of Congress
itself, you rarely see real people lobbying. They're used to the professional
lobbyists on Capitol Hill."[48]

A complication to this legal battle for late amnesty was the passage in
1996 of the IIRIRA. Section 377 of IIRIRA addressed the review by the courts
of naturalization cases. Applicants for late amnesty whose cases had been

rejected by INS staff by a procedure called "front-desking" could no longer appeal their case in the courts. Because of IIRIRA's Section 377, "The court's jurisdiction over the applicants was retroactively removed and about 350,000 U.S. residents saw their status revert to illegal residency, many after residing in the country for 10 years."[49] Fortunately, the US Supreme Court ruled in 1999 on the 1992 Catholic Social Services case, mentioned earlier, and ordered INS to accept and process applicants who had been rejected by the front-desking procedure. ARCA continued its impressive and persistent efforts that eventually culminated in the Legal Immigration Family Equity (LIFE) Act of 2000 signed into law on December 21, 2000.[50] It offered a new residency period to accommodate the late amnesty applicants. LIFE stated that applicants needed to have resided continuously in the United States from November 6, 1986, until May 4, 1988. Importantly, the law also stated that brief periods out of the country did not disqualify applicants.

Jiménez and the activists of ARCA achieved their objective. President Clinton approved late amnesty shortly before he left office. Their efforts, which included many trips to Washington, DC, paid off and provided them with invaluable experience. As ARCA leader Adriana Fernández described it, "To visit the White House as an undocumented immigrant was a real honor." This major political victory was possible because of efforts by ARCA but also, according to the *Houston Chronicle*, the "help of U.S. Rep. Sheila Jackson Lee [1950–2024], D-Houston [Eighteenth District], and longtime activist Maria Jiménez."[51] Representative Jackson Lee organized a congressional hearing and Fernández testified.[52] The congresswoman said that she wanted to help the ARCA activists because "America must confront a broken immigration system . . . we must have policies that respond to human beings not only in our city [Houston], but here in the United States."[53]

Jiménez and the Killing of Serafin Olvera

In 2001 an unambiguous example of racism and callous violation of human rights occurred, committed by INS agents. It was another incident in which Jiménez helped to obtain justice following a senseless tragedy. In this case the family of the victim, a Mexican national, contacted Jiménez for advice.

The victim was Serafin Olvera, a Mexican laborer and long-time Houston resident. At the time of the incident, Olvera was working as a house painter in Bryan, Texas, about one hundred miles northwest of Houston. On March 21 INS agents raided the Bryan home that he shared with other Mexicans. During the raid agents tackled Olvera, breaking his neck. Either believing Olvera was faking or indifferent to his injury, the INS agents repeatedly picked him up from the floor and then dropped him. One agent even sprayed the immobile victim's eyes with pepper spray. INS agents later covered up the incident, claiming that his injury occurred earlier at work. Unfortunately, they did not take him to a hospital in San Antonio for several hours. Olvera never recovered from his injuries and died on February 24, 2002, eleven months after the raid. The medical examiner concluded that his death was a homicide.[54]

Jiménez provided crucial advice to Olivera's relatives during the difficult legal battle for justice. Olvera's family and friends needed her advice because justice was often denied to undocumented immigrants, according to UH law Professor Joseph A. Vail (1952–2008). He said that "much of the work of the INS is done outside the limelight. It's a problem. Rights are violated all the time, but the immigrant remains quiet or gets deported and the incident is just forgotten."[55] In Olvera's tragic case, however, the incident was not forgotten because of the relentless efforts of his US-born relatives, especially his sister-in-law Martha Olvera.[56] Serafin Olvera's family had to challenge a powerful and uncooperative federal agency. The INS, for example, deported the approximately twenty Mexicans who had witnessed the fatal incident in Bryan to Mexico before they could make statements about the raid. However, following their deportation, Serafin's brother Gelasio went to Veracruz, Mexico, and returned with these witnesses.

In addition to Jiménez and the advice she gave to family members, the witnesses also helped to get justice for Olvera when they gave their testimony to US investigators. Recalling Gelasio's undertaking, Jiménez said, "If the family didn't bring them back from Mexico, there would be no witnesses."[57] The border agents in the incident were tried and found guilty in February 2004. The agent most responsible for the injuries was convicted of "willful indifference for failing to get timely medical care for Serafin Olvera, 48, of

Houston."[58] The guilty verdicts were possibly the first time "federal agents were convicted for failing to provide medical aid to illegal immigrants," according to the prosecuting lawyer from the DOJ.[59] A week before the conviction, the Olvera family won their law suit against the INS and was awarded a settlement of $2.15 million.[60]

The AFSC and Jiménez Part Ways: Her Activism Takes a New Direction

Jiménez worked for the AFSC until 2003. Her termination, after sixteen and a half years, was not amicable, and her attempt to be reinstated failed. Her main concern was not herself but the immigrants she could help as director of ILEMP in Houston. In mid-April of 2003, after AFSC fired her, it permanently closed the ILEMP office in Houston. However, a few months before her termination, AFSC had reassigned her to Philadelphia to head Project Voice, a national immigrants' rights program.

Jiménez's unfortunate firing was a personal blow to her, but AFSC lost a highly productive director of ILEMP. Her termination followed an email she wrote after AFCS announced its decision to close the Houston office. According to Jiménez, the email was a parody. She explained, "I took the *Mexicana* attitude of political satire, which any Latino who read the email would just burst out laughing. But they didn't take it that way."[61] She further explained,

> This was an office that didn't have to close. The institution could have done fundraising, had people willing to do it freely. . . . But they chose to close the office because I raised my voice in protest . . . I was fired for writing an email to 20 people, of which the institution did not like the content, and that was it. . . . And I was directing—ironically—a project called Project Voice. And it's all the voices, my own as an immigrant and all the voices of the immigrants, that are not being heard and are being silenced."[62]

Groups and individuals familiar with Jiménez's activism and commitment to immigrant and human rights protested her firing. Pancho Arguelles of the National Organizers Alliance criticized the AFSC and said, "Today, they are not only making a big mistake, but also making an injustice. And a strong contradiction . . . of what AFSC has been for more than 50 years. There is a big lack of trust right now among some of the partners who were involved with AFSC."[63] Anna Nuñez complained that "they unjustly fired her because she spoke out. . . .That's who she is, she speaks up and she complained. She fights for things that are not just and they fired her for that."[64] A vigil in Houston following her firing took place February 2003 with speakers representing fifteen Hispanic-rights organizations, labor unions, and Mayor Lee Brown's office. Richard Shaw, head of the local AFL-CIO, told the *Houston Chronicle*, "There is not one single immigrant organization I deal with who does not hold her in the highest regard . . . I consider her the godmother of the local immigrant community."[65]

Jiménez objected to the closure, believing that the Houston location and the network she had built were critical to her advocacy of social justice for immigrants. However, she remained a committed activist. Interestingly, after her termination, she said that people asked her, "Why aren't you angry?" She responded, "These types of things happen all over the country every single day every worker is denied. This is a country where there's an 'at will' doctrine. So I'm one more person who was faced with that. . . . So it's not an unusual experience because [if] you look at it from the collective experience of the society that doesn't protect workers, it's going to happen. I mean it happens."[66] Employed or not, Jiménez's commitment to social justice remained firm. She once commented that "I am going to die doing this work whether I am paid for it or not!"[67]

Tragedy in Victoria, Texas

A tragic incident occurred a month after Jiménez left the AFSC that required her expertise as an advocate for immigrant and human rights. On May 14, 2003, local authorities in Victoria, near Houston, discovered a grisly scene. Described as the nation's deadliest smuggling case, at least seventy-four undocumented immigrants were abandoned in a hot trailer by the driver, a Jamaican legal resident, who was transporting them to Houston. Temperatures in the truck reached 173 degrees Fahrenheit. Testimony at the trial revealed that the driver heard his passengers banging on the walls of the truck before he fled the scene. Nineteen died from asphyxiation and heat-related conditions. Among the dead was a 5-year-old boy. Witnesses reported that the child cried in this father's arms, saying, "Daddy, Daddy, I'm dying."[68] Sadly, undocumented immigrants, in this case and others, knew that they took risks entering the country without documentation, but the Victoria incident was an especially shocking example of these risks. Jiménez had long advocated an immigration policy that facilitated legal movement across borders, a policy that could end smuggling by callous "coyotes" who brought immigrants into the country illegally. Remarking on the tragedy in Victoria, she said regretfully, "In a sense these were preventable deaths."[69] As for the truck driver, Tyrone Williams, he was finally resentenced in January 2011, after many trials, to 405 months in prison.[70]

The tragedy became a major news story. Alarmed officials in Washington, DC, took action in June 2003, only one month after the incident. Specifically, the House Judiciary Committee's Subcommittee on Immigration conducted a hearing to address the crime of smuggling. At this time Jiménez was the chair of the Advisory Committee for MOIRA, which sent her to Washington to speak at the hearing. In describing the immigrants' reliance on smugglers, Jiménez told the subcommittee, "From their perspective, these types of enterprises are a necessary evil." In her statement before Congress, she said:

> The choice to move for the opportunity of improving one's well-being in a stronger economy or a more open society is made by individuals responding to the driving forces of labor needs in an ever-integrating international economy. The shortcomings of current immigration law and policy that create obstacles to an orderly, safe, and legal movement of people across international borders to resolve these labor needs frame the context for increasing the profitability for international commercial enterprises to move persons clandestinely across borders. In the equation, human life, rights, and dignity are subordinated to profit. It is time to take the profit motive out of this illicit activity.

Jiménez concluded, "It is time to reclaim life, dignity and rights for all persons."[71]

The risk that the undocumented immigrants took resulted from their dire need for employment. When a tragic situation occurs, however, documented immigrants do not cooperate with the authorities investigating the crimes that victimize them. Even Jiménez could not convince the immigrants who were witnesses to another deadly incident, when three men died, to speak to authorities. As Jiménez explained, the immigrants feared that the smugglers would retaliate against relatives in Mexico.[72] As for the smugglers, if they are arrested and convicted, they usually serve only a few years in prison, even in the case of the death of immigrants they brought into the country. Lawmakers attempted to reduce the smugglers' dangerous business. For example, Representative Sheila Jackson Lee (D-TX) introduced the Commercial Alien Smuggling Elimination Act of 2003, CASE Act, H.R. 2630, and a similar bill two years later.[73] Neither were enacted. She also supported another bill that, like hers, providing incentives for immigrants to testify against smugglers, granting them a special visa. As Representative Jackson Lee explained later, the bill would establish "a rewards program . . . virtually the same one the State Department presently uses to obtain informants in cases involving terrorists."[74]

Labor Unions' New Interest in Immigrant Workers

In 2000 Jiménez participated directly in an unexpected decision by unions to attract immigrant workers. That year the Harris County AFL-CIO hired her to assist it in this goal. A specific nationwide AFL-CIO undertaking to attract immigrant workers was the Immigrant Worker Freedom Ride (IWFR) in 2004, discussed later. Jiménez led this project and was "instrumental in building a coalition that supported the IWFR in Houston."[75] Commenting on the AFL-CIO's new focus, Jiménez said, "It was quite a surprise to see the change. . . .We used to be on opposite sides."[76] She may not have been aware of earlier instances of the intense union activism among immigrant workers, including Mexicans, in the United States.[77] Nevertheless, Jiménez assumed that the AFL-CIO had finally decided that "the only way to eliminate them [undocumented workers] is to legalize them and unionize them, where before they were opposed to it." She concluded that unions finally "understood that . . . people who are here without documents will never go away because they are needed as part of the exploitation in profit-making companies and sectors."[78]

In one initiative Houston's AFL-CIO Council organized a meeting in November 2000 to instruct undocumented workers on how to sue in the case of wage theft. Wage theft, a common complaint by undocumented workers, is the practice of denying a worker all or some of his or her wages for work completed. Regarding the meeting in November, the president of the AFL-CIO Council in the Houston area, Dale Wortham, declared, "We believe we're breaking new ground. We're teaching them to sue."[79] For Wortham, a self-described "recovering redneck," the unions' new interest in immigrant laborers was significant.[80] Andy Levin of the AFL-CIO agreed and said, "You can't appreciate how big a sea change this is for the labor movement." He added, "I would say for some years, there was a fear of creating a race to the bottom by organizing low-wage workers."[81]

The unions' change in their opinion of immigrant labor, including undocumented workers, can be interpreted in different and valid ways. First, the unions' efforts to attract immigrant workers was less an advance in the racial attitudes of union members than a desire to increase union membership; in other words, the change was an example of interest convergence. Kris Axtman, a labor union scholar, offered a second explanation of the unions' involvement with immigrant workers. He asserted that unions wanted to expand beyond "a narrowly focused interest group" to represent a "social movement—one they can say [represents] the voice of working men and women."[82]

Whatever the reason for the help provided to vulnerable immigrant workers, Jiménez was pleased and took a significant role in the union's new direction. In 2001 Jiménez and a large coalition of Houston groups and organizations created the Justice and Equality in the Workplace Program (JEWP). This important organization wanted to help immigrant workers who were frequent victims of crime, especially wage theft. Although undocumented workers experienced wage theft the most, US citizens and legal residents did too. On wage theft Jiménez remarked, "It's because of the presence of immigrants in these trades where it's easy not to pay them—like landscaping or construction—because (employers) know they can get away with it."[83] JEWP aggressively targeted corrupt employers. By mid-2003 it had recovered "over $1.3 million in back wages for 1,900 workers" in Houston. It publicized its service on over thirty billboards in Spanish in different parts of Houston, including near the Oscar Romero Day Labor Center for documented and undocumented workers. [84] This unprecedented coalition consisted, initially, of the Mexican Consulate, the Salvadorian Consulate, the EEOC, the DOL's Wage and Hour Division, MOIRA, and MALDEF. The coalition later expanded significantly.

Immigrant Workers Freedom Ride and Recognition for Jiménez's Activism

In 2003 Jiménez helped plan a national event for immigrant workers that was an unambiguous call for social justice and equality. She and the AFL-CIO, specifically, hoped "to persuade Congress and the public to back legislation to give legal status to millions of illegal immigrants."[85] Jiménez and the labor organization, therefore, coordinated to organize the Immigrant Workers Freedom Ride. For one Houston resident, the Freedom Ride expressed to the nation that its participants wanted "to be equal and to have a voice. We just want decent and fair wages."[86] During the Freedom Ride—designed, in part, to highlight events of an earlier fight for social justice and equality—the immigrant workers traveled to twelve cities to visit historic sites of the Civil Rights Movement. For example, they traveled to Birmingham, Alabama and Atlanta, Georgia. The trip included eighteen buses and eight hundred persons from ten cities. Organizers planned stops "in more than 100 communities in 42 states so the riders can hold rallies and news conferences, meet with political leaders and seek public support."[87]

Jiménez and Richard Shaw of the AFL-CIO worked together to organize the participants from Houston. This project was Jiménez's first major achievement after leaving the AFSC. In fact she asserted, "If I hadn't been fired from AFSC I wouldn't have even been able to come on this trip because when I came back, I was hired by AFL and began organizing."[88] Later, after the Freedom Ride, Jiménez was delighted to be honored by a letter from the Southern Poverty Law Center (SPLC). She also received a certificate signed by SPLC's director Morris Dees and Rosa Parks, the famous civil rights activist who helped launch the Montgomery, Alabama, bus boycott in December 1955.

Just as the AFL-CIO's new pro-immigrant worker position was notable, so too was the critical and very public role taken by undocumented immigrants in the Immigrant Workers Freedom Ride. The San Antonio Spanish-language newspaper *La Prensa* quoted Jaime Contreras, a labor union leader, who told immigrants to participate "because if we do nothing, nothing will happen."[89] Jiménez recalled, "And interestingly enough, people got permission, got vacation, it was primarily immigrants who went . . . although unions and religious groups went, as well." On the buses Jiménez said that "we learned how to sing 'We shall overcome' in Spanish: '*No nos vencerán.*'"[90] According to the *New York Times*, the foreign-born workers traveled to Washington calling "for legalizing the status of illegal immigrants, increasing visas for family reunification and stepping up protections for immigrant workers."[91] The ten-day trip included stops at many places that were famous from the Civil Rights Movement, such as the Ebenezer Baptist Church, "the spiritual home of civil rights leader Reverend Dr. Martin Luther King, Jr."[92] Six participants, including Jiménez, took part in a wreath-laying ceremony at King's crypt. She recalled, "Six of us were allowed to put a wreath on Martin Luther King's grave. It was a wonderful experience!"[93]

In describing her experience during the Freedom Ride, Jiménez expressed great pride in the historic event. She had learned years earlier, when a young child in Mexico, the importance of historical knowledge. Jiménez remarked, "It was great for the immigrants to learn about the struggle of the African Americans because people didn't have an idea of what it took . . . to end segregation." In fact, one immigrant who took part in the Freedom Ride told Jiménez, "My God, when we worry just about being deported, some people here were killed!" When Jiménez and other participants reached Selma, Alabama, a local committee, she recalled, had "organized the march across Pettus Bridge. Just like the Civil Rights Movement. . . . We marched across with local people. . . . It was *exciting*! We met family members of the four little girls that were killed in the bomb[ing]. They received us in the church where Martin Luther King was pastor during the Montgomery Boycott. I mean it was *exciting!*"[94]

The Freedom Ride was an invaluable experience for its participants and renewed their resolve to continue with their struggle for social justice. The journey ended with stops in Washington, DC, on October 1, then on to New York. In DC Jiménez recalled, "We went to lobby. There were about two hundred lobbyists. From there, we went on to New York and it ended in a rally." In New York Jiménez was chosen to speak at the rally, but she received a greater honor later, she remarked, which was a letter about the Wall of Power in 2005 to commemorate the Fiftieth Anniversary Montgomery Boycott. Of this she said, "They're putting together a wall of tolerance. And they asked if it was okay if they listed my name of many people for their work on civil rights!"[95]

Jiménez's mission, to promote the human rights of immigrants, became critical in 2005 when a new danger to undocumented immigrants arose in Houston: Minutemen. The organization's full name was the Minuteman Civil Defense Coalition (MCDC). Its primary, though not exclusive, goal was to block unauthorized entry into the United States at the US-Mexico border. This anti-immigrant paramilitary group, based in Arizona, was headed by Chris Simcox, a colorful personality who was later arrested, in 2013, for allegedly sexually molesting three girls, and later found guilty of child molestation.[96] In Texas Bill Parmley founded an MCDC branch at Goliad in 2005. He later resigned from the group in July of that year because of the racist comments made by its members. For example, members expressed interest in "shooting illegal immigrants or letting them die of dehydration."[97] Another member asked point blank, "Can't we just shoot 'em?"[98] Some of the individuals who were attracted to the MCDC, according to one member, were "retired Houston police officers or Harris County sheriff's deputies, and . . . war veterans."[99]

Anti-immigrant racism reached a dangerous level in 2005 when the Houston branch of the MCDC decided to target undocumented workers in their city. The MCDC's decision prompted Jiménez, Juan Alvarez, and Benito Juárez to mobilize the Coalition against Intolerance and for Respect

(CAIFR). In addition to CAIFR and other pro-immigrant organizations, important groups and individuals who opposed the Minutemen's plans in Houston included The Metropolitan Organization, LULAC, Houston Councilman Gordon Quan (b.1939), and the Catholic archbishop Joseph A. Fiorenza (1931–2022).

Influential officials spoke up against the MCDC. For example, Archbishop Fiorenza told the *Houston Chronicle*, "We stand against any attempt of outsiders to come to Houston to abuse and intimidate our immigrant communities."[100] US Representative Sheila Jackson Lee also expressed concern in May 2005 about the organization's plans. She said, in referring to Governor Rick Perry, "I urge the governor to disinvite the Minuteman Project. Ask them not to come here."[101] Representative Jackson Lee also called a meeting in July 2005 with law enforcement officials in Houston. She told them that the Minutemen "are acting in an unauthorized way and may be characterized even as militia."[102] In mid-August 2005, Simcox, the Minutemen leader, came to Houston and reportedly trained thirty local Minutemen for Operation Spotlight, which was scheduled to start the first day of October.[103] The tactics that the Minutemen planned to use included videotaping and photographing immigrants at the approximately fifty locations where contractors picked them up and recording the license plates numbers of the contractors.[104]

In anticipation of Operation Spotlight, CAIFR and Jiménez offered training on August 7, 2005, for individuals who wanted to monitor the actions of the MCDC. She told the *Houston Chronicle*, "What we want to do is organize workers on all the corners."[105] Regarding the Minuteman group, she declared, "For every Minuteman patrolling, we will have at least 10 people patrolling them. . . . We will respond to your organization with our organization. We are not shy about it!" Also responding to the MCDC was Teodoro Aguiluz, head of CRECEN, an organization that helped immigrants become citizens. He "threatened to file a lawsuit if they observed the Minutemen doing anything illegal."[106]

Houston volunteer monitors, including this writer, received training by the ACLU. A second training session was offered to UH law students. Monitors were trained to use techniques that would diffuse tension at the "informal labor markets" that Jiménez mentioned, including physically stepping between the day laborers and MCDC members if necessary. The literature distributed by the ACLU included the following:

> During this event, legal observers will position themselves alongside Minutemen volunteers, but will remain separate from them. . . . Legal observers maintain impartiality and neutrality during the event. While most legal observers feel strongly about the issues, they have chosen to protect the rights of others at the sacrifice of our own personal expression. Your presence alone is your statement. While you may feel a strong impulse to engage in dialogue or be confrontational with the Minutemen volunteers, you must resist this temptation. We are not there to convince the Minutemen that what they are doing is either illegal or immoral.[107]

As was true at the border, where MCDC operated as well, volunteer monitors wore "clearly marked shirts."[108]

By early October CAIFR changed its tactics for several reasons, including the fact that the harassment by the Minutemen waned after a few months. Jiménez reported, "The Minutemen have stated they suspended their day labor operations in Houston. . . . The truth is they did not get the number of volunteers they thought they would have. . . . They're taking their Houston people to the border." However, the most important reason that CAIFR changed its tactics, Jiménez explained, was because the "day laborers themselves asked us to keep all activities at low key at the corners as visibility activity [of CAIFR volunteers] scared potential employers. . . .We needed to respect their wishes and rethink our strategy." CAIFR immediately changed its tactics and, instead, became more directly involved in reporting any abuse that the workers experienced and soliciting the help of the HPD in these cases. Jiménez reported that "in a meeting with the Chief of Police, HPD assured us that any act of violence should be reported immediately to them and they will attend to the matter."[109]

The MCDC operation in Houston lasted less than six months. A major factor that affected its plans was Hurricane Katrina, which struck Louisiana on August 29, 2005. Many day laborers left for Louisiana because more jobs were available there than in Houston. Estimates of the total number of migrant workers who went to the Gulf Coast area ranged from thirty thousand to one hundred thousand, and of all construction workers in New Orleans, approximately one-fourth were undocumented.[110] The Minutemen left Houston either for the US-Mexico border or for Louisiana. Fortunately, hurricane-struck Louisiana received much-needed aid from the federal government and NGOs. Even Mexico helped when it sent troops to San Antonio to a camp that had been established for displaced Louisianans. President George W. Bush (2001–2009) approved this assistance. The Mexican troops arrived in San Antonio on September 8 to feed storm victims there and, according to Stephen R. Kelly, the United States diplomat to Mexico (2004–2006), before returning to Mexico, "The Mexicans had served 170,000 meals, helped distribute more than 184,000 tons of supplies and conducted more than 500 medical consultations."[111] This presence of the troops was historic because, as historian Martha Menchaca observed, it was "the first time since the Mexican American War from 1846 to 1848 that Mexican troops entered U.S. territory."[112]

Jiménez: Professor and Essayist

In 2005 Jiménez received an offer to train future Mexican American activists for social justice, an ideal opportunity for someone with her extensive theoretical and practical knowledge of activism. That spring CMAS at UH offered Jiménez the opportunity to teach the course "Latino Activism and Organizing." The course became an invaluable addition to the course offerings of CMAS, but it also pleased and gratified Jiménez. She said that she brought, "30 years of experience in the field . . . I'll really enjoy sharing my knowledge with young people and learning from them as well."[113] Jiménez also believed that teaching what she had learned made sense at this phase of her life. She commented, "a lot of my work . . . in the last five years, and probably will continue, will be more to share with younger generations of activists . . . what I've learned."[114]

For Jiménez it was personally satisfying to teach young activists to be warriors for social justice. As CRT asserts, activists of color have a vital role in society: to point out social inequities, to demand an end to them, and to work to reduce racial discrimination. In her class Jiménez offered her perspective on activism, which included urging the voiceless to speak up for their rights. She insisted, "In terms of communities that are neglected or marginalized from opportunities, the only way to ensure that people and their rights are respected is to increase their participation in the political process. The only way to change those inequities is to organize the people so that they can do for themselves."[115]

Among her interests, in addition to teaching a new generation of activists, was the important topic of human rights. She believed that her interest evolved from her work for immigrant rights when she was the director of the ILEMP for AFSC. From this experience she noticed that "immigrants tend to talk less about civil rights . . . because they do come from frameworks of . . . human rights."[116] In other words, Jiménez believed that immigrants talk more about *los derechos humanos* (human rights) because they often originated from countries where civil rights did not exist or were restricted. She observed, "When we talked to groups on the Mexican side [of the border], they have no concept of civil rights or constitutional rights in practice. If you talk to most Latin Americans, they always talk about rights in terms of human rights, *los derechos humanos*."[117]

Her advocacy of social justice included the right to mobility, a crucial human right in her opinion. Her views on the right to mobility grew during her years with AFSC and after leaving that organization. Jiménez knew that even though civil rights, including citizenship requirements, varied from country to country, human rights were universal. Human rights should not be denied to anyone, even if they cross a border from one country to another. In addition to the Lockean rights of life, liberty, and property, Jiménez ardently believed that individuals and groups should have the right to mobility. She insisted that workers have the right to freedom and economic survival and should not have to forfeit basic human rights when entering another country.

Jiménez considered the right of mobility essential for today's workforce. She presented her views on this right as early as 1994 in a panel discussion on NAFTA. For example, she pressed for easier legal entry from Mexico into the United States. Legal entry would eliminate the necessity of unauthorized, dangerous, and sometimes deadly entries. Unauthorized entry into the United States benefited corrupt and heartless coyotes and stripped emigrants of their dignity. Addressing the matter of dignity, Jiménez wrote, "We must begin defending the Mexican worker, and his or her dignity, by allowing that Mexican worker to walk across a bridge, and not swim the river."[118] Another problem was the militarization of the border which presented an unconscionable barrier to the right to mobility. Heightened control at the border, she believed, benefited the powerful at the expense of the working poor.

A more recent articulation of her belief in the right of mobility appeared in the essay "On Freedom and Equality: The Struggle for Global Democracy" in a book by Arjun Makhijani entitled *Manifesto for Global Democracy.*[119] Makhijani's essay denounced globalization and the harm that major powers, especially the United States, inflicted on weaker countries. He also discussed problems created by nations' border policies, a topic that drew his attention to Jiménez's writings. Makhijani not only quoted her in his essay, but he also thanked her in the book's acknowledgements. Jiménez's comments specifically addressed the economic exploitation of immigrant workers and the use of coercive forces, like border agents, against workers. She wrote,

> It is restrictions to mobility through the use of force that is inherent in subduing, controlling and integrating populations into strategies of economic exploitation of labor forces. It was use of military force that obligated native populations in North America to be confined to reservations and in Latin America to encomiendas. It was the use of military force that led to enslavement of the African population that led to the economic growth of the conquering elites. The use of military force is a tacit indication of the high priority placed by the elites in their quest for dominance and wealth.[120]

The topic of borders and movement across them is not a modern one and will continue to be a delicate international and domestic issue. Indeed, the need grows each day for a universal plan to address the problem of mobility.

The Dreamers: Out of the Shadows

The pro-immigrant activist Jiménez followed with great interest the rise of a national movement led by undocumented youths called the Dreamers. Numerically, in 2006 they were a small and specific group that included college students. Of the undocumented college students in the country, full-time and part-time, the estimate was between fifty thousand and sixty thousand. The total did not include others who were potentially eligible—specifically, young undocumented men and women in the military.[121] In Houston the young Dreamer activists organized Jóvenes Inmigrantes por un Futuro Mejor (JIFM) or Young Immigrants for a Better Future. In 2001 Jiménez gladly offered advice to JIFM because she knew the emotional toll of discrimination against immigrants and how difficult the struggle was for social justice and equality. Across the country these activists mobilized to urge Congress to pass what became known as the DREAM Act (Development, Relief, and Education for Alien Minors Act). First introduced in 2001, the bill's goal was to provide a pathway to citizenship for undocumented immigrants who came to this country as minors when their parents entered the United States without documentation.

Jiménez knew the Dreamers' fight for a pathway to citizenship would include many disappointments. She remarked in 2004 that "the road we have ahead is not an easy one. Our struggle is a long and difficult one. We have to take advantage of the upcoming elections to pressure President Bush into supporting the (Dream Act)."[122] The DREAM Act, in fact, failed to pass "as stand-alone bills or as attachments to omnibus bills in 2003, 2004, and 2005."[123] As of mid-2021, at least eleven versions of the Dream Act were introduced in Congress. All failed to become law.

Although the DREAM Act did not become a federal law in 2001 or later, some positive changes emerged at the state level, first in Texas and then across the nation. Specifically, following the example of community college systems in Houston and Dallas, other community colleges in Texas began to offer in-state tuition for undocumented students.[124] Later, in 2001, the Texas legislature passed House Bill 1403, which allowed undocumented students to pay in-state tuition if they had resided in the state for three years and graduated from a high school in Texas. Legislators who opposed in-state tuition for undocumented students repeatedly tried to eliminate it.[125] Fortunately for the Dreamers, Texas Governor Rick Perry (R) supported it. Years later, during the 2012 Republican presidential primaries, candidate Perry defended his position even though it damaged him politically. He asserted in one televised debate, "If you say that we should not educate children who have come into our state for no other reason that they have been brought there by no fault of their own, I don't think you have a heart."[126] The intense political opposition to in-state tuition seemed disproportionate to total number of students it involved. Only .008 percent of full-time college students in Texas were undocumented—that is, 9,062 out of 1,102,572 in 2007.[127]

The Dreamer movement, led by an energetic and innovative generation of undocumented youth, was a welcome development for older activists like Jiménez, who turned 57 years old in 2007. The Dreamers' political activism contrasted sharply with the conduct that their parents taught them. Their more cautious parents, Tomás R. Jiménez, professor of sociology at the University of California, San Diego, explained, "are here without authorization [and] feel they don't have the same leverage. Their children do and they are coming of age politically."[128] For example, the Dreamers in the JIFM organized a letter writing campaign that contributed significantly to the passage of the Texas law on in-state tuition.[129]

The Dreamers also differed from their parents by coming "out of the shadows" and making their demands very public. The Dreamers, therefore, pursued a new strategy, one that is advocated by CRT: storytelling. They started telling their life stories because they wanted the public to see them as human beings and not as a despised stereotype. They were honest and hardworking. They loved and identified with the only country that they knew, the United States. Furthermore, Jiménez pointed out, the youth were "articulating what has been taught in government and civic classes."[130] Fortunately, a national network, Fair Immigration Reform Movement (FIRM), formed in 2004 by the Center for Community Change, provided vital guidance to the Dreamers.[131] FIRM offered training for the young immigrants to develop a narrative that was designed to gain public support for the DREAM Act. The Dreamers agreed with FIRM that "storytelling is the most important way of getting our message out."[132] The Dreamers wanted to make themselves known to the public as human beings and not a menacing "other."[133]

Jiménez was delighted when Dreamers changed their strategy later, in 2010, because she always believed that those who suffered discrimination should organize themselves. Specifically, following the defeats of the

DREAM Act in 2010, the Dreamers entered a new phase when they created their own narrative, insisting on the right to speak on their own terms and not following the narrative crafted by others. They took very personally the malicious attacks made against their families and culture by virulently anti-immigrant persons and organizations like FAIR. A pleased Jiménez said that the young adults in the social movement were "acting as a sort of bullhorn through which their parents' hopes and aspirations are voiced."[134] She also predicted that Dreamers and other Hispanics "will remember it [the invectives] as a personal attack on their families. They will vote."[135]

The young immigrants' new militancy clearly impressed Jiménez. She believed that the Dreamers were committed to forming a social movement that represented the best values of this country, such as the belief in social justice and equality. Another person impressed with the Dreamers was Professor Michael A. Olivas (1951–2022), the William B. Bates Distinguished Chair in Law at the UH Law Center. He described the political activities in 2006 as "the first national, substantial public displays of support on behalf of immigrants, and they energized supporters and opponent alike."[136] Jiménez added that, "What's different today is the sheer quantity of the immigrants. . . . We haven't seen mobilization of this type."[137] Also different, Jiménez noted, was the use of social media to organize protests and other forms of activism.

Peaceful nationwide protests took place in the spring of 2006 against the hostile anti-immigrant climax at the time. The protests occurred in 120 cities and included 3.5 million immigrants and US citizens.[138] Countless students and their supporters, an estimated half-million in Los Angeles alone, participated in a nationwide march on April 10. In the following month, on May 1, 2006, the young immigrant activists joined hundreds of thousands of other immigrants, both legal and undocumented, in the historic Day without an Immigrant March. They protested against the Border Protection, Anti-Terrorism, and Illegal Immigration Control Act (H.R. 4437), introduced in Congress by James Sensenbrenner (R-WI) on December 16, 2005. The bill, which did not become law, was described by historian Neil Foley as the "most draconian anti-immigrant legislation ever seriously proposed" and meant that fearful undocumented persons had to "live with the specter of deportation."[139]

Conclusion

As discussed in this chapter, Jiménez and other activists fought against social injustices that violated the rights and dignity of the immigrant community. Fortunately, Jiménez's unique background and skill at fighting racial discrimination prepared her well for such challenges. A major struggle, and victory, was her success in the ARCA's campaign for late amnesty that culminated with the LIFE Act of 2000. Jiménez guided the undocumented immigrants in the three-year legal battle, for example, by teaching them how to lobby and by taking them to the Pentagon and the Congress to meet with officials there. Fortunately, Congress passed the LIFE ACT in December 2000. As great as this victory was, Jiménez remained alarmed by the intense anti-immigrant, especially anti-Mexican, climate during the late 1990s and early 2000s. The persistence of commonplace racist prejudices maintained a tenacious hold on many Americans' minds and undermined the nation's value of justice. The consequences were significant, and the situation remained precarious for undocumented individuals and other Hispanics. Examples included the INS violence against undocumented immigrants, as in the case of Serafin Olvera; police killings, as in the case of Oregón Navarro; and the hundreds of hate crimes each year against Hispanics.

Jiménez helped the victims, and the immigrant community, in many ways. For example, she chaired the Advisory Committee of MOIRA that the city of Houston created to aid its immigrant residents. In addition, the Harris County AFL-CIO hired her when it decided to promote union membership among documented and undocumented workers. The union even provided training for immigrant workers on how to sue employers in the case of wage theft. Jiménez and the AFL-CIO also organized the historic Immigrant Workers Freedom Ride. The goal of the event was the passage of a federal law that extended a pathway to citizenship to undocumented immigrants. The Freedom Ride also inspired the participants to continue their struggle because they learned the history of the earlier activists, specifically African Americans during the Civil Rights Movement of the 1950s and 1960s.

A very positive development in the early 2000s, one that delighted Jiménez, was the impressive rise in assertiveness among young undocumented immigrants. They organized the Dreamer Movement. What Jiménez had long advocated, that discriminated individuals and groups must organize themselves to fight injustice and that minorities themselves should make their stories known, materialized with this group. In the Dreamer Movement, undocumented youth bravely stepped "out of the shadows" to tell the nation their personal stories, their accomplishments, and their dream to become US citizens.

Jiménez realized that the immigrant community, with the Dreamer Movement, had passed into a new and crucial stage of their fight for immigration reform and human rights. Having been a voice for the voiceless and an advocate for civil and human rights for decades, Jiménez welcomed the spirit and energy of the Dreamers. She was optimistic about the future for the immigrant community because of the young immigrants' willingness to pick up the torch for social justice and to seek the public support for their cause. As she told this writer in 2004, "I've always said that the biggest demonstration I have ever seen in Houston spontaneously felt by the majority of the peoples, was when the Rockets won the NBA Championship. There were 200,000 people outside in the streets of Houston, and I said, 'Wow, the day we can get people to do that on human rights issues . . .'" This writer then said, "Yeah, your work is done!" To which she added, "Yeah, I can go home and sleep!"[140]

Epilogue

> Our identity is partly shaped by recognition or its absence, often by the *mis*recognition of others, and so a person can suffer real damage, real distortion, if the people or society around them mirror back to them a confining or demeaning or contemptible picture of themselves. Nonrecognition or misrecognition can inflict harm, can be a form of oppression, imprisoning someone in a false, distorted, and reduced mode of being.
> —Charles Taylor[1]

> My students . . . knew even in their youth the pain of prejudice. They never seem to know why people disliked them. But they knew it was so. I saw it in their eyes.
> —Lyndon B. Johnson[2]

The quote above by philosopher Charles Taylor addresses the need to respect others because not to do so causes harm. In the second quote, President Lyndon B. Johnson recalled his personal observation of that harm when he was a schoolteacher for Mexican-origin students in Texas. The stories in this book were offered with the hope of reducing racial prejudices, which constitute a stain on the nation's values of equality and social justice for everyone. Prejudices, based on ignorance, are used to justify racial discrimination in multiple forms—for example, obstacles to voting, denial of jury duty, barriers to quality education, separating immigrant children from their parents and putting both in cages, and the tolerance of hate crimes and wage theft. The struggles to fight these wrongs have been waged by warriors for social justice like Maria Jiménez and the other activists discussed in this book. This book told their stories and their efforts to advance social justice and equality in the United States. Despite the forms of injustice that they experienced, these activists fought to advance equality and defend the dignity of all persons through collective efforts like protests, legal action, and labor organizing.

223

To provide an explanation for the racist discrimination that the Mexican-origin activists experienced and battled, this writer used concepts from CRT that Richard Delgado and Jean Stefancic presented in their book *Critical Race Theory: An Introduction*. The authors explained the persistence of racial animus and discrimination thus: individuals and groups live in their own normative universe, or "nomos," that sometimes includes racist prejudices that are pervasive and tenacious—that is, commonplace.[3]

In CRT racism is not considered an aberration but is believed to be normal. It is normal because it is pervasive, and not in the sense that it is morally, socially, and politically acceptable. Not everyone is racist, but racism is such a pervasive problem that everyone needs to be concerned about it and address it. It is not a problem associated only with, for example, a bigoted neighbor, a radical on the left or right, or a nativist militia member. It could be a characteristic of anyone—for example, oneself, a good friend, a school board member, a teacher, an employer, an office mate, or an elected official. Any solution to the problem of racism for a society that professes to believe in democracy, where the rights and dignity of others are respected and protected, begins by recognizing the existence of racism. At that point steps can be taken to eliminate obstacles to social justice, like negative and demeaning stereotypes and racial discrimination.

The injustices described in this book never would have happened had individuals believed in and enforced the concept expressed in the United Nations' Universal Declaration of Human Rights, article 1: "All human beings are born free and equal in dignity and rights." The rest of article 1 expresses what activists for social justice believe, that "[human begins] are endowed with reason and conscience and should act towards one another in a spirit of brotherhood."[4] For example, instead of restaurants posting "No Mexicans Served" signs, Mexican American veterans could have eaten in restaurants. Instead of Texas schools keeping Spanish-speaking students arbitrarily in the first two grades for four years, the schools would have offered these students an educational system that met their pedagogical needs and respected their culture. As for Mexican immigrants, the militarized Operation Wetback would not have forcibly deported, in only three months, over one million Mexicans, or, more recently, the federal government would not have placed immigrant children in cages. Few persons, including this writer, advocate open borders, but the nation needs a humane immigration policy.

History books, including this one, contain examples of anti-Mexican discrimination, but they also tell of activists who fought for social justice. Their activism represents two important concepts in CRT. First, activists of oppressed minority groups, particularly minorities of color, must present a counternarrative to society that considers white culture the norm and nonwhites as problematic, as the "other," even "alien." Second, the minority activists' life stories and struggles provide them with insights that whites do not share. From their firsthand experiences with racial discrimination, minority activists recognize oppressive words and deeds that nonminority individuals sometimes do not. Their perception derived from what W. E. B. Du Bois called "double-consciousness." Minorities develop it from living in parallel societies wherein the dominant white culture, Du Bois wrote, considers them a "problem." It is a society where, he wrote, the marginalized person looks "at one's self through the eyes of others, of measuring one's soul by the [measuring] tape of a world that looks on in amused contempt and pity. One ever feels his twoness—an American, a Negro; two souls, two thoughts, two unreconciled strivings."[5]

This book also addressed the important topic of immigration, an exceptionally complex topic. What is certain is that emigration to the United States will continue, legally and illegally. Therefore, there is a critical need today for immigration reform. The events described in this book make this need clear. Throughout the nation's history, its position on immigration has always been Janus-faced. On the one hand, the United States has embraced immigrants, and on the other it has rejected them. When rejection occurred, newcomers were denied their dignity and civil rights.[6] This tension over immigrants and immigration is not new. For example, Benjamin Franklin (1706–1790) expressed his concern about German immigrants when he remarked that "unless the stream of their importation could be tamed . . . our government will become precarious."[7] Despite disparaging views on immigrants from the time of Franklin, wave after wave of persons from distant lands joined their predecessors to improve their lives in a nation rich with opportunities and a society with rights protected by its constitution.

"Reclaiming Our History" and Mexican American Activism

Jiménez once commented that part of the excitement among participants of the Chicano Movement of the 1960s and 1970s was the opportunity to celebrate their history. The period was, she said, "like a cultural renaissance . . . [and] you were recuperating this identity everybody denied us."[8] Participants in the Chicano Movement eagerly learned their history, which, unfortunately, had been absent or distorted in classrooms and historical literature. This was the kind of neglect that Charles Taylor, quoted above, considered immoral. Chicano and Chicana activists, including Jiménez, sought to correct this form of injustice. They proudly wrote about leaders in their community and their accomplishments. These activists practiced another important belief in CRT—that, through storytelling, the lives of minority groups become better known to whites and contribute, at least in part, to improved racial relations.

Although this book has focused on Jiménez, it also highlighted the activism and accomplishments of her many predecessors. It has told their stories. They often took risks and suffered the consequences. For example, in antebellum Texas, whites drove Mexican residents out of several towns because the Mexicans socialized with African Americans, then enslaved Black people. In the following century, the Texas Rangers, when summoned by powerful white businessmen and politicians, assaulted or threatened violence against union activists of Mexican descent. In 1937 Houston society harassed members of the woman's organization El Club Feminino Chapultepec when the club publicly criticized racism in the city. In the case of one of its members, Stella Quintenella, the FBI kept her under surveillance until 1942, suspecting that she was a Communist. In the case of Mexican immigrant women in the Pecan Shellers' Strike in San Antonio in 1938, the boss of the company fired the striking workers. Finally, the Mexican American lawyers for Pete Hernández suffered the indignity of not being able to remain overnight in the town where his trial took place because of the anti-Mexican hostility in rural towns in Texas.

Texans of Mexican descent, however, believed in the nation's highest virtues, including social justice and equality. Their activism advanced these virtues when they challenged racial discrimination. Sometimes, after considerable efforts, their protests and pressures culminated in legal cases. In *Hernández v. Texas* (1954), argued before the US Supreme Court, the highly skilled Mexican Americans lawyers for Hernández were victorious when the court ruled in their favor and extended protection of the Fourteenth Amendment to Hispanics as a "class." Activists, both students and parents, demanded the desegregation of public-school systems in Texas. Years after the *Brown v. Board of Education Topeka Kansas* (1954), HISD reluctantly desegregated following *Cisneros v. Corpus Christi ISD* (1970). Even immigrant parents dared to sue public school systems for charging prohibitively high tuition for their children. Again, the court helped, this time in *Plyler v. Doe* (1982). Not all victories for social justice required court decisions, however. Jiménez insisted, first and foremost, on the need for people who had "concrete" experiences of discrimination to worked collectively to create a more just society.

Maria Jiménez: The "Weary Soldier"[9]

The individuals and groups that challenged injustice served as invaluable models to emulate, and there is no better example than Maria Jiménez. Her life as an activist followed in the footsteps of her predecessors, whom she, in turn, admired. The inequities and racial discrimination that she had personally encountered angered her, but this anger became a positive motivation to fight for the rights and dignity of the marginalized. She made it her mission in life to try to reduce social injustice and help others do the same. Much of her sense of commitment derived from her family. The activism of her father and other relatives inspired her. Another major source of inspiration and optimism for Jiménez, despite many historical examples of racism, was the tolerance of the American people. As she once commented, "I think historically there's conflict between intolerance and tolerance, but there's still questioning. There's a soul-searching in the American people on that."[10] The soul-searching did not exist in other countries, she added, including Mexico, where she was born.

Starting with her years at UH, Jiménez became known as a fearless advocate for social justice and equality. For example, some of the events that

she organized in the early 1970s when the first Hispanic and first woman
president of the SA at UH included inviting César Chávez to her university,
supporting the national lettuce boycott that the UFW organized, and arranging at UH for the first conference in the nation for gays. In 1974, persuaded
by RUP, she ran as their candidate to represent the Mexican-origin community in east Houston's District 87 in the Texas House of Representatives.
Despite an energetic campaign, she lost to a well-connected incumbent. She
then left electoral politics behind and moved to Mexico. There her political
education continued and her organizational skills matured.

Jiménez returned to the United States in 1985 and, in 1987 she became
the director of the ILEMP for the AFSC. The organization and its funds
enabled Jiménez to help the immigrant community, especially the undocumented. Her return was timely because from the late 1980s into the 1990s the
level of the anti-immigrant rhetoric rose sharply, restrictive federal immigration laws began to multiply, and the militarization of the border between the
United States and Mexico violated human and civil rights. Jiménez's alarm
over the violation of the civil and human rights of undocumented immigrants,
legal residents, and US citizens near the border was the reason she called this
area a "deconstitutional zone."

Jiménez always believed that if one saw an injustice, he or she must act
to remove it. This included abuse by border authorities at the US-Mexico
border. Their violations of immigrant dignity and rights became an impetus
for the creation of the ILEMP. Her first initiative as its director was to create
a training program to teach local communities to monitor and record abuses
that border authorities committed. As a warrior for justice, Jiménez enjoyed
several victories, and she told this writer of the three accomplishments that
gratified her the most. Two of the major accomplishments dealt directly with
the violence at the border. One of her major concerns, which angered her
the most, was the lack of accountability of border authorities, especially the
Border Patrol, who inflicted physical harm on, even caused the death of their
victims. Jiménez, therefore, organized study groups and directed the groups
and specialists to investigate these abuses. She then presented the findings of
this important research to the US Congress. There she insisted that Border
Patrol agents be held accountable for their violent actions. Jiménez, with

other like-minded groups, ultimately succeeded in getting Congress to pass Section 503 of the Immigration Act of 1990. It required border agents to be instructed on the authority that the 1990 law granted them and the standards of conduct required of them in their assignments.

The second major accomplishment led to the suspension of military operations at the southern border in 1997. The suspension followed the killing in Redford in South Texas near the Mexican border of Esequiel Hernández, a high school student and American citizen. The presence of these troops, Jiménez pointed out when she testified before Congress, was a violation of the Posse Comitatus Act because the act prohibited the use of the nation's military in civilian matters. Jiménez organized the Redford community shortly after Hernández's death and took several residents to Washington, DC, to meet with officials. The Redford group and Jiménez pressured Congress and the Pentagon to end the use of troops at the border. The federal government ordered the troops to withdraw from the border in July 1997, two months after the fatal incident at Redford.

Jiménez's third major accomplishment, which happened after she left her position as director of ILEMP, was initiating a process that created ARCA. Jiménez's involvement was critical and included, for example, organizing the ARCA activists, teaching them how to lobby legislators, traveling with them to Washington, DC, to lobby, and arranging meetings with officials there. The need for ARCA arose when INS denied a pathway to citizenship to undocumented immigrants who had received the legal right to become naturalized citizens by the IRCA of 1986. Fortunately, ARCA's successful three-year legal battle granted them, again, the right to apply for US citizenship. The change became possible when President Bill Clinton signed the LIFE Act into law on December 21, 2000. Without doubt, ARCA's campaign benefited greatly from the knowledge and strategies that Jiménez had acquired over many years.

The Right of Mobility

Jiménez's strong belief in the importance of rights and dignity drew her to the debate about mobility as a universal right. If she were alive today, she would continue to assert the right for individuals to migrate to where living wages exist. Absent the right of mobility or a policy that offers legal entry to honest job seekers, especially from Mexico, individuals are denied the dignity of providing even the most basic necessities of life for themselves and their loved ones. Unfortunately, most Americans do not consider the unauthorized entry into the country of desperate job seekers an economic issue. They view it as a major threat to national security and demand greater control of the border. Border crossing, previously accepted as a "circular migration" between Mexico and the United States, became a crime. Citizens' fears were and are based, in large part, on misinformation and racial prejudices. Consequently, the militarization of the border has resulted in the violation of the human rights of unauthorized emigrants.[11] Tragically, in addition to the dangers of crossing borders, the federal "deterrence" policy since Operation Hold the Line (1993)—still in place and designed to divert border crossers into scorching deserts in Arizona—results in one or more deaths of unauthorized border crossers every day.

Jiménez understood the complex situation that border crossers faced. She regretted the weak position of migrant workers who were adversely impacted by globalization. They were exploited workers in the United States or in foreign assembly plants in Mexico. Jiménez believed this exploitation represented a form of slavery. The Border Patrol even reminded her, she said, of the "slave patrols of the deep South [whose] function was to impede the mobility of the slaves . . . [and] reinforce the existing social and economic structure."[12] After slavery was abolished, the exploitation of labor conditions did not end, but continued in the form of convict leasing.[13] In 2014, when referencing undocumented workers, Jiménez asserted that the "regulatory schemes that guarantee control, high profits and low wages, and the criminalization of human mobility, are essential for the neoliberal model of global economic development. Military integration in border policing, and the denial of rights of displaced populations domestically and internationally, reproduce a *de facto* system of slavery for marginalized economic and social sectors, particularly unauthorized international migrants."[14] Surprisingly, a spokesperson for FAIR, a major anti-immigration organization, also referred to slavery when discussing the exploitation of undocumented workers in the United States. In 2007

Ira Mehlman commented that "it's the next best thing to slavery. . . . They [employers] have a whole class of workers who have a limited ability to complain about conditions they're faced with."[15]

Jiménez confronted the problem of mobility for immigrants during the negotiations for NAFTA. During the debate on the proposed treaty, Jiménez, the director of the ILEMP, and AFSC, the parent organization of the ILEMP, became the voice for the working-class immigrant. Jiménez argued, "We should ask our government officials why, if we are talking about the breaking of barriers for the circulation of commodities along international borders, labor is not being included in the dialogue." In the hearings on NAFTA, Jiménez wrote, her organization was "asking that the issues of migration and labor mobility be included in NAFTA negotiations. The only way that we can diminish much of the suffering that we see on the United States-Mexico border is to make the movement, the mobility, a legal but regulated process."[16] Unfortunately, NAFTA did not grant workers the right of mobility.

Jiménez's fight for justice began long before her advocacy for the right of mobility. She has received numerous awards for her activism, the earliest from the National Organization of Women in 1971.[17] She accepted this award and other awards with grace, but for her it was not any one individual but people working collectively who made positive social, economic, and political changes. People working collectively, she insisted, made change for the better possible. In 1998 she remarked, "I believe that it doesn't matter who is in office. If we don't have active groups of citizens, then we don't have what we want."[18]

The style of leadership that Jiménez preferred, in fact, was to remain behind the scenes, organizing and guiding others in their struggles to promote civil and human rights and dignity. One person who praised her guidance was Eddie Canales (1948–2024), the founder of the nonprofit South Texas Human Rights Center in 2013, based in Falfurrias in Brooks County, in South Texas. The organization's goal is to save the lives of undocumented immigrants entering the nation by having water stations available for them. An accessible supply of water is critically important because many migrants die each year when passing through harsh terrain in hot weather. Regarding his new mission, and Jiménez's influence, Canales exclaimed, "My friend Maria the organizer organized me!"[19]

Looking Forward

Despite pervasive racial discrimination, Jiménez remained hopeful her whole life. Sadly, she died after a battle with cancer on December 1, 2020. An atheist, Jiménez held the conviction that a "perfect society . . . a creation of heaven here and now" was possible when humans worked collectively toward that end. She added, "My spirituality has always been my belief that human history moves towards progress and that it is that experiential material experience that has moved humanity toward the creation of more just worlds."[20] She also believed that dignity was one of the most important traits of a "perfect society" and that it must be extended to everyone.[21]

The significance of dignity, and its relation to rights and social justice, explained why Jiménez admired article 1 of the Universal Declaration of Human Rights. The statement addressed, Jiménez said, "the dilemma that I many times faced in the years of struggle around women's rights, or immigration rights, or Chicano rights, etc.—the issue of how do you deal with other people that are different. And we talked about equality, but it was a confused understanding of equality . . . article 1 resolves it because it allows for diversity while defining our equality in the areas of rights and dignity." These two areas in recent years have been diminished by politicians and many others who fomented commonplace racist prejudices and made vicious ad hominem attacks that reflected a depraved sense of morality. Consequently, the fabric of the nation's democracy has been weakened. It must be revived. Maria Jiménez, if she were to speak to our divisive nation today, would offer some positive words. As she once told this writer, it was important to believe that "our equality, [the] basis of our equality is in rights and dignity, we can have ethnic difference, we can have religious differences, we can have national differences. But where all of it lands—it lands in the areas of rights and dignity."[22]

Endnotes

Notes for Chapter 1

1. Rudolfo Anaya, *Bless Me, Ultima* (New York: Warner Books, 1972), 111.
2. Maria Jiménez, interview by Linda J. Quintanilla, September 10, 2004.
3. Martha Liebram, "Maria Jiménez: She's an 'Objective Leftist' Who Hasn't Given Up on the System," *Houston Post*, March 17, 1971.
4. Michelle Ye Hee Lee, "Donald Trump's False Comments Connecting Mexican Immigrants and Crime," *Washington Post*, July 8, 2015, https://www.washingtonpost.com/news/fact-checker/wp/2015/07/08/donald-trumps-false-comments-connecting-mexican-immigrants-and-crime/.
5. Linda Qiu, "The Context Behind Trump's 'Animals' Comment," *New York Times*, May 18, 2018, https://www.nytimes.com/2018/05/18/us/politics/fact-check-trump-animals-immigration-ms13-sanctuary-cities.html.
6. Patrick J. Buchanan, *State of Emergency: The Third World Invasion and Conquest of America* (New York: St. Martin's Press, 2006), 5. See also Samuel P. Huntington, *Who Are We? The Challenges to America's National Identity* (New York: Simon & Schuster, 2004), xvi–xvii.
7. "Houston City, Texas: Population Estimates, July 1, 2023," *QuickFacts, United States Census Bureau*, http://quickfacts.census.gov/qfd/states/48/4835000.html. Reuters, "Houston Set to Replace Chicago as 3rd Largest City by 2025," *Huffington Post*, September 14, 2015. http://www.huffingtonpost.com/entry/Houston-chicago-largest-city-in-america_55f6d6f10e0634bcebfacebf.
8. Doris Meissner, "5 Myths about Immigration," *Washington Post*, May 2, 2010.
9. Julia Preston, "In Report, 63% Back Way to Get Citizenship," *New York Times*, November 25, 2013, http://www.nytimes.com/2013/11/25/us/in-report-63-back-way-to-get-citizenship.html; Joel Rose, "Despite Concerns about Border, Poll Finds Support for Pathway to Citizenship," *The Hill*, May 20, 2021.
10. Alejandra Gomez and Bob Worsley, "Even Trump Backers Support Legalizing Undocumented Immigrants," azcentral.com, October 18, 2021; Victoria Balara, "Fox News Poll: Voters Continue to Prefer Pathway to Citizenship," *Fox News*, August 23, 2018. https://www.foxnews.com/politics/fox-news-poll-voters.

11. Richard Delgado and Jean Stefancic, *Critical Race Theory: An Intro-duction*, 2nd ed. (New York: New York University Press, 2012), 171.

12. Maria Jiménez, interview by José Angel Gutiérrez, January 22, 1998, *Tejano Voices* 96, Center for Mexican American Studies, University of Texas at Austin, https://library.uta.edu/tejanovoices/xml/CMAS_096.xml.

13. *Hernández v. Texas*, 347 U.S. 475 (1954).

14. For recent information, see Matt Dempsey and Karen Chen, "Analysis: Hispanics Rare on Grand Juries: Panels' Indictments May be Invalid under Ruling by U.S. Supreme Court," *Houston Chronicle,* December 20, 2014.

15. UN General Assembly, Resolution 217A (III), *Universal Declaration of Human Rights*, December 10, 1948.

16. Article 1: "All human beings are born free and equal in dignity and rights. They are endowed with reason and conscience and should act towards one another in a spirit of brotherhood"; UN General Assembly, *Universal Declaration of Human Rights*.

17. Jiménez, interview by Quintanilla, September 10, 2004.

18. Jiménez, interview by Quintanilla, September 10, 2004, emphasis hers.

19. Lu-in Wang, *Discrimination by Default: How Racism Becomes Routine* (New York: New York University Press, 2006). The book was banned in a school district in Arizona, as was "The Tempest" by William Shakespeare. Most books were about and/or written by Mexican Americans. In response to the banning, Tony Díaz, a Mexican American college instructor in Houston, collected banned books in 2012, organized a caravan, and took the books to Arizona. Laura Steiner, "*Librotraficante*' Caravan Set to Smuggle Books Back into Arizona Following Ethnic Studies Ban," *Huffington Post*, January 31, 2012, https://www.huffpost.com/entry/arizona-ethnic-studies-ban-controversy_n_1243975.

20. Wang, *Discrimination by Default*, 11.

21. Josh Dawsey and Jeff Stein, "White House Directs Federal Agencies to Cancel Race-related Training Sessions It Calls 'Un-American Propa-ganda," *Washington Post*, September 5, 2020, https://www.washington-post.com/politics/2020/09/04/white-house-racial-sensitivity-training/.

22. Delgado and Stefancic, *Critical Race Theory*, 3.

23. On the dichotomy, Richard Delgado points out that "Blacks do not suffer discrimination based on a foreign sounding accent, national origin, immigration status, or inability to speak English proficiently"; "The Current Landscape of Race: Old Targets, New Opportunities," *Michigan Law Review* 104 (2006): 1272.

24. Antonio Gramsci, "Culture and Ideological Hegemony," in *Culture and Society: Contemporary Debates*, ed. Jeffrey C. Alexander and Steven Seidman (New York: Cambridge University Press, 1990), 48.

25. Delgado and Stefancic, *Critical Race Theory*, 5.

26. Berta Esperanza Hernandez-Truyol, "Latinas—Everywhere Alien: Culture, Gender, and Sex," in *Critical Race Feminism: A Reader*, 2nd ed., ed. Adrien Katherine Wing (New York: New York University Press, 2003), 59.

27. Maylei Blackwell, *Chicana Power! Contested Histories of Feminism in the Chicano Movement* (Austin: University of Texas Press, 2011), 98–99.

28. Legal storytelling and narrative are methods that use "stories, parables, and first-person accounts to understand and analyze racial issues"; Delgado and Stefancic, *Critical Race Theory*, 178.

29. In the legal field, they serve as a countermeasure to inequities. Gloria Ladson-Billings, "Racialized Discourses and Ethnic Epistemologies," in *Handbook of Qualitative Research*, 2nd ed., ed. Norman K. Denzin and Yvonna S. Lincoln (Thousand Oaks, CA: Sage Publications, 2000), 265.

30. David M. Kennedy, "The Art of the Tale: Story-Telling and History Teaching," *History Teacher* 31, no. 3 (May 1998): 323.

31. Delgado and Stefancic, *Critical Race Theory*, 49.

32. Timothy J. Dunn, *Blockading the Border and Human Rights: The El Paso Operation That Remade Immigration Enforcement* (Austin: University of Texas Press, 2009), 26.

33. Jiménez, interview by Quintanilla, July 19, 2001, emphasis hers.

34. Jiménez, interview by Quintanilla, July 19, 2001.

35. David Glenn, "Our Hidden Prejudices, on Trial," *Chronicle Review*, April 25, 2008.

36. Ladson-Billings, "Racialized Discourses," 264.

37. Lee, quoted in Wang, *Discrimination by Default*, 12.

38. Derrick A. Bell Jr., "*Brown v. Board of Education* and the Interest-Convergence Dilemma," *Harvard Law Review* 93, no. 3 (January 1980): 523.

39. Delgado and Stefancic, *Critical Race Theory*, 177.

40. Concepts like "whiteness" are "products of social thought and relations. Not objective, inherent, or fixed, they correspond to no biological or genetic reality; rather, races are categories that society invents, manipulates, or retires when convenient"; Delgado and Stefancic, *Critical Race Theory*, 9.

41. George A. Martínez, "Mexican Americans and Whiteness," in *The Latino/a Condition: A Critical Reader*, ed. Richard Delgado and Jean Stefancic (New York: New York University Press, 1998), 175.

42. Alice Kessler-Harris, "AHR Roundtable: Why Biography?" *American Historical Review* 114, no. 3 (June 2009): 626.

43. Lois W. Banner, "AHR Roundtable: Biography as History," *American Historical Review* 114, no. 3 (June 2009): 580.

44. Yolanda Broyles-González, *Lydia Mendoza's Life in Music: La historia de Lydia Mendoza*, Norteño Tejano Legacies (New York: Oxford University Press, 2001). Lydia Mendoza, *Lydia Mendoza: A Family Autobiography*, complied and introduced by Chris Strachwitz with James Nicolopulos (Houston: Arte Publico Press, 1993).

45. Mary Dodson Wade, *Guadalupe Quintanilla: Leader of the Hispanic Community* (Springfield, NJ: Enslow, 1995).

46. Richard Delgado, "Storytelling for Oppositionists and Others," in Delgado and Stefancic, *Latino/a Condition*, 268.

47. Teresa Cordova, "Roots and Resistance: The Emergent Writings of Twenty Years of Chicana Feminist Struggle," in *Handbook of Hispanic Cultures in the United States: Sociology*, ed. Felix Padilla (Houston: Arte Publico Press, 1994): 189.

48. Thomas H. Kreneck, *Del Pueblo: A Pictorial History of Houston's Hispanic Community* (Houston: Houston International University, 1989); *Del Pueblo: A History of Houston's Hispanic Community* (College Station: Texas A&M University Press, 2012).

49. Arnoldo de León, *Ethnicity in the Sunbelt: A History of Mexican Americans in Houston* (Houston: Mexican American Studies Program, University of Houston, 1989); *Ethnicity in the Sunbelt: Mexican Americans in Houston* (College Station: Texas A&M University Press, 2001).

50. Grisel Gómez-Cano and James Ross-Nazzal, *The Spirit of Magnolia Park: Ethnic Pride in a Mexican Barrio, 1909–2009* (Boston: Pearson Learning Solutions, 2013).

51. Guadalupe San Miguel Jr., *Brown, Not White: School Integration and the Chicano Movement in Houston* (College Station: Texas A&M University Press, 2005).

52. Thomas H. Kreneck, *Mexican American Odyssey: Felix Tijerina, Entrepreneur and Civic Leader, 1905–1965* (College Station: Texas A&M University Press, 2001).

53. Teresa Palomo Acosta and Ruthe Winegarten, *Las Tejanas: 300 Years of History* (Austin: University of Texas, 2003).

54. Texas State Historical Association, https://www.tshaonline.org/handbook.

55. Emma Pérez, *The Decolonial Imaginary: Writing Chicanas into History* (Bloomington: Indiana University Press, 1999).

56. José Angel Gutiérrez, Michelle Meléndez, and Sonia Adriana Noyola, *Chicanas in Charge: Texas Women in the Public Arena* (Lanham, MD: AltaMira Press, 2007).

57. Samantha Rodriguez and Stalina Emmanuelle Villareal, "Maria Jiménez: *Reflexiones* on Transversing Multiple Fronteras in the South," in *Chicana Movidas: New Narratives of Activism and Feminism in the Movement Era*, ed. Dionne Espinoza, Maria Eugenia Cotera, and Maylei Blackwell, 276–89 (Austin: University of Texas Press, 2018).

58. David G. Gutiérrez, *Walls and Mirrors: Mexican Americans, Mexican Immigrants, and the Politics of Ethnicity* (Berkeley: University of California Press, 1995).

59. Mae M. Ngai, *Impossible Subjects: Illegal Aliens and the Making of Modern America* (Princeton: Princeton University Press, 2004).

60. Dunn, *Blockading the Border*.

Notes for Chapter 2

1. Maria Jiménez, editorial, *Houston Chronicle*, October 29, 1995.

2. Mrs. Cruz Valdez, interview by Thomas H. Kreneck, May 17, 1989, Houston Metropolitan Research Center, Houston Public Library, Houston, TX.

3. The term *Texas Revolt* is used in Bryan Burrough, Chris Tomlinson, and Jason Stanford's book *Forget the Alamo: The Rise and Fall of an American Myth* (New York: Penguin Press, 2021).

4. Terry G. Jordan, "Population Origins in Texas, 1850," *Geographical Review* 59 (January 1969): 85.

5. Mark Allen Goldberg, "'It Can Be Cultivated Where Nothing but Cactus Will Grow': Local Knowledge and Healing on the Texas Military Frontier," in *Recovering the Hispanic History of Texas*, ed. Monica Perales and Raúl A. Ramos (Houston: Arte Publico Press, 2010), 27

6. Carlin Romano, "Indian Scholars and the Rise of Native American Philosophy," *Chronicle of Higher Education*, May 5, 2000, B9.

7. Gary Clayton Anderson, *The Conquest of Texas: Ethnic Cleansing in the Promised Land, 1820–1875* (Norman: University of Oklahoma Press, 2005).

8. W. Marvin Dulaney, "African Americans," *Handbook of Texas Online*, updated August 24, 2023, https://tshaonline.org/handbook/entries/african-americans.

9. Dulaney, "African Americans."

10. Paul D. Lack, "Slavery and Vigilantism in Austin, Texas, 1840–1860," *Southwestern Historical Quarterly* 85, no. 1 (July 1981): 9.

11. David Montejano, *Anglos and Mexicans in the Making of Texas, 1836–1986* (Austin: University of Texas Press, 1987), 28.

12. Noah Smithwick and Nanna Smithwick Donaldson, *The Evolution of a State, by Noah Smithwick* (Austin: Steck, 1935), 45.

13. Whites murdered a Mexican because he refused to play his fiddle for them. Arnold de León, *The Tejano Community, 1836–1900* (Dallas: Southern Methodist University Press, 1997), 19.

14. William D. Carrigan and Clive Webb, "The Lynching of Persons of Mexican Origin or Descent in the United States, 1848–1928," *Journal of Social History* (Winter 2003): 417. Also see, Benjamin Heber Johnson, *Revolution in Texas: How a Forgotten Rebellion and Its Bloody Suppression Turned Mexicans into Americans* (New Haven: Yale University Press, 2003).

15. Arnoldo de León, *They Called Them Greasers: Anglo Attitudes toward Mexicans in Texas, 1821–1900* (Austin: University of Texas Press, 1983), 127n33.

16. Robert J. Rosenbaum, *Mexican Resistance in the Southwest: "The Sacred Right of Self-Preservation."* (Austin: University of Texas Press, 1981), 42.

17. Carrigan and Webb, "Lynching of Persons of Mexican Origin or Descent," 417.

18. Katherine S. Mangan, "White Hats, Black Tales: A Texas Scholar Digs into the Dark Truths about the Role of the Texas Rangers in the Early 20th Century Border Wars," *Chronicle of Higher Education*, August 5, 2005, A12; Richard Henry Ribb, "José Tomás Canales and the Texas Rangers: Myth, Identity, and Power in South Texas, 1900–1920" (PhD dissertation, University of Texas at Austin, 2001), 369. Also see Texas Senate and House, *Proceedings of the Joint Committee of the Senate and House in the Investigation of the Texas State Ranger Force* Austin: no publisher, 1919. The online document of *1919 Texas Rangers* (*Canales Investigation*) is at https://www.tsl.texas.gov/treasures/law/index.html#Canales, accessed April 11, 2021.

19. Lynching was made a federal hate crime with the Emmett Till Anti-lynching Act. Jeffery A. Jenkins and Justin Peck, "Congress Finally Passed a Federal Anti-Lynching Bill—after 120 Years of Failure,"

Washington Post, March 9, 2022, https://www.washingtonpost.com/politics/2022/03/09/congress-finally-passed-federal-anti-lynching-law-after-120-years-failure/.

20. De León, *Tejano Community*, 18–19. Regarding Texas Rangers' and white vigilantes' violence, see Monica Muñoz Martínez, *The Injustice Never Leaves You: Anti-Mexican Violence in Texas* (Cambridge, MA: Harvard University Press, 2018), 121–22; and Nicholas Villanueva Jr., *The Lynching of Mexicans in the Texas Borderlands* (Albuquerque: University of New Mexico Press, 2017), 126–27.

21. "Table 2: Lynchings of Mexicans by State," in Carrigan and Webb, "Lynching of Persons of Mexican Origin," 415. For states in the west and southwest this total was at least 597.

22. Timothy J. Dunn, *The Militarization of the U.S.-Mexico Border, 1978–1992: Low-Intensity Conflict Comes Home* (Austin: Center for Mexican American Studies, University of Texas Press, 1996), 7.

23. The Mutualista La Asamblea Mexicana protested white supremist activities and provided legal aid to Mexican nationals. "Ultimo Informe de la actuación de la Asamblea Mexicana," *La Gaceta Mexicana*, May 1, 1928; and F. Arturo Rosales, "Mexicans in Houston: The Struggle to Survive, 1908–1975," *Houston Review: History and Culture of the Gulf Coast* 3, no. 2 (1981): 230.
    Lynching is defined as "to put to death (as by hanging) by mob action without legal approval or permission," "Lynching," *Merriam Webster*, accessed November 7, 2024, https://www.merriam-webster.com/dictionary/lynch.

24. Villanueva, *Lynching of Mexicans*, 71.

25. Cynthia E. Orozco, *No Mexicans, Women, or Dogs Allowed: The Rise of the Mexican American Civil Rights Movement* (Austin: University of Texas Press, 2009), 10.

26. Emilio Zamora, *The World of the Mexican Worker in Texas* (College Station: Texas A&M University Press, 1993), 110.

27. Juan Gómez-Quiñones, *Mexican American Labor, 1790–1990* (Albuquerque: University of New México Press, 1994), 67–68.

28. United States Naturalization Law of March 26, 1790, 1 Statutes at Large 103.

29. Chinese Exclusion Act of 1882, 22 Statutes at Large 600.

30. Maria Jiménez, "Labor, Mobility and the North American Free Trade Agreement," *Immigration Newsletter* 19, no. 4 (March 1992): 4.

31. This was the first and last time Mexicans received refugee status. Jorge Durand, "Migration Policy and the Asymmetry of Power: The Mexican Case, 1900–2000," in *Citizenship and Those Who Leave: The Politics*

of Emigration and Expatriation, ed. Nancy L. Green and Francois Weil (Urbana and Chicago: University of Illinois Press, 2007), 226.

32. Maria Jiménez, "War in the Borderlands," *Report on the Americas, North American Congress on Latin America (NACLA)* 26, no. 1 (July 1992): 30.

33. Carole E. Christian, "Joining the American Mainstream: Texas's Mexican Americans during World War I," *Southwestern Historical Quarterly* 92, no. 4 (April 1989): 566–67.

34. His family—parents, two sons, and one daughter—settled in Austin Texas in 1920. Consuelo Martinez, interview by Linda J. Quintanilla, February 12, 2002.

35. José A. Ramírez, *To the Line of Fire! Mexican Texans and World War I* (College Station: Texas A&M University Press, 2009), 22; "Mexican Laborers Coming into to Texas not to Be Drafted," *Austin American*, July 13, 1918.

36. "Mexican Laborers Coming into Texas."

37. *Houston Daily Post*, September 16, 1918, in Ramírez, *To the Line of Fire!*, 35n70.

38. Alanis Enciso, *El Primer Programa Bracero*, in Durand, "Migration Policy and the Asymmetry of Power," in Green and Weil, *Citizenship and Those Who Leave*, 226.

39. Mae M. Ngai, *Impossible Subjects: Illegal Aliens and the Making of Modern America* (Princeton and Oxford: Princeton University Press: 2004), 10.

40. George J. Sánchez, *Becoming Mexican American: Ethnicity, Culture, and Identity in Chicano Los Angeles, 1900–1945* (New York: Oxford University Press, 1993), 52.

41. Manuel Garcia y Griego, "The Importation of Mexican Contract Laborers to the United States, 1942–1964: Antecedents, Operation, and Legacy," in *The Border That Joins: Mexican Migrants and the U.S. Responsibility*, ed. Peter G. Brown and Henry Shue (Totowa, NJ: Rowman and Littlefield, 1983), 51.

42. Mark Reisler, *By the Sweat of Their Brow: Mexican Immigrant Labor in the United States, 1900–1940* (Westpoint, CT: Greenwood Press, 1976), 58.

43. Gómez-Quiñones, *Mexican American Labor*, 131.

44. Montejano, *Anglos and Mexicans in the Making of Texas*, 211.

45. Zamora, *World of the Mexican Worker in Texas*, 39.

46. Montejano, *Anglos and Mexicans in the Making of Texas*, 211.

47. Nicole Narea, "A Woman in ICE Detention Says Her Fallopian Tube Was Removed Without Her Consent," *Vox*, September 17, 2020, https://www.vox.com/2020/9/17/21440001/ice-hysterectomies-whistleblower-irwin-fallopian; Rosa Tuirán and Nick Roberts, "Farmworkers Are among Those at Highest Risk for COVID-19, Studies Show," *Frontline*, July 21, 2020, https://www.pbs.org/wgbh/frontline/article/covid-19-farmworkers-among-highest-risk-studies-show/.

48. Maria Jiménez, "Mobility, Human Rights, and Economic Development: Lessons of the International Mexican Migrant Experience and United States Immigration Policies," *In Motion Magazine*, July 12, 1999, http://www.inmotionmagazine.com/mj3.html.

49. Sánchez, *Becoming Mexican American*, 57.

50. Ngai, *Impossible Subjects*, 7.

51. Alexandra Minna Stern, "Buildings, Boundaries, and Blood: Medicalization and Nation-Building on the U.S.-Mexico Border, 1910–1930," *Hispanic American Historical Review* 79, no. 1 (February 1999): 42, 49.

52. Stern, "Buildings, Boundaries, and Blood," 69.

53. Stern, "Buildings, Boundaries, and Blood," 68–69.

54. Sánchez, *Becoming Mexican American*, 55.

55. Ngai, *Impossible Subjects*, 68.

56. Persons who were eligible at that time, according to the Naturalization Act of 1790 and the Fourteenth Amendment, were free whites and persons of African ancestry.

57. Dillingham Commission Report, S. Doc. No. 758, 61st Cong. (3d sess. 1911). The commission described Italians and Jewish immigrants as having "a particular propensity from criminality."

58. Leo R. Chavez, "Immigration Reform and Nativism: The Nationalist Response to the Transnationalist Challenge," in *Immigrants Out! The New Nativism and the Anti-Immigrant Impulse in the United States*, ed. Juan F. Perea (New York: New York University Press, 1997), 72.

59. Ngai, *Impossible Subjects*, 52–53.

60. Eileen Sullivan, "A Rise in Deadly Border Patrol Chases Renews Concerns About Accountability," *New York Times*, January 9, 2022, https://www.nytimes.com/2022/01/09/us/politics/border-patrol-migrant-deaths.html; Eileen Sullivan, "Democrats in Congress Seek Review of Teams within the Border Patrol," *New York Times*, January 24, 2022, https://www.nytimes.com/2011/01/24/us/politics/border-patrol-critical-incident-teams.html.

61. Patrick Ettinger, *Imaginary Lines: Border Enforcement and the Origins of Undocumented Immigration, 1882–1930* (Austin: University of Texas Press, 2009), 162; Juan Ramón Garcia, *Operation Wetback: The Mass Deportation of Mexican Undocumented Workers in 1954*, Contribution in Ethnic Studies 2 (Westport, CT: Greenwood Press, 1980), 108.

62. Leonel Castillo, "The Growth of Hispanic Political Power in the Houston Area," in *Hispanics in Houston and Harris County, 1519–1968: A Sesquicentennial Celebration,* ed. Dorothy F. Caram, Anthony G. Dworkin, and Nestor Rodríguez (Houston: Houston Hispanic Forum, 1989), 98.

63. Ngai, *Impossible Subjects*, 68.

64. Sánchez, *Becoming Mexican American*, 59.

65. Neil Foley, *The White Scourge: Mexicans, Blacks, and Poor Whites in Texas Cotton Culture* (Berkeley: University of California Press, 1997), 87.

66. George Brown Tindall and David E. Shi, *America: A Narrative History* (New York: W. W. Norton, 2007), A95, "Immigration by Region and Selected Country of Last Residence, Fiscal Years 1820–2004." For all of Europe for the same decades, the totals were 4,321,887 and 2,463,194, respectively, A90–A91.

67. Orozco, *No Mexicans, Women, or Dogs Allowed*, 2.

68. Don E. Carleton, *Red Scare! Right-Wing Hysteria, Fifties Fanaticism, and Their Legacy in Texas* (Austin: Texas Monthly Press, 1985), 10.

69. Charles C. Alexander, *The Ku Klux Klan in the Southwest* (Lexington: University of Kentucky Press, 1965), 247.

70. Louis J. Marchiafava, "Law Enforcement on the Urban Frontier: Houston, 1878–1928," in *Houston: A Twentieth Century Urban Frontier*, ed. Francisco A. Rosales and Berry J. Kaplan (Port Washington, NY: Associated Faculty, 1983), 80.

71. Casey Greene, "Guardians against Change: The Ku Klux Klan in Houston and Harris County, 1920–25," *Houston History* 8, no. 1 (Fall 2010): 4.

72. Alexander, *Ku Klux Klan*, 41.

73. John J. Herrera, interview by Thomas J. Kreneck, n.d., Houston Metropolitan Research Center, Houston Public Library, Houston, TX.

74. For example, the author's father, Sam V. Quintanilla (1916–2005), did not attend school when he needed to help support his family. To do this, he recalled, he "picked feathers off turkeys at a produce house." Sam V. Quintanilla, interview by Linda J. Quintanilla, May 28, 2000.

75. Francisco E. Balderrama and Raymond Rodríguez, *Decade of Betrayal: Mexican Repatriation in the 1930s*, rev. ed. (Albuquerque: University of New Mexico Press, 2006), 97.
76. William E. Montgomery, "The Depression in Houston, 1929–1933," in *Texas Cities and the Great Depression*, ed. Robert C. Cotner (and others) (Austin: Texas Memorial Museum, 1973), 154.
77. Robert Calvert, Arnoldo de León, and Gregg Cantrell, *The History of Texas*, 3rd ed. (Wheeling, IL: Harlan Davidson, 2002), 321.
78. Balderrama and Rodríguez, *Decade of Betrayal*, 90.
79. Mrs. Cruz Valdez, interview by Thomas H. Kreneck, May 17, 1989, Houston Metropolitan Research Center, Houston Public Library, Houston, TX.
80. Balderrama and Rodríguez, *Decade of Betrayal*, 97.
81. Fernando Saúl Alanis Enciso, "Cuantos Fueron? La reparación de mexicanos en los Estados Unidos durante la Gran Depresión: Una interpretación cuantitativa 1930–1934," *Aztlán: Journal of Chicano Studies* 32, no. 2 (Fall 2007): 67.
82. Jiménez, "Labor, Mobility and the North American Free Trade Agreement," 5.
83. Alanis Enciso, "Cuantos Fueron?"; and Abraham Hoffman, *Unwanted Mexican Americans in the Great Depression: Repatriation Pressures, 1929–1939* (Tucson: University of Arizona Press, 1974), chart, 174–75.
84. Emily Priest, "Herman R. Cortéz," Voces Oral History Center, Moody College of Communication, University of Texas at Austin, accessed November 7, 2024, https://voces.moody.utexas.edu/collections/stories/herman-r-cortez.
85. Angelina (Mrs. Félix) Morales, interview by Thomas H. Kreneck and Emma Pérez, March 24, 1989, Houston Metropolitan Research Center, Houston Public Library, Houston, TX.
86. Ernest Eguía, interviewed by Claudia Garcia, February 2, 2001, in Stephen Stetson, "Soldier Led Charge for Hispanic Rights in Houston," *Narratives: Stories of U.S. Latino and Latinas and World War II* (Fall 2001): 36.
87. Stephanie Scalco, "Domingo Treviño," Voces Oral History Center, accessed November 7, 2024, https://voces.moody.utexas.edu/collections/stories/domingo-trevino; Maggie Rivas-Rodríguez et al., *A Legacy Greater than Words: Stories of the U.S. Latinos and Latinas of the World War II Generation* (Austin: U.S. Latino & Latina WWII Oral History Project Group, University of Texas at Austin, School of Journalism, 2006), "Domingo Treviño," 169.

88. Cynthia Agnew, "Jesús G. Reyes," Voces Oral History, accessed November 7, 2024, https://voces.moody.utexas.edu/collections/stories/jesus-g-reyes; Rivas-Rodríguez, *Legacy Greater than Words*, 74.

89. Carmen Cortés, interview by Thomas H. Kreneck and Cynthia Rosca, December 16, 1983, Houston Metropolitan Research Center, Houston Public Library, Houston, Texas.

90. Marilyn D. Rhinehart and Thomas H. Kreneck, "'In the Shadow of Uncertainty': Texas Mexicans and Repatriation in Houston During the Great Depression," *Houston Review: History and Culture of the Gulf Coast* 10, no. 1 (1988): 24–25.

91. Rhinehart and Kreneck, "In the Shadow of Uncertainty," 22.

92. Jesús Jesse Esparza, "La Colonia Mexicana: A History of Mexican Americans in Houston," *Houston History* 9, no. 1 (Fall 2011): 4.

93. "25 Mexican Families Will Go Back Home to Settle on Farms," *Dallas Morning News*, June 2, 1939.

94. De León, *Mexican Americans in Houston*, 30.

95. Pérez, *Decolonial Imaginary*, 97.

96. Robert R. Treviño, "In Their Own Way: Parish Funding and Mexican-American Ethnicity in Catholic Houston, 1911–1972," *Latino Studies Journal* 5, no. 3 (September 1994): 91–93.

97. Félix Fraga, interview by Frank Michel, September 14, 2007, Houston Metropolitan Research Center, Houston Public Library, Houston, TX.

98. A. B. Olmos, "History of Hispanics in the Second Ward," in Caram, Dworkin, and Rodríguez, *Hispanics in Houston and Harris County*, 23.

99. Rhinehart and Kreneck, "In the Shadow of Uncertainty," 27.

100. Pérez, *Decolonial Imaginary*, 96–97.

101. Mamie Garcia, interview by Linda J. Quintanilla, March 27, 2000.

102. US Congress, Committee on Immigration and Naturalization, "Mexican Immigration: A Report by Roy I. Garis for the Information of the Members of Congress," *Western Hemisphere Immigration*, H.R. 8523, H.R. 8530, H.R. 8702, 71st Cong., 2d sess., 1930, p. 436, quoted in Rodolfo Acuña, *Occupied America: The Chicano's Struggle toward Liberation* (San Francisco: Canfield Press, 1972), 141.

103. Zaragosa Vargas, *Labor Rights Are Civil Rights: Mexican American Workers in Twentieth-Century America* (Princeton and Oxford: Princeton University Press, 2005), 31. My father said that one of his teachers "hated Mexicans down to the bone . . . you would think she was a hero at the Alamo, or something"; Sam V. Quintanilla, interview by Linda J. Quintanilla, May 28, 2000.

104. Richard A. Garcia, "Class, Consciousness, and Ideology: The Mexican Community of San Antonio, Texas, 1930–1940," *Aztlan: Journal of Chicano Studies* 9 (1978): 23.

105. Irene Ledesma, "Texas Newspapers and Chicana Workers' Activism, 1919–1974," *Western Historical Quarterly* 26, no. 4 (Autumn 1995): 311.

106. Ledesma, "Texas Newspapers and Chicana Workers' Activism," 314.

107. Acosta and Winegarten, *Las Tejanas*, 137–40.

108. See Roberto R. Calderón and Emilio Zamora, "Manuela Solis Sager and Emma B. Tenayuca: A Tribute," in *Between Borders: Essays on Mexicana/Chicana History*, ed. Adelaida R. Del Castillo (Encino, CA: Floricanto Press, 1990); Julia Kirk Blackwelder, *Women of the Depression: Case and Culture in San Antonio, 1929–1939* (College Station: Texas A&M University Press, 1984), 132–35; Ledesma, "Texas Newspapers and Chicana Workers' Activism," 317; Gabriela González, "Carolina Munguia and Emma Tenayuca: The Politics of Benevolence and Radical Reform," *Frontiers* 24, nos. 2 & 3 (2003): 216; and Gómez-Quiñones, *Mexican American Labor*, 127

109. The Agricultural Adjustment Act of 1933 excluded the same workers. Gómez-Quiñones, *Mexican American Labor*, 130.

110. Gutiérrez, *Walls and Mirrors*, 147.

111. George N. Green, "Texas State Industrial Union Council," *Handbook of Texas Online*, updated April 28, 2021, https://www.tshaonline.org/handbook/entries/texas-state-industrial-union-council.

112. See Emma Tenayuca and Homer Brooks, "The Mexican Question in the Southwest," *Communist* 18, no. 3 (March 1939).

113. González, "Carolina Munguía and Emma Tenayuca," 209.

114. See Zaragoza Vargas, "Tejana Radical: Emma Tenayuca and the San Antonio Labor Movement during the Great Depression," *Pacific Historical Review* 66 (1997): 553–80.

115. Juan Gómez-Quiñones, *Roots of Chicano Politics, 1600–1940* (Albuquerque: University of New Mexico Press, 1994), 393.

116. At least 597 persons of Mexican descent were lynched between 1848 and 1928; Carrigan and Webb, "Lynching of Persons of Mexican Origin or Descent," 413. Lynching was not a problem of the distant past. At a banquet in 1932 honoring the Texas Rangers, Governor Ross S. Sterling "complimented the rangers . . . on a 'lynchless' year, just completed"; "Gov. Sterling Lauds Ranger Enforcement," *Austin American Statesman*, February 13, 1932.

117. Juvencio Rodríguez, interview by Thomas H. Kreneck, August 14, 1980, Houston Metropolitan Research Center, Houston Public Library, Houston, Texas.

118. "Severe Jim Crow segregation in Texas encouraged Mexicans to assert white identity more aggressively there"; Ian F. Haney-López, *Racism on Trial: The Chicano Fight for Justice* (Cambridge, MA: Belknap Press of Harvard University Press, 2003), 79–80.

119. Richard A. Garcia, "Alonso S. Perales: The Voice and Visions of a Citizen Intellectual," in *Leaders of the Mexican American Generation: Biographical Essays*, ed. Anthony Quiroz (Boulder: University Press of Colorado, 2015), 99.

120. Betsy Clickman, "Antonio Campos," Voces Oral History Center, accessed November 7, 2024, https://voces.moody.utexas.edu/collections/stories/antonio-campos.

121. Juvencio Rodríguez, interview by Thomas H. Kreneck, August 14, 1980, Houston Metropolitan Research Center, Houston Public Library, Houston, TX.

122. F. Arturo Rosales, "Shifting Self Perceptions and Ethnic Consciousness Among Mexicans in Houston, 1908–1946," *Aztlan: Journal of Chicano Studies* 16, nos. 1–2 (Spring & Fall 1987): 86. Rosales does not provide a date for this incident.

123. Rosales, "Shifting Self Perceptions," 86–87.

124. "Remark by Starkey Draws Latin-American Protest," *Houston Chronicle,* May 11, 1938.

125. Juvencio Rodríguez, interview by Thomas H. Kreneck, August 14, 1980.

126. Rudy Vara, interview by Thomas H. Kreneck, January 16, 1984, Houston Metropolitan Research Center, Houston Public Library, Houston, Texas.

127. Rosales, "Shifting Perceptions," 87.

128. Pérez, *Decolonial Imaginary*, 85.

129. Carmen Cortéz, interview by Thomas H. Kreneck and Emma Pérez, May 2, 1989, Houston Metropolitan Research Center, Houston Public Library, Houston, TX.

130. Thomas H. Kreneck, "The Letter from Chapultepec," *Houston Review*: *History and Culture of the Gulf Coast* 3, no. 2 (Summer 1981): 270.

131. Kreneck, "The Letter from Chapultepec," 270.

132. Paul Alejandro Levengood, "For the Duration and Beyond: World War II and the Creation of Modern Houston, Texas" (PhD diss., Rice University, 1999), 406.

133. Marie Dauplaise, "I.G.N. Alley Far from the City's East Street," *Houston Chronicle*, December 4, 1958.

134. Pérez, *Decolonial Imaginary*, 88.

135. For a discussion of the letter and its repercussion see Pérez, *Decolonial Imaginary*, 87–91.

136. Pérez, *Decolonial Imaginary*, 90.

Notes for Chapter 3

1. Maria Jiménez, "Panel 3: The North American Free Trade Agreement: Open Borders or Closed Dreams?" Comments by María de Los Angeles Jiménez," *La Raza Law Journal* 7, no. 1 (1994): 138.

2. Jiménez, "Labor Mobility and the North American Free Trade Agreement," 5.

3. Ernest Eguía, interview by Paul R. Zepeda, December 23, 2002, in Stetson, "Soldier Led Charge," 36.

4. Matt S. Meier and Feliciano Rivera, *Mexican Americans, American Mexicans: From Conquistadors to Chicanos*, rev. ed. (New York: Hill and Wang, 1993), 160.

5. These were, from Texas, Luciano Adams, Macario Garcia, Silvestre Herrera, José M. López, and Cleto L. Rodríguez; from California, Harold Gonsalves, David M. Gonzales, and Ysmael R. Villegas; from New Mexico, José P. Martínez, Alejandro R. Ruiz, and José F. Valdez; and from Oklahoma, and Manuel Pérez Jr. See Manuel G. Gonzáles, *Mexicanos: A History of Mexicans in the United States* (Bloomington: Indiana University Press, 1999), 162.

6. See VA Watchdog.org, "Flap Over Ken Burns' World War II Documentary, Part I," *YouTube*, May 14, 2007, www.youtube/watch?vRJH-UV-GoXs. On the Defend the Honor campaign, see David Bauder, "Burns' World War II Documentary is Under Fire by Some Latino Leaders," Associated Press, April 8, 2007, https://www.seattlepi.com/entertainment/tv/article/burns-world-war-ii-documentary-is-under-fire-by-1233591.php; Gary Strauss, "Activists: More Latino Voices Needed," *USA Today*, September 20, 2007, http://usatoday.com/life/television/news/2007-09-20-was-latinos_N.htm; Lynn Elber, "Ken Burns Adds Half-Hour to 'The War' Series to Include Hispanic, American Indian Veterans," *Deseret News* (Salt Lake City, UT), July 13, 2007, https://www.deseret.com/2007/7/13/20029455/ken-burns-adds-half-hour-to-the-war-series-to-include-hispanic-american-indian-veterans/; Elizabeth Jensen, "Arts,

Briefly: Ken Burns and Hispanic Groups Reach Agreement," *New York Times*, May 11, 2007, https://archive.nytimes.com/query.nytimes.com/gst/fullpage-940CE3D61431F932A25756C0A9619C8B63.html.

7. Gonzáles, *Mexicanos*, 183–84.

8. Acosta and Winegarten, *Las Tejanas*, 217–18.

9. Henry A. J. Ramos, *The American GI Forum: In Pursuit of the Dream, 1948–1983* (Houston: Arte Publico Press, 1998), 29.

10. Herminia Quiñones, interview by Thomas H. Kreneck and Cynthia Rosco, December 16, 1983, Houston Metropolitan Research Center, Houston Public Library, Houston, TX.

11. Patrick J. Carroll, *Félix Longoria's Wake: Bereavement, Racism, and the Rise of Mexican American Activism* (Austin: University of Texas Press, 2003), 162.

12. Carroll, *Félix Longoria's Wake*, 55.

13. Julie Leininger Pycior, *LBJ & Mexican Americans: The Paradox of Power* (Austin: University of Texas, 1997), 70.

14. Patrick J. Carroll, "Separate Tejano/Texan Worlds: The Felix Longoria Controversy, Racism, and Patriotism in Post WWII South Texas," in Quiroz, *Leaders of the Mexican American Generation*, 178–79.

15. Gonzales, *Mexicanos*, 173. For an eyewitness account of the abuses of contract workers in Texas, see José Angel Gutiérrez, *The Making of a Chicano Militant: Lessons from Cristal* (Madison: University of Wisconsin Press, 1998), 18–19; and in California, see Ernesto Galarza, *Barrio Boy* (Notre Dame: University of Notre Dame Press, 1971), 262–65.

16. Gutiérrez, *Walls and Mirrors*, 138.

17. Gutiérrez, *Walls and Mirrors*, 143–46.

18. John J. Herrera, interview by Thomas J. Kreneck, n.d., Houston Metropolitan Research Center.

19. Durand, "Migration Policy and the Asymmetry of Power," in Green and Weil, *Citizenship and Those Who Leave*, 228; and Matthew Gritter, *Mexican Inclusion: The Origins of Anti-Discrimination Policy in Texas and the Southwest* (College Station: Texas A&M University Press, 2012), 27.

20. Garcia y Griego, "Importation of Mexican Contract Laborers," 60.

21. Meier and Rivera, *Mexican Americans,* 178.

22. Gutiérrez, *Walls and Mirrors*, 139.

23. Vargas, *Labor Rights are Civil Rights*, 205.

24. Gutiérrez, *Walls and Mirror*, 140.

25. Gritter, *Mexican Inclusion*, 25. The Texas legislature passed the Caucasian Race Resolution, which made racial discrimination against "Caucasians," which included Mexicans, a crime. The resolution had little effect because it was not a law, only a resolution. Montejano, *Anglos and Mexicans in the Making of Texas*, 268–69.

26. Jorge A. Bustamante, *Población y Desarrollo: A Virtual Contradiction between International Migration and Human Right* (Santiago, Chile: United Nations, Economic Commission for Latin America and the Caribbean and Inter-American Development Bank, 2003), 11.

27. Garcia, *Operation Wetback*, 187.

28. García y Griego, "Importation of Mexican Contract Laborers," 65.

29. Garcia, *Operation Wetback*, 84.

30. Ernesto Galarza, *Merchants of Labor: The Mexican Bracero Story* (San Jose: Rosicrucian Press, 1964), 63. A specific "drying out the wetback" incident, the El Paso Incident, occurred in 1948. In response Mexico abrogated the 1948 bracero agreement. See US Congress, Senate Committee on the Judiciary, *History of the Immigration and Naturalization Service*, report prepared by the Congressional Research Service, Library of Congress, 96th Congress 2d sess.1980, Committee Print, Table 24: "Illegal Aliens Apprehended, Total Aliens Deported, Aliens Deported to Mexico Only, and Aliens Departing Voluntarily under Proceedings, Fiscal Years 1946-52," 54; and Table 25: "Mexican Agricultural Laborers Admitted and Contracted, Fiscal Years 1950-52," 58.

31. Ramos, *American GI Forum*, 72.

32. Gutiérrez, *Walls and Mirror*, 153.

33. Garcia, *Operation Wetback*, 231.

34. American Committee for the Protection of the Foreign Born, "Our Badge of Infamy," in Carlos Cortes, *The Mexican American and the Law* (New York: Arno Press, 1974), 33–34. This selection of the anthology is a petition submitted to the United Nations on April 17, 1959.

35. García, *Operation Wetback*, 212.

36. Gladwin Hill, "'Wetback' Drive in the Valley: Texas' Lower Rio Grande Area Cites 'Rights' on Keeping Illegal Mexican Labor," *New York Times*, August 2, 1954.

37. Residents protested immigration authorities by, for example, making it difficult for the Border Patrol to get meals, lodging, and gasoline for their cars. Restaurants posted "Dogs and Border Patrolmen not allowed" signs. Garcia, *Operation Wetback*, 214–19.

38. García, *Operation Wetback*, 219.

39. Immigration and Nationality Act of 1952, 66 Statutes-at-Large 163. The act stipulated that half of the immigration quota went to relatives of persons already in the United States who were either citizens or legal residents and the other half of the quota to immigrants with valued skills. Katherine M. Donato, Jorge Durand, and Douglas S. Massey, "Changing Conditions in the US Labor Market: Effects of the Immigration Reform and Control Act of 1986," *Population Research and Policy Review* 11, no. 2 (January 1992): 95.

40. Ngai, *Impossible Subjects*, 237.

41. Ngai, *Impossible Subjects*, 239.

42. Gutiérrez, *Walls and Mirrors*, 166. Criticism of the act was also raised at the 1958 annual meeting in Laredo, Texas. *Walls and Mirrors*, 260n38.

43. David Montejano, "The Demise of 'Jim Crow' for Texas Mexicans, 1940–1970," *Aztlan: Journal of Chicano Studies* 16, nos. 1–2 (1987): 50.

44. Montejano, "Demise of 'Jim Crow,'" 29. In the same period, Texas established the Mexican school system that segregated Mexican-origin students from white students.

45. Illustrating white attitudes toward Mexicans is the experience of Juan José Herrera when inquiring about a job on a farm. The farmer informed Herrera that he and his family would sleep in a chicken house. According to Herrera's son John H. Herrera, the coop had "a dirt floor . . . there was chicken shit all over the walls and everything." Herrera's father turned down the job offer and told the farmer angrily, "Why don't you move *your* family in there you son of a bitch!" John H. Herrera, interview by Thomas H. Kreneck, May 22, 1981, Houston Metropolitan Research Center.

46. Montejano, "Demise of 'Jim Crow,'" 29.

47. Montejano, "Demise of 'Jim Crow,'" 30.

48. The lawyers and their dates are James de Anda (1925–2006), Gus Garcia (1915–1964), John J. Herrera (1910–1986), and Carlos Cadena (1917–2001).

49. Ian F. Haney-López, "Race and Erasure: The Salience of Race to Latinos/as," in Delgado and Stefancic *Latino/a Condition*, 180.

50. However, the US Bureau of the Census, the public schools, and the state government recognized them as a separate class. Ricardo Romo, "George I. Sánchez and the Civil Rights Movement: 1940–1960," *La Raza Law Journal* 1 (1986): 356.

51. Michael A. Olivas, *"Hernández v. Texas*: A Litigation History," in *"Colored Men" and "Hombres Aquí"*: Hernández v. Texas *and the Emergence of Mexican-American Lawyering*, ed. Michael A. Olivas (Houston: Arte Publico Press, 2006), 215.

52. Olivas, *"Hernández v. Texas*," 221.

53. Lori Rodríguez, "Little-Known Case was Landmark for Hispanics: 50 Years Ago, A Texan's Trial Helped Bring Latinos Equity," *Houston Chronicle*, November 18, 2004.

54. Haney-López, "Race and Erasure," 181.

55. Anthony Quiroz, "'I Can See No Alternative Except to Battle It Out in Court': Gus García and the Spirit of the Mexican American Generation," in Quiroz, *Leaders of the Mexican American Generation*, 216.

56. Quiroz, "I Can See No Alternative," in Quiroz, *Leaders of the Mexican American Generation*, 218.

57. Calvert, de León, and Cantrell, *History of Texas*, 373.

58. June Melby Benowitz, "Minute Women of the U.S.A.," *Handbook of Texas Online*, updated November 30, 2023, http://www.tshaonline.org/handbook/online/articles/pwm01.

59. V. Carl Allsup, *"Hernández v. Driscoll CISD*," *Handbook of Texas Online*, updated August 3, 2020, http://www.tshaonline.org/handbook/online/articles/jrh02.

60. Guadalupe San Miguel Jr. *"Let All of Them Take Heed": Mexican Americans and the Campaign for Educational Equality in Texas, 1910–1981* (Austin: University of Texas Press, 1987), 134.

61. Montejano, *Anglos and Mexicans,* 276.

62. Acosta and Winegarten, *Las Tejanas*, 226.

63. Shafeq Patel, "Houston's Population Is Still Booming," *Axios,* March 18, 2024, https://www.axios.com/local/houston/2024/03/19/texas-population-increase-htx.

64. "2040 Regional Transportation Plan Demographics," h-gac.com, accessed November 7, 2024, https://www.h-gac.com/regional-transportation-plan/2040/demographics.

65. Joe R. Feagin, "The Global Context of Metropolitan Growth: Houston and the Oil Industry," *American Journal of Sociology* 90, no. 6 (1985): 1216–17.

66. In the greater Houston metropolitan area, the total was 646, 869 in 1940. Feagin, "Global Context of Metropolitan Growth," 1206.

67. Beth Ann Shelton, "Patterns of Racial and Ethnic Disparity and Conflict: Hispanic Communities," in *Houston: Growth and Decline in*

a Sunbelt Boomtown, ed. Beth Ann Shelton et al. (Philadelphia: Temple University Press, 1989): 96.

68. Marie Dauplaise, "Houston's Latin American: 50,000 Latins Pose Paradox, Challenge," *Houston Chronicle*, December 1, 1958.
69. Dauplaise, "Houston's Latin American."
70. Levengood, "For the Duration and Beyond," 409–10.
71. The committee functioned during WWII. It was the predecessor to the Equal Employment Opportunity Commission (EEOC) that later modeled its forms and procedures after those established by the FEPC. Gritter, *Mexican Inclusion*, 2.
72. President Roosevelt's Executive Order 9346 prohibited this form of discrimination.
73. Gómez-Quiñones, *Mexican American Labor*, 165.
74. Gritter, *Mexican Inclusion*, 79.
75. Gritter, *Mexican Inclusion*, 79.
76. Gritter, *Mexican Inclusion*, 6.
77. Emilio Zamora, *Claiming Rights and Righting Wrongs in Texas: Mexican Workers and Job Politics during World War II* (College Station: Texas A&M University Press, 2009), 159.
78. Zamora, *Claiming Rights and Righting Wrongs*, chap. 5 (125–57).
79. Gritter, *Mexican Inclusion*, 72.
80. Gritter, *Mexican Inclusion*, 75.
81. Levengood, "For the Duration and Beyond," 413.
82. Levengood, "For the Duration and Beyond," 414.
83. Zamora, *Claiming Rights and Righting Wrongs*, chap. 6, 158–80. The refineries included Humble (now Exxon Mobil) and Shell.
84. Zamora, *Claiming Rights and Righting Wrongs*, 159.
85. Zamora, *Claiming Rights and Righting Wrongs*, 161.
86. Zamora, *Claiming Rights and Righting Wrongs*, 178. A specific case for the FEPC involved the Shell Oil Company's Deer Park Refinery, east of Houston. Shell made minimal efforts in early 1945 to ameliorate the work situation for the complainants. However, angry white union workers of Local 367 of the Oil Workers' International Union went on strike. Gómez-Quiñones, *Mexican American Labor*, 165; Levengood, "For the Duration and Beyond," 416.
87. In Los Angeles racial tension between Mexican American "zooters" and whites culminated in the violent Zoot Suit Riots in June 1943.
88. Manuel Crespo, interview by Thomas H. Kreneck, August 2, 1984, Houston Metropolitan Research Center, Houston Public Library, Houston, TX.

89. "Police Squad to Deal with Latin-American Problems Selected," *Houston Press,* July 12, 1944.

90. "Two Councilmen Doubt Chief Can Stop Thugs," *Houston Chronicle*, March 7, 1950.

91. Orie Collins, "Wave of Latin-American Gang Crimes Stir Cries for Fast, Efficient Action," *Houston Chronicle*, March 8, 1950.

92. "Latin-American Gangs in Houston Now Eliminated," *Houston Chronicle*, December 2, 1945.

93. Kreneck, *History of Houston's Hispanic Community*, 51. Félix Fraga was the Ripley House's manager from 1977 to 1990.

94. Another helpful organization, the Good Citizens League, was formed by whites and Mexican Americans, including the civic leader and restaurateur Félix Tijerina. De Leon, *Mexican Americans in Houston*, 109.

95. Kreneck, *History of Houston's Hispanic Community*, 49.

96. Kreneck, *History of Houston's Hispanic Community*, 55.

97. Mary Ellen Goodman and Don des Jarlais, *The Spanish Surname Population of Houston: A Demographic Sketch*, Project Houston, Report 2 (Houston: Center for Research in Social Change and Economic Development, Rice University, 1968), 2.

98. Marie Dauplaise, "Houston's Latin American: Future Holds Fear and Doubt," *Houston Chronicle,* December 9, 1958.

99. Goodman and Jarlais, *Spanish Surname Population of Houston*, 5.

100. "Felicitas Cerda Flores," in Rivas-Rodriguez et al., *Legacy Greater Than Words*, 186.

101. Ernest Eguía, interviewed by Claudia Garcia, February 2, 2001, in Stetson, "Soldier Led Charge," 36.

102. Goodman and Jarlais, *Spanish Surname Population of Houston*, 2.

103. Marie Dauplaise, "Houston's Latin American: All Living Here Dealt Blow by Sex Attacker," *Houston Chronicle*, December 7, 1958.

104. Dauplaise, "Houston's Latin American: Job Chances in Big Firm Poor," *Houston Chronicle*, December 5, 1958.

105. Goodman and Jarlais, *Spanish Surname Population of Houston*, 9–10.

106. Dauplaise, "Houston's Latin American Schools Give Children Too Little, Too Late," *Houston Chronicle*, December 3, 1958.

107. The school was bounded by Paige, Garrow, and Delano Streets. Maria Puentes, interview by Thomas H. Kreneck, October 26, 1978, Houston Metropolitan Research Center, Houston Public Library, Houston, TX.

108. María-Cristina Garcia, "Reyna, María Torres," *Handbook of Texas Online*, updated November 1, 2017, https://www.tshaonline.org/handbook/entries/reyna-maria-torres. Also, "Fiestas Award Winners," *Houston Chronicle*, September 14, 1973.

109. Angie (Mrs. Felix) Morales, interview by Thomas Kreneck, February 5, 1979, Houston Metropolitan Research Center.

110. De León, *Mexican Americans in Houston*, 69.

111. Morales, interview by Kreneck, February 5, 1979, Houston Metropolitan Research Center.

112. De León, *Mexican Americans in Houston*, 114.

113. Lydia Mendoza, interview by Joe I. Torres, October 16, 1978, in Lydia Mendoza Collection, MSS 0123, Houston Metropolitan Research Center.

114. Broyles-González, *Lydia Mendoza's Life in Music*, x.

115. Interestingly, the policy created a controversy for Tijerina, a problem thoroughly described by historian and archivist Thomas H. Kreneck in *Mexican American Odyssey*, chap. 7. Kreneck revealed that although Tijerina always claimed he had been born in Texas, he was actually born in Mexico.

116. Kreneck in *Mexican American Odyssey*, 93–94.

117. Morales, interview by Kreneck and Emma Pérez, March 24, 1989, Houston Metropolitan Research Center.

118. Dauplais, "Houston's Latin American: Pupils Who Can't Speak English in Sad Plight," *Houston Chronicle*, December 2, 1958.

119. Claudia Feldman, "The Woman She Came to Be," *Texas: Houston Chronicle Magazine*, January 12, 2000, 10.

120. Guadalupe Quintanilla, "The Little School of the 400 and Its Impact on Education for the Spanish Dominant Bilingual Children of Texas" (EdD diss., University of Houston, 1976).

121. San Miguel, *Brown, Not White*, 55.

122. San Miguel, *Brown, Not White*, 55–56.

Notes for Chapter 4

1. Maria Jiménez, interview by José Angel Gutiérrez, January 22, 1998, *Tejano Voices*, no. 96, Center for Mexican American Studies, University of Texas, Austin, Texas.

2. Maria Jiménez, interview by Linda J. Quintanilla, September 10, 2004.

3. Joe R. Feagin, *Free Enterprise City: Houston in Political and Economic Perspective* (New Brunswick, NJ: Rutgers University Press, 1988), 254.

4. By 2010 the Asian population reached 129,098 or 6.1 percent of Houston's population; "Population by Race/Ethnicity, City of Houston: 1980–2010," accessed February 19, 2012, http://www.houstontx.gov/planning/Demographics/docs_pdfs/Cy/2010-CensusByRace.pdfr.

5. Jiménez, interview by Quintanilla, July 19, 2001.

6. Jo Ann Zuniga, "A Weary Soldier: Activist Grows Frustrated in Her Battle for Hispanic Rights," *Houston Chronicle*, February 7, 1999.

7. Jiménez, interview by Quintanilla, July 19, 2001.

8. Jiménez, interview by Quintanilla, July 19, 2001.

9. Jiménez, interview by Quintanilla, July 19, 2001.

10. Jiménez, interview by, September 10, 2004.

11. In the Houston metropolitan area, all Hispanics totaled 212,444 in 1970 and 424,903 in 1980; Nestor P. Rodríguez, "Economic Restructuring and Latino Growth in Houston," in *In the Barrios: Latinos and the Underclass Debate*, ed. Joan Moore and Raquel Pinderhughes (New York: Russell Sage Foundation,1993), 103

12. She attended Franklin Elementary, Edison Middle, and Milby High Schools.

13. Jiménez, interview by Quintanilla, September 10, 2004.

14. Kreneck, *History of Houston's Hispanic Community*, 78.

15. Shelton, "Patterns of Racial and Ethnic Disparity," 97. In 1949 the chairman of the school said the lunch program would impose unwanted "federal inspection, regulation, and uniformity"; David G. McComb, *Houston: A History* (Austin: University of Texas Press, 1981), 164.

16. Henry B. González (1916–2000) was born in San Antonio, Texas. He was elected in a special election in 1961, filling a vacancy to the US House of Representatives when Representative Paul J. Kilday resigned.

17. John J. Herrera, rerecording of a memorial service program on November 22, 1964, given November 28, 1983, Houston Metropolitan Research Center.

18. Pycior, *LJB & Mexican Americans*, 18.

19. Excerpt of the March 15, 1965, speech at: www.youtube.com/watch?v=NEOtGRi_w.

20. Luis Cano, interview by Thomas H. Kreneck, April 22, 1987, Houston Metropolitan Research Center.

21. Jiménez, interview by Quintanilla, September 10, 2004. The lie was credible to the grandmother because Jiménez was light complected.

22. Jiménez, interview by Quintanilla, July 19, 2001.

23. Tatcho Mindiola Jr., "A Personal Comment on Assimilation," *Houston Review: History and Culture of the Gulf Coast* (Summer 1981): 261.

24. Mindiola, "Personal Comment on Assimilation," 262.

25. Jiménez, interview by Quintanilla, July 19, 2001.

26. Zuniga, "A Weary Soldier"; and Rodriguez and Villareal, "Maria Jiménez," in Espinoza, Cotera, and Blackwell, *Chicana Movidas*, 280.

27. Jiménez, interview by Quintanilla, July 19, 2001. She applied in 1968 to become a naturalized citizen on her eighteenth birthday, August 2.

28. Jiménez, interview by Quintanilla, September 10, 2004.

29. Jiménez, interview by Quintanilla, July 19, 2001.

30. Martha Liberum, "Maria Jiménez. She's an 'Objective Leftist' Who Hasn't Given Up on the System," *Houston Post*, March 17, 1971. Professor Tatcho Mindiola Jr. also experienced considerable "social discrimination, especially in high school." Tatcho Mindiola Jr., interview by David Goldstein, June 4, 2008, Houston Metropolitan Research Center.

31. Jiménez, interview by Quintanilla, September 10, 2004.

32. George Xavier Cruz, "Being Hispanic in Houston: From the 'Barrio' and Back Again," *Americas Review* 16, no. 1 (Spring 1988): 57.

33. Mary M. Moody, "'Chicano' Call Pleases Some, Irks Others, Suit Yourself," *Austin American-Statesmen*, July 10, 1971.

34. Félix Ramírez, interviewer unknown, February 21, year unknown, Houston Metropolitan Research Center.

35. Jiménez, interview by Quintanilla, September 10, 2004.

36. Jiménez, interview by Quintanilla, September 10, 2004.

37. "Barrios of Houston: Houston Hispanics Refuse to Be Categorized, Typified," *Houston Post*, June 13, 1979.

38. Bob Sherrill, "Migrant Misery: 100,000 Texans," *Austin Statesman*, September 1, 1960.

39. Alfonso Vasquez, interview by Thomas H. Kreneck, November 15, 1978, Houston Metropolitan Research Center.

40. James C. Harrington, "From La Casita to LUPE," *Texas Observer*, December 3, 2004.

41. Sherrill, "Migrant Misery."

42. "Los Huelguistas y Sus Problemas," *El Sol* (Houston), July15, 1966.

43. Gómez-Quiñones, *Mexican American Labor*, 255.

44. Sherrill, "Migrant Misery."

45. *El Sol*, July 22, 1966, quoted in Robert S. Guerra and Mary Ellen Goodman, *A Content Assessment of El Sol, A Community Newspaper* (Houston: Center for Research in Social Change and Economic Development, Rice University, 1968), 20.

46. Ernest Stromberger, "La Marcha: How a Strike Became a Cause," *Dallas Times Herald*, September 4, 1966.

47. De León, *History of Mexican Americans in Houston*, 170–71.

48. Martin Dreyer, "Critics Cry: 'Abolish the Rangers!'" *Houston Chronicle*, February 9, 1969, 31–32.

49. Richard Bailey, "The Starr County Strike," *Red River Valley Historical Review* 4, no. 1 (Winter 1979): 44.

50. Ronnie Dugger, "The Rangers and La Huelga," *Texas Observer*, June 9–23, 1967, 28.

51. Dryer, "Critics Cry," 33.

52. United States Commission on Civil Rights, *Mexican Americans and the Administration of Justice in the Southwest* (Washington, DC: Government Printing Office, 1970), 17.

53. *Allee v. Medrano*, 416 U.S. 802 (1974), http://supreme.justia.com/us/416/802, accessed April 30, 2006. Allee was a Texas Ranger.

54. Nick Cooper, "Interview with Longtime Houston Activist Maria Jiménez," *Houston Free Press*, February 11, 2014, https://freepresshouston.com/interview-with-longtime-houston-activist-maria-jimenez/.

55. Cooper, "Interview with Longtime Houston Activist Maria Jiménez."

56. Maria Jiménez, interview by Natalie Garza, Oral History of Houston History Project, June 14, 2010, Mexican-American History Migrant Rights, University of Houston, Houston, TX.

57. "Los huelguistas y Sus Problemas," *El Sol*, July 15, 1966.

58. Kreneck, *Del Pueblo*, 83.

59. Marilyn D. Rhinehart and Thomas H. Kreneck, "The Minimum Wage March of 1966: A Case Study in Mexican-American Politics, Labor, and Identity," *Houston Review: History and Culture of the Gulf Coast* 11, 1 (1989): 37.

60. Kreneck, *History of Houston's Hispanic Community*, 84.

61. Roberto R. Treviño, *The Church in the Barrio: Mexican American Ethno-Catholicism in Houston* (Chapel Hill: University of North Carolina Press, 2006), 193.

62. Alfred J. Hernández, interview by Thomas H. Kreneck, November 27, 1984, Houston Metropolitan Research Center.

63. Félix Ramírez, interviewer unknown, February 21, year unknown, Houston Metropolitan Research Center.

64. Tom Milligan, "Rally at Capitol, Climaxes March," *Dallas News*, September 6, 1966.

65. Alfonso Vásquez, interview by Thomas H. Kreneck, November 15, 1984, Houston Metropolitan Research Center. Growers preferred

Mexican nationals, the so-called green carders who received visas from the federal government and accepted lower wages. "Los Huelgistas y Sus Problemas," *El Sol,* July 15, 1966. It should be noted that anyone born "on the farms in Texas" is not a "wetback" but a US citizen.

66. Rhinehart and Kreneck, "Minimum Wage March," 37.
67. Dorothy Lillard, "Farm Wage Group Opens Capitol Vigil," *Dallas News,* September 7, 1966.
68. Dreyer, "Critics Cry," 33.
69. Treviño, *Church in the Barrio,* 190, 192.
70. Leonel Castillo, "Community Gains from School Boycott," *Papel Chicano,* October 10–23, 1970.
71. Ignacio M. García, *Chicanismo: The Forging of a Militant Ethos among Mexican Americans* (Tucson: University of Arizona Press, 1997), 3.
72. García, *Chicanismo,* 12.
73. Jiménez, interview by José Angel Gutiérrez, January 22, 1998.
74. Martha Liebrum, "Maria Jiménez: She's an 'Objective Leftist' Who Hasn't Given Up on the System," *Houston Chronicle,* March 17, 1971.
75. Carlos Calbillo "The Chicano Movement in Houston and Texas: A Personal Memory," *Houston History* 9, no. 1 (Fall 2011): 27.
76. Connie Lunnen, "Chicanos and the Church. A Woman Has to Fight Back," *Houston Chronicle,* February 19, 1970.
77. Yolanda Birdwell, interview by Ernesto Valdez, May 4, 2007, Oral Histories of Houston History Project, University of Houston, Houston, TX.
78. "Chicano Power," *Echo News Magazine,* March 17, 1970.
79. J. D. Arnold, "Chicanos Promised Compromise," *Houston Chronicle,* March 6, 1970.
80. Jiménez, interview by Quintanilla, July 19, 2001.
81. Wade Roberts, "Traffic Court Rules T&S Tickets Invalid," *Daily Cougar* (Houston), February 17, 1971.
82. Jiménez, interview by Quintanilla, July 19, 2001. Emphasis is hers.
83. Maria Jiménez, "Women Still Powerless," *Papel Chicano,* September 26–October 9, 1970.
84. Jiménez, interview by Quintanilla, July 19, 2001.
85. Sor Juana Inéz de la Cruz (d. 1695), known as the "Tenth Muse," was an erudite Mexican nun. Asunción Lavrin, "Women in Colonial Mexico," in *The Oxford History of Mexico,* ed. Michael C. Meyer and William H. Beezley (Oxford: Oxford University Press, 2000), 271–72.
86. Jiménez, interview by Quintanilla, July 19, 2001. Emphasis made by Maria.

87. Rodríguez and Villarreal, "Maria Jiménez," in Espinoza, Cotera, and Blackwell, *Chicana Movidas*, 282. She did not have a romantic relationship with any Chicano while at the university. She married after graduating from the University of Houston to a Mexican national and moved to Mexico.

88. Jiménez, "Women Still Powerless."

89. In the 1930s Sam V. Quintanilla's school sent him to work in an office in Austin, Texas. He recalled, "I would type jillions of letters . . . jillions of envelopes." Sam V. Quintanilla, interview by Linda J. Quintanilla, May 28, 2000.

90. Jiménez, "Women Still Powerless."

91. "La Madre de Familia se Debe Cuidar," *El Mexica*, December 24, 1975. *"En su esfuerzo porque los demás miembros de la familia comiencen el día con un desayuno nutritivo, ella descuida el suyo."* (In her effort so that the other members of the family begin the day with a nutritious breakfast, she neglects her own.) My translation.

92. Jiménez, "Women Still Powerless."

93. Jiménez, interview by Quintanilla, July 19, 2001.

94. Jiménez, interview by Quintanilla, July 19, 2001. Emphasis by Jiménez.

95. Jiménez, interview by Quintanilla, July 19, 2001.

96. Stan McLendon, "New SA Pres. Plans Executive Reforms," *Daily Cougar*, November 22, 1971.

97. Rodríguez and Villarreal, "Maria Jiménez," in Espinoza, Cotera, and Blackwell, *Chicana Movidas*, 283–84.

98. "Houston Activists to Honor SA Prez," *Daily Cougar*, February 16, 1972.

99. Jiménez, interview by Quintanilla, July 19, 2001.

100. Maria Jiménez, interview by Samantha Rodríguez, February 25, 2012, Oral History of Houston History Project.

101. Jiménez, interview by Quintanilla, July 19, 2001.

102. Peggy Reid, "Funding Questioned: Solon Investigates SA," *Daily Cougar*, November 9, 1971.

103. "Committee Sponsors Anti-War Rally," *Daily Cougar*, October 13, 1971.

104. Gloria Smith, "UWC Denounces Asia War," *Daily Cougar*, April 21, 1971.

105. Jiménez, interview by Rodríguez, February 25, 2012, Oral History of Houston History Project.

106. Cooper, "Interview with Longtime Houston Activist Maria Jiménez."

107. "Students Picket Supermart," *Daily Cougar*, September 21, 1971.
108. In East Texas, where Blacks were concentrated, resistance to integra-
     tion was substantial, even violent. "Racial Terror Charged in East Texas
     Slaying," *Austin Statesman*, November 5, 1955.
109. Rodríguez and Villareal, "Maria Jiménez," in Espinoza, Cotera, and
     Blackwell, *Chicana Movidas*, 279.
110. Gómez-Cano and Ross-Nazzal, *Spirit of Magnolia Park*, 93.
111. Jiménez, interview by Quintanilla, July 19, 2001.
112. San Miguel, *Brown, Not White*, 209.
113. "Houston Looks for Support in Race Issue," *Austin Statesman*, Septem-
     ber 1, 1960.
114. The African American attorney Weldon Berry said, "We met a great
     deal of opposition from the early school boards [that] adopted many
     delaying tactics." Jorjanna Price, "HISD Litigation: June Hearing
     Another Step in Long Hunt for Solution," *Houston Post*, May 13,
     1979.
115. Delgado and Stefancic, *Critical Race Theory*, 29.
116. US Commission on Civil Rights, Texas State Advisory Committee,
     *Civil Rights in Texas: A Report of the Texas Advisory Committee to the
     U.S. Commission on Civil Rights* ([Austin?]: 1970), 7.
117. McComb, *Houston*, 167.
118. McComb, *Houston*, 166.
119. Allan Turner, "Beneva Williams Nyamu, 1932–2014: An Early Fighter
     for Desegregation," *Houston Chronicle*, January 14, 2014.
120. "Rice Seeking to End Negro Student Ban," *Austin Statesman*, February
     9, 1964.
121. John B. Boles, *A University So Conceived: A Brief History of Rice*
     (Houston: Rice University, 1992), 52–53.
122. Black students first attended Rice University in 1965. The pragmatic
     argument in favor of ending segregation at Rice University is an
     example of what crits call "interest convergence."
123. Guadalupe San Miguel Jr., "'The Community Is Beginning to Rumble:'
     The Origins of Chicano Educational Protest in Houston, 1965–1970,"
     Houston Review: History and Culture of the Gulf Coast 13, no. 3
     (1991): 141.
124. Marie Dauplaise, "Houston's Latin American: Education Key to
     Tomorrow," *Houston Chronicle*, December 10, 1958.
125. Marie Dauplaise, "Houston's Latin American: Schools Give Children
     Too Little, Too Late," *Houston Chronicle*, December 3, 1958.

126. As Lu-in Wang explained, research revealed that, "the teachers' behavior contributed to changes in the children's self-concept, expectations, and motivations and even the children's cognitive skills." Wang, *Discrimination by Default*, 58.

127. "Chale! We Are Not Brown Monkeys," *Papel Chicano*, October 10–23, 1970.

128. De León, *Mexican Americans in Houston*, 159.

129. San Miguel, *Brown, Not White*, 60.

130. San Miguel, *Brown, Not White*, 61–63.

131. San Miguel, *Brown, Not White*, 63.

132. Raúl Gutiérrez, "Mexican-Americans Boycott Elsa High School: Greater Houston—Uneasy?" *Compass* 2, no. 9 (December 1968): 2.

133. San Miguel, *Brown, Not White*, 66.

134. September 16 has historical significance in Mexico's history because it was the day in 1821 that Mexico declared its independence from Spain.

135. MALDEF filed an amicus curiae (friend of the court) brief in August 1970 with the US Fifth Circuit of Appeals asking that Mexican American students be classified as an identifiable minority group in the desegregation process. The court, located in New Orleans, Louisiana, denied MALDEF's request.

136. A thorough description of this episode is found San Miguel, *Brown, Not White*, chap. 5.

137. Price, "HISD Litigation."

138. *Cisneros v. Corpus Christi ISD*, "Mexican-Americans and the Desegregation of Schools in the Southwest," *Houston Law Review* 8 (1970–1971): 943.

139. In his ruling Connally wrote, sarcastically, "Content to be 'White' for these many years, now, when the shoe begins to pinch, the would-be Intervenors wish to be treated not as White but as an 'identifiable group.' In short, they wish to be 'integrated' with Whites, not Blacks." Donald R. McAdams, *Fighting to Save Our Urban Schools . . . and Winning! Lessons from Houston* (New York: Teachers College, Columbia University, 2000), 20.

140. The first strike ended after only two and a half weeks because the HISD board agreed to most of the demands by MAEC, the most important being "identifying Mexican Americans as an ethnic group and appealing the pairing decision to the Supreme Court." San Miguel, *Brown, Not White*, 116.

141. San Miguel, *Brown, Not White*, 97.

142. San Miguel, *Brown, Not White*, 98.

143. The MAEC and other groups tried, without success, to be placed on the agenda of the HISD council meeting. Leonel J. Castillo, "Confusion at HISD," *Papel Chicano*, September 26–October 9, 1970.

144. Salazar recalled that "they [the police] handcuffed everyone except Yolanda Birdwell for some reason. I don't know how she got away with it, she was the worst one." Gregorio Salazar, interview by Thomas H. Kreneck, May 9, 1989, Houston Metropolitan Research Center. Birdwell, however, recalled she was arrested at the "riot" and at other MAYO events. Yolanda Birdwell, interview by Ernesto Valdez, May 4, 2007, Oral History of Houston History Project.

145. San Miguel, *Brown, Not White*, 180.

146. "LULACS Where Are You," *Papel Chicano*, November 9, 1971.

147. Jiménez, interview by Rodríguez, February 25, 2012, Oral History of Houston History Project.

148. Tom Curtis, "Blacks, Chicanos Say Integration is Not Working," *Houston Chronicle*, February 22, 1972.

149. The lower court was the US Court of Appeals for the Tenth Circuit, which includes the states of Oklahoma, Kansas, New Mexico, Colorado, Wyoming, and Utah.

150. Ruben Donato, *The Other Struggle for Equal Schools: Mexican Americans during the Civil Rights Era* (New York: State University of New York Press, 1997), 124.

151. Luis Cano, interview by Thomas H. Kreneck, April 22, 1987, Houston Metropolitan Research Center.

152. Cano, interview by Kreneck, April 22, 1987, Houston Metropolitan Research Center.

153. John Brandstetter and Charles R. Foster, "'Quality Integrated Education' in Houston's Magnet Schools," *Phi Delta Kappan* (April 1976): 503.

154. Angela Valenzuela, *Subtractive Schooling: U.S.-Mexican Youth and the Politics of Caring* (Albany: State University of New York Press, 1999), 49.

155. Valenzuela, *Subtractive Schooling*, 50.

156. Richard Vara, "Alternative Education: Frustrated Chicanos Now Receiving Some Extra Help at Special Schools," *Houston Post*, May 13, 1979.

157. Jiménez, interview by Quintanilla, September 10, 2004.

158. Margaret B. Melville, "Mexican Women Adapt to Migration," in *Mexican Immigrant Workers in the U.S.*, ed. Antonio Rios-Bustamante (Los Angeles: Chicano Studies Research Center, University of California, 1981), 121.

159. Barbara Belejack, "A Lesson in Equal Protection: The Texas Cases That Opened the Schoolhouse Door to Undocumented Immigrant Children," *Texas Observer*, July 13, 2007, 15.

160. Nancy Stancill, "A Question of Free Education for Illegal Alien Children in Texas: Case before U.S. Court Here May Affect Estimated 111,284," *Houston Chronicle*, February 2, 1980.

161. Belejack, "Lesson in Equal Protection."

162. Michael A. Olivas, *No Undocumented Child Left Behind:* Plyler v. Doe *and the Education of Undocumented Schoolchildren* (New York: New York University Press, 2012), 15 and 109n22, 23.

163. Belejack, "Lesson in Equal Protection," 19.

164. Belejack, "Lesson in Equal Protection," 19–20.

165. From the perspective of historians, life stories are an important means to "understanding broad social and cultural phenomena." Kessler-Harris, "Why Biography?," 626.

166. Jiménez, interview by Quintanilla, September 10, 2004.

Notes for Chapter 5

1. Maria Jiménez, interview by José Angel Gutiérrez, January 22, 1998.

2. Maria Jiménez, interview by Linda J. Quintanilla, September 10, 2004.

3. Quotas were first set by the Quota Law of May 19, 1921. Persons from Western Europe were granted many more visas than from other regions. Quota Law of May 19, 1921 (42 Statutes-at-Large 5).

4. The nation was shocked recently, for example, by the police killing of George Floyd on May 25, 2020. "What to Know about the Death of George Floyd in Minneapolis," *New York Times*, March 23, 2021.

5. Armando Villafranca, "Immigrants' Role Being Seen in New Light," *Houston Chronicle*, April 20,1998.

6. "Campaign 2024: Former President Trump Campaigns in Green Bay, Wisconsin," *C-Span*, October 30, 2024, https://www.c-span.org/video/?539547-1/president-trump-campaigns-green-bay wisconsin.

7. The Eastern Hemisphere (i.e., most of Europe, Africa, and Asia) had a cap of twenty thousand visas for any country per year, but there was no fixed cap for the Western Hemisphere.

8. Steven M. Gillon, *"That's Not What We Meant to Do:" Reform and Its Unintended Consequences in Twentieth Century America* (New York: W. W. Norton, 2000), 176–77.

9. Martha Menchaca, *Naturalizing Mexican Immigrants: A Texas History* (Austin: University of Texas Press, 2011), 262–63.

10. Marcela Cerrutti and Douglas S. Massey, "Trends in Mexican Migration to the United States, 1965 to 1995," *Crossing the Border: Research from the Mexican Migration Project*, ed. Jorge Durand and Douglas S. Massey (New York: Russell Sage Foundation, 2004), 25.

11. Maria Jiménez, interviewed by Rebecca Phares, "The U.S.-Mexico Border: A Strategy of Low-Intensity Conflict," *Social Justice* 27, no. 4 (2000): 35.

12. Houston-Galveston Area Council, *Population Growth and Ethnicity in the H-GAC Region, 1970–1980*, Analytic Report No. 1 (December 1981), 11.

13. "Used Car Business Rip-off for 'Illegals,' but Many Don't Complain," *Houston Post*, August 12, 1979.

14. Shelton, "Patterns of Racial and Ethnic Disparity," 104.

15. Rodríguez, "Economic Restructuring," in Moore and Pinderhughes, *In the Barrios*, 109.

16. Feagin, *Free Enterprise City*, 253.

17. Jiménez, interview by Quintanilla, July 19, 2001.

18. Ngai, *Impossible Subjects*, 261.

19. "Leader Says 170 Klansmen are Patrolling the Texas Border," *Houston Chronicle*, October 30, 1977.

20. "Klan, Chicanos Stay Apart," *Houston Chronicle*, November 1, 1977.

21. "Troops Said Patrolling Mexican Side of Border," *Houston Chronicle*, October 31, 1977.

22. "LULAC Calls for Latins in Two Posts," *Houston Chronicle*, April 18, 1977.

23. Christine Marie Sierra, "In Search of National Power: Chicanos Working the System on Immigration Reform, 1976–1986," *Chicano Politics and Society in the Late Twentieth Century*, ed. David Montejano (Austin: University of Texas Press, 1999), 132.

24. Sierra, "In Search of National Power," in Montejano, *Chicano Politics and Society*, 135.

25. Gutiérrez, *Walls and Mirrors*, 179.

26. Gutiérrez, *Walls and Mirrors*, 201.

27. Jiménez, interview by Samantha Rodriguez, February 25, 2012, Oral History of Houston History Project.

28. Jiménez, interview by Quintanilla, October 15, 2004.

29. Quoted in Haney-López, *Racism on Trial*, 218.

30. Jiménez, interview by José Angel Gutiérrez, January 22, 1998.

31. Jiménez, interview by Samantha Rodriguez, February 25, 2012, Oral History of Houston History Project.

32. Martha Liebrum, "Maria Jiménez: She's an 'Objective Leftist' Who Hasn't Given Up on the System," *Houston Post*, March 17, 1971.

33. "MAYO Committee Works to Create Chicano Studies," *Daily Cougar*, March 24, 1972.

34. Kreneck, *History of Houston's Hispanic Community*, 90.

35. Gonzáles, *Mexicanos*, 212.

36. "College Info Aids Minority Groups," *Daily Cougar*, January 21, 1971.

37. "Umoff Gets Backings," *Daily Cougar*, March 3, 1971, and Pedro Vasquez, "Maria Jiménez, Vice-President, U of H Students" *Papel Chicano*, April 1, 1971.

38. Jiménez, interview by Quintanilla, October 15, 2004.

39. Constance Cooper, "Chicano Studies: Full-time Teachers Are Hard to Find," *Daily Cougar*, October 27, 1972.

40. Tatcho Mindiola Jr., "Finding a Way: Developing the Center for Mexican American Studies at UH," *Houston History* 9, no. 1 (Fall 2011): 38–40. Dr. Mindiola skillfully directed the center from 1980 to 2015. His successor is Dr. Pamela A. Quiroz.

41. Mindiola, "Finding a Way," 40.

42. See Alma M. García, "Introduction," in *Chicana Feminist Thought: The Basic Historical Writings*, ed. Alma M. García (New York: Routledge, 1997), 1–16.

43. "Houston Chicana Conference," *La Gente* 1, no. 6 (May 31, 1971): 6.

44. Jiménez, interview by Samantha Rodríguez, February 25, 2012, Oral History of Houston History Project.

45. Jiménez, interview by Quintanilla, July 19, 2001.

46. District 87 represented the ship channel area in the eastern section of Houston. Jiménez graduated from the University of Houston in 1974 with a Bachelor of Arts degree in Political Science.

47. Jo Ann Zuniga, "A Weary Soldier: Activist Grows Frustrated in Her Battle for Hispanic Rights," *Houston Chronicle*, February 7, 1999.

48. Jiménez, interview by Quintanilla, July 19, 2001. Emphasis made by Jiménez.

49. Tatcho Mindiola Jr., interview by Louis J. Marchiafava, April 21, 1975, Houston Metropolitan Research Center, Houston Public Library, Houston, TX.

50. Daniel Bustamante, interview by Thomas H. Kreneck, February 24, 1982, Houston Metropolitan Research Center.

51. Carlos Muñoz Jr., *Youth, Identity, Power: The Chicano Movement* (London: Verso, 1989), 102.

52. "Voter Percentage Lowest Since World War II Days," *Houston Chronicle*, November 6, 1974.

53. Bustamante, interview by Kreneck, February 24, 1982, Houston Metropolitan Research Center.

54. Rodríguez and Villarreal, "Maria Jiménez," in Espinoza, Cotera, and Blackwell, *Chicana Movidas*, 286.

55. Jiménez, interview by Quintanilla, July 19, 2001.

56. Bustamante, interview by Kreneck, February 24, 1982, Houston Metropolitan Research Center.

57. Mindiola, interview by Marchiafava, April 21, 1975, Houston Metropolitan Research Center.

58. Zuniga, "Weary Soldier."

59. Tony Castro, "Muñiz Charges Briscoe Received Lobbyist Funds," *Houston Post*, November 1, 1974.

60. Jiménez, interview by Quintanilla, July 19, 2001.

61. Bustamante, interview by Kreneck, February 24, 1982, Houston Metropolitan Research Center.

62. Mindiola, interview by Marchiafava, April 21, 1975, Houston Metropolitan Research Center.

63. Jiménez, interview by José Angel Gutiérrez, January 22, 1998.

64. Jiménez, interview by Quintanilla, July 19, 2001.

65. Jiménez, interview by Gutiérrez, January 22, 1998.

66. Mindiola, interview by Marchiafava, April 21, 1975, Houston Metropolitan Research Center.

67. Jiménez, interview by Gutiérrez, January 22, 1998.

68. For a firsthand account of RUP's efforts and success in Crystal City, see Gutiérrez, *Making of a Chicano Militant*.

69. Richard Santillan, "An Analysis of the 1974 General Elections," *La Gente*, February 1975.

70. Bustamante, interview by Kreneck, February 24, 1982, Houston Metropolitan Research Center.

71. Jiménez, interview by Gutiérrez, January 22, 1994.

72. Jiménez, interview by Quintanilla, July 19, 2001.
73. Jiménez, interview by Gutiérrez, January 22, 1994.
74. Jiménez, interview by Quintanilla, July 19, 2001.
75. Zuniga, "Weary Soldier."
76. Jiménez, interview by Quintanilla, July 19, 2001.
77. Jiménez, interview by Quintanilla, October 15, 2004.
78. Jiménez, interview by Quintanilla, July 19, 2001.
79. Pancho Arguelles, interview by Quintanilla, September 16, 2009.
80. Jiménez, interview by Gutiérrez, January 22, 1994.
81. Zuniga, "Weary Soldier."
82. Jiménez, interview by Quintanilla, March 26, 2013. From 1979 to 1983, her employer was the Banrural-Fideicomiso de Organizaciones. She worked as a project director.
83. Jiménez, interview by Quintanilla, October 15, 2005.
84. Jiménez, interview by Quintanilla, September 10, 2004.
85. Zuniga, "Weary Soldier."
86. Jiménez, interview by Quintanilla, July 19, 2001. Jiménez did not provide the year of the incident.
87. Jiménez, interview by Gutiérrez, January 22, 1998.
88. Jiménez, interview by Quintanilla, July 19, 2001.
89. Jiménez, interview by Quintanilla, July 19, 2001.
90. Jiménez, interview by Quintanilla, September 10, 2001.
91. Jiménez, interview by Quintanilla, September 10, 2001. Emphasis made by Jiménez.
92. Thomas R. Cole, *No Color Is My Kind: The Life of Eldrewey Stearns and the Integration of Houston* (Austin: University of Texas Press, 1997), 26, 30.
93. Serbino Sandifer-Walker, "A Sit-in to Face Down Jim Crow," *Houston Chronicle*, March 2, 2008; and William Henry Keller, "Race Relations and School Desegregation in Houston, Texas" (Master's Thesis, University of Houston, December 1990), 73; and Cole, *No Color Is My Kind*, 26.
94. Michael Anderson, "Eldrewey Stearns and Houston's Student Civil Rights Movement," *Houston History* 14, no. 2 (May 2017): 26.
95. NASA selected Houston in 1961 for the Manned Spacecraft Center, later renamed the Lyndon B. Johnson Space Center in 1973. Houston's first MLB team, from 1962 to 1964, was the Houston Colt .45s. In 1965 the team was renamed the Houston Astros.
96. A very important individual who worked to avoid violence in Houston was Bob Dundas, in charge of public relations at Foleys, a major department

store based in Houston. He successfully blocked media coverage of the desegregation of seventy lunch counters and other places to avoid protests by white Houstonians. Cole, *No Color Is My Kind*, 55.

97. "Police Story: Two Hard Towns, Lawless Cops?" *Time*, September 19, 1977.

98. Mike Yuen, "Moody Park Rioters of '78 Might Not Recognize HPD of '88," *Houston Post*, May 2, 1988.

99. Rick Nelson, "'Search and Kill' Policy Once Used, Canales Says," *Houston Post*, March 4, 1979.

100. Edward Hegstrom, "Looking Back on Integration; In Houston Money Spoke Louder than Parks," *Houston Chronicle*, October 26, 2005.

101. Keller, "Race Relations," 70. See also Dwight Watson, *Race and the Houston Police Department, 1930–1990: A Change Did Come* (College Station: Texas A&M University, 2005), 86.

102. Christy Drennan, "The Hole: A Quiet Place Where Police Go for Various Reasons—Sometimes to Talk with a Suspect," *Houston Chronicle*, May 14, 1977.

103. Janice Blue, "Torres' Death Sparks Call for Unity," *Houston Breakthrough*, June 1977; and Pete Wittenberg, "Janish Spoke of Having 'Fun' Harassing Mexicans, Witness Says," *Houston Post*, February 6, 1978.

104. "'My God, They've Thrown Him (Torres) In!' Officer Tells about Splash, Man Floating in the Bayou," *Houston Chronicle*, September 15, 1977.

105. The autopsy report said Torres "had a fractured skull, broken ribs, a broken arm and leg." Blue, "Torres' Death."

106. Janet Sanders, "Torres' Ability to Swim Is Focus of the Defense," *Houston Chronicle*, September 17, 1977. The police officers were Terry Denson and Stephen Orlando.

107. Sanders, "My God, They've Thrown Him In!"

108. Among the Chicano newspapers that reported on the killing were *Semanario El Mexica* (Houston), and *Para La Gente* (Austin).

109. Tom Moran, "Reyes Says LULAC Request to Halt Torres Trial was Misunderstanding," *Houston Chronicle*, September 10, 1977.

110. Janet Sanders, "2 Ex-Policemen Get Probation," *Houston Chronicle*, October 8, 1977.

111. Mamie Garcia, interview by Linda Quintanilla, July 20, 2001.

112. Steven Harmon Wilson, *The Rise of Judicial Management in the U.S. District Court, Southern District of Texas, 1955–2000* (Athens: University of Georgia Press, 2002), 257.

113. Pete Wittenberg, "3 Ex-officers Given One-year Terms. Torres' Mother Unhappy," *Houston Post*, March 29, 1978.

114. Wilson, *Rise of Judicial Management*, 256, 265.

115. Garcia, interview by Quintanilla, July 20, 2001.

116. "Morales, 2 Others Held on Riot Charges," *Houston Post*, May 13, 1978; and Lori Rodríguez, "Moody Park: 10 Years After; Lives of Many People Changed After Riot," *Houston Chronicle*, May 8, 1988.

117. "*Los Indocumentados Son Víctimas*," *El Voz*, August 1979.

118. García, interview by Quintanilla, July 20, 2001.

119. Adriana Castro, "Guadalupe Quintanilla: Defying the Odds," *Houston History* 14, no. 2 (May 2017): 16–17.

120. Lisa Teachey, "25 Years Later, Distrust Remains," *Houston Chronicle*, May 6, 2002. Matt Schwartz, "HPD Weathers another Storm: Recent Revelations Have Not Sullied Public Opinion about Police," *Houston Chronicle*, June 22, 2003. Marialuisa Rincon, "40 Years Ago Police Killed Joe Campos Torres Sparking Massive Moody Park Riots," *Houston Chronicle*, May 4, 2018.

121. Russell Contreras, "Scoop: Houston Apologizes to Hispanic Family for 1977 Police Killing," *Axios*, June 2, 2021, https://www.axios.com/2021/06/02/houston-apologizes-latino-1977-police-killing. Contreras worked for the Associated Press in Albuquerque and Boston and, since 2020, has been the Race and Justice Reporter at Axios.

122. "*Que es nuestra obligación y nuestra responsabilidad crear socie-dades que, en todas sus leyes, en todas sus políticas, en todas sus prácticas, reconozcan ese principio: que todos los seres humanos somos igual en dignidad y derechos. Y si no existe hay que crearlo.*" Elena Vega, "*Entre Nosotros: María Jiménez, Por La Justicia Social,*" *Houston Chronicle*, February 28, 2008, https://www.chron.com/news/article/mar-a-jimenez-1542902.php.

123. In 1973 activists helped to create a school for dropouts, the George I. Sánchez Junior and Senior High School.

124. Vilma S. Martínez, "Velma S. Martínez Testifies Before the U.S. Commission on Civil Rights About the Mexican American Legal Defense and Educational Fund (MALDEF), 1975," in *Major Problems in Mexican American History: Documents and Essays*, ed. Zaragosa Vargas (Boston: Houghton Mifflin Company, 1999), 420.

125. "*La Juez Rosemary Saucido Recibe Mención Honorífica,*" *La Prensa* (México City), May 24, 1978.

126. Richard Delgado, "Book Review Essay: Crossroads and Blind Alleys: A Critical Examination of Recent Writings about Race," *Texas Law Review* 82, no. 1 (2003): 130.

127. Jiménez, interview by Quintanilla, July 19, 2001.

128. David Montejano, "Introduction: On the Question of Inclusion," in Montejano, *Chicano Politics and Society*, ix.

129. Montejano, "Introduction," in Montejano, *Chicano Politics and Society*, xiv.

130. H-GAC, *Population Growth and Ethnicity*, 11.

131. Wayne King, "Houston's Spanish Accent Gets More Pronounced," *New York Times*, June 10, 1985. http://www.nytimes.com/1985/06/10/us/houston-s-spanish-accent-gets-more-pronounced.html.

132. Peggy O'Hare, "HPD's Chicano Squad Ready to Mark 25 Years of Successes," *Houston Chronicle*, August 16, 2004, http://www.chron.com/news/houston-texas/article/HPD-s-Chicano-Squad-marks-25-years-of-success-1960865.php.

133. Brown "imposed education requirements on police officers and started a Neighborhood Oriented Policing strategy to build community ties." John Williams, "Fires of Racial Hate Fail to Ignite Here," *Houston Chronicle*, May 3, 1992. Brown became the first African American mayor of Houston. Amy D'Onofrio, "Today in Texas History: Lee Brown Becomes Houston's First African American Police Chief," *Houston Chronicle*, June 24, 2009.

134. Yuen, "Moody Park Rioters."

135. Juan R. Palomo and Jim Simmon, "Houston Hispanics: Future Could Be Bright but Road Will Be Tough," *Houston Post*, March 1, 1987.

136. Mike Morris, "More Diversity Urged at HPD," *Houston Chronicle*, October 6, 2014.

137. Feagin, *Free Enterprise City*, 257.

138. De León, *Mexican Americans in Houston*, 214.

139. Shelton, "Patterns of Racial and Ethnic Disparity," 96.

140. Jiménez, interview by Gutiérrez, January 22, 1998.

141. Quote in Gómez-Cano and Ross-Nazzal, *Spirit of Magnolia Park*, 150.

Notes for Chapter 6

1. Jiménez, "Mobility, Human Rights, and Economic Development," 5.

2. Jiménez, "War in the Borderlands," 31.

3. An egregious killing by border authorities occurred in 2010 in San Ysidro. See Pedro Ríos, "Opinion: Revisiting the 2010 killing of

Anastacio Hernández Rojas May Lead to Changes," *San Diego Union-Tribune*, November 30, 2022, https://www.sandiegouniontribune.com/2022/11/30/revisiting-the-2010-killing-of-anastasio-hernndez-rojas-may-lead-to-big-changes/.

4. Edward Hegstrom, "Better Late than Never; After Court Battle, Amnesty Plan Makes Immigrants Legal," *Houston Chronicle*, February 15, 2002.

5. Nestor P. Rodríguez, "Undocumented Central Americans in Houston: Diverse Populations," *International Migration Review* 21, no. 1 (Spring 1987): 4.

6. Juan González, *Harvest of Empire: A History of Latinos in America* (New York: Penguin Books, 2001), 134–35. John Mack Faragher, ed, *Out of Many: A History of the American People*, 2nd ed. (Upper Saddle River, NJ: Prentice Hall, 1997), 992.

7. Rodríguez, "Economic Restructuring," in Moore and Pinderhughes, *In the Barrios*, 118

8. Shelton, "Patterns of Racial and Ethnic Disparity," 98.

9. Feagin, *Free Enterprise City*, 255.

10. Rodríguez, "Economic Restructuring," in Moore and Pinderhughes, *In the Barrios*, 116.

11. Rodríguez, "Economic Restructuring," in Moore and Pinderhughes, *In the Barrios*, 117.

12. Jiménez, interview by José Angel Gutiérrez, January 22, 1998.

13. Shelton, "Patterns of Racial and Ethnic Disparity," 104.

14. Rodríguez, "Economic Restructuring," in Moore and Pinderhughes, *In the Barrios*, 113.

15. Rodríguez, "Undocumented Central Americans,"18.

16. Ripley House of the Neighborhood Center dates from 1940.

17. Cerrutti and Massey, "Trends in Mexican Migration," in Durand and Massey, *Crossing the Border*, 21.

18. Roderic Ai Camp, "The Time of the Technocrats and Deconstruction of the Revolution," in *The Oxford History of Mexico*, ed. Michael C. Meyer and William H. Beezley (Oxford: Oxford University Press, 2000), 614.

19. David Thelen, "Rethinking History and the Nation-State: Mexico and the United States," *Journal of American History* 86, no. 2 (September 1999): 442.

20. Camp, "Time of the Technocrats," in Meyer and Beezley, *Oxford History of Mexico*, 610.

21. Diego Cevallos, "Rights-Mexico: Tlatelolco Massacre—40 Years of Impunity," *IPS (Inter Press Service)* October 1, 2008, http:/www.ipsnews. net/2008/10/rights-mexico-tlatelolco-massacre-40-years-of-impunity.

22. Camp, "Time of the Technocrats," in Meyer and Beezley, *Oxford History of Mexico*, 611.

23. William H. Beezley, *Mexico in World History* (New York: Oxford University Press, 2011), 132.

24. The Arab Oil Boycott lasted from October 17, 1973, to March 18, 1974.

25. Marc Lacey, "Miguel de la Madrid, President of Mexico in the 1980s, Dies at 77," *New York Times*, April 1, 2012, https://www.nytimes. com/2012/04/02/world/americas/miguel-de-la-madrid-president-of-mexico-in-1980s-dies-at-77.html.

26. Beezley, *Mexico in World History*, 137.

27. Beezley, *Mexico in World History*, 137.

28. Camp, "Time of the Technocrats," in Meyer and Beezley, *Oxford History of Mexico*, 614.

29. Jiménez, personal communication with author, March 26, 2013.

30. Jiménez, interview by Quintanilla, July 19, 2001. Similarly, following the earthquake, according to Camp, self-help groups "would later become part of a larger grassroots movement of human rights and civic action groups in the late 1980s and 1990s." Camp, "Time of the Technocrats," in Meyer and Beezley, *Oxford History of Mexico*.

31. Cerrutti and Massey, "Trends in Mexican Migration," in Durand and Massey, *Crossing the Border*, 28.

32. Susan Warren, "Experts Say Amnesty Won't Affect Illegal Immigration," *Houston Chronicle*, May 2, 1988.

33. Warren, "Experts Say Amnesty"; Roberto Suro, "1986 Amnesty Law Is Seen as Failing to Slow Alien Tide," *New York Times*, June 18, 1989; Katherine M. Donato, Jorge Durand, and Douglas S. Massey, "Stemming the Tide?: Assessing the Deterrent Effects of the Immigration Reform and Control Act," *Demography* 29, no. 2 (May 1992): 156.

34. Jiménez, "Mobility, Human Rights, and Economic Development," 5.

35. Susan Warren, "Battle Lines Firm on Amnesty; One Side Claims It's a Success, the Other Labels It a Failure," *Houston Chronicle*, April 30, 1989.

36. Mike Tolson, "INS Reporting Huge Increase of Applications for Citizenship," *Houston Chronicle*, February 17, 1995.

37. Juan Palomo and Jim Simmon, "Houston's Hispanics: Future Can Be Bright but Road Will Be Tough," *Houston Post*, March 1, 1987.

38. R. G. Ratcliffe, "Hobby Raps Law on Aliens; Official Urges an Open Border," *Houston Chronicle*, September 19, 1989.

39. Feagin, *Free Enterprise City*, 255.

40. Gina Seay, "Task Force Sets Up Hot Line to Handle Immigrants' Queries," *Houston Chronicle*, August 28, 1988.

41. Jiménez, interview by José Angel Gutiérrez, January 22, 1998.

42. United Nations General Assembly, Resolution 217A (III), "Universal Declaration of Human Rights," December 10, 1948.

43. Jiménez, "Labor Mobility and the North American Free Trade Agreement," 5.

44. Bill Coulter, "Group Urges Repeal of Employer Sanctions," *Houston Chronicle*, March 30, 1990.

45. Seay, "Task Force Sets Up Hot Line.

46. Chet Burchett, "Immigration Law Sparks Firings: Jobless Aliens Ponder Dwindling Options," *Houston Post*, March 1, 1987.

47. Chet Burchett, "U.S. 'Amnesty' Turning Aliens toward Canada," *Houston Post*, March 1, 1987.

48. Jiménez, "Mobility, Human Rights, and Economic Development," 5.

49. Donato, Durand, and Massey, "Changing Conditions in the U.S. Labor Market," 110.

50. Jiménez, "Mobility, Human Rights, and Economic Development."

51. Donato, Durand, and Massey, "Changing Conditions in the U.S. Labor Market," 95–96.

52. Lori A. Flores, *Grounds for Dreaming: Mexican Americans, Mexican Immigrants, and the California Farmworkers Movement* (New Haven: Yale University Press, 2016), 93.

53. Donato, "U.S. Policy and Mexican Migration to the United States, 1942–92," *Social Science Quarterly* 75, no. 4 (December 1994): 720. Luna quote in Susan Warren, "Alien Legalization Draws Fire; Advocates Challenge Notion There's a Farm Worker Shortage," *Houston Chronicle*, September 5, 1989.

54. Warren, "Alien Legalization,"

55. Cerrutti and Massey, "Trends in Mexican Migration," in Durand and Massey, *Crossing the Border*, 25.

56. Susan Warren, "Local INS Waging War on Fraud; Amnesty Papers Being Scrutinized," *Houston Chronicle*, August 6, 1989.

57. Susan Warren, "City to Get Border Patrol Office; Deportations Likely to Rise," *Houston Chronicle*, April 23, 1988.

58. Warren, "Battle Lines Firm on Amnesty."

59. Donato, Durand, and Massey, "Changing Conditions in the U.S. Labor Market," 95.
60. Warren, "Battle Lines Firm on Amnesty."
61. R. A. Dyer, "2 Face Criminal Charges in Hiring of Aliens," *Houston Chronicle*, April 28, 1989.
62. Jim Zook, "Ex-NFL player is Sentenced: Former Running Back Gets 60 days in Illegal Alien Case," *Houston Chronicle*, March 20, 1990,.
63. Jiménez, interview by Quintanilla, July 19, 2001.
64. Jiménez, interview by Quintanilla, July 19, 2001.
65. Jiménez, interview by José Angel Gutiérrez, January 22, 1998.
66. Maria Jiménez, "Border Militarization: The History, the Effect, and the Response," *Immigration Newsletter* 16, no. 4 (July–August 1987): 11.
67. Jiménez, interview by Quintanilla, July 19, 2001.
68. Jiménez, interview by Quintanilla, July 19, 2001.
69. Jiménez, interview by Quintanilla, July 19, 2001.
70. Jiménez, interview by Quintanilla, July 19, 2001.
71. Maria Jiménez, "Police Policies and Practices: The Case of the Border Patrol," *Immigration Newsletter* 17, no. 4 (1988): 1.
72. Jiménez, "Police Policies and Practices," 5.
73. *Murrillo et al. v. Musegades, INS et al.*
74. Douglas S. Massey, Jorge Durand, and Nolan J. Malone, *Beyond Smoke and Mirrors: Mexican Immigration in an Era of Economic Integration* (New York: Russell Sage Foundation, 2002), 99–100.
75. Ira J. Kurzban, "Democracy and Immigration," in *Keeping Out the Other: A Critical Introduction to Immigration Enforcement Today*, ed. David C. Brotherton and Philip Kretsedemas (New York: Columbia University, 2008), 64.
76. Jiménez, "Border Militarization," 1.
77. Jiménez, "War in the Borderlands," 30. It is not certain if Jiménez originated the term "deconstitutional zones." Of her writings, it probably first appeared in 1992 in "War in the Borderlands."
78. Jiménez, "War in the Borderlands," 29.
79. Dunn, *Blockading the Border*, 21.
80. Dunn, *Blockading the Border*, 23–24.
81. Sharon Shahid, "Charges of Abuse at the Border," *USA Today*, February 26, 1992.
82. Maria Jiménez, interview by Nic Paget-Clarke, "The Militarization of the U.S.-Mexico Border," *In Motion Magazine*, February 2, 1998, http://www.inmotionmagazine.com/mj1.html.

83. Dunn, *Blockading the Border*, 23.

84. Jiménez, interview by Gutiérrez, January 22, 1998.

85. Jiménez, interview by Quintanilla, July 19, 2001.

86. Jiménez, "Militarization of the U.S.-Mexico Border."

87. Dunn, *Blockading the Border*, 129–30.

88. Jiménez, interview by Quintanilla, July 19, 2001.

89. Robert Lee Maril, *Patrolling Chaos: The U.S. Border Patrol in Deep South Texas* (Lubbock: Texas Tech University Press, 2004), 96.

90. American Friends Service Committee, *Sealing Our Border: The Human Toll*, 3rd report, Immigration Law Enforcement Monitoring Project (ILEMP), A Project of the Mexico-US Border Program (Philadelphia: American Friends Service Committee, 1992), 21.

91. Jiménez, "War in the Borderlands," 29. The detained refugees were not permitted to speak to nonprofit groups offering legal aid. Ana Puga and Jo Ann Zuniga, "INS Starts Detention amid Heated Protests," *Houston Chronicle*, February 22, 1989.

92. Lisa Belkins, "Wave of Immigrant Children Strains Schools and Housing," *New York Times*, January 29, 1989.

93. Belkins, "Wave of Immigrant Children."

94. Jiménez, "War in the Borderlands," 31.

95. Lori Rodriguez, "Hispanic Influx Adds Dimension to Bias," *Houston Chronicle*, May 14, 1989,.

96. Rodríguez, "Hispanic Influx."

97. Rodríguez, "Hispanic Influx."

98. Judy Wiessler, "Many Newly Legal Aliens Refuse State Aid, Report Says," *Houston Chronicle*, July 11, 1989.

99. Executive Office of the President, Council of Economic Advisors, "Immigration's Economic Impact," *White House*, June 20, 2007, https://georgewbush-whitehouse.archives.gov/cea/cea_immigration_062007.html.

100. Jiménez, editorial, *Houston Chronicle*, October 29, 1995.

101. Rodríguez, "Hispanics Influx."

102. Rodríguez, "Hispanic Immigrants in Study Take Active Role in U.S. Politics," *Houston Chronicle,* September 7, 1989.

103. Susan Warren, "Flood of Immigrants: Top-choice in Texas; Application by Asylum Seekers Skyrocket Here," *Houston Chronicle*, March 23, 1989.

104. Warren, "City to Get Border Patrol Office."

105. Warren, "Battle Lines Firm on Amnesty."

106. Jo Ann Zuniga, "Protesters Blast INS Alien Raid," *Houston Chronicle*, April 12, 1989.

107. Carol Ellis, "The Houston Catholic Worker: Casa Juan Diego, 1981–2004," *Houston Review of History and Culture* 3, 1 (Fall 2005): 59.

108. Lori Rodríguez, "New Immigrants Here Ask for Understanding," *Houston Chronicle*, October 6, 1994.

109. Thom Marshall, "Casa His Home Away from Home," *Houston Chronicle*, April 8, 2001.

110. Rodríguez, "New Immigrants Here Ask for Understanding."

111. For the immigrants wanting to learn English, even the INS was helpful. It provided funds for English classes to over fifty organizations in Houston. In 1989 about 30,000 immigrants were enrolled in these classes. "Free Classes to Aid Legalized Immigrants: Students Study for Residency Test," *Houston Chronicle*, September 10, 1989.

112. Nancy Rytina, "IRCA Legalization Effects: Lawful Permanent Residence and Naturalization through 2001" (paper presented at The Effects of Immigrant Legalization Programs on the United States: Scientific Evidence on Immigrant Adaptation and Impacts on US Economy and Society, October 25, 2002).

113. Jiménez, interview by Quintanilla, July 19, 2001.

Notes for Chapter 7

1. Jiménez, "Mobility, Human Rights, and Economic Development."

2. Martha Liebrum, "Maria Jiménez: She's an 'Objective Leftist' Who Hasn't Given Up on the System," *Houston Chronicle*, March 17, 1971.

3. Joan Raymond, superintendent of HISD, was a controversial figure and HISD board meetings were sometimes tense. "Trustee Denies Slapping Mincberg During Dispute," *Houston Chronicle*, January 8, 1988.

4. Valenzuela, *Subtractive Schooling*, 50.

5. Wang, *Discrimination by Default*, 58–59.

6. Valenzuela, *Subtractive Schooling*, 51.

7. Valenzuela, *Subtractive Schooling*, 58.

8. William Pack, "Austin High Conditions Better, but Community Still Fragmented," *Houston Post*, November 4, 1989.

9. Valenzuela, *Subtractive Schooling*, 300–301n1.

10. Valenzuela, *Subtractive Schooling*, 57.

11. Jo Ann Zuniga, "Group Seeks Solutions to City's Racial Tensions," *Houston Chronicle*, February 18, 1995.

12. Maria Jiménez, interview by Linda J. Quintanilla, October 15, 2004.
13. Jennifer Silva, "District's Migrant Education Program Helps Students," *Houston Chronicle, Viva Magazine,* August 12, 1994.
14. Dudley Althaus, "Twilight's Children,'" *Houston Chronicle,* December 17, 1995.
15. Valenzuela, *Subtractive Schooling,* 20.
16. Lori Rodríguez, "Houston's Hispanic Destiny," *Houston Chronicle,* July 8, 1990.
17. See Ted Brader, Nicholas A. Valentino, and Elizabeth Suhay, "What Triggers Public Opposition to Immigration? Anxiety, Group Cues, and Immigration Threat," *American Journal of Political Science* 52, no. 4 (October 2008): 959–78.
18. Susan Warren, "Anti-alien Ads Not Fair, Hispanics Say," *Houston Chronicle,* January 17, 1990.
19. Warren, "Anti-alien Ads Not Fair."
20. Susan Warren and Jennifer Liebrum, "Anti-immigration Ads Ripped; Catholic Church, Hispanics Label Radio Spots Racist," *Houston Chronicle,* January 18, 1990.
21. Warren and Liebrum, "Anti-immigration Ads Ripped."
22. Warren and Liebrum, "Anti-immigration Ads Ripped." See Steve McVicker, "Dead, Dead, Dead," *Houston Press,* May 6, 1999 http://www.houstonpress.com/1999-05/news/dead-dead-dead/full.
23. Warren and Liebrum, "Anti-immigration Ads Ripped."
24. Susan Warren, "More Radio Stations Here Drop Controversial Immigration Ads," *Houston Chronicle,* January 20, 1990.
25. Bill Coulter, "Group Urges Repeal of Employer Sanctions," *Houston Chronicle,* March 30, 1990.
26. Coulter, "Group Urges Repeal."
27. Staff, "Around Houston," *Houston Chronicle,* February 27, 1990.
28. Staff, "Around Houston."
29. R. A. Dyer, "Workers Who 'Slaved' Sue; Suit Names Houston Job-Recruiting Firm," *Houston Chronicle,* May 26, 1992.
30. "News Briefs, Area; Slavery Lawsuit Filed," *Houston Chronicle,* May 28, 1992.
31. Associated Press, "Indentured Servants Awarded $300,000 against Company," *Prescott (AZ) Courier,* November 1, 1992.
32. Public Law 101-649, November 29, 1990, amendment to the Immigration and Nationality Act. With the amendment family-based visas were granted, and family-preference immigration visas were increased.

33. Warren R. Leiden and David L. Neal, "Highlights of the U.S. Immigration Act of 1990," *Fordham International Law Journal* 14, no. 1 (1990): 336.

34. Maria Jiménez, Testimony, *Allegations of Violence along the United States-Mexico Border: Hearing Before the Subcommittee on Human Rights and International Organizations of the Committee on Foreign Affairs,* U.S. Congress, House Committee on Foreign Affairs, 101st Cong., 2nd sess., April 18, 1990, 15.

35. Maria Jiménez, "Introduction," in American Friends Service Committee, *Human Rights at the Mexico-US Border*, 2nd Annual Report, Immigration Law Enforcement Monitoring Project (ILEMP) (Philadelphia: American Friends Service Committee, 1990), 4–6.

36. Jiménez, "Introduction," in AFSC, *Human Rights at the Mexico-US Border*, 5.

37. Wang, *Discrimination by Default*, 18.

38. Jiménez, "Introduction," in AFSC, *Human Rights at the Mexico-US Border*, 4.

39. Jiménez, interview by José Angel Gutiérrez, January 22, 1998.

40. AFSC, *Human Rights at the Mexico-US Border*, 34.

41. Jiménez, interview by Gutiérrez, January 22, 1998.

42. Jiménez, interview by Gutiérrez, January 22, 1998.

43. In 2014 the US Customs and Border Protection published another guide on the correct use of force. Damien Cave, "Complaints of Abuse by Border Agents Often Ignored, Records Show," *New York Times*, May 5, 2014, http://www.nytimes.com/2014/05/05/us/complaints-of-abuse-by-border-agents-often-ignored-records-show.html?_y=0. Julia Preston, "Book Guiding Border Agents on Force Released," *New York Times*, May 31, 2014, http://www.nytimes.com/book-guiding-border-agents-on-force-is-released.html.

44. Immigration Act of 1990, Section 503-PL 101–649.

45. Jiménez, "Introduction," in AFSC, *Human Rights at the Mexico-US Border*, 7.

46. Jiménez, "Introduction," in AFSC, *Human Rights at the Mexico-US Border*, 9.

47. Jiménez, "Introduction," in AFSC, *Human Rights at the Mexico-US Border*, 26.

48. Jiménez, "Introduction," in AFSC, *Human Rights at the Mexico-US Border*, 11. An organization in Mexico received three hundred complaints by undocumented individuals of abuse by US border

authorities between April 1997 and March 1998. Rubén Barrera Ventura, "Pide Amnistía Internacional Cesar Impunidad de Agentes Migratorios," *Notimex* (México City), May 20, 1998.

49. Jiménez, Testimony, *Allegations of Violence along the United States-Mexico Border*, 29–30.
50. Sam Howe Verhovek, "Border Patrol Is Criticized as Abusive," *New York Times*, May 20, 1998.
51. Roberto Rodríguez, "A New Search for Ways to Curb Border Death and Violence," *San Diego Union-Tribune*, July 1, 1990.
52. Rodríguez, "New Search."
53. Jordan Dey, "U.S. Agents Accused of Border Violence," *Houston Chronicle*, April 19, 1990, p. 6.6, 2005).
54. Dey, "U.S. Agents Accused of Border Violence."
55. Debbie Nathan, "Racist Shop Talk Common along U.S.-Mexico Border," *Pacific News Service*, April 10, 1991, https://digitalrepository. unm.edu/cgi/viewcontent.cgi?article=1579&context=sourcemex.
56. R. Rodríguez, "A New Search."
57. Jiménez, "Panel 3," 135.
58. Rodriguez, "New Search."
59. Dey, "U.S. Agents." See also "Rights Group Cites INS for Abuses Along Border; Agents Said to Have No Accountability," *Houston Chronicle*, February 25, 1992.
60. Dey, "U.S. Agents."
61. "The *Orantes* Injunction and Expedited Removal," *National Immigration Law Center*, July 2006, 2.
62. Dan Freedman, "Trouble at INS; INS Foul-ups Point to Borderline Management: In-fighting, Inefficiency Hobble Agency," *Houston Chronicle*, April 7, 1991.
63. Jesús A. Treviño, "Border Violence against Illegal Immigrants and the Need to Change the Border Patrol's Current Complaint Review Process," *Houston Journal of International Law* 21, no. 1 (Fall 1998): 95.
64. Jiménez, "War in the Borderlands," 32.
65. Jiménez, "War in the Borderlands," 30.
66. Dunn, *Blockading the*, 21.
67. Dennis Bixler-Márquez, "La Preparatoria Bowie versus la Patrulla Fronteriza," *Aztlan: Journal of Chicano Studies* 30, no. 2 (Fall 2005): 162.
68. *Murillo v. Musegades*, 809 F. Supp. 487 (W. Texas, 1992).
69. Dunn, *Blockading the Border*, 20.

70. Dunn, *Blockading the Border*, 22–23.
71. Dunn, *Blockading the Border*, 24.
72. Bixler-Márquez, *"La Preparatoria Bowie."*
73. Tina Plaza, "'Let's See Some Papers': In El Paso, Looking Latin Is a Crime," *Progressive* 57, no. 4 (April 1993): 18–23.
74. Dunn, *Blockading the Border*, 41–42. "Solely" is italicized in the original court decision.
75. Dunn, *Blockading the Border*, 47.
76. Dunn, *Militarization of the U.S.-Mexico Border*, 3.
77. AFSC, *Sealing Our Border*, 18–19.
78. "Rights Group Cites INS for Abuse along Border; Agents Said to Have No Accountability," *Houston Chronicle*, February 25, 1992.
79. See, for example, Amnesty International, *Human Rights Concerns in the Border Region with Mexico*, May 1, 1998, https://www.refworld.org/reference/countryrep/amnesty/1998/en/77967, accessed May 29, 2022. Also, *Federal Immigration Law Enforcement in the Southwest: Civil Rights Impacts on Border Communities,* Arizona, California, New Mexico, and Texas Advisory Committees to the U.S. Commission on Civil Rights, March 1997. The Human Rights Watch reports included: *Brutality Unchecked: Human Rights Abuses Along the US Border with Mexico,* June 1, 1992; *Frontier Injustice: Human Rights Abuse Along the US Border with Mexico Persist Amid Climate of Impunity,* May 1, 1993; *Crossing the Line: Human Rights Abuses Along the US Border Persists Amid Climate of Impunity,* April 1, 1995; *Slipping Through the Cracks: Unaccompanied Children Detained by the US Immigration and Naturalization Service,* April 1, 1997.
80. *"Tenemos que reconocer el peso que tiene Amnistia y es por ello que hay esperanza de que este reporte tenga repercusiones no (no) solo entre las agencias de Migración, pero también ante el Congreso."* Ventura, "Pide Amnistía Internacional Cesar Impunidad." My translation.
81. Treviño, "Border Violence against Illegal Immigrants," 100.
82. AFSC, *Sealing Our Borders*, 45–46.
83. Jiménez, "Border Militarization," 10. The act is U.S. Code Title 18, Part 1, Chapter 67, Section 1385. Use of the Army and Air Force as posse comitatus. It states: "Whoever, except in cases and under circumstances expressly authorized by the Constitution or Act of Congress, willfully uses any part of the Army or the Air Force as a posse comitatus or otherwise to execute the laws shall be fined under this title or imprisoned not more than two years, or both."

84. Bert Tussing, "New Requirements for a New Challenge: The Military's Role in Border Security," *Homeland Security Affairs: Journal of the Naval Post Graduate School Center for Homeland Defense and Security* 4, no. 3 (October 2008): 4. The act was progressively weakened over the years by, for example, the National Defense Authorization Act for Fiscal Year 2008, signed into law by President George W. Bush on January 28, 2008.

85. Jiménez, "Border Militarization."

86. Dunn, *Militarization of the U.S.-Mexico Border*, 4.

87. Quote in Arjun Makhijani, *Manifesto for Global Democracy: Two Essays on Imperialism and the Struggle for Freedom* (New York: Apex Press, 2004), 35, 32.

88. Maria Jiménez, *Humanitarian Crisis: Migrant Deaths at the U.S.-Mexico Border,* American Civil Liberties Union of San Diego & Imperial Counties and Mexico's National Commission of Human Rights (San Diego: ACLU, 2009), 15–16, http://www.aclu.org/immigrants/gen/41186pub20091001.html. See also Jiménez, "U.S.-Mexico Border," 34.

89. "Agua Prieta, Punto más Activo," *Novedades*, March 22, 1999.

90. Cerrutti and Massey, "Trends in Mexican Migration," in Durand and Massey, *Crossing the Border*, 23.

91. Border agents did not like "doing X's" because it was boring. Maril, *Patrolling Chaos*, 163–66.

92. Dunn, *Blockading the Border*, 66–67.

93. Pauline Arrillaga, "Immigrants Apprehensions Decrease during Operation Rio Grande," January 7, 1998, http://www.texnews.com/1998/texas/border0107.html.

94. Jo Ann Zuniga, "For Immigrants Given Amnesty, the Wait Is Over: Surge of New Citizens to Have Impact," *Houston Chronicle*, February 13, 1994.

95. Lori Rodríguez and Lad Salle, "City's Hispanic Poor Nearly Double in Decade," *Houston Chronicle*, May 29, 1992.

96. Lori Rodríguez, "Houston's Hispanic Destiny," *Houston Chronicle*, July 9, 1990.

97. Jim Simmon, "Houston's Hispanic Destiny," *Houston Chronicle*, July 10, 1990.

98. Stephanie Asin, "Census Deflates Hispanic Clout; Almost Half of Those of Voting Age Here Are Not Citizens," *Houston Chronicle*, July 7, 1993.

99. Nestor P. Rodríguez et al., "Political Mobilization in Houston's Magnolia," in *Barrio Ballots: Latino Politics in the 1990 Elections,*

ed. Rodólfo O. de la Garza, Martha Menchaca, and Louis DeSipio (Boulder, CO: Westview Press, 1994), 111.

100. Lori Rodríguez, "Houston's Hispanic Destiny," *Houston Chronicle*, July 8, 1990.

101. Jo Ann Zuniga, "Katy Police Harassed Hispanics, Groups Say," *Houston Chronicle*, May 26, 1994.

102. Jo Ann Zuniga, "LULAC Protests Police Tactics in Katy Roundup," *Houston Chronicle*, May 25, 1994.

103. Zuniga, "Katy Police."

104. Deborah Tedford and Jerry Urban, "Raid Detainees Sue INS, Katy: 12 Allege Illegal Questioning," *Houston Chronicle*, July 21, 1994.

105. Zuniga, "Katy Police."

106. Tedford and Urban, "Raid Detainees."

107. Zuniga, "LULAC Protests."

108. Jiménez, interview by Quintanilla, September 10, 2001.

109. Tedford and Urban, "Raid Detainees."

110. Terry Kliewer, "Settlement OK'd in Raid Suits; Hispanics Expect 'Civilized Treatment,'" *Houston Chronicle*, February 22, 1997.

111. Kliewer, "Settlement OK'd."

112. See interview, Doris Meissner, the Commissioner of the INS from 1993 to 2000, Gatekeeper Foundation, *The 800 Mile Wall* (Los Angeles: 2009). www.GatekeeperFound.org.

Notes for Chapter 8

1. Maria Jiménez, interview by José Angel Gutiérrez, January 22, 1998.

2. Delgado and Stefancic, *Critical Race Theory*, 48.

3. Jo Ann Zuniga and staff, "Minorities Plan Rally, March for Tolerance; Growing Anti-Immigrant Mood Cited," *Houston Chronicle*, September 30, 1993.

4. Kenneth B. Noble, "The 1994 Elections," *New York Times*, November 9, 1994.

5. Kevin R. Johnson, *Opening the Floodgates: Why America Needs to Rethink Its Border and Immigration Laws* (New York: New York University Press, 2007), 150.

6. "Deportations at High, but Sanctions Down," *Houston Chronicle*, November 19, 1996.

7. Jo Ann Zuniga, "Protesters Call for 'Justice' and Right to 'Dignity'; Marchers Contend Proposed Policies for Illegal Immigrants are Biased," *Houston Chronicle*, October 17, 1994.

8. Zuniga, "Protesters Call for 'Justice.'"

9. Sam Howe Verhovek, "Immigrants' Anxieties Spur a Surge in Natural-izations," *New York Times*, September 13, 1996, https://www.nytimes.com/1996/09/13/us/immigrants-anxieties-spur-a-surge-in-naturalizations.html.

10. Elena R. Gutiérrez, *Fertile Matters: The Politics of Mexican-Origin Women's Reproduction* (Austin: University of Texas Press, 2008): xi, 117, 119.

11. Paul Feldman and Rich Connell, "Wilson Acts to Enforce Parts of Prop 187," *Los Angeles Times*, November 10, 1994, https://www.latimes.com/archives/la-xpm-1994-11-10-mn-61147-story.html.

12. "Prenatal Care: Davis Preserves Program for Immigrants," *California Healthline Daily Edition: Summary of Health Policy Coverage from Major News Organization*, July 27, 1999.

13. Mike Tolson, "Election '94: Groups Decry California Move to Bar Aid to Illegal Immigrants," *Houston Chronicle*, November 10, 1994.

14. Joe Garofoli, "Wilson's Return May Hurt GOP Latino Outreach," *SFGate*, March 20, 2010, https://www.sfgate.com/politics/joegarofoli/article/Wilson-s-return-may-hurt-GOP-Latino-outreach-3195789.php.

15. Johnson, *Opening the Floodgates,* 171.

16. Kathy Walt, "Morales' Immigration Suit Draws Criticism from Groups," *Houston Chronicle*, September 17, 1994.

17. Claudia Kolker, "No.1 in Uninsured," *Houston Chronicle*, July 10, 1998. Judy Wiessler, "Many Newly Legal Aliens Refuse State Aid, Report Says," *Houston Chronicle*, July 11, 1989.

18. Kolker, "No. 1 in Uninsured."

19. Thaddeus Herrick, "Immigrant Study Finds Poverty Shadows Many Recipients," *Houston Chronicle*, July 9, 1996.

20. Herrick, "Immigrant Study."

21. Mike Tolson, "Against the Current," *Houston Chronicle*, January 29, 1995.

22. The circumstances in Texas were different from those in California "which absorbed the greatest number of illegal immigrants, an esti-mated 43 percent." Tolson, "Against the Current."

23. Tolson, "Against the Current."

24. Kolker, "No. 1 in Uninsured."

25. Edward Hegstrom, "Immigrants Lacking Health Coverage," *Houston Chronicle*, July 19, 2000.

26. Sam Howe Verhovek, "In a Shift, U.S. Grants Asylum for Mexicans," *New York Times*, December 1, 1995.

27. Verhovek, "In a Shift." Until 1994, the granting of political asylum to Mexican nationals was rare.
28. Thaddeus Herrick, "U.S. Grants Asylum to Mexican Woman; Tacit Recognition of Rights Abuse," *Houston Chronicle*, November 29, 1995.
29. Verhovek, "In a Shift."
30. Jiménez, "Panel 3," 138.
31. Jiménez, "Panel 3," 135.
32. Jiménez, "Panel 3," 138.
33. Jiménez, "Panel 3," 136.
34. Jiménez, "Panel 3," 137.
35. Anna Gonzalez-Barrera, "Before COVID-19, More Mexicans Came to the U.S. than Left for Mexico for the First Time in Years," *Pew Research Center*, July 9, 2021, 3. Gary Martin, "Employment and Unemployment in Mexico in the 1990s," *Monthly Labor Review*, November 2000, 1, https://www.bls.gov/opub/mlr/2000/11/art1full.pdf.
36. Jo Ann Zuniga, "Houston's Hispanic Chamber Backs Loan Package for Mexico," *Houston Chronicle,* January 27, 1995.
37. Zuniga, "Houston's Hispanic Chamber"; and Chris Woodyard and Andrew Downie, "Mexico Moves to Pay Off U.S. Loans 3 Years Early," *Houston Chronicle*, January 16, 1997.
38. Also South Texas Human Rights Center, founded in 2013.
39. Mark Collette, "Civil Rights Group: Texas Authorities Fail to Do Part Identifying Remains of Undocumented," *Corpus Christi Caller-Times,* February 3, 2013.
40. Edward Hegstrom, "Search for Missing Immigrants Is Long and Lonely for Relatives," *Houston Chronicle*, May 3, 2004.
41. Stanley Bailey et al., "The Human Costs of Border Enforcement: Migrant Deaths at the Texas-Mexico Border," *Migration World Magazine* 24, no. 4 (1996): 16–21.
42. American Friends Service Committee, "New Study Documents Hundreds of Immigrant Deaths at Texas-Mexico Border," news release, March 14, 1996, http://www.hartford-hwp.com/archives/45/123.html.
43. Jiménez, *Humanitarian Crisis*. Photos were provided by John Carlos Frey, the writer and director of the excellent documentary *The 800 Mile Wall* (Los Angeles: Gatekeeper Productions, 2009).
44. Jiménez, *Humanitarian Crisis*, 15. This is the estimate of the US Department of Homeland Security Border Safety Initiative.
45. Jiménez, *Humanitarian Crisis*, 55.

46. *"1996 ha sido un año violento . . . Las altas temperaturas provocadas por la sequía vinieron a agravar el difícil camino de cientos de hombres y mujeres que vienen a este país a trabajar, y que muchas veces lo que encuentran es la muerte."* Rubén Barrera Ventura, "Temen más Muertes de Indocumentados en Frontera Texas-México en 1997," *Diario de Juárez* (Juárez, Mexico), December 23, 1996. My translation.

47. Ventura, "Temen más Muertes"; and, Debbie Nathan, "Racist Shop Talk Common Along U.S.-Mexico Border," *Pacific News Service,* April 10, 1991.

48. Karl Eschbach, Jacqueline Hagan, and Nestor Rodríguez, "Death at the Border," *International Migration Review* 33, no. 2 (Summer 1999): 431.

49. Eschbach, Hagan, and Rodríguez, "Death at the Border," 430–31.

50. *"en el centro del debate nacional al presentar otra cara humana de la inmigración que parece querer negarse."* Ventura, *"Temen más Muertes."*

51. Bob Ortega, "Border Patrol Failed to Count Hundreds of Migrant Deaths on US Soil," CNN, May 15, 2018.

52. Carlos Byars, "Hundreds Die Annually Trying to Cross Rio Grande, Study Finds," *Houston Chronicle*, March 15, 1996. Also, AFSC, "New Study Documents Hundreds of Immigrant Deaths."

53. The INS agreed to collect statistics on those who perished and send this information to Mexico. Mexico expanded its rescue efforts, already provided by Grupos de Protección de Migrantes (Migrant Protection Group) commonly called Beta.

54. Jim Cason and David Brooks, "Acuerdan México y EU Campana de Protección a Los Migrantes," *La Jornada* (México City), June 17, 1998, my translation.

55. Susan Carroll, "Dilemma of the Dead: Illegal Immigrants' Deaths Put Burden on Texas Counties," *Houston Chronicle*, September 27, 2007. Baylor University and Mexico are working together to identify the deceased using DNA samples. "For the Living and the Dead," baylor. edu, August 27, 2019, https://research.baylor.edu/news/story/2019/living-and-dead.

56. Karla Zabludovosky, "Hunting Humans: The Americans Taking Immigration into Their Own Hands," *Newsweek*, July 23, 2014, https://www.newsweek.com/2014/08/01/hunting-humans-americans-go-war-migrants-260642.html. John Cormack, "South Texas Deaths Belie Migrant Statistics," *Houston Chronicle*, January 2, 2013, https://www.

houstonchronicle.com/news/houston-texas/texas/article/south-tex-as-deaths-belie-migrant-statistics-4160175.php.

57. John Carlos Frey, "Graves of Shame," *Texas Observer*, July 6, 2015, https://www.texasobserver.org/illegal-mass-graves-of-migrant-remains-found-in-south-texas/.

58. Ronnie Crocker, "Attorney Says Marine Fired at Border Teen as 'Last Resort," *Houston Chronicle*, July 24, 1997.

59. "The Ballad of Esequiel Hernandez," *POV*, season 21, episode 1, directed by Kieran Fitzgerald, aired July 8, 2008, www.pbs.org/pov/ballad. Hernández's mother "never came out of shock. She died without coming out of shock." Manny Fernández, "U.S. Troops Went to the Border in 1997. They Killed an American boy," *New York Times*, November 27, 2018.

60. Dunn, *Blockading the Border*, 166.

61. "A series of failures" by the Justice and Defense departments led to Hernandez's death. Roberto Suro, "Report: U.S. 'Failures' Led to Border Death," *Washington Post*, November 13, 1998.

62. Thaddeus Herrick, "Family to Receive $1.9 million in Border Shooting," *Houston Chronicle*, August 12, 1998.

63. Dunn, *Blocking the Border and Human Rights*, 166.

64. Gómez-Cano and Ross-Nazzal, *Spirit of Magnolia Park*, 130.

65. Jo Ann Zuniga, "A Weary Soldier: Activist Grows Frustrated in Her Battle for Hispanic Rights," *Houston Chronicle*, February 7, 1999.

66. Jiménez, interview by José Angel Gutiérrez, January 22, 1998.

67. Judy Wiessler, "House Panel Plans Probe of S. Texas Border Killing," *Houston Chronicle*, July 17, 1997.

68. Wiessler, "House Panel Plans Probe."

69. Herrick, "Family to Receive," and "Recordaran a Joven Asesinado Hace Seis Meses en EU por un Militar," *Notimex*, October 17, 1997.

70. Jiménez, interview by Natalie Garza, June 14, 2010, Oral History of Houston History Project, Mexican-American History—Migrant Rights, University of Houston, Houston, TX.

71. Jim Cason and David Brooks, "Retira el Pentágono Tropas de la Frontera Sur por Falta de Protección Legal," *La Jornada*, July 30, 1997.

72. Dunn, *Blockading the Border*, 180.

73. Thaddeus Herrick, "Another Border Shooting Disputed; Paralyzed Illegal Immigrant, 18, Is Seeking $25 Million from U.S.," *Houston Chronicle*, March 8, 1999.

74. "Former Agent Admits Shooting Immigrant," *Houston Chronicle*, November 3, 2000.

75. Edward Hegstrom and James Pinkerton, "Newcomers Blamed for Upsetting Rio Grande Peace," *Houston Chronicle*, May 22, 2000.

76. Ross E. Milloy, "Incidents Renew Ranch's Border Patron Ban," *New York Times*, April 2, 2000.

77. These and other laws can be found at the website of the U.S. Citizenship and Immigration Services: http://www.uscis.gov/portal/site/uscis.

78. Jo Ann Zuniga, "Hispanic, Immigrant Groups to March," *Houston Chronicle*, February 21,1997.

79. Public Law 104–193.

80. Verhovek, "Immigrants' Anxieties Spur a Surge in Naturalizations."

81. Zuniga, "Hispanic, Immigrant Groups to March."

82. Jennifer C. Wang, "New Welfare Rules to Take Toll on Texas Immigrants," *Houston Chronicle*, August 6, 1996.

83. Laws ameliorating the Welfare Act included, for example, P.L.105-18 and P.L.107-171 for food stamps, and P.L.105-33 for SSI.

84. Steve Brewer, "Care Continues for Illegal Aliens," *Houston Chronicle*, July 31, 2001.

85. Jim Cason and David Brooks, "Entro en Vigor le Ley Antiinmigrante," *La Jornada*, April 2, 1997.

86. Scott Phillips, Nestor Rodríguez, and Jacqueline Hagan, "Brutality at the Border? Use of Force in the Arrest of Immigrants in the United States," *International Journal of the Sociology of Law* 30 (2003): 287.

87. R. A. Dyer, "Immigrants Feel Heat and Helping Hand as Well," *Houston Chronicle*, June 29, 1997.

88. Mirta Ojito, "Change in Laws Sets off Big Wave of Deportations; Nearly 300,000 Are Expelled in 2 Years, a Record," *New York Times*, December 15, 1998.

89. Dyer, "Immigrants Feel Heat."

90. Zuniga, "Immigration Laws."

91. Phillips, Rodríguez, and Hagan, "Brutality at the Border."

92. Ngai, *Impossible Subjects*, 275n1. *INS*. v. *St. Cyr,* 121 S. Ct. 2271 (2001)

93. Arturo Solís, "Cientos de Residentes en EU Realizan Tramites de Ultima Hora para Evitar la Deportación," *Crónica*, April 1, 1997.

94. Treviño, "Border Violence against Illegal Immigrants," 100.

95. E. Meza, "Controversia por Disparos de Boinas Verdes a Mexicano," *Diario de Juárez*, January 29, 1997.

96. American Friends Service Committee, "News Release," June 10, 1997. http://www.afsc.org/news/1997/nrredfrd.htm, accessed May 26, 2013.

97. Richard Estrada, "Who's Minding the Border?" *Dallas Morning News*, April 15, 1997.

98. Jo Ann Zuniga, "Hispanic Groups Prepare to March on Washington," *Houston Chronicle*, September 28, 1996.

99. "Illegal Aliens Beat by Riverside County California Police Caught on Tape," *YouTube*, December 2, 2011, https://www.youtube.com/watch?v=R29pH0C9uRE.

100. Joseph Torres, "Latinos Speak Out," *Hispanic*, December 1996.

101. Steven A. Holmes, "Hispanic March Draws Crowd to Capitol," *New York Times*, October 13, 1996, https://www.nytimes.com/1996/10/13/us/hispanic-march-draws-crowd-to-capital.html.

102. Torres, "Latinos Speak Out."

103. Zuniga, "March Should Lead to Hispanic Activism."

104. James Cason and David Brooks, "Demandan Respeto a Derechos Humanos; Llegaron el próximo Sábado," *La Jornada*, October 10, 1996. My translation.

105. Carey Goldberg, "Hispanic Groups Prepare to March to Washington," *New York Times*, October 9, 1996, https://www.nytimes.com/1996/10/09/us/hispanic-groups-prepare-to-march-to-washington.html.

106. Armando Villafranca, "Houston Hispanics March; Diversity of Groups Demonstrates a Strong Sense of Unity," *Houston Chronicle*, October 13, 1996.

107. Jo Ann Zuniga, "Immigrants' Rights Marches Planned," *Houston Chronicle*, May 25, 1995.

108. Gómez-Cano and Ross-Nazzal, *Spirit of Magnolia Park*, 130.

109. Cason and Brooks, "Demandan Respeto."

110. Jiménez, interview by Natalie Garza, June 14, 2010.

111. "Recibirá Activista de EU Declaración de Nacionalidad Mexicana," *Notimex,* June 1, 1998.

112. Jiménez, email communication to author, May 19, 2009.

113. Zuniga, "'We Can Be Loyal to Both Countries," *Houston Chronicle*, June 3, 1998.

114. Dudley Althaus, "Dual Nationality Now Reality, Houstonians Among 100 Celebrating Mexican Law," *Houston Chronicle*, June 5, 1998.

115. "Recibirá Activista de EU Declaración de Nacionalidad Mexicana," *Notimex,* June 1, 1998.

116. Durand, "Migration Policy and the Asymmetry of Power," in Green and Weil, *Citizenship and Those Who Leave*, 235. Durand is a professor in the Department for the Study of Social Movements, University of Guadalajara, Mexico.

117. Lennox Samuels, "Mexican, American – or Both?," *Dallas Morning News*, October 11, 2006.
118. Alma M. Garcia, "Still Coming North from Mexico: Immigration Constraints and Contestations," in *North from Mexico: The Spanish-Speaking People of the United States*, by Carey McWilliams, 3rd ed., updated by Alma M. Garcia (Santa Barbara, CA: Praeger, 2015), 346.
119. Garcia, "Still Coming North," in McWilliams, *North from Mexico*, 346–47.
120. Althaus, "Dual Nationality Now Reality."
121. Althaus, "Dual Nationality Now Reality."
122. John Arquilla and David Ronfeldt, "The Advent of Netwar (Revisited)," in *Networks and Netwars: The Future of Terror, Crime, and Militancy*, ed. John Arquilla and David Ronfeldt (Santa Monica, CA: Rand, 2001), 6.
123. Ronfeldt and Arquilla, "Emergence and Influence of the Zapatista Social Netwar," in Arquilla and Ronfeldt, *Networks and Netwars*, 175.
124. Roberto Rodríguez and Patrisia González, "We're Witnessing Global Shift in Political Culture," *Houston Chronicle*, August 23, 1996.
125. Jiménez, interview by Quintanilla, October 15, 2004.
126. Dudley Althaus, "Mayan Rebels' Tour Brings Out Crowds in Mexico," *Houston Chronicle*, March 11, 2001.
127. Jiménez, interview by Quintanilla, October 25, 2004.
128. Rodríguez and González, "We're Witnessing Global Shift."
129. Jiménez, interview by Quintanilla, October 25, 2004.
130. Jiménez, interview by Quintanilla, July 19, 2001.
131. Bill Weinberg, "Zapatistas and Globalization of Resistance," *Yes Magazine*, May 20, 2004.
132. Jenalia Moreno, "Trade Tariffs Ends in NAFTA Milestone," *Houston Chronicle*, January 2, 2008. Laura Carlsen, *Americas Policy Program: NAFTA Inequality and Immigration*, CIP Americans Policy Program (Washington, DC: Center for International Policy, 2007).
133. Robert Martínez, interviewed by Nic Paget-Clarke, "Border Operations/Migrant Life/Organizing for Human Rights," *In Motion Magazine*, July 7, 2001, http://inmotionmagazine.com/hrcr/rm2001a.html.
134. "Chiapas Relief Convoy Seeking Donations," *Houston Chronicle*, November 2, 1995.
135. Philip Kretsedemas, "What Does an Undocumented Immigrant Look Like? Local Enforcement and the New Immigrant Profiling" in *Keeping Out the Other: A Critical Introduction to Immigration Enforcement Today*,

ed. David C. Brotherton and Philip Kretsedemas (New York: Columbia University Press, 2008), 342–43.

136. Rodríguez and Gonzáles, "We're Witnessing Global Shift."

137. Farhan Haq, "Mexico-U.S.: Rape of EZLN Official Part of a Pattern, Group Says," *Inter Press Service*, New Agency, November 6, 1995, https://www.ipsnews.net/1995/11/mexico-us-rape-of-ezln-official-part-of-a-pattern-group-says/#google_vignette.

138. Melissa Fletcher Stoeltje, "Activist Appeals to End War Rape," *Houston Chronicle*, March 8, 1996. The resolution was 1993/46 of 3 March.

139. Frank Michel, "Houston Victory Over Bigotry Point of Pride," *Houston Chronicle*, July 28, 1997. The report is titled *The New American: Diversity Works*.

140. Stephen L. Klineberg, *Houston Ethnic Communities*, 3rd ed. (Houston: Rice University, 1996), 1.

141. Armando Villafranca, "Immigrants' Role Being Seen in New Light," *Houston Chronicle*, April 20, 1998. Parenthesis original.

142. Villafranca, "Immigrants' Role."

143. Jo Ann Zuniga, "Hispanics Leading the Way as County Population Rises," *Houston Chronicle*, December 19, 1997.

144. Steve Lash, "Ad Drive for Census Aims at Hispanics; Effort Seeks a Full Count in 2000," *Houston Chronicle*, September 16, 1996.

Notes for Chapter 9

1. Nick Cooper, "Interview with Longtime Houston Activist Maria Jiménez," *Free Press Houston*, February 11, 2014, 3.

2. Cooper, "Interview," 4.

3. Simon During, "Introduction," in *The Cultural Studies Reader*, ed. Simon During (London: Routledge, 1993): 5.

4. Wang, *Discrimination by Default*, 88.

5. Jo Ann Zuniga, "DA Dismisses Charges in '82 Police Slaying; Case Against Aldape Guerra Too Weak Now, Holmes Says," *Houston Chronicle*, April 16, 1997.

6. Jerry Urban, "Group Mourns, Remembers Aldape Guerra; Former Death Row Inmate Called a Symbol of Justice at Memorial at Hidalgo Park," *Houston Chronicle*, August 25, 1997.

7. Lisa M. Chmiola, "People React to Ironic Death on Heels of Freedom," *Houston Chronicle*, August 23, 1997.

8. Zuniga, "DA Dismisses Charges in '82 Police Slaying."

9. Stephen Johnson and Steve Brewer, "Man Released from Death Row Dies in Accident; Aldape Guerra is Killed in Car Wreck in Mexico," *Houston Chronicle*, August 22, 1997.

10. Edward Hegstrom, "Mexican Consul Files Complaint about Shootings," *Houston Chronicle*, July 27, 2000.

11. S. K. Bardwell, "Police Shot Man 12 Times in Raid," *Houston Chronicle*, July 21, 1998.

12. Peggy O'Hare, "Embattled Bradford Plans Early Retirement," *Houston Chronicle*, July 18, 2003.

13. Lisa Teachey, "Six Officers in Oregón Case Fired," *Houston Chronicle*, November 3, 1998.

14. Robert Crowe, "HPD Told Officer Must Be Reinstated," *Houston Chronicle,* December 11, 2004.

15. Allan Turner, "'Railroad Killer' Offers Apology at Execution" *Houston Chronicle*, June 28, 2006, https://www.chron.com/news/houston-texas/article/railroad-killer-offers-apology-at-execution-1891401.php. He said, "*Les pido que me perdonen. No están obligado a hacerlo . . . Dios mío, perdóname.*" (I ask you to forgive me. You are not obligated to do it. . . . My God, forgive me.") My translation. "*El mexicano 'asesino' de ferrocarril' es ejecutado en Texas,*" *Ahora Si!*

16. Reuters News Service, "Buchanan Links Immigration, Crime," *Houston Chronicle*, July 8, 1999.

17. Edward Hegstrom, Maria Luisa Peres, and Jo Ann Zuniga, "Suspect Surrenders," *Houston Chronicle*, July 14, 1999.

18. Jo Ann Zuniga and Lisa Teachey, "Some Hispanics Upset over Tactics in Rail Killer Hunt," *Houston Chronicle*, June 30, 1999.

19. Jim Yardley, "Some Texans Tiring of Stops by Border Patrol," *New York Times*, January 26, 2000; and Zuniga and Teachey, "Some Hispanics Upset."

20. Lori Rodríguez, "Hate Crimes on the Rise, Says La Raza," *Houston Chronicle*, July 27, 1999.

21. Patricia González and Roberto Rodríguez, "Police Involved in Immigration Duties Means Trouble," *Houston Chronicle*, August 7, 1998.

22. Rodríguez, "Hate Crimes on the Rise."

23. Rachel Graves, "Labor-Intensive Care: Day Workers Urged to Congregate at City-Funded Sites," *Houston Chronicle*, April 16, 2001; and Ana Babin, Franklin Olson, and Richard C. Shaw, "Another Chance to Support City's Day Laborers," *Labor in the News*, June 4, 2002. http://www.hcaflcio.org/vol8.htm.

24. Janette Rodrígues, "Mayor Unveils Office for Immigrant-Refugee Affairs," *Houston Chronicle*, May 20, 2001.

25. Tal Kopan, "What Are Sanctuary Cities and Can They be Defunded?" CNN, March 26, 2018, https://www.cnn.com/2017/01/25/politics/sanctuary-cities-explained/index.html.

26. Benito Juárez, conversation with Linda J. Quintanilla, August 21, 2015.

27. Tom Karson, "Confronting Houston's Demographic Shift: The Harris County AFL-CIO," *WorkingUSA: Journal of Labor and Society* 8 (December 2004): 212.

28. Steven Greenhouse, "Suit Claims Discrimination Against Hispanics on Job," *New York Times*, February 9, 2003, http://www.nytimes.com/2003/02/09/us/suit-claims-discrimination-against-hispanics-on-job.html.

29. L. M. Silex, "EEOC sues to get Quietflex papers," *Houston Chronicle*, April 1, 2000.

30. Mexican American Legal Defense and Education Fund, "MALDEF, Quietflex Manufacturing Company, L.P., Announce Final Approval of Settlement with Latino Employees on Discrimination Claims," maldef.org, January 23, 2007, https://www.maldef.org/2007/01/maldef-quietflex-manufacturing-company-l-p-announce-final-approval-of-settlement-with-latino-employees-on-discrimination-claims/.

31. Edward Hegstrom, "Immigrants Embracing Activism," *Houston Chronicle*, July 25, 2001.

32. *Reno v. Catholic Social Services* and *LULAC v. INS*. The LULAC case latter became *Newman v. INS* (1987). Both cases were combined in the US Supreme Court case *Catholic Social Services, Inc. v. Thornberg* 956 F. 2d 914 (1992).

33. Tracy Wilkinson, "INS Ordered to Accept Late Amnesty Filings," *LA Times*, February 14, 1992, https://www.latimes.com/archives/la-xpm-1992-02-14-mn-2155-story.html.

34. Lisa M. Chmiola, "Living in Fear of Deportation," *Houston Chronicle*, December 13, 1998.

35. "'A Hostage in This Country,' Late Amnesty Applicants Face Arrest, Deportation," *AFSC Quaker Service Bulletin* (Spring 2000).

36. Claudia Kolker, "Longtime Residents Lose Work Permits in Suit's Dismissal," *Houston Chronicle*, April 4, 1998.

37. Edward Hegstrom, "Better Late than Never," *Houston Chronicle*, February 15, 2002.

38. "Miles de Ilegales Deberán Salir de EU al Cerrarse el Plaza para la Regularización," *El Excelsior*, January 16, 1998. My translation.

39. League of United Latin American Citizens, "LULAC: American Friends Service Committee (AFSC) & Association for Residency and Citizenship of America (ARCA)," news release, December 1, 1998, http://lulac.org/news/pr/immigration_afsc_arca/index.html.

40. Pancho Arguelles, interview by Quintanilla, September 16, 2009.

41. Anna Nuñez, interview by Linda J. Quintanilla, August 7, 2009.

42. Denise Gómez, "A Life of Activism: Maria Jiménez," *Houston History* 12, no. 3 (Summer 2015): 17.

43. Gómez, "Life of Activism," 18.

44. Arguelles, interview by Quintanilla, September 16, 2009.

45. Jiménez, interview by Quintanilla, September 10, 2004.

46. Gómez, "Life of Activism," 18.

47. Hegstrom, "Better Later than Never."

48. Jiménez, interview by Quintanilla, September 10, 2004.

49. Chmiola, "Living in Fear of Deportation."

50. LIFE Act Amendment of 2000 (Pub. L.106-553 and -554).

51. Hegstrom, "Better Late than Never."

52. Jiménez, interviewed by Natalie Garza, June 14, 2010, Oral History of Houston History Project.

53. Cynthia Leonor Garza, "Houston Leaders Push for Immigration Reform," *Houston Chronicle*, June 6, 2006.

54. Edward Hegstrom, "Family Looking for Justice after Deadly INS Raid," *Houston Chronicle*, July 28, 2002.

55. Hegstrom, "Family Looking for Justice."

56. Martha has the same last name as her brother-in-law because she married Serafin's brother.

57. Hegstrom, "Family Looking for Justice."

58. Harvey Rice, "Agent Remorseful over Death," *Houston Chronicle*, January 30, 2004.

59. Rod Nissimov, "Ex-immigration Agents Get Prison Time," *Houston Chronicle*, February 3, 2004.

60. Rice, "Agent Remorseful."

61. Jiménez, interview by Quintanilla, September 10, 2004.

62. Anna Nuñez, "AFSC Closes Houston Office Amidst Protest," *KPFT News*, April 18, 2003.

63. Nuñez, "AFSC Closes."

64. Anna Nuñez, interview by Quintanilla, August 7, 2009. Nuñez was the host and producer of the radio program "Latino Voices" for KPFT, Pacifica radio.

65. Edward Hegstrom and Lucas Wall, "Activists Protests Firing of Local Immigrant Rights Leader," *Houston Chronicle*, February 19, 2003.

66. Jiménez, interview by Quintanilla, September 10, 2004. A definition of the employment-at-will doctrine is: "At-will employment refers to an employment agreement stating that employment is for an indefinite period of time and may be terminated either by employer or employee. If an employment is at-will, such an agreement would typically be expressly included in the relevant employment contract," https://www.law.cornell.edu/wex/employment-at-will_doctrine.

67. Gutiérrez, Meléndez, and Noyola, *Chicanas in Charge*, 131.

68. Ralph Blumenthal, "Truck Driver Found Guilty in Deaths of 19 Immigrants in Texas in 2003," *New York Times*, November 5, 2006.

69. Mary Flood, "Sentence Ends Case in 2003 South Texas Migrant Deaths," *Houston Chronicle*, June 8, 2010.

70. "Trucker Resentenced for '03 Smuggling Deaths," ABC, January 24, 2011, http://abc13.com/archive/7915107.

71. Maria Jiménez, Testimony, "*Deadly Consequences of Illegal Alien Smuggling.*" *Hearing of the Subcommittee on Immigration, Border Security and Claims of the Committee on the Judiciary, House of Representatives.* 108th Cong. 1st sess. June 24, 2003, 31.

72. Edward Hegstrom, "Deadly Crossing: Proposed Bill Touts Bounties; House Measure Targets Smugglers," *Houston Chronicle*, July 25, 2003.

73. Kris Axtman, "Changing Landscape of an Underground Trade," *Christian Science Monitor,* July 17, 2003, https://www.csmonitor.com/2003/0717/p03s01-usgn.html; and Edward Hegstrom, "Deadly Crossing: Talk Is Tough; Sentences Aren't; Lawmakers Seek Harsher Penalties for Transporting Human Cargo," *Houston Chronicle*, July 28, 2003.

74. *Pushing the Border Out on Alien Smuggling: New Tools and Intelligence Initiatives. Congressional Hearing before the Subcommittee on Immigration, Border Security, and Claims of the Committee on the Judiciary, House of Representatives,* U.S. Congress, House Committee of the Judiciary. 108th Cong., 2nd sess., May 18, 2004, 13.

75. Karson, "Confronting Houston's Demographic Shift," 215.

76. Axtman, "Why Unions Embrace Illegal Immigrants."

77. Brian Burgoon and Janice Fine, "Immigration and the Transformation of American Unionism," *International Migration Review* 44, no. 4 (Winter 2010): 935.

78. Jiménez, interview by Quintanilla, July 19, 2001.

79. Edward Hegstrom, "Fighting Back: Immigrants Taught to Sue for Unpaid Wages," *Houston Chronicle*, November 30, 2000.

80. Axtman, "Why Unions Embrace Illegal Immigrants."

81. Jenalia Moreno, "Union Forging a Voice for Immigrant Workers," *Houston Chronicle*, September 1, 2003.

82. Axtman, "Why Unions Embrace Illegal Immigrants."

83. James Pinkerton, "Day Workers Plagued by Wage Theft: Advocates Try to Recoup Pay for Victims Here as Exploitation Grows in U.S.," *Houston Chronicle*, July 30, 2007.

84. Jo Ann Zuniga, "Committee of Peers Fights for Fair Pay, Job Safety for Immigrants," *Houston Chronicle*, August 10, 2001, http://www.chron. com/news/houston-texas/article/Committee-fights-for-fair-pay-safety-for-2015113.php. Unpaid back wages in 2006 reached $2.9 million in the Houston area. The DOL recovered $475,000. Sandy Smith, "Labor Department Launches Hispanic Workers Protection Program," *EHS (Environmental Health Safety)*, http://ehstoday.com/print/news/ehs_ imp_36420, accessed January 18, 2013.

85. Steven Greenhouse, "Riding across America for Immigrant Workers," *New York Times*, September 17, 2003, https://www.nytimes.com/2003/09/17/ us/riding-across-america-for-immigrant-workers.html.

86. David Stokes, "Immigrants' Freedom Rider Seeks Workplace Equity," *Atlanta Inquirer*, October 4, 2003.

87. Greenhouse, "Riding Across America."

88. Jiménez, interview by Quintanilla, September 10, 2004.

89. " . . . *porque si no hacemos nada, nada va a pasar.*" Rubén Funes, "Marcha por La Libertad; Arriba a Orlando la Caravana de Inmigrantes," *La Prensa* (México City), September 25, 2003. My translation.

90. Jiménez, interview by Quintanilla, September 10, 2004.

91. Steven Greenhouse, "Immigrant Workers Share a Bus and Hope," *New York Times*, September 28, 2003.

92. Stokes, "Immigrants' Freedom Ride Seeks Workplace Equity."

93. Jiménez, interview by Quintanilla, September 10, 2004.

94. Jiménez, interview by Quintanilla, September 10, 2004.

95. Jiménez, interview by Quintanilla, September 10, 2004.

96. David Neiwert, "Arizona Judge Rules that Simcox Can Cross-Examine Young Alleged Victims," *Southern Poverty Law Center*, April 3, 2015, https://www.splcenter.org/hatewatch/2015/04/03/arizona-judge-rules-simcox-can-cross-examine-young-alleged-victims. Megan Cassidy, "Ex-Minuteman Chris Simcox Sentenced to 19.5 Years in Child Sex-Abuse Case," *AZ Central*, July 11, 2016, https://www.azcentral.com/ story/news/local/phoenix/2016/07/11/chris-simcox-sentenced-child-sex-abuse/86948200/.

97. Edward Hegstrom, "Head of Texas Minutemen Quits, Cites Racism," *Houston Chronicle*, July 28, 2005, https://www.chron.com/news/houston-texas/article/Head-of-Texas-Minutemen-quits-cites-racism-1929889.php.

98. Edward Hegstrom, "Minutemen Headed Here Warned They, Too, Will be Watched," *Houston Chronicle*, July 9, 2005.

99. Edward Hegstrom, "Minutemen Head Clarifies Plans for Houston," *Houston Chronicle*, July 17, 2005, https://www.chron.com/news/houston-texas/article/minutemen-head-clarifies-plans-for-houston-1941619.php.

100. Hegstrom, "Minutemen Headed Here."

101. "Jackson Lee Urges Perry to 'Disinvite' Minutemen," *Houston Chronicle*, May 16, 2005.

102. Melanie Markley, "Officials Prepare for Visit by Minutemen," *Houston Chronicle*, July 10, 2005.

103. Pam Easton, "Minuteman Civil Defense Corps. Holding Training in Houston," Associated Press, August 14, 2005.

104. Edward Hegstrom, "Activists Hope to Educate, Unify Day Laborers," *Houston Chronicle*, August 13, 2005, https://www.chron.com/news/houston-texas/article/Activists-hope-to-educate-unify-day-laborers-1937544.php.

105. Hegstrom, "Activists Hope to Educate."

106. Hegstrom, "Minutemen Headed Here."

107. American Civil Liberties Union of Arizona and American Friends Service Committee, "Legal Observing Vigilantes: A Guide for Observers from the Minutemen Project – October 2005."

108. Associated Press, "Activists Say Minutemen Causing Fear," August 22, 2005, https://www.chron.com/news/houston-texas/article/activists-say-minutemen-causing-fear-aclu-offers-1944685.php.

109. Maria Jiménez, email, October 5, 2005.

110. Jenalia Moreno, "Immigrants Helping Rebuild New Orleans Say They're Making Less," *Houston Chronicle*, October 29, 2006.

111. Stephen R. Kelly, "When Mexicans Crossed Our Border to Feed Americans in Need, *Washington Post*, August 28, 2015, https://www.washingtonpost.com/opinions/when-mexicans-crossed-our-border-to-feed-our-hungry/2015/08/28/347342e4-4cee-11e5-84df-923b3ef1a64b_story.html.

112. Menchaca, *Naturalizing Mexican Immigrants*, 303.

113. University of Houston (UH), "Latino Activist Demonstrates Commitment to the Field and to UH: Maria Jiménez Brings 30 Years of Community Activism to the Classroom," news release, January 20, 2005.

114. Jiménez, interview by Quintanilla, October 15, 2004.

115. UH, "Latino Activist Demonstrated Commitment."

116. Jiménez, interview by Quintanilla, October 15, 2004.

117. Jiménez, interview by Quintanilla, September 10, 2004.

118. Jiménez, "Panel 3," 138.

119. The essay is one of two in Makhijani's book *Manifesto for Global Democracy.*

120. Makhijani's book *Manifesto for Global Democracy*, 35.

121. Michael Olivas, "The Political Economy of the DREAM Act and the Legislative Process: A Case Study of Comprehensive Immigration Reform," *Wayne Law Review* 55 (Winter 2009): 1758.

122. Juan Alanis, "Undocumented Students, Parents Gather at UH," *Houston Chronicle*, March 25, 2004.

123. Walters J. Nicholls, *The DREAMers: How the Undocumented Youth Movement Transformed the Immigrant Rights Debate* (Stanford: Stanford University Press, 2013), 35.

124. Olivas, "Political Economy of the DREAM Act," 1773. Other states passed similar laws, including California, Massachusetts, and New York.

125. The last effort to deny in-state tuition failed in 2015. Enrique Rangel, "Controversial Immigration Bill Dies in Texas Senate," *Amarillo Globe*, May 26, 2015.

126. Nicholls, *DREAMers,* 55. Also, Tom Curry, "How Immigration Blew Up on Rick Perry," *NBC*, September 27, 2011, www.nbcnews.com/id/44675117/ns/politics-decisions_2012/t/how-immigration-blew-rick-perry/#WEzG1n2vg!k.

127. Olivas, "Political Economy of the DREAM Act," 1783.

128. Eyder Peralta and Cynthia Garza, "Young Hispanics Stepping Out, Speaking out for Elders," *Houston Chronicle*, April 1, 2006.

129. The JIFM's "letter writing campaign was vital in getting House Bill 1403 legislation passed." Alanis, "Undocumented Students, Parents Gather at UH."

130. Peralta and Garza, "Young Hispanics Stepping Out."

131. FIRM was formed in 2004.

132. Nicholls, *DREAMers*, 63.

133. Rinku Sen, "Immigrants are Losing the Policy Fight. But That's Beside the Point," *Colorlines*, September 17, 2012, https://colorlines.com/article/immigrants-are-losing-policy-fight-thats-beside-point/.

134. Peralta and Garza, "Young Hispanics Stepping Out."

135. Cynthia Leonor Garza, "Teenagers Say Any Repercussions of the Walkout Will Be Worth It," *Houston Chronicle*, March 28, 2006.

136. Olivas, "Political Economy of the DREAM Act," 1775.

137. Alexis Grant, "Student Protest Plan for Tighter Federal Rules," *Houston Chronicle*, March 28, 2006.

138. Neil Foley, *Mexicans in the Making of America* (Cambridge, MA: Belknap Press of Harvard University Press, 2014), 215.

139. Natalie Molina, *How Race Is Made in America: Immigration, Citizenship, and the Historical Power of Racial Scripts* (Berkeley: University of California Press, 2014), 144. The proposed law categorized any undocumented immigrant as a felon and made it a "federal crime to knowingly help any undocumented person."

140. Jiménez, interview by Quintanilla, October 15, 2004.

Notes for Epilogue

1. Charles Taylor, *Multiculturalism and "The Politics of Recognition": An Essay by Charles Taylor* (Princeton, NJ: Princeton University Press, 1992), 25.

2. Pycior, *LBJ & Mexican Americans*, 3–4.

3. Delgado and Stefancic, *Critical Race Theory*.

4. United Nations General Assembly, Resolution 217A (III), "Universal Declaration of Human Rights," December 10, 1948.

5. W. E. B. Du Bois, "Double-Consciousness and the Veil," in *Social Theory: The Multicultural and Classical Readings,* ed. Charles Lemert (Boulder: Westview Pres, 1993), 179.

6. An extreme form of violence is "Mexican hopping," "bean hopping," also called "beaner jumping." Young males, usually white, find Mexican immigrants to beat or to kill. Cara Buckley, "Teenagers' Violent 'Sport' Led to Killing on Long Island, Officials Say," *New York Times*, November 21, 2008, http://www.nytimes.com/2008/11/21/nyregion/21immigrant.html?=etal.

7. Cristina Constantini, "Fear of Immigrants Is as Old as America Itself," ABC News, May 14, 2013, http://abcnews.go.com/ABS_Univision/fear-immigrants-america/story/id=19177944.

8. Maria Jiménez, interview by Linda J. Quintanilla, July 19, 2001.

9. Jo Ann Zuniga, "A Weary Soldier: Activist Grows Frustrated in Her Battle for Hispanic Rights," *Houston Chronicle*, February 7, 1999.

10. Jiménez, interview by Quintanilla, September 10, 2004.

11. Restrictive movement across borders dates only from the nineteenth century. Satvinder S. Juss, "Free Movement and the World Order," *International Journal of Refugee Law* 16, no. 3 (2004): 298–99.

12. Jiménez, "Mobility, Human Rights, and Economic Development."

13. Bryan Stevenson, *Just Mercy: A Story of Justice and Redemption* (New York: Spiegel & Grau, 2014), 299.

14. Nick Cooper, "Interview with Longtime Houston Activist Maria Jiménez," *Free Press Houston*, February 11, 2014, https://freepresshouston.com/interview-with-longtime-houston-activist-maria-jimenez/.

15. James Pinkerton, "Day Workers Plagued by Wage Theft," *Houston Chronicle*, July 30, 2007.

16. Jiménez, "Panel 3," 135. The AFSC addressed their concerns in the hearing on NAFTA in San Diego and in Houston.

17. Jiménez has received numerous awards: "Houston Activists to Honor SA Prez," *Daily Cougar*, February 16, 1971; "News and Notable," *Houston Chronicle*, June 12, 1999; "Partners in Preaching Award," June 4, 1999; "Event to Honor Hispanic Leaders Planned," *Houston Chronicle*, August 12, 2004; "Mayor Parker Announces 2010 Hispanic Heritage Awards, Recipients and Mayor's Advisory Board," Press Release, October 1, 2010; "La Universidad de Houston Nombra Decano Latino," *La Voz*, July 8, 2015.

18. Jiménez, interview by José Angel Gutiérrez, January 22, 1998.

19. Melissa del Bosque, "Tyrant's Foe: Eddie Canales is Saving Lives of Undocumented Immigrants," *Texas Observer*, January 1, 2017. Also see Jason de León, *The Land of Open Graves: Living and Dying on the Migrant Trail* (Oakland: University of California Press, 2015).

20. Jiménez, interview by Natalie Garza, June 14, 2010.

21. "Dignidad" was her email address.

22. Jiménez, interview by Quintanilla, September 10, 2004.

Bibliography

Archives and Collections

Austin History Center, Austin Public Library, Austin, TX.
    Frank Caldwell Texana Collection
    Neal Douglass Photograph Archive
Houston Metropolitan Research Center. Houston Public Library, Houston, TX.
Leonard Nadel Photographs and Scrapbooks, Archives Center. National Museum of American History, Smithsonian Institution.
Maria Jiménez Collection
Oral History of Houston History Project. University of Houston, Houston, TX.
Tejano Voices 96. Center for Mexican American Studies. University of Texas at Austin, Austin, TX.
Voces Oral History Center. Moody College of Communication, University of Texas at Austin, Austin, TX.

News Sources

Ahora Sí! (Austin, TX)
Amarillo Globe
Associated Press
Atlanta Inquirer
Austin American
Austin American Statesman
Austin Statesman
Axios
Christian Science Monitor
CNN
Corpus Christi Caller-Times
Daily Cougar (Houston)
Dallas Morning News
Dallas Times Herald
Deseret News (Salt Lake City, UT)
Diario de Juárez (Juárez, Mexico)
El Excelsior (Mexico City, Mexico)
El Mexica (Houston)

El Sol (Houston)
El Voz (Houston)
Fox News
Free Press Houston
Frontline
The Hill
Houston Breakthrough
Houston Chronicle
Houston Free Press
Houston Post
Huffington Post
La Gaceta Mexicana (Houston, TX)
La Gente (Houston, TX)
La Jornada (México City)
La Prensa (México City)
Los Angeles Times
New York Times
Newsweek
Notimex (México City)
Papel Chicano (Houston, TX)
Prescott (AZ) Courier
San Diego Union-Tribune
Time
USA Today
Vox
Washington Post

Books, Reports, Theses, Dissertations, Documentary

Acosta, Teresa Palomo. "In Re Ricardo Rodríguez." *Handbook of Texas Online*,
    updated November 11, 2020. https://www.tshaonline.org/handbook/entries/
    in-re-ricardo-rodriguez.

Acosta, Teresa Palomo, and Ruthe Winegarten. *Las Tejanas: 300 Years of
    History*. Austin: University of Texas Press, 2003.

Acuña, Rodolfo. *Occupied America: The Chicano's Struggle toward Liberation*.
    San Francisco: Canfield Press, 1972.

Alexander, Charles C. *The Ku Klux Klan in the Southwest*. Lexington:
    University of Kentucky Press, 1965.

Allen, Dr. O. F. *The City of Houston, from Wilderness to Wonder*. Temple,
    TX: O. F. Allen, 1936.

Allen, Ruth A., George N. Green, and James V. Reese. "Labor Organizations." *Handbook of Texas Online*, updated December 15, 2021. https://www.tshaonline.org/handbook/entries/labor-organizations.

American Friends Service Committee. *Human Rights at the Mexico-US Border.* 2nd Annual Report. Immigration Law Enforcement Monitoring Project (ILEMP). Philadelphia: American Friends Service Committee, 1990.

American Friends Service Committee. *Sealing Our Borders: The Human Toll.* 3rd Annual Report. Immigration Law Enforcement Monitoring Project (ILEMP). A Project of the Mexico-US Border Program. Philadelphia: American Friends Service Committee, 1992.

Anaya, Rudolfo. *Bless Me, Ultima.* New York: Warner Books, 1972.

Anderson, Gary Clayton. *The Conquest of Texas: Ethnic Cleansing in the Promised Land, 1820–1875.* Norman: University of Oklahoma Press, 2005.

Balderrama, Francisco E., and Raymond Rodríguez. *Decade of Betrayal: Mexican Repatriation in the 1930s.* Rev. ed. Albuquerque: University of New Mexico Press, 2006.

Beezley, William H., *Mexico in World History.* Oxford: Oxford University Press, 2011.

Blackwelder, Julia Kirk. *Women of the Depression: Case and Culture in San Antonio, 1929–1939.* College Station: Texas A&M University Press, 1984.

Blackwell, Maylei. *Chicana Power! Contested Histories of Feminism in the Chicano Movement.* Austin: University of Texas Press, 2011.

Blanton, Carlos Kevin. *George I. Sánchez: The Long Fight for Mexican American Integration.* New Haven: Yale University Press, 2014.

Boles, John B. *A University So Conceived: A Brief History of Rice.* Houston: Rice University, 1992.

Broyles-González, Yolanda. *Lydia Mendoza's Life in Music: La historia de Lydia Mendoza.* Norteño Tejano Legacies. New York: Oxford University Press, 2001.

Buchanan, Patrick J. *State of Emergency: The Third World Invasion and Conquest of America.* New York: St. Martin's Press, 2006.

Burrough, Bryan, Chris Tomlinson, and Jason Stanford. *Forget the Alamo: The Rise and Fall of an American Myth.* New York: Penguin Press, 2021.

Bustamante, Jorge A. *Población y Desarrollo: A Virtual Contradiction between International Migration and Human Right.* Santiago, Chile: United

Nations, Economic Commission for Latin America and the Caribbean and Inter-American Development Bank, 2003.

Calvert, Robert A., Arnoldo de León, and Gregg Cantrell. *The History of Texas*. 3rd ed. Wheeling, IL: Harlan Davidson, 2002.

Caram, Dorothy F., Anthony G. Dworkin, and Nestor P. Rodríguez. *Hispanics in Houston and Harris County, 1510–1986: A Sesquicentennial Celebration*. Houston: Houston Hispanic Forum, 1989.

Carleton, Don E. *Red Scare! Right-Wing Hysteria, Fifties Fanaticism, and Their Legacy in Texas*. Austin: Texas Monthly Press, 1985.

Carlsen, Laura. *Americas Policy Program: NAFTA Inequality and Immigration*. CIP Americans Policy Program. Washington, DC: Center for International Policy, 2007.

Carroll, Patrick J. *Félix Longoria's Wake: Bereavement, Racism, and the Rise of Mexican American Activism*. Austin: University of Texas Press, 2003.

Cole, Thomas R. *No Color Is My Kind: The Life of Eldrewey Stearns and the Integration of Houston*. Austin: University of Texas Press, 1997.

Cortes, Carlos. *The Mexican American and the Law*. New York: Arno Press, 1974.

De León, Arnoldo. *Ethnicity in the Sunbelt: A History of Mexican Americans in Houston*. Houston: Mexican American Studies Program, University of Houston, 1989.

De León, Arnoldo. *Ethnicity in the Sunbelt: Mexican Americans in Houston*. College Station: Texas A&M University Press, 2001.

De León, Arnoldo. *The Tejano Community, 1836–1900*. Dallas: Southern Methodist University Press, 1997.

De León, Arnoldo. *They Called Them Greasers: Anglo Attitudes toward Mexicans in Texas, 1821–1900*. Austin: University of Texas Press, 1983.

De León, Jason. *The Land of Open Graves: Living and Dying on the Migrant Trail*. Oakland: University of California Press, 2015.

Delgado, Richard, and Jean Stefancic. *Critical Race Theory: An Introduction*. 2nd ed. New York: New York University Press, 2012.

Delgado, Richard, and Jean Stefancic, eds. *The Latino/a Condition: A Critical Reader*. New York: New York University Press, 1998.

Donato, Ruben. *The Other Struggle for Equal Schools: Mexican Americans during the Civil Rights Era*. New York: State University of New York Press, 1997.

Du Bois, W. E. B. "Double-Consciousness and the Veil." In *Social Theory: The Multicultural and Classic Reading*, edited by Charles Lemert, 177–82. Boulder: Westview Press, 1993.

Dunn, Timothy J. *Blockading the Border and Human Rights: The El Paso Operation That Remade Immigration Enforcement.* Austin: University of Texas Press, 2009.

Dunn, Timothy J. *The Militarization of the U.S.-Mexico Border, 1978–1992: Low-Intensity Conflict Comes Home.* Austin: Center for Mexican American Studies, University of Texas at Austin, 1996.

Durand, Jorge, and Douglas S. Massey, eds. *Crossing the Border: Research from the Mexican Migration Project.* New York: Russell Sage Foundation, 2004.

Ettinger, Patrick. *Imaginary Lines: Border Enforcement and the Origins of Undocumented Immigration, 1882–1930.* Austin: University of Texas Press, 2009.

Faragher, John Mack, ed. *Out of Many: A History of the American People.* 2nd ed. Upper Saddle River, NJ: Prentice Hall, 1997.

Feagin, Joe R. *Free Enterprise City: Houston in Political and Economic Perspective.* New Brunswick, NJ: Rutgers University Press, 1988.

Flores, Lori A. *Grounds for Dreaming: Mexican Americans, Mexican Immigrants, and the California Farmworkers Movement.* New Haven: Yale University Press, 2016.

Foley, Neil. *Mexicans in the Making of America.* Cambridge, MA: Belknap Press of Harvard University Press, 2014.

Foley, Neil. *The White Scourge: Mexicans, Blacks, and Poor Whites in Texas Cotton Culture.* Berkeley: University of California Press, 1997.

Galarza, Ernesto. *Barrio Boy.* Notre Dame: University of Notre Dame Press, 1971.

Galarza, Ernesto. *Merchants of Labor: The Mexican Bracero Story.* San Jose: Rosicrucian Press, 1964.

García, Ignacio M. *Chicanismo: The Forging of a Militant Ethos among Mexican Americans.* Tucson: University of Arizona Press, 1997.

Garcia, Juan Ramón. *Operation Wetback: The Mass Deportation of Mexican Undocumented Workers in 1954.* Contribution in Ethnic Studies 2. Westport, CT: Greenwood Press, 1980.

Gillon, Steven M. *"That's Not What We Meant to Do": Reform and Its Unintended Consequences in Twentieth-Century America.* New York: W. W. Norton, 2000.

Gómez-Cano, Grisel, and James Ross-Nazzal. *The Spirit of Magnolia Park: Ethnic Pride in a Mexican Barrio, 1909–2009.* Boston: Pearson Learning Solutions, 2013.

Gómez-Quiñones, Juan. *Mexican American Labor, 1790–1990.* Albuquerque: University of New Mexico Press, 1994.

Gómez-Quiñones, Juan. *Roots of Chicano Politics, 1600–1940*. Albuquerque: University of New Mexico Press, 1994.

González, Juan. *Harvest of Empire: A History of Latinos in America*. New York: Penguin Books, 2001.

Gonzáles, Manuel G. *Mexicanos: A History of Mexicans in the United States*. Bloomington: Indiana University Press, 1999.

Goodman, Mary Ellen, and Don des Jarlais. *The Spanish Surname Population of Houston: A Demographic Sketch*. Project Houston, Report 2. Houston: Center for Research in Social Change and Economic Development, Rice University, 1968.

Gritter, Matthew. *Mexican Inclusion: The Origins of Anti-Discrimination Policy in Texas and the Southwest*. College Station: Texas A&M University Press, 2012.

Guerra, Roberto S., and Mary Ellen Goodman. *A Content Assessment of El Sol, A Community Newspaper*. Houston: Center for Research in Social Change and Economic Development, Rice University, 1968.

Gutiérrez, David G. *Walls and Mirrors: Mexican Americans, Mexican Immigrants, and the Politics of Ethnicity*. Berkeley: University of California Press, 1995.

Gutiérrez, Elena R. *Fertile Matters: The Politics of Mexican-Origin Women's Reproduction*. Austin: University of Texas Press, 2008.

Gutiérrez, José Angél. *The Making of a Chicano Militant: Lessons from Cristal*. Madison: University of Wisconsin Press, 1998.

Gutiérrez, José Angél, Michelle Meléndez, and Sonia Ariana Noyola. *Chicanas in Charge: Texas Women in the Public Arena*. Lanham, MD: AltaMira Press, 2007.

Haney-Lopez, Ian F. *Racism on Trial: The Chicano Fight for Justice*. Cambridge, MA: Belknap Press of Harvard University Press, 2003.

Hoffman, Abraham. *Unwanted Mexican Americans in the Great Depression: Repatriation Pressures, 1929–1939*. Tucson: University of Arizona Press, 1974.

Houston-Galveston Area Council. *Population Growth and Ethnicity in the H-GAC Region, 1970– 1980*. Analytic Report No. 1. December 1981.

Huntington, Samuel P. *Who Are We? The Challenges to America's National Identity*. New York: Simon & Schuster, 2004.

Jiménez, Maria. *Humanitarian Crisis: Migrant Deaths at the U.S.-Mexico Border*. American Civil Liberties Union of San Diego (ACLU) & Imperial Counties and Mexico's National Commission of Human Rights. San Diego: ACLU, 2009. http://www.aclu.org/immigrants/gen/41186pub 200911001.html.

Jiménez, Maria. Introduction. *Human Rights at the Mexico-US Border.* American Friends Service Committee, Immigration Enforcement Monitoring Project (ILEMP). 2nd Annual Report. March 1990.

Johnson, Benjamin Heber. *Revolution in Texas: How a Forgotten Rebellion and Its Bloody Suppression Turned Mexicans into Americans.* New Haven: Yale University Press, 2003.

Johnson, Kevin R. *Opening the Floodgates: Why America Needs to Rethink Its Borders and Immigration Laws.* New York: New York University Press, 2007.

Keller, William Henry. "Race Relations and School Desegregation in Houston, Texas." Master's Thesis. University of Houston, 1990.

Klineberg, Stephen L. *Houston Ethnic Communities.* 3rd ed. Houston: Rice University, 1996.

Kreneck, Thomas H. *Del Pueblo: A History of Houston's Hispanic Community.* College Station: Texas A&M University Press, 2012.

Kreneck, Thomas H. *Del Pueblo: A Pictorial History of Houston's Hispanic Community.* Houston: Houston International University, 1989.

Kreneck, Thomas H. *Mexican American Odyssey: Felix Tijerina, Entrepreneur and Civil Leader, 1905–1965.* College Station: Texas A&M University Press, 2001.

Levengood, Paul Alejandro. "For the Duration and Beyond: World War II and the Creation of Modern Houston, Texas." PhD diss., Rice University, 1999.

Makhijani, Arjan. *Manifesto for Global Democracy: Two Essays on Imperialism and the Struggle for Freedom.* New York: Apex Press, 2004.

Maril, Robert Lee. *Patrolling Chaos: The U.S. Border Patrol in Deep South Texas.* Lubbock: Texas Tech University Press, 2004.

Martínez, Monica Muñoz. *The Injustice Never Leaves You: Anti-Mexican Violence in Texas.* Cambridge, MA: Harvard University Press, 2018.

Massey, Douglas S., Jorge Durand, and Nolan J. Malone. *Beyond Smoke and Mirrors: Mexican Immigration in an Era of Economic Integration.* New York: Russell Sage Foundation, 2002.

McAdams, Donald R. *Fighting to Save Our Urban Schools . . . and Winning! Lessons from Houston.* New York: Teachers College, Columbia University, 2000.

McComb, David G. *Houston: A History.* Austin: University of Texas Press, 1981.

Meier, Matt S., and Feliciano Rivera. *Mexican Americans, American Mexicans: From Conquistadors to Chicanos.* Rev. ed. New York: Hill and Wang, 1993.

Menchaca, Martha. *Naturalizing Mexican Immigrants: A Texas History*. Austin: University of Texas Press, 2011.

Mendoza, Lydia. *Lydia Mendoza: A Family Autobiography*. Compiled and introduced by Chris Strachwitz with James Nicolopulos. Houston: Arte Publico Press, 1993.

Molina, Natalia. *How Race Is Made in America: Immigration, Citizenship, and the Historical Power of Racial Scripts*. Berkeley: University of California Press, 2014.

Montejano, David. *Anglos and Mexicans in the Making of Texas, 1836–1986*. Austin: University of Texas Press, 1987.

Montejano, David, ed. *Chicano Politics and Society in the Late Twentieth Century*. Austin: University of Texas Press, 1999

Muñoz, Carlos, Jr. *Youth, Identity, Power: The Chicano Movement*. London: Verso, 1989.

Ngai, Mae M. *Impossible Subjects: Illegal Aliens and the Making of Modern America*. Princeton: Princeton University Press, 2004.

Nicholls, Walter J. *The DREAMers: How the Undocumented Youth Movement Transformed the Immigrant Rights Debate*. Stanford: Stanford University Press, 2013.

Olivas, Michael A. *No Undocumented Child Left Behind:* Plyler v. Doe *and the Education of Undocumented Schoolchildren*. New York: New York University Press, 2012.

Orozco, Cynthia E. *No Mexicans, Women, or Dogs Allowed: The Rise of the Mexican American Civil Rights Movement*. Austin: University of Texas Press, 2009.

Pérez, Emma. *The Decolonial Imaginary: Writing Chicanas into History*. Bloomington: Indiana University Press, 1999.

Pycior, Julie Leininger. *LBJ & Mexican Americans: The Paradox of Power*. Austin: University of Texas Press, 1997.

Quintanilla, Guadalupe. "The Little School of the 400 and Its Impact on Education for the Spanish Dominant Bilingual Children of Texas." EdD diss., University of Houston, 1976.

Quiroz, Anthony. *Leaders of the Mexican American Generation: Biographical Essays, ed. Anthony Quiroz*. Boulder: University Press of Colorado, 2015.

Ramírez, José A. *To the Line of Fire! Mexican Texans and World War I*. College Station: Texas A&M University Press, 2009.

Ramos, Henry A. J. *The American GI Forum: In Pursuit of the Dream, 1948–1983*. Houston: Arte Publico Press, 1998.

Reisler, Mark. *By the Sweat of Their Brow: Mexican Immigrant Labor in the United States, 1900–1940.* Westport, CT: Greenwood Press, 1976.

Ribb, Richard Henry. "José Tomás Canales and the Texas Rangers: Myth, Identity, and Power in South Texas, 1900–1920." PhD diss., University of Texas at Austin, 2001.

Rivas-Rodríguez, Maggie, Juliana Torres, Melissa Dipiero-D'Sa, and Lindsay Fitzpatrick. *A Legacy Greater than Words: Stories of U.S. Latinos & Latinas of the World War II Generations.* Austin: U.S. Latino & Latina WWII Oral History Project Group, University of Austin, School of Journalism, 2006.

Rosenbaum, Robert J. *Mexican Resistance in the Southwest: "The Sacred Right of Self-Preservation."* Austin: University of Texas Press, 1981.

Sánchez, George J. *Becoming Mexican American: Ethnicity, Culture, and Identity in Chicano Los Angeles, 1900–1945.* New York: Oxford University Press, 1993.

San Miguel, Guadalupe, Jr. *Brown, Not White: School Integration and the Chicano Movement in Houston.* College Station: Texas A&M University Press, 2005.

San Miguel, Guadalupe, Jr. *"Let All of Them Take Heed": Mexican Americans and the Campaign for Educational Equality in Texas, 1910–1981.* Austin: University of Texas Press, 1987.

Smithwick, Noah, and Nanna Smithwick Donaldson. *The Evolution of a State, by Noah Smithwick.* Austin: Steck, 1935.

Stevenson, Bryan. *Just Mercy: A Story of Justice and Redemption.* New York: Spiegel & Grau, 2014.

Taylor, Charles. *Multiculturalism and "The Politics of Recognition": An Essay by Charles Taylor.* Princeton, NJ: Princeton University Press, 1992.

Tindall, George Brown, and David E. Shi. *America: A Narrative History.* New York: W. W. Norton, 2007.

Treviño, Roberto R. *The Church in the Barrio: Mexican American Ethno-Catholicism in Houston.* Chapel Hill: University of North Carolina Press, 2006.

United States Commission on Civil Rights, Texas State Advisory Committee. *Civil Rights in Texas: A Report of the Texas Advisory Committee to the U.S. Commission on Civil Rights.* [Austin?], 1970.

United States Commission on Civil Rights. *Mexican Americans and the Administration of Justice in the Southwest.* Washington, DC: Government Printing Office, 1970.

Valenzuela, Angela. *Subtractive Schooling: U.S.-Mexican Youth and the Politics of Caring.* Albany: State University of New York Press, 1999.

Vargas, Zaragosa. *Labor Rights Are Civil Rights: Mexican American Workers in Twentieth-Century America.* Princeton: Princeton University Press, 2005.

Villanueva, Nicholas, Jr. *The Lynching of Mexicans in the Texas Borderlands.* Albuquerque: University of New Mexico Press, 2017.

Wade, Mary Dodson. *Guadalupe Quintanilla: Leader of the Hispanic Community.* Springfield, NJ: Enslow, 1995.

Wang, Lu-in. *Discrimination by Default: How Racism Becomes Routine.* New York: New York University Press, 2006.

Watson, Dwight. *Race and the Houston Police Department, 1930–1990: A Change Did Come.* College Station: Texas A&M University Press, 2005.

Wilson, Steven Harmon. *The Rise of Judicial Management in the U.S. District Court, Southern District of Texas, 1955–2000.* Athens: University of Georgia Press, 2002.

Zamora, Emilio. *Claiming Rights and Righting Wrongs in Texas: Mexican Workers and Job Politics during World War II.* College Station: Texas A&M University Press, 2009.

Zamora, Emilio. *The World of the Mexican Worker in Texas.* College Station: Texas A&M University Press, 1993.

Articles, Chapters, and Papers

Alanis Enciso, Fernando Saúl. "Cuántos Fueron? La reparación de mexicanos en los Estados Unidos durante la Gran Depresión: Una interpretación cuantitativa 1930–1934." *Aztlan: Journal of Chicano Studies* 32, no. 2 (Fall 2007): 65–91.

Allsup, V. Carl. "*Hernandez v. Driscoll CISD*." *Handbook of Texas Online*, updated August 3, 2020. https://www.tshaonline.org/handbook/entries/hernandez-v-driscoll-cisd.

American Committee for the Protection of the Foreign Born. "Our Badge of Infamy." In Cortes, *Mexican American and the Law*, 33–34.

Anderson, Michael. "Eldrewey Stearns and Houston's Student Civil Rights Movement." *Houston History* 14, no. 2 (May 2017): 26.

Arquilla, John, and David Ronfeldt. "The Advent of Netwar (Revisited)." In *Networks and Netwars: The Future of Terror, Crime, and Militancy*, edited by John Arquilla and David Ronfeldt, 1–25. Santa Monica, CA: Rand, 2001.

Bailey, Richard. "The Starr County Strike." *Red River Valley Historical Review* 4, no. 1 (Winter 1979): 42–61.

Bailey, Stanley, Karl Eschbach, Jacqueline Hagan, and Nestor Rodríguez. "The Human Costs of Border Enforcement: Migrant Deaths at the Texas-Mexico Border." *Migration World Review* 24, no. 4 (1996): 16–20.

Banner, Lois W. "AHR Roundtable: Biography as History." *American Historical Review* 114, no. 3 (June 2009): 579–86.

Belejack, Barbara. "A Lesson in Equal Protection: The Texas Cases That Opened the Schoolhouse Door to Undocumented Immigrant Children." *Texas Observer*, July 13, 2007.

Bell, Derrick A., Jr. "*Brown v. Board of Education* and the Interest-Convergence Dilemma." *Harvard Law Review* 93, no. 3 (January 1980): 518–33.

Benowitz, June Melby. "Minute Women of the U.S.A." *Handbook of Texas Online*, updated November 30, 2023. https://www.tshaonline.org/handbook/entries/minute-women-of-the-usa.

Bixler-Márquez, Dennis. "La Preparatoria Bowie versus la Patrulla Fronteriza." *Aztlan: Journal of Chicano Studies* 30, no. 2 (Fall 2005): 157–68.

Brader, Ted, Nicholas A. Valentino, and Elizabeth Suhay. "What Triggers Public Opposition to Immigration? Anxiety, Group Cues, and Immigration Threat." *American Journal of Political Science* 52, no. 4 (October 2008): 959–78.

Brandstetter, John, and Charles R. Foster. "'Quality Integrated Education' in Houston's Magnet Schools." *Phi Delta Kappan* (April 1976): 502–6.

Burgoon, Brian, and Janice Fine. "Immigration and the Transformation of American Unionism." *International Migration Review* 44, no. 4 (Winter 2010): 933–73.

Calbillo, Carlos. "The Chicano Movement in Houston and Texas: A Personal Memory." *Houston History* 9, no. 1 (Fall 2011): 25–29.

Calderón, Robert R., and Emilio Zamora. "Manuela Solis Sager and Emma B. Tenayuca: A Tribute." In *Between Borders: Essays on Mexicana/Chicana History*, edited by Adelaida R. Del Castillo, 269–79. Encino, CA: Floricanto Press, 1990.

Camp, Roderic Ai. "The Time of the Technocrats and Deconstruction of the Revolution." In *The Oxford History of Mexico*, edited by Michael C. Meyer and William H. Beezley, 609–36. Oxford: Oxford University Press, 2000.

Carrigan, William D., and Clive Webb. "The Lynching of Persons of Mexican Origin or Descent in the United States, 1848–1928." *Journal of Social History* (Winter 2003): 411–38.

Carroll, Patrick J. "Separate Tejano/Texan Worlds: The Félix Longoria Controversy, Racism, and Patriotism in Post-World War II South Texas." In Quiroz, *Leaders of the Mexican American Generation*, 163–87.

Castillo, Leonel. "The Growth of Hispanic Political Power in the Houston Area." In Caram, Dworkin, and Rodríguez, *Hispanics in Houston and Harris County*, 98–99.

Castro, Adriana. "Guadalupe Quintanilla: Defying the Odds." *Houston History* 14, no. 2 (May 2017): 13–17.

Cerrutti, Marcela, and Douglas S. Massey. "Trends in Mexican Migration to the United States, 1965 to 1995." In *Crossing the Border: Research from the Mexican Migration Project*, edited by Jorge Durand and Douglas S. Massey, 17–44. New York: Russell Sage Foundation, 2004.

Chavez, Leo R. "Immigration Reform and Nativism: The Nationalist Response to the Transnationalist Challenge." In *Immigrants Out! The New Nativism and the Anti-Immigrant Impulse in the United States*, edited by Juan F. Perea, 61–77. New York: New York University Press, 1997.

Christian, Carole E. "Joining the American Mainstream: Texas's Mexican Americans during World War I." *Southwestern Historical Quarterly* 92, no. 4 (April 1989): 559–95.

Cordova, Teresa. "Roots and Resistance: The Emergent Writings of Twenty Years of Chicana Feminist Struggle." In *Handbook of Hispanic Cultures in the United States: Sociology*, edited by Felix Padilla, 175–202. Houston: Arte Publico Press, 1994.

Cruz, George Xavier. "Being Hispanic in Houston: From the 'Barrio' and Back Again." *Americas Review* 16, no. 1 (Spring 1988): 53–63.

Delgado, Richard. "Book Review Essay: Crossroads and Blind Alleys: A Critical Examination of Recent Writings about Race." *Texas Law Review* 82, no. 1 (2003): 130.

Delgado, Richard. "The Current Landscape of Race: Old Targets, New Opportunities." *Michigan Law Review* 104 (2006): 1269–86.

Delgado, Richard. "Storytelling for Oppositionists and Others." In Delgado and Stefancic, *Latino/a Condition*, 259–70.

Donato, Katherine M. "U.S. Policy and Mexican Migration to the United States, 1942–92." *Social Science Quarterly* 75, no. 4 (December 1994): 705–29.

Donato, Katherine M., Jorge Durand, and Douglas S. Massey. "Changing Conditions in the US Labor Market: Effects of the Immigration Reform and Control Act of 1986." *Population Research and Policy Review* 11, no. 2 (January 1992): 93–115.

Donato, Katherine M., Jorge Durand, and Douglas S. Massey. "Stemming the Tide? Assessing the Deterrent Effects of the Immigration and Reform and Control Act." *Demography* 29, no. 2 (May 1992): 139–57.

Dugger, Ronnie. "The Rangers and La Huelga." *Texas Observer*, June 9–23, 1967.

Dulaney, W. Marvin. "African Americans." *Handbook of Texas Online*, updated August 24, 2023. https://tshaonline.org/handbook/entries/african-americans.

Durand, Jorge. "Migration Policy and the Asymmetry of Power: The Mexican Case, 1900–2000." In *Citizenship and Those Who Leave: The Politics of Emigration and Expatriation*, edited by Nancy L. Green and Francois Weil, 224–42. Urbana: University of Illinois Press, 2007.

During, Simon. "Introduction." In *The Cultural Studies Reader*, edited by Simon During, 1–25. London: Routledge, 1993.

Ellis, Carol. "The Houston Catholic Worker: Casa Juan Diego, 1981–2004." *Houston Review of History and Culture* 3, no. 1 (Fall 2005): 20–21, 59–62.

Eschbach, Karl, Jacqueline Hagan, and Nestor Rodríguez. "Death at the Border." *International Migration Review* 33, no. 2 (Summer 1999): 430–54.

Esparza, Jesús Jesse. "La Colonia Mexicana: A History or Mexican Americans in Houston." *Houston History* 9, no. 1 (Fall 2011): 2–8.

Feagin, Joe R. "The Global Context of Metropolitan Growth: Houston and the Oil Industry." *American Journal of Sociology* 90, no. 6 (1985): 1204–30.

Frey, John Carlos. "Graves of Shame." *Texas Observer*, July 6, 2015. https://www.texasobserver.org/illegal-mass-graves-of-migrant-remains-found-in-south-texas/.

García, Alma M. "Introduction." In *Chicana Feminist Thought: The Basic Historical Writings*, edited by Alma M. Garcia, 1–16. New York: Routledge, 1997.

García, Alma M. "Still Coming North from Mexico: Immigration Constraints and Contestations." In *North from Mexico: The Spanish-Speaking People of the United States*, by Carey McWilliams, 3rd ed., updated by Alma M. Garcia, 329–60. Santa Barbara, CA: Praeger, 2016.

Garcia, Maria Cristina. "La Gaceta Mexicana." *Handbook of Texas Online*, updated April 13, 2017. https://www.tshaonline.org/handbook/entries/la-gaceta-mexicana.

Garcia, Maria Cristina. "Reyna, Maria Torres." *Handbook of Texas Online*, updated November 1, 2017. https://www.tshaonline.org/handbook/entries/reyna-maria-torres.

Garcia, Richard A. "Alonso C. Perales: The Voice and Visions of a Citizen Intellectual." In Quiroz, *Leaders of the Mexican American Generation*, 85–117.

Garcia, Richard A. "Class, Consciousness, and Identity: The Mexican Community of San Antonio, Texas, 1930–1940." *Aztlan: Journal of Chicano Studies* 9 (1978): 23–69.

Garcia y Griego, Manuel. "The Importation of Mexican Contract Laborers to the United States, 1942–1964: Antecedents, Operations, and Legacy." In *The Border That Joins: Mexican Migrants and U.S. Responsibility*, edited by Peter G. Brown and Henry Shue, 49–98. Totowa, NJ: Rowman and Littlefield, 1983.

Glenn, David. "Our Hidden Prejudices, on Trial." *Chronicle Review*, April 25, 2008.

Glickman, Betsy. "Fighting the Good Fight: Antonio Campos Saw Many Signs of Second-Class Citizenship—Before and After WWII: the Ex-Paratrooper Stormed the Texas System and Changed It." *Narratives: U.S. Latinos and Latinas & WWII Oral History Project*, 2002.

Goldberg, Mark Allen. "'It Can Be Cultivated Where Nothing but Cactus Will Grow': Local Knowledge and Healing on the Texas Military Frontier." In *Recovering the Hispanic History of Texas*, edited by Monica Perales and Raúl A. Ramos, 19–37. Houston: Arte Publico Press, 2010.

Gómez, Denise. "A Life of Activism: Maria Jiménez." *Houston History* 12, no. 3 (Summer 2015): 14–18.

González, Gabriela. "Carolina Munguia and Emma Tenayuca: The Politics of Benevolence and Radical Reform." *Frontiers* 24, nos. 2 & 3 (2003): 200–229.

Gonzalez-Barrera, Ana "Before COVID-19, More Mexicans Came to the U.S. than Left for Mexico for the First Time in Years." *Pew Research Center*, July 9, 2021.

Gramsci, Antonio. "Culture and Ideological Hegemony." In *Culture and Society: Contemporary Debates*, edited by Jeffrey C. Alexander and Steven Seidman, 47–54. New York: Cambridge University Press, 1990.

Green, George N. "Texas State Industrial Union Council." *Handbook of Texas Online*, updated April 28, 2021. https://www.tshaonline.org/handbook/entries/texas-state-industrial-union-council.

Greene, Casey. "Guardians against Change: The Ku Klux Klan in Houston and Harris County, 1920–25." *Houston History* 8, no. 1 (Fall 2010): 2–5.

Gutiérrez, Raúl. "Mexican-Americans Boycott Elsa High School: Greater Houston—Uneasy?" *Compass* 2, no. 9 (December 1968): 2

Haney-Lopez, Ian F. "Race and Erasure: The Salience of Race to Latinos/as." In Delgado and Stefancic, *Latino/a Condition*, 180–95.

Harrington, James C. "From La Casita to LUPE." *Texas Observer*, December 3, 2004.

Hernández-Truyol, Berta Esperanza. "Latinas—Everywhere Alien: Culture, Gender, and Sex." In *Critical Race Feminism: A Reader*, 2nd ed., edited by Adrien Katherine Wing, 57–69. New York: New York University Press, 2003.

Jiménez, Maria. "Border Militarization: The History, the Effect, the Response." *Immigration Newsletter* 16, no. 4 (July–August 1987): 1, 11.

Jiménez, Maria. "Labor, Mobility and the North American Free Trade Agreement." *Immigration Newsletter* 19, no. 4 (March 1992): 5–8.

Jiménez, Maria. Interviewed by Nic Paget-Clarke. "The Militarization of the U.S.-Mexico Border." *In Motion Magazine*, February 2, 1998. http://www.inmotionmagazine.com/mj1.html.

Jiménez, Maria. "Mobility, Human Rights, and Economic Development: Lessons of the International Mexican Migrant Experience and United States Immigration Policies." *In Motion Magazine*, July 12, 1999.

Jiménez, Maria. "Panel 3: The North American Free Trade Agreement: Open Borders or Closed Dreams?" *La Raza Law Journal* 7, no. 1 (1994): 134–43.

Jiménez, Maria. "Police Policies and Practices: The Case of the Border Patrol." *Immigration Newsletter* 17, no. 4 (1988): 1–5

Jiménez, Maria. Interviewed by Rebecca Phares. "The U.S.-Mexico Border: A Strategy of Low-Intensity Conflict." *Social Justice* 27, no. 4 (2000): 32–36.

Jiménez, Maria. "War in the Borderlands." *Report on the Americas, North American Congress on Latin America (NACLA)* 26, no. 1 (July 1992): 29–33.

Jordan, Terry G. "Population Origins in Texas, 1850." *Geographical Review* 59 (January 1969): 83–103.

Karson, Tom. "Confronting Houston's Demographic Shift: The Harris County AFL-CIO." *WorkingUSA: Journal of Labor and Society* 8 (December 2004): 207–27.

Kennedy, David M. "The Art of the Tale: Story-Telling and History Teaching." *History Teacher* 31, no. 3 (May 1998): 319–30.

Kessler-Harris, Alice. "AHR Roundtable: Why Biography?" *American Historical Review* 114, no. 3 (June 2009): 624–30.

Kreneck, Thomas H. "The Letter from Chapultepec." *Houston Review: History and Culture of the Gulf Coast* 3, no. 2 (Summer 1981): 267–71.

Kretsedemas, Philip. "What Does an Undocumented Immigrant Look Like? Local Enforcement and the New Immigrant Profiling." In *Keeping Out the Other: A Critical Introduction to Immigration Enforcement Today*, edited by David C. Brotherton and Philip Kretsedemas, 334–64. New York: Columbia University Press, 2008.

Kurzban, Ira J. "Democracy and Immigration." In *Keeping Out the Other: A Critical Introduction to Enforcement Today*, edited by David C. Brotherton and Philip Kretsedemas, 63–78. New York: Columbia University Press, 2008.

Lack, Paul D. "Slavery and Vigilantism in Austin, Texas, 1840–1860." *Southwestern Historical Quarterly* 85, no. 1 (July 1981): 1–20.

Ladson-Billings, Gloria. "Racialized Discourses and Ethnic Epistemologies." In *Handbook of Qualitative Research*, 2nd ed, edited by Norman K. Denzin and Yvonna S. Lincoln, 257–78. Thousand Oaks, CA: Sage Publications, 2000.

Lavrin, Asunción. "Women in Colonial Mexico." In *The Oxford History of Mexico*, edited by Michael C. Meyer and William H. Beezley, 245–73. Oxford: Oxford University Press, 2000.

Ledesma, Irene. "Texas Newspapers and Chicana Workers' Activism, 1919–1974." *Western Historical Quarterly* 26, no. 4 (Autumn 1995): 309–31.

Leiden, Warren R., and David L. Neal. "Highlights of the U.S. Immigration Act of 1990." *Fordham International Law Journal* 14, no. 1 (1990): 328–39.

Mangan, Katherine S. "White Hats, Black Tales: A Texas Scholar Digs into the Dark Truths about the Role of the Texas Rangers in the Early 20th Century Border Wars." *Chronicle of Higher Education*, August 5, 2005.

Marchiafava, Louis J. "Law Enforcement on the Urban Frontier: Houston, 1878–1928." In *Houston: A Twentieth Century Urban Frontier*, edited by Francisco A. Rosales and Berry J. Kaplan, 78–99. Port Washington, NY: Associated Faculty, 1983.

Martin, Gary. "Employment and Unemployment in Mexico in the 1990s." *Monthly Labor Review*, November 2000.

Martínez, George A. "Mexican Americans and Whiteness." In Delgado and Stefancic, *Latino/a Condition*, 175–79.

Martínez, Roberto. Interview by Nic Paget-Clarke. "Border Operations/ Migrant Life/Organizing for Human Rights." *In Motion Magazine*, July 7, 2001. http://inmotionmagazine.com/hrcr/rm2001a.html.

Martínez, Vilma S. "Vilma S. Martínez Testifies Before the U.S. Commission on Civil Rights about the Mexican American Legal Defense and

Educational Fund (MALDEF), 1975." In *Major Problems in Mexican American History: Documents and Essays*, edited by Zaragosa Vargas, 419–21. Boston: Houghton Mifflin Company, 1999.

Melville, Margarita B. "Mexican Women Adapt to Migration." In *Mexican Immigrant Workers in the U.S.*, edited by Antonio Rios-Bustamante, 119–24. Los Angeles: Chicano Studies Research Center, University of California, 1981.

Mindiola, Tatcho, Jr. "Finding a Way: Developing the Center for Mexican American Studies at UH." *Houston History* 9, no. 1 (Fall 2011): 38–43.

Mindiola, Tatcho, Jr. "A Personal Comment on Assimilation." *Houston Review: History and Culture of the Gulf Coast* (Summer 1981): 261–66.

Montejano, David. "The Demise of 'Jim Crow' for Texas Mexicans, 1940–1970." *Aztlan: Journal of Chicano Studies* 16, nos. 1–2 (1987): 27–60.

Montejano, David. "Introduction: On the Question of Inclusion." In Montejano, *Chicano Politics and Society*, xi–xxvi.

Montgomery, William E. "The Depression in Houston, 1929–1933." In *Texas Cities and the Great Depression*, edited by Robert C. Cotner (and others), 153–69. Austin: Texas Memorial Museum, 1973.

Olivas, Michael A. *"Hernández v. Texas*: A Litigation History." In *"Colored Men" and "Hombres Aquí"*: Hernández v. Texas *and the Emergence of Mexican-American Lawyering*, edited by Michael A. Olivas, 209–22. Houston: Arte Publico Press, 2006.

Olivas, Michael A. "The Political Economy of the DREAM Act and the Legislative Process: A Case Study of Comprehensive Immigration Reform." *Wayne Law Review* 55 (Winter 2009): 1757–810.

Olmos, A. B. "History of Hispanics in the Second Ward." In Caram, Dworkin, and Rodríguez, *Hispanics in Houston and Harris County*, 23.

"The *Orantes* Injunction and Expedited Removal." *National Immigration Law Center* (July 2006): 1–5.

Phillips, Scott, Nestor P. Rodriguez, and Jacquelin Hagan. "Brutality at the Border? Use of Force in the Arrest of Immigrants in the United States." *International Journal of the Sociology of Law* 30 (2003): 285–306.

Plaza, Tina. "'Let's See Some Papers': In El Paso, Looking Latin Is a Crime." *Progressive* 57, no. 4 (April 1993): 18–23.

Rhinehart, Marilyn D., and Thomas H. Kreneck. "'In the Shadow of Uncertainty': Texas Mexicans and Repatriation in Houston During the Great Depression." *Houston Review: History and Culture of the Gulf Coast* 10, no. 1 (1988): 21–33.

Rhinehart, Marilyn D., and Thomas H. Kreneck. "The Minimum Wage March of 1966: A Case Study in Mexican-American Politics, Labor, and Identity." *Houston Review: History and Culture of the Gulf Coast* 11, no. 1 (1989): 27–44.

Rodríguez, Nestor. "Economic Restructuring and Latino Growth in Houston." In *In the Barrios: Latinos and the Underclass Debate*, edited by Joan Moore and Raquel Pinderhughes, 101–27. New York: Russell Sage Foundation, 1993.

Rodríguez, Nestor. "Growth of Houston's Hispanic Population." In Caram, Dworkin, and Rodríguez, *Hispanics in Houston and Harris County*, 49–54.

Rodríguez, Nestor P. "Undocumented Central Americans in Houston: Diverse Populations." *International Migration Review* 21, no. 1 (Spring 1987): 4–26.

Rodríguez, Nestor, Noelia Elizondo, David Mena, Ricardo Rojas, Adolfo Vasquez, and Frank Yeverino. "Political Mobilization in Houston's Magnolia." In *Barrio Ballots: Latino Politics in the 1990 Election*, edited by Rodolfo O. de la Garza, Martha Menchaca, and Louis De Sipio, 83–114. Boulder, CO: Westview Press, 1994.

Rodríguez, Samantha, and Stalina Emmanuelle Villareal. "Maria Jiménez: *Reflexiones* on Transversing Multiple Fronteras in the South." In *Chicana Movidas: New Narratives of Activism and Feminism in the Movement Era*, edited by Dionne Espinoza, Maria Eugenia Cotera, and Maylei Blackwell, 276–89. Austin: University of Texas Press, 2018.

Romano, Carlin. "Indian Scholars and the Rise of Native American Philosophy." *Chronicle of Higher Education*, May 5, 2000.

Romo, Ricardo. "George I. Sánchez and the Civil Rights Movement: 1940–1960." *La Raza Law Journal* 1 (1986): 342–62.

Ronfeldt, David, and John Arquilla. "Emergence and Influence of the Zapatista Social Netwar." In *Networks and Netwars: The Future of Terror, Crime, and Militancy*, edited by John Arquilla and David Ronfeldt, 171–99. Santa Monica, CA: Rand, 2001.

Rosales, F. Arturo. "Mexicans in Houston: The Struggle to Survive, 1908–1975." *Houston Review: History and Culture of the Gulf Coast* 3, no. 2 (1981): 224–48.

Rosales, F. Arturo. "Shifting Self Perceptions and Ethnic Consciousness among Mexicans in Houston, 1908–1946." *Aztlan: Journal of Chicano Studies* 16, nos. 1–2 (Spring & Fall 1987): 71–94.

Rytina, Nancy. "IRCA Legalization Effects: Lawful Permanent Residence and Naturalization through 2001." Paper presented at Effects of Immigrant Legalization Programs on the United States: Scientific Evidence on Immigrant Adaptation and Impacts on US Economy and Society, October 25, 2002.

San Miguel, Guadalupe, Jr. "'The Community Is Beginning to Rumble': The Origins of Chicano Educational Protests in Houston, 1965–1970." *Houston Review: History and Culture of the Gulf Coast* 13, no. 3 (1991): 127–47.

Satvinder, Juss S. "Free Movement and the World Order." *International Journal of Refugee Law* 16, no. 3 (2004): 289–335.

Shelton, Beth Anne. "Patterns of Racial and Ethnic Disparity and Conflict: Hispanic Communities." In *Houston: Growth and Decline in a Sunbelt Boomtown*, edited by Beth Ann Shelton, Nestor P. Rodriguez, Joe R. Feagin, Robert D. Bullard, and Robert D. Thomas, 93–122. Philadelphia: Temple University Press, 1989.

Sierra, Christine Marie. "In Search of National Power: Chicanos Working the System on Immigration Reform, 1976–1986." In Montejano, *Chicano Politics and Society*, 131–53.

Stern, Alexandra Minna. "Buildings, Boundaries, and Blood: Medicalization and Nation-Building on the U.S.-Mexico Border, 1910–1930." *Hispanic American Historical Review* 79, no. 1 (February 1999): 41–81.

Stetson, Stephen. "Soldier Led Charge for Hispanic Rights in Houston." *Narratives: Stories of U.S. Latino and Latinas and World War II* (Fall 2001): 36.

Tenayuca, Emma, and Homer Brooks. "The Mexican Question in the Southwest." *Communist* 118, no. 3 (March 1939): 257–68.

Thelen, David. "Rethinking History and the Nation-State: Mexico and the United States." *Journal of American History* 86, no. 2 (September 1999): 438–52.

Torres, Joseph. "Latinos Speak Out." *Hispanic*, December 1996.

Treviño, Jesús A. "Border Violence against Illegal Immigrants and the Need to Change the Border Patrol's Current Complaint Review Process." *Houston Journal of International Law* 21, no. 1 (Fall 1998): 85–116.

Treviño, Roberto R. "In Their Own Way: Parish Funding and Mexican American Ethnicity in Catholic Houston, 1911–1972." *Latino Studies Journal* 5, no. 3 (September 1994): 87–107.

Tussing, Bert. "New Requirements for a New Challenge: The Military's Role in Border Security." *Homeland Security Affairs: Journal of the Naval Post Graduate School Center for Homeland Defense and Security* 4, no. 3 (October 2008): 1–22.

Vargas, Zaragosa. "Tejana Radical: Emma Tenayuca and the San Antonio Labor Movement during the Great Depression." *Pacific Historical Review*, no. 66 (1997): 553–80.

Weinberg, Bill. "Zapatistas and Globalization of Resistance." *Yes Magazine*, May 20, 2004.

Index